John Silber

Kant's Ethics

John Silber

Kant's Ethics

The Good, Freedom, and the Will

DE GRUYTER

ISBN 978-1-61451-071-0
e-ISBN 978-1-61451-074-1

Library of Congress Cataloging-in-Publication Data
A CIP catalog record for this book has been applied for at the Library of Congress.

Bibliographic information published by the Deutsche Nationalbibliothek
The Deutsche Nationalbibliothek lists this publication in the Deutsche Nationalbibliografie; detailed bibliographic data are available in the Internet at http://dnb.dnb.de

Cover image: akg-images
Typesetting: jürgen ullrich typosatz, Nördlingen
Printing: Hubert & Co. GmbH & Co. KG, Göttingen
⊗ Printed on acid-free paper
Printed in Germany

www.degruyter.com

In memory of my parents
Paul George Silber
and
Jewell Joslin Silber
and my dear friend and colleague
Klaus Hartmann

Preface

Most of the chapters of this book have appeared as separate articles or, in one case, as a book chapter. One might therefore be led to the conclusion that *Kant's Ethics: The Good, Freedom and the Will* is pieced together or *bloßes Stückwerk*. This would be a fundamental mistake. This book not only represents a unified interpretation of Kant's ethics, it is itself a work *aus einem Guß*, that is, a solid piece of Kant-scholarship that coheres in its own right and presents a *fresh* interpretation of Kant. As such it is a significant contribution to Kant scholarship which will now be available for the first time in its entirety. To use a somewhat hackneyed phrase, this book is far more than the sum of its previously published parts.

While *Kant's Ethics* represents fifty years of work and thought, it is in no way a work that is dated or of merely antiquarian interest. The book is highly relevant to the contemporary discussion of Kant. Its emphasis on the importance of the concept of the good in Kant's ethics represents an important alternative to most interpretations advanced today. Ignoring "the essential role of the good, happiness and sensible desires in Kant" remains a powerful motive today, and if anything, it stands even more in the way of the appropriation of Kant's ethics as a whole. This book convincingly argues that while Kant rejected any attempt to begin with the idea of the good, he did mean to define the good in such a way that it could be recognized as an essential feature of the moral experience from which he had to begin. Furthermore, "the concept of the good pulls together so many strands of Kant's ethics that Kant organized the *Critique of Practical Reason* around it." It is Silber's attentiveness to Kant's text and Kant's own project that differentiates his account from vaguely Kantian projects that emphasize the "priority of the right over the good." Indeed, it is a welcome corrective to such popular views.

Silber's book is also a welcome corrective to the current sometimes all-too-facile attempts at showing that Kant's ethics can be understood without invoking metaphysics altogether. Silber forcefully argues that ethics is *not* "an addendum to Kant's other metaphysical interests." Ethics is the very heart of Kant's philosophical enterprise. Kant's philosophy is indeed "based on the centrality of the practical as a guide to reason." Indeed, the "full significance of the highest good cannot be understood even as an ethical concept of practical reason until it is also understood as a metaphysical concept of pure reason." The metaphysical interpretation of Kant's ethics may be controversial today, but this is *precisely* why it is important today. Silber's excellent discussion of this position needs to be heard.

The distinction between "*Wille*," "*Willkür*" and "Freedom" in Chapter III of *Kant's Ethics* is perhaps familiar by now, but I believe that Silber's discussion still repays the most careful study. It is especially the insistence that we must make a distinction between the freedom of the human individual and the freedom of a pure will that deserves to be taken seriously. Kant, in the context of his *Groundwork*, is not so much concerned with the morality of human agents as he is with the necessary conditions of the morality of any rational being. He meant to analyze what is involved in the morality of human individuals as finite beings more in his *Religion*, *Anthropology* and *Metaphysics of Morals*, and not so much in his *Groundwork* and the *Critique of Practical Reason*. Accordingly, the *Religion* and the *Anthropology* must be given more prominence when we discuss Kant's ethical project as a whole. While Silber concentrates on religion and does not pursue the anthropological dimension to its full extent, his sophisticated discussion points in the right direction, and one may hope that this book will provide further impetus for exploring these issues.

Another feature of Kant's thought that Silber emphasizes at the beginning of his book and in Chapter VIII, namely the cosmopolitan background or intent of Kant's ethical theory, would perhaps have needed even more attention. In any case, it is very suggestive and does deserve further development.

There are many other aspects of this book that remain important. There is, for instance, no better discussion of the "symbolic schematization of the highest good" than the one presented in Chapter VII. Silber's treatment of the Hegelian criticisms of Kant's ethics in Chapter IX also seems unsurpassed to me. The Appendix on Kant at Auschwitz is a vivid reminder that those who make it their business to think and write about Kant cannot legitimately insulate themselves from political evil. It may well be that "Kant's ethics is inadequate to the understanding of Auschwitz because Kant denies the possibility of the deliberate rejection of the moral law." Yet, understanding is one thing, moral judgment is another. Rather to die than to burden one's conscience with the terrible (and immoral) things the Nazis asked for is not just a real possibility for anyone who considers himself or herself subject to the categorical imperative. I would say it is not just a real possibility of action, but what the categorical imperative demands. However that may be, we should heed Silber's advice that philosophers should not forget the Holocaust.

Kant's Ethics is an impressive contribution to philosophical scholarship to be enjoyed by present and future students of Kantian philosophy. We are fortunate that the fragments or individual chapters are now available for the first time in the context in which they belong, that is, a thorough, unified and convincing interpretation of Kant's theory of the good. Like all good scholarship, it has not aged but remains highly relevant.

Manfred Kühn

Foreword

This book represents more than fifty years of work and reflection on Kant's ethics. It began with a manuscript in 1956, one which, while I thought it substantial, also seemed to me to require additional chapters. Over the years, the work has expanded and developed, at each turn taking account of the recent scholarship. In the last two years, it has been brought into accord with my latest thinking on the subject. I note that I have inadvertently followed Plato's dictum that philosophical thinking must mature over at least fifty years.

The manuscript has literally been through the fire: in the first year of my presidency at Boston University, a time of student unrest, our home was set on fire; all footnotes and some text were lost and had to be recreated. In a way this may have been a good thing, as the restoration gave me an opportunity to develop and widen my approach. As this book has developed, I have taken account of more and more recent points of view on Kant. I have also broadened my study of his ethics in various directions that seem to me important, until this work has reached a point, I believe, which has been the goal of all my studies of Kant.

This goal is to offer a comprehensive account of Kant's ethics, drawing on the entirety of his work. To this end, the opening chapter sets the criteria on which students of Kant must rely as they endeavor to resolve the puzzles that result from contradictions, real or seeming, or from isolated statements that seem at odds with Kant's basic point of view. As will be seen, such problems can only be resolved by a comprehensive reading of Kant's work on ethics and, indeed, of his metaphysics as well.

As my thinking on Kant has developed, parts of this book have appeared as articles. They are listed in the Bibliography. With the benefit of the responses these have generated, as well as my own ongoing thinking about Kant, and with an eye to the integration and interrelation of different areas of Kant's ethics, all of these articles have been revised for this book, and play a part along with new and previously unpublished material.

Taking into account the scholarly work on Kant up to the present, I do not see that my basic position has been refuted or eclipsed, although it is certainly fair to say that, along with extensive discussion of my published views, there has been some disagreement. There has also been some important borrowing, particularly of the important distinction, for the first time in English translation, of *Wille*, *Willkür* and *Gesinnung* and their dynamic function in the act of volition.

Despite the questionings of some scholars, in particular Lewis Beck, I find it crucial to insist on the importance of the highest good in Kant's ethics. It is a striking fact that, in the first *Critique*, Kant held that the highest good was the canon of pure reason; and it is otherwise impossible to explain why Kant, in the second *Critique*, laid such emphasis on the good, including the highest good. Clearly the good was of central importance to his ethics, only slightly less central than the concept of duty. Ignoring the role of the good in Kant's ethics leads one to interpret him as a single-minded deontologist who ignored or minimized the nature of the moral agent as a sensible, no less than a rational, being. This, I think, gets Kant wrong: ignoring the essential role of the good, of happiness and sensible desires, leaves Kant open to criticism for an empty formalism, that is, for lack of content in his ethics. I think I have shown that this is demonstrably not the case. Such observations as these are one example, to my mind, of the importance of an integrated approach to Kant's ethics such as I have undertaken in this book.

Given that my overall views guide the thinking throughout the book, some readers may find certain chapters of greater interest than others. Judging from the frequency of references in recent literature to Kant's discussion of will, of *Wille*, *Willkür* and *Gesinnung* and their functional relation, many will find Chapter III of particular importance. Readers interested in the role of the highest good will find Chapters V and VI congenial, while the emphasis in Chapter VII on Kant's moral schematism and in Chapter VIII on his procedural formalism may perhaps be more congenial to others. Chapter X assesses the overall effectiveness of Kant's treatment of ethics and draws on a good deal of recent scholarship. "Kant at Auschwitz" is, I believe, of current significance and importance, drawing as it does on Hannah Arendt's interpretation of Kant's ethics in the context of Eichmann's testimony and trial.

Through the years as this work developed, many of my citations were from untranslated texts; most of these are now available in English, and I have therefore added citations both to Kant's German and to the English translations.

Now a word of acknowledgement. I owe much to professors now deceased: George A. Schrader, Charles Hendel, Theodore M. Greene, Brand Blanshard, Paul Weiss, Robert L. Calhoun, F.S.C. Northrop, and Lewis W. Beck. Without their instruction and especially their criticism and encouragement, this book would never have been started. In addition I must acknowledge my gratitude to the late Klaus Hartmann of the University of Tübingen, Thomas Seebohm of the University of Mainz, and Elie Wiesel, whose influence is apparent in my discussion of evil.

I also want to thank Loni Hayman, who laboriously assisted in replacing citations from the Cassirer edition with citations from the *Akademie-Ausgabe*. Ted Harwood, a consummate editor, offered excellent suggestions concerning the organization of the book along with many textual changes. He also assisted in reviewing articles and books on Kant's ethics published since 1970 and calling relevant works to my attention. Professor Wolfgang Haase, director of Boston University's Institute for the Classical Tradition, generously reviewed my final manuscript. I also wish to thank Brian Jorgensen for his help in the final editing.

Finally I express my gratitude to my executive assistant, Kelly O'Connor, and my research assistant, Chandler Rosenberger, for their support in researching texts, typing and proofreading, and above all for their keen questions and criticisms.

Despite the best efforts of all I have mentioned, I am sure that shortcomings remain for which I am fully responsible.

Nevertheless I fancy – I hope with some plausibility – that Kant would have been pleased with this interpretation of his ethics. I always felt that he was peering over my shoulder, sometimes surprised, sometimes distressed, but for the most part nodding his approval.

Table of Contents

Preface (Manfred Kühn) — **VII**
Foreword — **IX**
Introduction — **1**

Chapter I: The Context Of Kant's Ethics — 11
1 Kant's Conception Of Philosophy — **11**
2 Kant's Philosophical Method: Logical and Transcendental — **20**
3 The Chief Characteristics of Kant's Critical Thought — **33**

Chapter II: The Copernican Revolution In Ethics: The Good Reexamined — 46
1 The Primacy of the Moral Law in the Determination of the Good — **46**
2 The Heterogeneity of the Good — **54**
3 The Good as the Object of the Moral Law — **61**

Chapter III: Kant's Analysis Of The Will — 64
1 The Theoretical Background and Importance of the Religion — **64**
2 Freedom — **69**
3 The Human Will — **78**
4 The Contribution of the Religion to Ethics — **114**

Chapter IV: The Moral Good And The Natural Good — 116
1 Terminological Problems — **116**
2 The Intrinsic Goodness of Both the Natural Good and the Moral Good — **119**
3 Particular Natural Goods and the Natural Good — **129**
4 Particular Natural Goods as Extrinsic, Relational Goods — **134**
5 The Qualification of the Natural Good by the Moral Good — **141**
6 Summary — **148**

Chapter V: The Highest Good As The Material Object Of Moral Volition — 152
1 The Centrality of the Highest Good in Kant's Ethics — **152**
2 Perfection (the Moral Good) as a Component of the Highest Good — **156**
3 Happiness (the Natural Good) as a Component of the Highest Good — **164**
4 The Unity of Perfection and Happiness in the Highest Good — **167**

Chapter VI: The Highest Good As Immanent And As Transcendent — 173
1 The Highest Good as the Canon of Pure Reason — **173**
2 The Immanence of the Highest Good — **184**
3 The Transcendence of the Highest Good — **192**

4 The Constitutive Immanence and Regulative Transcendence of the Highest Good — **197**

Chapter VII: The Moral Task: The Embodiment Of The Highest Good — 203
1 The Moral Task as the Creation of Moral Schemata — **203**
2 The Symbolic Schematism of the Highest Good — **211**

Chapter VIII: The Role Of Judgment In Kant's Procedural Formalism — 225
1 The Procedure of Judgment in All Employments — **225**
2 The Procedures of Judgment in Ethics — **231**
3 The Procedural Formalism of Kant's Ethics — **246**

Chapter IX: The Role Of Judgment In The Embodiment Of The Highest Good — 261
1 Moral Feeling — **261**
2 The Cultivation of Moral Feeling — **272**

Chapter X: Summary And Assessment — 281
1 Kant's Attempt to Reconcile the Christian and Scientific Worldviews — **281**
2 The Heterogeneity of the Good — **282**
3 The Clarification of the Concept of Freedom — **283**
4 Kant's Response to Diderot's Demand for Moral Guidance — **287**
5 Kant's Absolute Concept of Freedom — **290**
6 Moral Incentive in Kant's Ethics — **298**
7 Ethical Orthodoxy in Religious Education — **307**

Appendix: Kant at Auschwitz — 314
1 The Holocaust — **314**
2 Eichmann's Claim to be a Kantian — **317**
3 Absolute Obedience in Kant's Ethics — **323**
4 Devilishness as an Actual Mode of Freedom — **329**
5 Alternative Explanations of Moral Responsibility — **335**

Kant's Works And Their Abbreviations — 343
Other translations of Kant's works — **345**

Bibliography — 346

Acknowledgements — 350

Index — 351

Introduction

Kant's ethical doctrines continue to have uncommon relevance and vitality in our time for they continue to challenge philosophers and all persons interested in ethics and in living in accordance with ethical principles. This is true not just in America and Western Europe, where Kant's philosophy has been argued with Talmudic-like exegesis near to the point of exhaustion, but among philosophers throughout the globe, as shown by the increasing participation of multi-national contributors to recent international Kant symposia and congresses.

This should come as no surprise. Kant's doctrines are as relevant today as they were in his own time because his examination of our moral experience has a scope and depth unequalled by his predecessors and, I would argue, unrivalled in the two hundred years since his death. His investigations led him not merely to a systematic theory of ethics but to a theory intended to be of practical assistance to individuals without regard to their cultural or temporal position. Kant considered his life's work to be of little or no value and himself as worthless if he failed to contribute to the well-being of ordinary people: "I learn to honor human beings, and would consider myself less useful than the common worker if I did not believe that this contemplation can give worth to all others and establish the rights of humankind."[1]

The value of Kant's ethics is not based solely, or even primarily, on the fact that Kant tested his ideas against a storehouse of anthropological and historical evidence or by the fact that he also rested his doctrines of duty and virtue on a comprehensive metaphysics of human knowledge and action. The enduring vitality and relevance of his ethics owes much more to the fact that Kant intended to clarify and facilitate the moral lives of all men and women in any time or place. Although Kant departed fundamentally in his ethical theory from the ancient Greeks – "die Alten" as he called them – as I discuss in Chapter II, his work resembles in purpose the ethical investigations of Socrates and Plato. Kant was not motivated in ethics by a narrow professional vision of how his philosophical inquiry should proceed. Rather, he labored with ethical concerns in all three *Critiques* and in most other writings because he viewed ethics as the overriding concern of humankind in the quest for knowledge in all spheres no less than in the quest for virtue.

Kant's ethics is not, therefore, merely an addendum to his other metaphysical interests – an add-on compendium of insights into ethical theory and

---

1 HN (A20), 44. "Bemerkungen zu den Betrachtungen über das Gefühl des Schönen und Erhabenen." My translation.

practice, an approach taken by some philosophers who write on ethical issues only as a sideline to inquiries they regard as more fundamental. Unfortunately, many intellectuals view ethics with something akin to disdain as an "applied field" subject to religious and ideological contamination. Or, they view it as a social science in which the objective study of moral life has succeeded only in subjectivizing and relativizing ethical principles. Even among those philosophers who consider ethics a legitimate philosophical concern, many view ethical inquiry as just one among several sub-disciplines – e.g. business ethics, medical ethics, military ethics, etc. – a view in keeping with the contemporary interest in "professionalizing" philosophy.

These, however, were not Kant's views. To the contrary, for Kant ethics is central to the philosophic enterprise because reason is practical, that is, ethically guided, in all its employments. Understanding the moral law as universally applicable in human affairs and showing how human conduct can be tested by that law was for Kant the most important use of practical reason. But practical reason is also required in the quest for theoretical knowledge. Scientific inquiry, for example, unless guided by ethical practice can lead to error. To be sure, Kant's important epistemological investigation into the possibilities and limits of pure reason is of continuing interest to philosophers and remains of lasting value to the philosophical enterprise. But it is the moral or practical use of reason that was for Kant primary in all human activity.[2]

There are two ironies, however, at the heart of Kant's universalism and his contemporary international appeal. Although Kant treated ethics as a discipline built on rules relevant to all human beings at all times, it was concerns peculiar to his own time and culture that moved him to write. And although Kant thought that his ethics was integrated completely into his larger metaphysics, especially his deep interest in the discoveries of the natural sciences, he was determined to construct a system that would leave room for that which many thought that reason necessarily excluded – religious faith.

Kant's philosophy exhibits that transcendence on which great philosophy depends even though that ability to write and think, as Spinoza said, *sub specie aeternitatis*, can never be fully attained. Indeed, the finest philosopher may be the one who, rather than withdrawing from the movements of his times, includes all of them in his intellectual grasp and assigns to each its proper weight and influence.

Kant was such a philosopher: revolutionary thinker in the age of revolution, quintessential child of the eighteenth century. He caught the spirit of the

2 See Chapter VI.

Enlightenment in writing "*Sapere aude*! Have courage to use your *own* reason! – that is the motto of enlightenment,"[3] and in Kant most of the complex and often conflicting movements that gave the eighteenth century its distinctive character were present and held in a balance of extraordinary coherence.

A pietism that emphasized moral practice over abstract theology – a religious tradition that asserted the still powerful influence of the Christian *Weltanschauung* – was dominant in Kant's home and in his early schooling. Reflecting the intellectual balance of the eighteenth century, the influence of this powerful motivational force was checked in Kant by the rising influence of a new *Weltanschauung* based on Newtonian science, to which Kant was himself a significant contributor. Kant believed that "the heavens declare the glory of God," but those "starry heavens above" continued to fill Kant's mind "with ever new and increasing admiration and awe" not through revealed mystery but through Newton's revelation of a God of reason who had created a natural order devoid of mystery and miracle that was comprehensible through human reason. As Pope had written:

> Nature and Nature's laws lay hid in Night:
> God said, *Let Newton be!* and All was *Light*.[4]

1 The Clash of Worldviews in the Enlightenment

The most significant intellectual work of the eighteenth century involved the assimilation of the Christian and Newtonian worldviews into some coherent or at least plausible synthesis.

But the Enlightenment cannot be understood simply as an age of reason, any more than the seventeenth century, dominated though it was by Descartes. As Carl Becker correctly observed, the thirteenth century, the century of Dante and St. Thomas, could with equal or greater plausibility be called the Age of Reason. Any true Age of Faith, which at its core is instinctual, had reached and long passed its zenith by the thirteenth century. In a true age of faith, questions do not arise, for there is no basis for doubt. In an age of faith the religious *Weltanschauung* appears factual and mundane: the faithful would no more wonder about the existence of God or ask for proof of God's existence than a middle-class Victorian child would wonder if his parents were married and ask

3 WA, 35: WE, 286.
4 "Epigram on Sir Isaac Newton" Pope, 808.

to see their marriage license. Such an age of faith might more aptly be called an age of belief or even an age of credulity. And if in such an age an imponderable question should arise, all doubt would be dispelled with Tertullian's response, *credo quia absurdum*. In a true age of faith we believe what has been told us by our fathers and by their fathers before them. The character of such an age is expressed by the chorus in Euripides's *Bacchae:*

> Beyond the old beliefs,
> no thought, no act shall go.
> Small, small is the cost,
> to believe in this:
> whatever is god is strong;
> whatever long time has sanctioned,
> that is a law forever;
> the law tradition makes
> is the law of nature.[5]

By this criterion the thirteenth century could hardly be described as the Age of Faith; it was rather an age of increasing doubt in which justification by reason became increasingly important to the preservation of faith and faith became increasingly dependent upon justification by reason. As Becker writes:

> Thus it was possible for the 13th century, employing a highly intricate dialectic supported on occasion by a symbolic interpretation, to justify the ways of God to man. Paradise lost and paradise regained – such was the theme of the drama of existence as understood in that age; and all the best minds of the time were devoted to its explication. Theology related and expounded the history of the world. Philosophy was the science that rationalized and reconciled nature and history. Logic provided both theology and philosophy with an adequate methodology.[6]

In an age of reason, like the thirteenth century and the two following centuries, reason was sufficiently effective in supporting faith in the Christian worldview. Reason was able to check the doubts of the most penetrating critics of the mythic tradition.

But in the seventeenth century, the scientific method, that mixture of rationalism and empiricism, that melding of Baconian observation of nature and Cartesian clarity of mathematical thought, triumphed in Newton's *Principia*. The implications of the Newtonian synthesis were so profound that they struck at and loosened the roots of the Christian *Weltanschauung* itself. From the point

---

5 Euripides, *The Bacchae*, lines 891–899, pp. 194–5.
6 Becker, 10.

of view of traditional Christian theology, reason, which in the thirteenth century had been a faithful handmaiden, had become first a rebellious servant and finally a dangerous usurper.

The new worldview was given the name of Newtonianism because, as Becker sums up,

> Newton, more than any other man had banished mystery from the world by discovering a "*universal law of nature,*" thus demonstrating, what others had only asserted, that the universe was rational and intelligible through and through, and capable, therefore, of being subdued to the uses of men.[7]

Newton, a lifelong believer in traditional Christianity, was not so confident. He said:

> I do not know what I appear to the world, but to myself I seem to have been only a boy playing on the seashore, and diverting myself and now and then finding a smoother pebble or prettier shell than ordinary, whilst the great ocean of Truth lay all undiscovered before me.[8]

But Newton's younger contemporary, Alexander Pope, offered in the *Dunciad* a dramatic assessment of the impact that Newton had had on the intellectual life of his age:

> See skulking *Truth* to her old Cavern fled,
> Mountains of Casuistry heap'd o'er her head!
> *Philosophy*, that lean'd on Heav'n before,
> Shrinks to her second cause, and is no more.
> *Physic* of *Metaphysic* begs defense,
> And *Metaphysic* calls for aid on *Sense*!
> See *Mystery* to *Mathematics* fly!
> In vain! They gaze, turn giddy, rave, and die.
> *Religion* blushing veils her sacred fires,
> And unawares *Morality* expires.[9]

The scientific *Weltanschauung* only began to take form in the public mind in the early seventeenth century. But everywhere in the eighteenth century, men and women who lacked the mathematical and scientific education to read Newton with understanding read of Newton's views in popular restatements. And even

7 Ibid, 60.
8 Brewster, 407.
9 *The Dunciad*, Book III, lines 641–650. Pope, 800.

those who had never read on the subject spoke freely of it, as the general public speak today of Einstein's theory of relativity and quantum mechanics without any genuine comprehension.

Intoxicated by the apparent simplicity, elegance, and power of the Newtonian synthesis, philosophers and intellectuals of the eighteenth century "renounced the authority of church and Bible, but exhibited a naïve faith in the authority of nature and reason."[10] The Laws of God metamorphosed into the Laws of Nature, disclosed not by revelation but by reason and sense. In a world free from the miraculous lay the opportunity for human advancement and improvement.

Among the literate, the scientific worldview gradually displaced the Christian worldview as the dominant climate of opinion. Aristophanes' commentary on the collapse of Greek religion in the face of natural philosophy at the end of the fifth century B.C. was, as Becker remarked, equally descriptive of this transition from the medieval to the scientific worldview: "Whirl is king, having cast out Zeus."[11]

Newtonianism held forth the promise of understanding and ultimate control of nature, but it placed in doubt the spiritual and moral foundations on which the meaning of human existence depends. The fear that Pope had expressed of the eclipse of religion and the expiration of morality was widely shared. The emergence of the scientific worldview revealed implications destructive to religion and morality that, in turn, gave rise to a new appreciation of the religious worldview and thereby, as in the thirteenth century but with perhaps greater urgency, pressed theological issues on the minds of the most advanced thinkers of the age.

As the century wore on, even the most skeptical – fearing the consequences of the new philosophy – restrained their skepticism. Those less skeptical offered religious interpretations of the new philosophy. In sense experience, for example, Bishop George Berkeley found the *divine* language of nature that could be read by thoughtful, rational human beings to reveal knowledge of the real world, which was also the world of God. A similar view was expressed by Hume, through the persona of Cleanthes, in his *Dialogues Concerning Natural Religion.* Cleanthes points out that the mind of a human being is congruous with the Author of Nature who has so arranged the grandeur of the universe that the human mind can comprehend it. Natural law does not, thus, cease to be God's

---

10 Becker, 30.
11 "The Clouds," l. 828, Aristophanes, 121.

law, but God's law is immanent in Nature rather than imposed upon it, As Newton put it,

> These Principles I consider not as occult Qualities, supposed to result from the specific Forms of Things, but as general Laws of Nature, by which the Things themselves are form'd.[12]

But if nature was the expression of God, and moved in accordance with inexorable laws, then whatever evil exists in the world was the consequence of God's creation, the result of either God's incompetence or indifference, if not of God's malevolence.[13] This dilemma posed by the new philosophy drove many to reconsider the relationship of reason and religion, the very question that had preoccupied the gFreat scholastic philosophers of the later Middle Ages. But now the apparent moral indifference of the universe, which seemed to many the inescapable consequence of the work of Newton and his followers, posed a terrible dilemma for thinkers who feared that Whirl might truly be king, and that by a cruel irony truth itself might overthrow virtue. Concerned about the effect his *Dialogues* might have, Hume voluntarily withheld them from publication during his lifetime and he revised his published work so that, as he said in 1737, "it shall give as little offense as possible."[14]

2 The Search for a New Synthesis

Diderot, like Hume, also wrote works he refused to publish. But unlike Hume he was personally distressed by his inability to find "any sufficient reason for virtuous conduct, his heart unable to renounce the conviction that nothing is better in this world than to be a good man."[15] Diderot could intellectually articulate, but could not ultimately believe, the moral indifference that appeared to follow from the Newtonian philosophy. Diderot was profoundly troubled by his inability to establish morality on a rational foundation, and was not content

---

12 Dampier, 183–184.

13 The Lisbon earthquake of 1755 produced a flood of theodicy and a bumper crop of critics of theodicy.

14 Burton, 64; Becker, 38.

15 Becker, 80. Note the expression of Diderot's view in Kant's famous statement, "It is impossible to conceive anything at all in the world, or even out of it, which can be taken as good without qualification, except a *good will*." (GMS, 393; GMM, 61). This point is elaborated below.

to attack the Christian faith and doctrine without offering something positive and superior to take its place. Diderot concluded, "It is not enough to know more than they [theologians] do; it is necessary to show them that we are better, and that *philosophy makes more good men than sufficient or efficacious grace*."[16] To put it another way, Diderot was troubled by his inability to incorporate what he regarded as the new truths discovered by Newton and others into a satisfactory and comprehensive synthesis that could do for his age what Thomism had done for the later Middle Ages.

Although Diderot devoted years of effort to the establishment of morality on rational foundations, he never published on the subject. He said, "I have not even dared to write the first line; I say to myself, if I do not come out of the attempt victorious, I become the apologist of wickedness; I will have betrayed the cause of virtue ... I do not feel equal to this sublime work; I have uselessly consecrated my whole life to it."[17]

Diderot may have been unusual in honestly recognizing his inability to solve the problem he had framed, but he was right – and hardly alone – in his diagnosis: the eighteenth century lacked a comprehensive and coherent worldview, and its construction was the central intellectual project of the age. As Becker rightly concludes,

> [T]he underlying preconceptions of 18th-Century thought were still, allowance made for certain important alterations in the bias, essentially the same as those of the 13th Century ... the *philosophes* demolished the heavenly city of St. Augustine only to rebuild it with more up-to-date material.[18]

While the *philosophes* welcomed Newtonianism, and while they sought through the use of reason to understand the laws of nature and thereby to gain control of it, they nonetheless recognized that an adequate natural philosophy must also provide guidance for the affairs of men and women and give meaning to human life. In the opinion of the most sensitive of the *philosophes*, one could not abandon the mythic roots of Christianity until the problem of evil had been dealt with and a rational foundation for morality had been provided. Diderot framed the problem: a "sufficient reason for just conduct" must be found.

---

16 Diderot, Vol. 19, 464; Becker, 81.
17 Diderot, Vol. 23, 45; Becker, 80.
18 Becker, 31.

3 Kant's Attempt to Reconcile Newtonianism and Morality

Clearly, it is in this spirit that Kant wrote his first *Critique* and established the limits of knowledge "in order to make room for faith."[19] In particular, it was in this spirit that Kant sought not to discover or invent morality, but to complete that "sublime work" that Diderot found beyond his powers – that is, "to seek out and establish *the supreme principle of morality*"[20] along with the principles and doctrines of religion on the basis of reason to ensure that the laws of practical reason have "access to the human mind and an influence on its maxims."[21]

Although the chapters that follow explore many important issues posed by Kant's ethical writings – among them Kant's critique of the deficiencies in classical ethical theory as well as in the rationalistic and naturalistic theories of his time – they have as their objective a single theoretical problem. The problem I have undertaken to examine is posed for Kant's ethical theory by his metaphysical doctrines taken as a whole. It is the problem of how the individual in accordance with Kant's views can understand the requirements of the moral law in a way that enables him or her to know concretely and objectively, rather than merely subjectively and in the abstract, what action is required or proscribed by the moral law – that is, the problem of how in the light of all of Kant's writings one can live a moral life in this world.

4 Principles of Interpretation

This is a problem in Kant's ethics, for, as any student knows, Kant wrote copiously and with concreteness not only on duty, on virtue and vice, on the good, on the moral education of the young, on the duties of statesmen and judges, and on much else that involves "real world" applications of ethical principles, but also on metaphysical doctrines that appear at odds with some of his ethical positions. In short, a clear consistent picture of Kant's ethics is not immediately apparent.

This problem is by no means unique to Kant's philosophy. No satisfactory exposition of the views of any great thinker, especially one with Kant's scope, can be derived from the mere examination of texts. No matter how carefully this

---

19 KrV, Bxxx: CpR, 29.
20 GMS, 392: GMM, 60.
21 KpV, 151: CprR, 249.

textual research is carried out, sound exposition requires many decisions, selections and evaluations. This is particularly true if one attempts a systematic exposition of Kant's ethics. Kant's ethical writings contain numerous contradictory passages that can easily distort the conception of the whole of his ethical theory if their importance is either exaggerated or minimized. In rare cases some of these passages must be disregarded as mistaken.

In order to present a convincing view of Kant's ethics worthy of Kant's labors, one must go beyond the citing of texts. Rather, a sound, comprehensive interpretation of Kant's ethics must be grounded in the context of Kant's ethical thought *taken as a whole*. That is, the criteria for selection, evaluation and interpretation of Kant's writings must stem from one's knowledge of a) Kant's conception of philosophy, b) his philosophical methods, and c) his central problems and doctrines. As Kant said in regard to theoretical knowledge, we may say in regard to the understanding of all his works: "Accidental observations, made in obedience to no previously thought out plan, can never be made to yield a universal law."[22] Nor, we may add, a universally valid interpretation. Prior, then, to any exposition of Kant's ethical theory that can hope to be sound, a review of the context of Kant's ethics must be attempted. That is the subject of Chapter I. Devoted as it is to an overview of Kant's approach to philosophy, most of it will be well known to Kant scholars. Its importance lies in its illumination of the context of Kant's ethics, and the provision of criteria essential to the sound interpretation of Kant's ethical writings.

---

22 KrV, Bx111: CpR, 20.

Chapter I: The Context Of Kant's Ethics

1 Kant's Conception Of Philosophy

Kant's conception of the philosophic enterprise is not new – its roots can be traced back to Socrates. But Kant's exposition of his view of philosophy reveals emphases that are original and of fundamental importance in the development of his philosophy. Philosophy, according to Kant, is rational, discursive knowledge.

In both the first *Critique* and the *Logic*,[1] Kant classifies knowledge according to its two modes of origination : first, from the standpoint of its objective origin, that is, by reference to the sources from which the knowledge comes, and second, from the standpoint of its subjective origin, by reference to the manner in which knowledge is acquired. In regard to the first, knowledge is either rational or empirical, since these are its only objective sources. In regard to the second, the way in which the individual knower acquires knowledge is either rational or historical regardless of its objective origin.

Under the subjective mode of origination, Kant explains that historical knowledge is knowledge acquired from data derived in turn from sense experience. In relation to the knower, this knowledge comes from without and the knower adds nothing substantial to it. One has historical knowledge, not rational knowledge, if when one has been told something, one remembers what one has been told so that one can repeat it. (With slight variations in degree, this is the character of most learning, and one can even learn philosophy in this manner.) Knowledge so acquired may have been rational knowledge for the original observer, scholar or scientist, but for the student it is merely historical. Whatever rationality is present in it was put there by someone else. One acquiring historical knowledge "has grasped and kept; that is, he has learnt well, and is merely the plaster-cast of a living man."[2]

Rational knowledge, however, must come from inward effort. Its objective source must lie in principles which, when employed by the individual, can provide for the criticism and even the rejection of historical knowledge. Knowledge cannot be acquired rationally without an active and free mind that is

---

1 This work is the collection of Kant's lectures on logic which was compiled under Kant's direction by G. B. Jasche and published in 1800. The *Logic* is both pre- and post-critical since the lectures were composed over the years from 1755–1796, during which period Kant lectured on logic fifty-four times. See Paulsen, 57.

2 KrV, B864: CpR, 656 ; see also, Log, 22: Logic, 536.

neither imitative nor mechanical – precisely the mental qualifications for competent performance as a judge, legislator, scientist or philosopher.[3] The philosopher, however, is distinguished by the fact that, according to Kant, the knowledge he or she acquires rationally is from principles only. Philosophical knowledge, therefore, is for Kant rational knowledge both in terms of objective origin (source) and subjective origin (acquisition).

Philosophy shares with mathematics knowledge that is rational both subjectively and in point of origin. It is distinguished from mathematics by being derived from concepts, whereas mathematics is derived from *a priori* intuition in space and time from which its concepts are constructed. Mathematics provides intuitive knowledge while philosophy contributes discursive knowledge. Mathematics enjoys an advantage in certainty, but it pays the price of being restricted to quantitative considerations by its inability to present qualities in *a priori* intuition.[4]

Having defined philosophy as rational, discursive knowledge from concepts, Kant notes the two fundamentally different conceptions of this discipline: the "scholastic" and the "cosmic". Philosophy has generally been pursued under a scholastic conception which aims at the systematic unity of all philosophical concepts and is satisfied with the merely logical perfection of a philosophical system of knowledge. A philosopher who adopts this approach aims at dialectical skills and subtlety of argument, "striv[ing] only for speculative knowledge, without looking to see how much the knowledge contributes to the final end of human reason."[5]

Kant, however, believed genuine philosophy can be carried out only under the cosmic conception,[6] which regards philosophy as "the science of the final ends of human reason." Not dialectical skills or subtlety of reasoning but usefulness *(Nützlichkeit)* is the goal. The philosopher is a practical person who teaches wisdom "by doctrine and example." The philosopher is not a practitioner of clever arguments, but through his or her own rational insight is a lawgiver. As such, the true philosopher

---

3 Log, 22: Logic, 536. We shall see that in this concept of rational knowledge are contained the seeds of the idea of the Copernican Revolution and of the idea of autonomy in wider than moral application.

4 Ibid., 23: ibid., 536.

5 Ibid., 24: ibid., 537.

6 It is strange that Kant should have referred to this humanistic, Socratic conception of philosophy as the "cosmic" conception (*in sensu cosmico*). I suppose he wanted to stress the breadth of his philosophic concern in his use of the word "cosmic." He clearly did not intend to emphasize cosmology. Kant's meaning is better conveyed by "cosmopolitan," the usage I shall adopt.

> as one who thinks for himself, must therefore make a free use of his reason on his own, not a slavishly imitative use of his reason. But not a dialectical use, i.e. not one that aims only at giving cognitions the illusion *of truth and wisdom*. This is the business of the mere Sophist, thoroughly incompatible with the dignity of the philosopher, as one who is acquainted with and is a teacher of wisdom.[7]

In favoring the cosmopolitan conception, Kant strives to follow in the Socratic tradition which directs attention to the ultimate concerns of humankind. Philosophy, so conceived, must take as its essential ends those which are of concern not just to professional philosophers but to everyone. If humankind's essential ends are viewed systematically, one end may be regarded as ultimate while the others are subordinate to it as means to its fulfillment. This ultimate end, which it is the task of philosophy to pursue, to examine, and to clarify, "is no other than the whole vocation of man, and the philosophy that deals with it is entitled moral philosophy."[8]

As early as the first *Critique*, after having examined the sources of theoretical knowledge and the limits of reason, Kant clearly states the priority of moral philosophy and insists on the primacy of this practical employment of reason.[9] But if the vocation of humankind is the ultimate end of reason, any inquiry into reason itself cannot be the ultimate end of philosophy. Indeed, Kant tells us that reason itself is instrumental, acquiring value only as it benefits humankind. In the final analysis, Kant argues,

> Everything ... comes down to the *practical*, and the practical worth of our own cognition consists in this tendency of everything theoretical and all speculation in regard to its use. This worth is *unconditioned, however, only if* the *end* toward which the practical use of the cognition is directed is an *unconditioned* end. The sole unconditioned and final end (ultimate end) to which all practical use of our cognition must finally relate is Morality, which on this account we may also call the *practical without qualification* or the *absolutely practical.*[10]

---

7 Ibid., 26: ibid., 539; cf. KrV, B867: CpR, 657–658.

8 KrV, B868: CpR, 658. Vaihinger has pertinently remarked *"Wie Sokrates ... so habe Kant die Nichtigkeit des Erkennens bewiesen und das Primat des Handelns gelehrt."* Vaihinger, 2–3.

9 When I published a version of this chapter in 1959 this point was not widely held among Kant scholars. It has, however, become more widely acknowledged. See, for example, Sullivan, 17, and Velkley, 2–5. Velkley notes that for Kant "the role of theoretical inquiry is to provide, above all else, the preparatory foundation for such a metaphysical morality." In short, the goodness of reason for humanity emerges early in Kant's writings, even before the *Critiques*, as a central metaphysical preoccupation. What Velkley shows is the deep impact Rousseau had on Kant's attitude toward reason and the Enlightenment project taken as a whole.

10 Log, 87: Logic, 587–8. Note also, "In the last resort all the elaborate work of our faculties must issue in and unite in the practical as its goal." (KU, 274: CoAJ, 44).

While philosophy has both its pure and its empirical aspects, depending on whether its knowledge is derived *a priori* or from experience, its ultimate concern under the cosmopolitan conception is always practical. It is not surprising, therefore, that Kant should conclude that all the interests of reason, both speculative and practical, and the entire field of philosophy, are encompassed in the following questions:

1. What can I know?
2. What ought I to do?
3. What may I hope?
4. What is man?[11]

Of these questions, Kant explains:

> Metaphysics answers the first question, *Morals* the second, *Religion* the third, and *Anthropology* the fourth. Fundamentally, however, we could reckon all of this as anthropology, because the first three questions relate to the last one.[12]

In this way Kant repudiates any fundamental bifurcation of his philosophy into a theoretical part and a practical part. While Kant does recognize that the understanding finds satisfaction in mere insight, he does not overlook the ultimate usefulness *(Nützlichkeit)* of such insight, and he heartily rejects the intellectual dilettante who delights in ideas that will never emerge from the schools to influence the way a person lives. Consequently, any chasm which may seem to separate Kant's theoretical from his practical philosophy must be taken as a challenge to his readers. Kant's intention is clear: to have theoretical philosophy serve all other inquiries and to have all philosophical knowledge culminate in the understanding of humanity, i.e., in philosophical anthropology.[13]

---

11 Log, 25: Logic, 538; cf. KrV, B833: CpR, 635 ff. The word *Mensch* refers to man or to human beings without regard to gender. Like the English word *man* it includes both males and females.

12 Ibid, 25; ibid, 538.

13 The close relationship of the theoretical and practical employments of reason and the primacy of the latter employment is seen in the following passage from Kant's Logic:
"Practical cognitions are, namely, either: (1) imperatives, and are to this extent opposed to theoretical cognitions; or they contain (2) the grounds for possible imperatives and are to this extent opposed to speculative cognitions."
"By imperative is to be understood in general every proposition that expresses a possible free action, whereby a certain end is to be made real. Every cognition that contains imperatives is

Although the philosophic enterprise under the cosmopolitan conception is motivated primarily by the practical goal of morality, Kant has other motives for seeking the unity of all the branches of philosophical inquiry. Reason itself is practical and seeks as its own end the unity of all its various employments. In contemplating a critique of pure reason, Kant first intended to include both reason's theoretical and its practical employments as parts of a *single* critique of reason as a unitary faculty. In 1772, he wrote to Marcus Herz:

> Without going into details here about the whole series of investigations that has continued right down to this last goal, I can say that, so far as my essential purpose is concerned, I have succeeded and that now I am in a position to bring out a critique of pure reason that will deal with the nature of theoretical as well as *practical* knowledge – in so far as the latter is purely *intellectual*. Of this, I will first work out the first part, which will deal with the sources of metaphysics, its *method* and limits. After that I will work out the pure *principles* of morality. With respect to the first part, I should be in a position to publish it within three months."[14]

Despite Kant's efforts to develop a unified treatment of the limits of reason, a project he assumed would require only three months, nine years elapsed before he was able to present even the first part of the planned critique of pure reason. In the first *Critique*, which bore the title of the entire original project, Kant was unable to provide a unitary examination of reason in all its aspects. He was able to present only the first of two distinct systems that follow from the application of legislative reason to its two main objects – nature (the philosophy of nature) and freedom (the philosophy of morality). The very idea of two systems, moreover, left him dissatisfied, for he realized that reason would not rest until it had unified these two systems "ultimately in one single philosophical system."[15]

---

practical, then, and is to be called practical in opposition to theoretical cognition." (Log, 86: Logic, 587).

It is clear that scientific investigation itself falls under the practical domain since it involves "free actions by which a certain end is to be attained," and scientific method prescribes imperatives for this free action. In the context of the primacy of practical reason these hypothetical imperatives will be caught up again in the categorical imperative to direct the entire scientific program towards the attainment of the practical end of humankind.

14 Letter to Marcus Herz, dated February 21, 1772, Br (AA10) 132: Corr, 134–5.

15 KrV, B868: CpR, 659. According to Richard Velkley, Kant viewed the unity of freedom and nature as the "ideal goal or telos of man as rational" and as an ideal that precedes the theoretical inquiries required to support its realization. Velkley claims, with justification, that the question of how happiness and nature can have moral significance, and form an essential

A unified system, however, proved elusive, and was a continual source of both aspiration and frustration. Having completed the first *Critique,* Kant was anxious to present his ethical views in a metaphysic of morals. But he realized that such a treatise would have to rest on the foundation of a completed critique of pure practical reason. Here again the unity of reason was a stumbling block. As he stated the problem in the "Preface" to the *Groundwork of the Metaphysic of Morals:*

> ... a critique of [pure] practical reason, if it is to be complete, requires, on my view, that we should be able at the same time to show the unity of practical and theoretical reason in a common principle, since in the end there can only be one and the same reason, which must be differentiated solely in its application.[16]

Apparently at this point Kant was no longer content to write a critique of practical reason parallel to the *Critique of Pure Reason.* In the proposed second *Critique* he hoped rather to provide the philosophical system based on the moral law and also to demonstrate the ultimate unity of the two systems of nature and morality. Since this work was not yet ready, Kant published the less ambitious *Groundwork.*

The goal of unity still eluded Kant even after he had written the second *Critique.* Kant's awareness of his failure to demonstrate this unity between nature and morality in the second *Critique* is revealed in the "Introduction" to the second edition of the third *Critique* – the *Critique of Judgment.* Here he speaks of the understanding (*Verstand*) and of reason (*Vernunft*) as, thus far, having two distinct jurisdictions – the former pertaining to nature, the latter to freedom – and neither interfering with the other.[17] Dissatisfied with this division of the rational life into two distinct and mutually exclusive compartments, Kant presents the third *Critique* as a "means of linking the two parts of philosophy in a whole."[18] Thus, in his twenty-year search, from the time of the letter to Herz until the completion of the *Critique of Judgment,* Kant's own thinking provides evidence of how reason itself was for Kant a force driving toward the unity of all philosophical inquiry in one system.

component of the highest end of reason, is an issue that continues to bedevil Kant scholars. Velkley, 10–14.

16 GMS, 247: GMM, 59.

17 For a cogent discussion of Kant's three-fold classification of humanity's cognitive powers into sensibility, understanding and reason, see Sullivan, 302–303, note 11.

18 KU, 176, cf. 174ff.: CoAJ, 14, cf. 12ff.

Throughout Kant's writings we see a dedication to reason and an *ultimate* dedication of that reason to the service of humankind. Kant's cosmopolitan conception of philosophy does not call for the development of reason for reason's sake alone – as does the scholastic conception. That would be of little use to anyone. Nor does it call for the pursuit of the ultimately practical goal of philosophy apart from the development of the unity of reason – such a pursuit would be deficient in design, direction, and structure. Kant's cosmopolitan conception of philosophy calls rather for a development of *practical* reason, a development in which the proper demands of both reason and practice are fulfilled.

Kant's cosmopolitan conception of philosophy has generally been overlooked, and the motives that guided Kant's philosophical creativity have been misunderstood. Many scholars have assumed that Kant pursued rational knowledge primarily for its own sake. As a result, his theoretical writings acquired primary importance and have received the overwhelming share of critical attention. His ethical concern has consequently been placed in the background as a secondary though important interest. This traditional view of Kant was reinforced by the caricature of Kant as the "*Verstandesmensch*" and a more or less typical child of the "*Aufklärung*," the "Age of Reason."

Schopenhauer's interpretation of Kant is a case in point. In Schopenhauer's view, the first *Critique* provides the measure by which all of Kant's other writings are to be interpreted and judged. Any divergence from its doctrines in Kant's later works indicates not advance in insight, but only an advance in garrulity or senility. In *The Basis of Morality*, his most thorough examination of Kant's ethics, Schopenhauer for two reasons bases his interpretation of Kant's ethics on the *Grundlegung* rather than the second *Critique*. First, he takes for granted that Kant did not seriously and competently address himself to moral questions until he had completed the first *Critique* (the *Grundlegung* thus being taken mistakenly as the first of Kant's ethical writings). Second, he assumes that the *Grundlegung* was the only writing on ethics that was completed before Kant's intellectual power began to wane.[19] Schopenhauer does give serious consideration to two sections of the second *Critique* – the sections on the relation of freedom to necessity and on moral theology – since their quality and agreement with the doctrines of the first *Critique* indicate to him that they were written in earlier years.[20] That Schopenhauer should accept these two parts of the second

19 Schopenhauer, *On The Basis of Morality*, 47, 50–51.

20 As evidence of Kant's failing powers of mind, Schopenhauer argues that Kant seriously marred his first critique, on the *Critique of Pure Reason*, by publishing the *Prolegomena to any Future Metaphysics* and then by rendering on the *Critique of Pure Reason* incoherent and self-

Critique (after insisting that it is a work which has marred the *Grundlegung*) just because they harmonize with the doctrines of the first *Critique*, clearly shows that he considers the *Grundlegung* a complete theory of ethics rather than only a statement of the formal components of an ethical theory.[21] Since Schopenhauer also rejects Kant's cosmopolitan conception of philosophy he can accept the *Grundlegung* as separate from Kant's theoretical concerns. The practical inquiry into morality, Schopenhauer asserts, should serve the theoretical interests of reason; that is, the practical concern should be viewed from the standpoint of the theoretical.

This influential point of view, for which Schopenhauer was so articulate a spokesman, must be challenged. It ignores Kant's early and continuing concern with morality; it overlooks the gradual development of Kant's ethical position from his pre-critical period; and it pre-supposes a conception of the theoretical goals of the first *Critique* that Kant expressly repudiates.

In a brief but brilliant chapter in his study of Kant's pre-critical ethics, Paul Schilpp pulled together evidence from Kant's life, correspondence and lectures to show Kant's early and continued interest in ethical questions.[22] Schilpp rejected Paul Menzer's view that Kant's distinctive ethical position did not emerge until 1770, when, according to Menzer, Kant freed himself from the domination of Rousseau and the English moralists.[23] By close examination of the *Untersuchung* of 1762 and the essays immediately following (which are cited

---

contradictory through an unfortunate second edition disfigurement. In addition, Schopenhauer believes Kant marred the *Groundwork of the Metaphysic of Morals* by the publication of the second critique, on the *Critique of Practical Reason*, in which, Schopenhauer says, Kant "gave more scope to the garrulity of old age." (Ibid., 50–51).

The Metaphysics of Morals is dismissed by Schopenhauer. He viewed the first part, the Doctrine of Law, as deplorable, and the second part, the Doctrine of Virtue, which Schopenhauer believes was written in 1797, as revealing the debility of old age in luxuriant manifestation.

21 The absence of any extended discussion of the concept of the good in the *Groundwork* is sufficient proof of Schopenhauer's mistake.

22 Schilpp, 1–14. Many other critics, Paul Menzer among them, have carefully demonstrated the gradual development of Kant's ethical thought, the central ideas of which were expressed before the publication of the *Critique of Pure Reason*. Schilpp must be credited for showing the continuity of Kant's thought from his pre-critical ethical writings through the major ethical treatises of his critical period. But Schilpp noted in his foreword to the third printing of his book (1977, 1–14) that Josef Schmucker's *Die Ursprünge der Ethik Kants* (1961) may prove to be a more accurate account of the evolution of Kant's ethical theory prior to his critical period.

23 Menzer, "Der Entwicklungsgang der Kantischen Ethik in den Jahren 1760–1785." Among Kant's important early ethical treatises are the following: *Untersuchung über die Deutlichkeit der Grundsätze der Theologie und Moral* (1764), *Versuch den Begriff der negativen Grössen in*

by Menzer and others to prove Kant's complete dependence on Rousseau, Hutcheson, Shaftesbury, and Hume), Schilpp pointed out the embryonic formulations of Kant's distinctive concept of duty and the distinction between hypothetical and categorical imperatives. Schilpp proved, beyond question, Kant's independence and originality from the very outset of his ethical investigations.[24]

That Kant did not publish any prolonged or systematic examination of moral questions prior to 1785 did not prove that only theoretical concerns were of importance to him. This proved merely, as Schilpp argues, that Kant "realized that until he had determined what was the nature of knowledge and what it was possible for man to know, it was useless to try to answer questions requiring *ethical* knowledge."[25]

To prove that Kant's concern even in the preparation of the first *Critique* sprang from practical motives, Schilpp included a fragment from a letter Kant wrote in 1773 to Markus Herz:

> ... I have come this far in my projected reworking of the science that has been so long cultivated in vain by half the philosophical world, since I see myself in possession of a principle that will completely solve what has hitherto been a riddle and that will bring the misleading qualities of the self alienating understanding under certain and easily applied rules, I therefore remain obstinate in my resolve not to let myself be seduced by any author's itch into seeking fame in easier, more popular fields, until I shall have freed my thorny and hard ground for general cultivation .... Nevertheless, it inspires me with the hope that, without fear of being suspected of the greatest vanity, I reveal to no one but you: the hope that by means of this work philosophy will be given durable form, a different and – for religion and morality – more favorable turn, but at the same time that philosophy will be given an appearance that will make her attractive to shy mathematicians, so that they may regard her pursuit as both possible and respectable."[26]

---

die Weltweisheit einzuführen (1763), and *Beobachtungen über das Gefühl des Schönen und Erhabenen* (1764) in AA 02.

24 Schilpp, chapters 3 and 4, (22–62) *passim*.

25 Ibid., 10.

26 Kant to Herz, late 1773, Br, (AA 10), 144; Corr, 140.
In the earlier letter to Herz (February 21, 1772), Kant indicated that he had already done more work on morality than on the theoretical problem in his proposed first critique of pure reason. As Schilpp notes, Kant told Herz that he had already distinguished the sensible and the intellectual aspects of morality, along with its principle and that he considered publishing these reflections in a work entitled "The Limits of Sensibility and Reason." This not only reveals Kant's early concern for morality but also his recognition that morality has a *sensible* aspect. (ibid., 129: ibid., 132) See also Schilpp, 108–109.

Schilpp further notes that the most unequivocal statement of Kant's insistence on the metaphysical foundation of morality is to be found in the *Grundlegung*. In its preface Kant says:

> The moral law in its purity and genuineness (and in the field of action it is precisely this that matters most) is to be looked for nowhere else than in a pure philosophy. Hence pure philosophy (that is, metaphysics) must come first, and without it there can be no moral philosophy at all.[27]

Armed with passages such as these – including Kant's own insistence in the first *Critique* on the primacy of moral philosophy[28] – Schilpp concludes that students of Kant should question the commonly held assumption that: 1. the *Critique of Pure Reason* brought about the Copernican Revolution; and 2. the importance of the first *Critique* far exceeds the second. Even apart from Schilpp's well-documented support, these conclusions are sufficiently evident when we reflect upon Kant's conception of philosophy as a rational knowledge requiring the agency of free, rational beings dedicated to the ultimate end of morality; that is, upon his insistence on the primacy of practical reason.[29]

2 Kant's Philosophical Method: Logical and Transcendental

Turning now from Kant's cosmopolitan view of the philosophical enterprise to the method he employs in philosophizing, we find that the fundamental dedication of reason to practice, required by the cosmopolitan conception, is present in Kant's methods both as a necessity and as a desideratum.

In the unified pursuit of philosophy, reason in logic provides the structure of possibility in all areas of practice – theoretical, moral, aesthetic. Because

---

27 GMS, 390: GMM, 56.

28 KrV, B867–68: CpR, 658.

29 Schopenhauer stands practically alone in rejecting the bulk of the *Critique of Practical Reason*; its quality demonstrates Kant's mental capacity at the time of its composition. While the Doctrine of Virtue (the second part of the Metaphysics of Morals) was published in 1797 and no doubt revised shortly before that time, it had in fact been largely written by 1780 since most of its contents are to be found in Kant's academic lectures on ethics, given in the years 1775–80.

Concerning Kant's alleged senility, accounts differ both as to the seriousness of his debilitation and the time of its appearance. The general consensus, however, is that Kant did not suffer a serious mental decline before 1796. (Paulsen, 51–52). See Manfred Kühn's definitive *Kant: A Biography*, 386ff.

logic is purely formal (that is, has no practical or material component beyond the formal demand that there be such a component), it is the science of the laws of thinking without restriction as to the objects thought about. Consequently, it delimits the right use of understanding in theoretical matters, reason in moral matters, and judgment in aesthetic matters. Since all areas of practice necessarily involve thinking, logic–as the science which provides rules necessary for sound thought–is itself practical and shares with all other branches of philosophy humankind's final end of morality.[30]

In providing the rules for the truth of cognitions in all areas of practice, logic imposes two requirements. First, it makes the negative demand that true cognitions be logically possible, i.e., not contradictory; second, it makes the positive demand that cognitions be logically well-founded, that is, as Kant states, that cognitions "(a) have grounds, and (b) not have false consequences."[31] It is this second criterion which provides for "*external* logical truth, or accessibility to reason *[Rationabilität]*" of a cognition.[32] In this way, logic provides the structure for direct disverification and indirect verification, both essential to scientific method. The formal criteria of truth, therefore, are found to be the principle of contradiction and the principle of sufficient reason.[33]

Though these two criteria are ineffectual until put into use, that is, until material content has been supplied to them, their demand is nonetheless plain. The demand of the universality of reason is one of the sources of the drive toward unity in philosophy. In putting these criteria to work, community in two related senses is demanded – a community of thoughts within an individual, and a community of individuals. For this reason Kant can say that common sense *(sensus communis)* is a touchstone for detecting errors in our use of understanding. How can one check on the full range of one's thought, on the truth or falsity of the consequences of one's thought? One can do so only by transcending not only the limitations of isolated thoughts within oneself, by recourse to all one's thoughts and experiences, but also by using the thoughts and experiences of others as a check on one's own. Reason in logic makes its ubiquitous demand for *totality* which is always a force breaking down the isolation of the individual and demanding a working community of those who would think correctly. Thus Kant writes:

---

30 Log, 11–16: Logic, 1–6.

31 Ibid., 51: ibid., 559.

32 Idem: idem.

33 Ibid., 51–53: ibid., 558–561.

> General rules and conditions of the avoidance of error are (1) to think for oneself; (2) to put oneself in thought in the place or point of view of another; and (3) always to think consistently. The first may be called *enlightened;* the second *enlarged;* and the third *consequent* or *coherent* thinking.[34]

We see that reason, which demands universality in logic as elsewhere, stands in need of implementation by the thinking community in order to achieve the universality which is the mark of truth. In fact, Kant is so impressed with the importance of community for the successful employment of reason that he asks those who deny men or women the freedom of speech or publication, while admitting their right to think, to tell him

> how much, and how correctly, would we think if we did not think as it were in common with others, with whom we mutually communicate! Thus one may well say that the external power which wrests from man the freedom publicly to communicate his thoughts also takes away the freedom to think.[35]

Kant discusses the inescapable dependence of human beings upon community for sound thinking and knowledge more systematically in the *Anthropology* where he distinguishes the different varieties of egoism and the risk that accompanies each variety. Egoism is based on the arrogance of the understanding, of taste, and of practical interest; accordingly, egoism can be logical, or aesthetic, or practical. The logical egoist is in danger of complete loss of intelligible contact with others because of failure to test his or her judgment and understanding against theirs. Egoists believe they do not need the touchstone of an external criterion of truth. But their isolation robs them of the use of the principle of sufficient reason because their internal application of this principle to their narrow experience (supposing that they do not further compartmentalize their egoism) by no means exploits its potential usefulness. This egoism runs the greatest risks where the senses are involved and illusion is frequent. In the final analysis, Kant holds, such logical egoism involves the failure to make use of one's reason at all, for:

---

34 Ibid, 57: Abbott, Logic, 48. I revert to the earlier translation of this passage from the Logic by T.K. Abbott, for his formulation is accurate and elegant and parallels Kant's formulation of the categorical imperative. Note the parallel between this statement of the conditions for the avoidance of error in cognition and the three formulations of the categorical imperative prescribing the conditions for the avoidance of error in morality. Cf. Orientiren, 144–45: Orient, 303–304.

35 Orientiren, 144: Orient, 303; cf. Anth, 128–9; AN, 16–17.

> To make use of one's own reason means nothing more than to ask one's self, with regard to everything that is to be assumed, whether he finds it practicable to make the ground of the assumption or the rule which follows from the assumption a universal principle of the use of his reason.[36]

As a logical egoist, one neither appeals to the thought and experience of the community, nor tests, by thinking for oneself, the suitability of one's thought in the community of other rational beings, a community which is encountered when the attempt is made to universalize fundamental assumptions and principles. The egoist thus fails to use "the maxim of the self-preservation of reason"[37] and falls victim to superstition and fanaticism.

The aesthetic egoist rests content with personal taste, not caring that others may find his or her verses, music, painting or whatever to be laughable. This sort of egoism precludes aesthetic improvement since the aesthetic egoist searches only within himself or herself for the touchstone of the artistically beautiful.

The moral egoist restricts all ends to self; no purpose is useful which does not serve him or her. Personal happiness alone constitutes the determining principle of such a person's will. As a result the moral egoist lacks a touchstone for the true concept of duty, which demands universality – that is, a concern for one's self and others as ends in themselves.

All forms of egoism are dangerous because they deprive the individual of the support to be derived from careful attention to the logical criteria for the truth of conceptions, criteria which cannot function properly in the isolation of individual reflection. In opposition to egoism Kant will settle for nothing less than the most extensive pluralism, a universalistic mode of thinking which does not regard the individual as a world in himself or herself, but recognizes the self as a citizen of the world.[38]

Kant also rejects egoism on the level of the nation when he insists on the subjection of all nations to a rule of law. Political egoism (though Kant does not use the term) involves the assumption by the state of its adequacy to be its own judge on all political questions, and the further assumption that its ends are the only ends that it need recognize or pursue. The danger from this egoism is perhaps the greatest of all – the danger of war. From this form of egoism there is no escape save in the federation of states in a community under international law.[39]

---

36 Orientiren, 146n-7n: Orient, 305n.

37 Idem: idem. This is important in the interpretation of the categorical imperative.

38 Anth, 128–30; AN, 10–12.

39 ZeF, 354ff.: TEP, 316ff.

In attempting to use the logical criteria of truth, we are led by reason itself to strive for the fulfillment of community, not only in politics, but in science, art, and morality. In applying these criteria, we see the unified drive of reason towards its ultimate goal – morality – and we see reason as practical at every stage. Kant has not been forced to concoct arguments proving that the ultimate end of reason is the vocation of humankind. He has simply shown that without the human community there can be no sound employment of reason and that any limitation on the totality of inclusion in this community compromises the universality of any judgment and is a limitation on the scope and usefulness of reason itself. For Kant there is no problem of making reason relevant to humanity because there is no functioning reason apart from rational beings and, consequently, so far as our *knowledge* extends, apart from human beings. Thus to talk of reason and its interest is to talk of humanity and its interests. They are inseparable.

To the question of subordination, whether humans shall live for reason, or whether reason shall serve humankind, Kant never wavers in his insistence that reason, like the Sabbath, exists for humankind.[40]

Thus Kant's conception of logic and logical method is found to harmonize with and support his conception of philosophy. In order to make use of the two criteria of logical truth, one is required: *(a)* to think for oneself – this reaffirms his conception of philosophy as rational; and *(b)* to think in total community with others – this reaffirms the universal character of reason and its dedication, under the cosmopolitan conception, to the end of morality.

Of equal importance to Kantian interpretation, we find the recognition in logic (in formal philosophy) of reason's ineluctable need for material content in its successful employment. We are thus driven by the method of formal philosophy (logic) to the starting point of material philosophy (metaphysics). This is the starting point of the transcendental method which begins with experience, with knowledge as an experienced fact. We begin with a real world which we can know. Kant never puts himself in the position of asking: Can there be knowledge? He knows that philosophers who ask this question never answer it successfully. Furthermore, since philosophy gains its knowledge discursively, it cannot start in a vacuum devoid of concepts to be examined, discussed, or related. Since, like Socrates, Kant believes that the nature of philosophy is discursive, he can inquire no further without recognizing knowledge as a fact

---

40 As Kant states the matter, "These highest aims [of pure reason] must, from the nature of reason, have a certain unity, in order that they may, as thus unified, further that interest of humanity which is subordinate to no higher interest." (KrV, B826: CpR, 631ff.)

than Socrates could argue without the presence of a person wise (or foolish) enough to make an assertion.

That we have knowledge of a world independent of our consciousness is Kant's point of departure in each of the *Critiques* and in the *Groundwork*. In the *Critique of Pure Reason*, Kant first justifies the question "How are the sciences of pure mathematics and of nature possible?" Then, pursuing immediately the conditions of their possibility, he remarks: "Since these sciences actually exist, it is quite proper to ask *how* they are possible; for that they must be possible is proved by the fact that they exist."[41] We start then in the *Critique of Pure Reason* with the givenness of mathematics and physics. Both sciences contain or presuppose necessarily true propositions whose truth is supplied in part by reason and in part by experience.[42]

Kant is less certain when he next asks how metaphysics is possible, for he realizes that the reality of metaphysics may be in doubt. In the first *Critique* he says metaphysical knowledge is given in experience either as a science or as a disposition of human reason to ask ultimate questions. So, even if we refuse to regard any of the answers to metaphysics as scientific, we must still confront and accept the reality of metaphysics as consisting of the metaphysical questions which reason asks when it probes the possibility of metaphysical answers. The question "How is metaphysics as a science possible?" cannot properly be asked, let alone answered, until we have seen how synthetic *a priori* judgments are possible. When that is accomplished, the reality of metaphysics is assured and the question can then be asked of it.[43]

Kant takes the same approach to the examination of morality. Here Kant proposes to begin with humanity's common moral experience and proceeds to the formulation of the first principles of morality. He insists that it would be foolish for him or anyone else to presume to have invented morality (although he does hope to offer a formula for it).[44] He assumes that morality is a given in human life and that it must be accepted as such. Hence Kant can employ humanity's universal experience of morality as the starting-point for his transcendental method in ethics.

We are not to suppose, however, that Kant intends to use moral examples – that is, individuals or actions commonly thought to be virtuous – as the foundation of his ethics. Moral principles, according to Kant, cannot be derived *a*

---

41 Ibid., B20: ibid., 56; cf. Prol, 280ff.: Prologue, 31ff. For Kant, whatever is actual is possible.
42 Prol, 274–5: Prologue, 25.
43 KrV, B19–23: CpR, 55–7; Prol, 275–80: Prologue, 26–31. Kant also considers metaphysics essential to reason. Cf. KrV, B18: CpR, 54–5.
44 GMS, 392: GMM, 57–58; KpV, 8: CprR, 123.

posteriori from experience; hence, any supposed example of a good moral person or good conduct, for example Jesus of Nazareth and his teachings, must be judged by *a priori* principles of morality arrived at by other means in order to determine whether or not an individual or specific actions can serve as such an example.[45] Nor does Kant believe that the common person possesses infallible judgment in the determination of morally good actions on which a theory of ethics can be based. Rather, the moral experience of the common person, the "fact" upon which moral theory must be constructed, is merely that person's consciousness of obligation in which

> the moral law is given, as an apodictically certain fact, as it were, of pure reason, a fact of which we are *a priori* conscious, even if it be granted that no example could be found in which it has been followed exactly.[46]

This is where Kant begins. Just as science is possible because scientific experience is actual, so morality is possible because moral obligation is actual.

This interpretation of the starting point of Kant's method in morality will not suit all students of Kant. Some will no doubt agree with Schopenhauer that

> Kant does not represent the so-called moral law *as a fact of consciousness*, as something empirically demonstrable; the philosophasters of recent times would, all and sundry, like to pass it off as such. By discarding every empirical basis of morals he rejects all inner, and even more definitely all outer, experience.[47]

Schopenhauer is right to insist that Kant does not say that an "empirical" proof of the moral law is possible. But Schopenhauer is mistaken if, as this passage suggests, he rejects the reality of moral obligation in inner experience as the primary fact in ethics. Kant insists that we are conscious of the moral law: i.e., we have an *a priori* experience of it that is not derived from sensible experiences. Schopenhauer refused to recognize the possibility of one's being conscious of something that is not sensible. Since Kant often identifies phenomenal experience (sensible experience) with Experience as such, it is not surprising that Schopenhauer should have made this mistake. We should recognize that only a part of our conscious awareness is sensory or phenomenal in this sense. Subjective experience (mere consciousness) teems with material that can never

---

45 GMS, 408: GMM, 72–3.
46 KpV, 47: CprR, 157.
47 Schopenhauer, *On the Basis of Morality*, 62.

be phenomenal, material which is not empirical but is derived subjectively from concepts or from the depths of the noumenal self. It is true that the actual, temporal state of mind in which one is conscious of moral obligation is an empirical state. But the components of this state are not all of empirical origin. Kant is free, then, to insist that the moral law "is not an empirical fact but the sole fact of pure reason, by which it [the law] proclaims itself as originally legislative."[48] This fact, Kant insists, is indubitable. To reassure oneself of it,

> One need only analyze the sentence which men pass upon the lawfulness of their actions to see in every case that their reason, incorruptible and self-constrained, in every action confronts the maxim of the will with the pure will, i.e., with itself regarded as *a priori* practical; and this it does regardless of what inclination may say to the contrary.[49]

Common sense can justify morality because, when we are aware of the moral demand, we are aware that it casts aside all our empirical desires and inclinations as incapable of determining what we *ought* to do. This is the empirical awareness of that which is not derived from sensibility and hence is not known empirically.[50] In full consistency, then, Kant appeals to humankind's consciousness of the moral law as the foundation of morality without resting morality on an empirical footing. Thus Kant's method in ethics parallels that used in the first *Critique*: he begins with the reality of experience, not, however, in the sense of *Erfahrung*, which in the first *Critique* usually refers only to phenomenal experience.[51]

In the field of artistic taste we find a continuation of this general methodological pattern. Kant begins once again with the actuality of a given aspect of human life whose nature he is inquiring into. And although in matters of taste we cannot speak of knowledge in its usual sense, since judgments of taste are strictly speaking non-cognitive, nevertheless, we must recognize the characteristic of necessity in aesthetic judgments as a fact of common experience in this

48 KpV, 31: CprR, 143. Kant notes: "… but as regards whatever there may be in him of pure activity (whatever comes into *consciousness*, not through affection of the senses, but immediately) he must count himself as belonging to the *intellectual world* of which, however, he knows nothing further." (GMS, 451: GMM, 112). My italics "consciousness" only.

49 KpV, 32: CprR, 143; cf. TP, 278–89: TaP, 45–56.

50 KpV, 91–92: CprR, 197–98.

51 This parallelism is, of course, not perfect. For example, Kant sometimes seeks to offer a transcendental deduction of the moral law, whereas usually he uses the awareness of this law as the foundation for a transcendental deduction of freedom. (GMS, 419ff.: GMM, 82ff.; KpV, 47: CprR, 157). For an excellent discussion of this question see Paton, *The Categorical Imperative*, 28, 202–205; cf. Kemp Smith, 272–273.

area of inquiry. Judgments of the beautiful are not matters of individual whimsy, for aesthetic judgments cannot be merely reports of agreeable sensations. In aesthetic experience we confront feelings of pleasure and pain which, since they result not from mere sensation but from the free play of the imagination with the understanding, are demanded of (if not shared by) all rational beings with sensibility of the sort we have.[52]

In science, morality, and art, Kant always starts from the foundation of human experience, knowledge, conviction, and judgment.[53]

In following the method of material philosophy (metaphysics) Kant faces the basic question: How is this knowledge and experience which we have possible? This question, following as it does from the assumption of the reality of that knowledge and experience, is answered by explaining how what is actual is possible. This starting point provides the material foundation for the transcendental method and reveals its essential structure.

The logical structure of the transcendental method may be understood as an adaptation of *modus ponens.* Take for granted the actuality of A; then by philosophical analysis show that B is required for the actuality of A, thereby showing the necessity of B. This method is transcendental in both a negative and a positive way. It is positive in establishing the necessity of conditions and principles entailed by the reality of whatever is given at the outset. It shows certain factors to be necessarily presupposed by the given knowledge or experience. It is negative in that the conditions and principles which are found to be necessarily presupposed by the directly given experience or knowledge are not themselves directly observable in either pure or empirical intuition.

In practice, the transcendental method, while remaining structurally constant, is differentiated into two modes, the analytic and the synthetic, depending on what is assumed as the given, i.e., as the reality which serves as the point of departure. The method begins either with the question, "How are synthetic propositions *a priori* possible?" or with the question, "How is experience possible?" If the first question is asked, the method is called the analytic; if the second question, it is the synthetic method. "The analytical method," Kant says, "so far as it is opposed to the synthetical [method] . . signifies only that we start

52 KU, 212–213, *passim*: CoAJ, 52–53, *passim*.

53 Kant did not follow this method, however, in religion. The answer to this apparent breakdown in Kant's application of the transcendental method requires an extended discussion. But since it is not essential to our present study, a brief answer may suffice: Kant holds that there is no knowledge of religious matters; there is only *hope* that the objects of religious faith may be true. We shall discuss his moral argument for God and immortality in Chapter VI.

from what is sought, as if it were given, and ascend to the only conditions under which it is possible."[54] Beginning with the reality of synthetic *a priori* judgments, the analytic method ascends to the conditions under which their possibility can be understood. The synthetic method, on the other hand, asking the broader, more fundamental question, "How is experience possible?" ascends to those conditions by reference to which we can understand the possibility of experience itself and, in addition, explain the actuality of synthetic *a priori* judgments.

If the analytic method were the only method that Kant employed, and if Hume and his followers were justified in denying the possibility of synthetic *a priori* judgments (on the ground that science offers only laws of empirical generalization, and mathematics only analytic propositions), Kant's position would indeed be indefensible, for the very foundation of this analytic argument, namely, the reality of synthetic *a priori* propositions, would have been properly denied.

Kant's analytic method is, however, supplemented by the synthetic method. When he uses the latter (which is not differentiated by structure from the former) Kant does not start by assuming the validity of synthetic *a priori* judgments. He begins, instead, with the fact of experience. In analyzing experience, the synthetic method leads to the determination of the fundamental compositional elements of knowledge and the conditions which generate it. From these elements and conditions it is possible to deduce the *a priori* principles which are necessary to sustain the scientific enterprise, even if one refuses to accept any law of science as a synthetic *a priori* judgment, and even if one refuses to acknowledge that scientific method is in any way dependent upon synthetic *a priori* conditions.[55] The synthetic method is thus seen to have greater power than the analytic method, since it is able to provide the starting-point for the latter.

---

54 Prol, 276n: Prologue, 27n.

55 Arthur Pap offers an interpretation of Kant's category of causality which preserves its synthetic *a priori* character while showing its continuing validity and usefulness for scientific inquiry. Although Pap does not hold that Kant's formulation of the causal principle is adequate, he does hold that synthetic *a priori* principles are necessary to the functioning of science. He would not argue that any specific principle is necessary. But his insistence that science necessarily depends upon the employment of some such principles as functionally necessary, commits him by implication to the view that synthetic *a priori* principles, as such, are transcendentally necessary and hence that the starting point of Kant's analytic method is adequately secured. Pap, 55–72. For the relevant sections in Kant's work, see KrV, B5, B218: CpR, 44–45, 208; Prol., 296–97: Prologue, 54.

The importance of the distinction between the analytic and synthetic methods is seen in the fact that Kant was himself at times confused about the nature of scientific certainty. In the *Proglomena* he says that in pure physics we can be confident of the existence of synthetic *a priori* propositions which are acknowledged to be apodictically certain and which must therefore have been established independently of experience even though they are derived in part from experience.[56] He singles out Newton's law of gravity as an example of such a synthetic *a priori* proposition.[57] But in so doing, Kant, quite unawares, was headed for trouble, for when Newton's law of gravity fell by the wayside Kant's transcendental argument fell with it. While it is possible to argue that specific laws of science would, if true, be synthetic *a priori* judgments, they can never be known to be true *a priori*; hence, specific scientific laws can never provide the basis for Kant's critical philosophy. It is strange that Kant should have been confused on this point since in his treatment of the principle of sufficient reason in his *Logic* he is quite explicit in regard to the indirection of any proof of a proposition supported by the truth of its consequences; this, of course, is the situation we face in the proof of scientific hypotheses.

In spite of such problems (and this is not the last difficulty we shall encounter in his examples), Kant does not rest his critical philosophy on so shaky a foundation. It is rather the synthetic method, the stronger of the two, on which he relies throughout most of the first *Critique*. This method, instead of assuming the validity of synthetic *a priori* knowledge as given, proves its validity as a consequence of conditions and principles which are independently established as necessary conditions of experience itself. In the "Introduction" to the first *Critique*, after noting examples of synthetic *a priori* propositions in mathematics and physics which he accepts as given, Kant disavows any ultimate dependence of critical philosophy on such examples. He says,

> Even without appealing to such examples, it is possible to show that pure *a priori* principles are indispensable for the possibility of experience, and so to prove their existence *a priori*. For whence could experience derive its certainty, if all the rules according to which it proceeds, were always themselves empirical, and therefore contingent?[58]

Here Kant relies on the reality of experience as the foundation of his critical philosophy rather than on the reality of synthetic *a priori* knowledge in the

56 Prol., 275: Prologue, 25.
57 Ibid., 321: ibid., 83.
58 KrV, B5: CpR, 44–5; cf. Prol, 297: Prologue, 54.

particular sciences. This synthetic method is applied so persistently throughout the Transcendental Deduction that, in spite of Kant's misguided opinion that scientific laws provide examples of synthetic *a priori* propositions, it is clear that he did not rely exclusively on these examples as the foundation of his philosophy. Rather, he attempted to show the necessity of synthetic *a priori* judgments for the explanation of the possibility of experience. In order to explain the capacity of science to produce merely useful hypotheses, Kant demonstrated that one must accept the actuality of certain synthetic *a priori* propositions. He summed this up in his well-known statement "Experience is possible only through the representation of a necessary connection of perceptions."[59]

Even under the synthetic method, the experience to be explained includes scientific cognition. But the distinction between the analytic and synthetic methods is nonetheless important because, thanks to the synthetic method, the success of Kant's critical philosophy no longer depends upon the validity of Newtonian science or even on the presence of science at all. With the synthetic method Kant can establish the critical philosophy on an experiential base no richer than that provided by the most primitive civilization. Kant's deduction of the category of causality, for example, does not rely essentially on the dubious assumption that there are necessary propositions in science. The transcendental deduction requires only that the scientist *claim* that certain laws are necessary. This the scientist must do if he or she does not want to sacrifice the methods of direct disverification and indirect verification of scientific laws.

Indeed, Kant might have ignored science altogether, for the component of necessity in experience which is vital to the transcendental deduction is found in many areas of experience other than the scientific. For example, it is found in the experiential fact that people can distinguish their dreams from reality. We have always conceived of the "objective" in terms of orderly behavior – the same yesterday, today and tomorrow. Had we done otherwise, the distinction between "subjective" and "objective" would never have been possible. The fact that the Masai always attack lions with spears, never with blades of grass, is all Kant needs to establish the category of causality as a synthetic *a priori* component of experience. This practice reveals the tacit assumption of the uniformity of nature, that is, the assumption of a synthetic *a priori* judgment.

The skeptic, therefore, who chooses to deny the synthetic *a priori* character of the principle of causality would, if Kant's synthetic method is employed

---

59 KrV, B218: CpR, 208.

correctly, be forced to deny the actuality not only of science but of all experience. Such a skeptic would have to deny all distinctions between dream life and waking life and even deny personal identity. In short, a skeptic would refute himself or herself in the attempt to refute Kant.[60]

Having seen the power of the synthetic method, we must not overlook the ease with which one can move from it to the analytic method. Starting from experience, the first achievement of the synthetic method is the establishment of the actuality of synthetic *a priori* judgments. And the judgment stating the conclusion of the transcendental argument under the synthetic method, that is, stating the necessity of *a priori* judgments, is itself a synthetic *a priori* judgment. As soon as we reach this point, we see that while the synthetic method carries over to the analytic method and supplies the latter with its material, it is not completely understood until the opening question of the analytic method has been answered. Thus the foundation of the critical philosophy as established by the synthetic method is obscure until the method itself has been explained with the help of the narrower analytic method, which seeks an answer to the question, "How are synthetic *a priori* judgments possible?"

At the same time, we should not overlook the added strength which the analytic method derives from the synthetic method. It can now move with confidence from the actuality of synthetic *a priori* judgments for they are known by means of the synthetic method to be as indubitable as experience itself. The two methods thus complement each other, the synthetic method providing the analytic method with its necessary starting point, the latter validating the type of proposition upon which the former essentially relies.

There is in both of these modes of the transcendental argument an important deductive moment. Kant repeatedly attempts to check the adequacy of any transcendental deduction by determining whether or not the basic experience from which the transcendental arguments start can be regained by combining the principles or conditions which were found to be necessarily presupposed. If any set of principles or conditions is essential to the foundational experience, we should be able to recover the initial experience by combining these factors. If we cannot do so, we cannot be sure that the allegedly derived conditions are in fact essential to the experience in question. They may, though essential, fail to account for experience only because an additional crucial component has been overlooked. Or the derived components may not be

---

60 As one student of Kant has so aptly stated the issue: "This constitutes as valid a proof as can be given of any principle, for it seems that the proof must in the last resort rest on the dilemma – believe this or believe nothing." Ewing, 48.

needed at all and one or more may even be inimical to the achievement of the initial experience.[61]

To recapitulate, Kant's philosophy is based on the centrality of the practical as a guide to reason. Reason is unable to procure the material of knowledge and the necessary checks on its employment apart from the initial assumption of, and attention to, the range of experience as given. Thus reason is inextricably enmeshed in the life of the human community as the locus of humanity's rational capacity and the only source of data for its employment. To answer the questions – What can we know?, What should we do?, What may we hope? – to answer the all-inclusive question – What is humankind? – we begin within the actuality of human knowledge and experience in the areas of science, morality, religion[62] and art. In carrying out this metaphysical inquiry of material philosophy the basic question then becomes: How is this knowledge and experience which we have actually possible? Or, more specifically: How are the synthetic *a priori* judgments which we make in all these areas of experience themselves possible?

3 The Chief Characteristics of Kant's Critical Thought

As Vaihinger has remarked, "One could, with full justice, entitle Kant's *Critique of Pure Reason*: Kant's *Theory of Experience*."[63] Accordingly, we shall succeed in pointing out the essential characteristics of Kant's critical philosophy if we can make clear the essential characteristics of the experience which provides his methodological starting-point.

We discern at the outset that neither form nor matter alone suffices to account for experience. Kant rejected the view that form alone could provide the

---

61 For parallel statements of Kant's method in his other writings see GMS, 392, 447: GMM, 57, 108. Also see KpV, 47: CprR, 157, which gives a transcendental deduction of freedom from the fact of the moral law.

62 Religion as discussed here and as referred to in the question "What may we hope?" is treated according to the transcendental method. But the starting point in this discussion of religion is not religious experience, but rather moral experience. I have already acknowledged the breakdown in the parallelism of Kant's method in the various employments of reason. In attempting to discuss religion Kant remains loyal to this parallelism; but he actually applies his method to morality, not to religion itself. Kant never addressed himself *directly* to the question of religious experience on its own terms as a parallel application of the transcendental method would seem to have required.

63 Vaihinger, 7.

given foundational experience[64] when he rejected rationalism in all its dogmatic forms. Under rationalism knowledge seemed secure for its judgments were thought to be *a priori*; that is, their truth was believed to depend not on the character of existent things but merely on the nature of reason and its concepts. The truth of such judgments was thought to be assured by the rational principle of contradiction, since the predicate concept could not be disassociated from the subject concept without contradiction. But Hume's clear thinking disclosed the fact that all *a priori* judgments of rationalism were analytic, while the connection between subject and predicate was always wholly contingent in judgments relating to matters of fact. By showing that it was quite possible to conceive the opposite of any matter of fact without contradiction, Hume showed that judgments of matters of fact were actually synthetic. In terms of his understanding that all propositions were either *a priori* or *a posteriori*, Hume concluded that since such propositions could not be *a priori* they were therefore *a posteriori*. Their truth depends entirely on an *observed* connection of subject and predicate. Thus Hume concluded that any confidence in the necessity of the connection between subject and predicate in any proposition regarding matters of fact depended solely on the learned habits of the observer, that is, on the observer's customary experience of such sequences. Hume here reasserted what Plato, Aristotle, and many other philosophers had known – that essence and existence are distinct,[65] and that the world of appearance is not the product of reason alone, coming into or going out of existence at reason's command. Hume thus confronted both rationalism and empiricism with this challenge : If you profess to speak with necessity you will be speaking only analytically and trivially.

We find support for Hume's position in human experience. Science cannot deduce from the concept of an axe-head the fact that it will or will not float. Only experience can validate these propositions. In science, experience is also the means of testing propositions, although the rigor of the experimental method is required. Moreover, Hume's rejection of rationalism is also borne out in morality. All that pure reason can deduce from the good as a basic concept of reason in ethics is that one should do good. This, as Kant noted, is merely an

---

64 We must not confuse a given experience with the given *in* experience. The given *in* experience is that material component in experience of which we are aware only by analysis. Given experience is experience as apprehended or lived through. It includes given elements and elements supplied by the knower; it is "given" in the sense that it is posited as the foundation of transcendental argument which is concerned to reveal the presuppositional conditions of such experience.

65 KrV, B279, B298: CpR, 247, 259; KU, 401: CoTJ, 56.

empty tautology.[66] Similarly, the demand of reason that happiness be commensurate with virtue is daily negated by both human beings and the weather.[67]

Or, consider aesthetic experience. It also cannot be understood in terms of form alone. Here, sole reliance on form involves us in a contradiction in terms, since under such a conception we would confront a formal (non-aesthetic) aesthetic experience. Kant selected the term "aesthetic judgment" for a judgment that was strictly speaking non-cognitive since he thought no one could claim that an aesthetic judgment is cognitive without encountering this contradiction.[68]

Thus the attempt to derive all knowledge and experience from reason alone is hopeless. As Kant says, "The reproach of aridity falls on understanding, which reaches the universal but must, because of this, put up with abstraction."[69] If reason attempts to give us knowledge about matters of fact, it must rest content with verbal definitions and triviality. Nor can it escape this triviality by drawing on the powers of the subjective imagination because this would be a direct appeal to mere fancy. Fancy need not be trivial, but neither is it necessary; it may be harmless, but it may also be pernicious if it is presented to us as knowledge of the external world. The distinction between the internal subjective world and the external objective world is one which cannot be maintained by reason alone. Knowledge and experience, however, depend essentially upon this distinction. Reason cannot be allowed to forget the limitations of essence in the presence of existence; it must, in its search for real knowledge, take into account the resisting influence of matter.

But Kant also rejected the view that matter alone could provide an adequate foundation for experience, and in so doing he rejected radical empiricism just as he had rejected dogmatic rationalism. This insight was not the discovery of any one philosopher; it was deeply imbedded in Kant's heterogeneous heritage from Plato, Aristotle, Leibniz, and Wolff. Just as the concepts of rationalism were found to be empty, so the data of empiricism were found to be blind.

All our material knowledge, Kant found, is both synthetic (based on judgments in which the predicate concept adds something not contained in the subject) and *a posteriori* (restricted to judgments based on observable instances which provide the connection between the subjects and the predicates of these synthetic propositions). Empiricism, in offering us merely synthetic *a posteriori*

66 VüE, 35–36: LoE, 25–26. Kant's rejection of ethical rationalism (formalism) has often been overlooked by students of Kantian ethics.

67 KU, 403–404: CoTJ, 58–59.

68 EEKU, 221–23: CoPJ, 24–25.

69 Anth, 146: AN, 25–26.

knowledge, is hopelessly blind and unstable, for one can know only what one has experienced.[70] It cannot enable us to anticipate the future in any way, or to establish contact with the past. It isolates us in a specious present which, shut off from past and future, finally disappears altogether. Nor can empiricism account for our errors in perception. If all knowledge comes from matters given in experience, what is given must be accepted at face value. As a consequence, the distinction between appearance and reality is lost and with it the possibility of error which is essential to knowledge.[71] The empiricist waits in vain for matter to present itself in a fashion so orderly that it is immediately clear and useable by the observer; the most obvious empirical fact is that raw sense data apart from epistemological interpretation are chaotic.

But human experience in manifold areas is not chaotic. The presence of order in experience forces us to reject empiricism even as it forced us to reject rationalism. Science, if denied all recourse to form and forced to depend solely on matter, on the sensuous given, would be a science without laws – a contradiction in terms.

In ethics, empiricism inevitably ends in subjectivism. Moral obligation is quickly reduced to the mere feeling of obligation. One is obligated only so long as one *feels* obligated, but no longer. Accordingly, any moral injunction or claim could be answered with: "I feel no obligation." Neither will this serve to account for legal obligations, since one could claim exemption from a law by not wanting to obey it.

In art, empiricism reduces aesthetic judgment to a mere judgment of agreeableness and thus once again to complete subjectivism. To judge that a painting is beautiful would be merely to remark "I am pleased." If one were revolted by the finest work of Bach, and found the greatest thrill in listening to "London Bridge," one would not be lacking in taste. One would be merely liking and disliking. This even elevates obscene performance art and the most vicious rap songs to the level of works by Michelangelo and Mozart. As in other areas of experience, here too we are finally reduced by empiricism to isolation in time, place, and thought.

Form without matter and matter without form lead the knower into the hopeless isolation which Kant described in his treatment of egoism, save that now the individual is lost even to self-knowledge, along with all knowledge and experience. Both form and matter, therefore, must be ingredient in experience.

70 Ibid., 144ff.: ibid., 35ff.

71 KrV, B235: CpR, 220. See Blanshard, *The Nature of Thought*, Chapters II and V.

The second characteristic of the given experience, whose reality we must presuppose and whose nature we are trying to explain, is correlative to the first: the formal and material components of experience must be different and distinct. This second feature differs from the first in that it exposes the mistake of conflating formal and material components in experience by postulating a formal-matter or material-form designed to avoid the difficulties of relating form and matter with necessity.

Rationalists, for example, may use the terms "form" and "matter," but in their analysis they tend to merge them into a formal-matter, as a purely rational unity of form and matter. On such a view the knower, in the act of knowing, is said to become aware of a given unity of form and matter by means of reason alone. This maneuver is of no avail, for the conditions which Kant found to be essential to experience are ignored. Essence and existence are once again identified. There is no restriction on fantasy, and thus, the "knowledge" of the external world which is alleged is in fact false. Hegel's "rational demonstration" that there could only be nine planets is a prime example of this error. Whatever is offered as knowledge of matters of fact can still be denied without contradiction.

In like manner, an empiricist may argue that there is material-form, that matter as presented to the knower is already impregnated with formal components. All one has to do is perceive, for a unitary experience of material-form is given in sensation. But this will not suffice either, because the object of knowledge is lost in the immediacy of sense. In the absence of the distinction between appearance and reality the possibility of negation and error essential to objectivity and knowledge is sacrificed. We are left again in the plight of the extreme realists.

Thus it is fundamental to Kantian philosophy that form and matter be epistemologically distinct. They must be brought together in the synthesis of knowledge as components which, as given, are essentially distinct. The effort to bring them together as a unity *before* the process of knowing takes place destroys the polarities essential to knowledge : appearance and reality, the one and the many, and essence and existence. To find a propositional vehicle adequate to these requirements, Kant combines in a new propositional form the synthetic character of the empiricist's *a posteriori* judgments with the *a priori* character of the rationalist's analytic judgments. In one proposition Kant combines synthesis – which provides for the multiplicity and diversity of parts (the many) – and *a priority* – which provides for the necessity of relating them in a unity (the one). Thus, the logical structure of propositions which are to articulate experience is the synthetic *a priori.*

We need, Kant argues, synthetic *a priori* judgments in which the subject is bound in a relation of *a priori* necessity to a predicate that is not contained in the subject by the principle of identity. This union cannot be achieved by either the subject or the predicate alone; sole reliance on the subject will give us only the inadequate analytic judgments, and sole reliance on the predicate, only synthetic *a posteriori* judgments. The union of subject and predicate in the mode of necessity can only be achieved with the help of a third thing, namely, the actuality of experience from which we started and in the perspective of which the proposition becomes transcendentally analytic. The given experience, then, which it is the task of critical philosophy to explain, is itself the *union* of diverse and distinct material and formal components. Because it is a necessary union, it can be articulated only by means of synthetic *a priori* propositions.

Our attempt to grasp the essential characteristics of experience, which is the starting point of Kant's synthetic method, has led us now to the starting point of his analytic method and to the central and specific problem of his critical philosophy in all three *Critiques*. In order to understand fully the nature of the given experience on which the synthetic transcendental method rests, we must now face the central question in Kantian philosophy – "How are *a priori* synthetic judgments possible?"[72] To understand the possibility of synthetic *a priori* judgments, we must recognize two factors of preeminent importance : (1) Kant's distinction between the phenomenal, the noumenal, the conceptual and the sensible; and (2) Kant's account of the agency of the individual knower.

(1) Our first task is to understand how the unity of subject and predicate can be attained without relinquishing the true distinctness and individuality of each by the appeal to a third thing.[73] After we have admitted that matter and form must be introduced as distinct components into experience, we must recognize that there is a difference between the "object" of experience – the derived unity of form and matter which is the "given experience" of the transcendental argument – and the ingredients that enter into it. That this object can be neither a concept nor a percept follows analytically from our recognition of the need for both form and matter as epistemologically distinct components brought together in a unity providing knowledge. If the parts, though distinct from one another, must yet be present in a unity, this unity cannot be identified with either original component. We must have a conceptual component (the categories, the ideas of reason) and a non-conceptual, material component (sensibility) *in addition to* the "object" of experience as the unified combination of these components.

---

72 KrV, B19: CpR, 55.
73 Ibid., B13ff.: ibid., 50ff.

This is how Kant acknowledges the need to maintain the separation of appearance and reality while avoiding the mistake of empiricism. By distinguishing the given *in* experience (not to be confused with "given experience" as a fact) from that which can be recognized *as* experience,[74] he allows for the possibility of confusion and error, for mistakes in perception. That which we take to be true is never known to be so with immediacy; that which is given in immediacy is never an object of experience. Thus the object of experience is only appearance in relation to the thing-in-itself (*Ding an sich*).[75]

This distinction of the object of experience from the *Ding an sich* and from the conceptual components is also required in order to avoid the mistakes of rationalism. This is evident in Kant's analysis of the antinomies and the paralogisms and in his insistence that concepts as such are empty.[76] If reason could legislate the object of experience and if the object of experience were not fundamentally different from its rational components, we could not account for the discrepancies between the world of experience and the demands of reason. For example, the world reveals an endless causal series whose first cause can never be reached. Yet reason demands a first cause to explain the causal chain.

Similarly, reason demands the complete good (*das vollendete Gut*), the perfect observance of the moral law and the just equivalence of happiness and the worthiness to be happy. Yet the world of experience does not honor these demands. The conceptual rational component of knowledge cannot be identified, then, with the object of experience. We must retain both the conceptual component and the object of experience. The conceptual component, furthermore, must adapt itself to the independence of the sensibility since it is unable to reshape the given according to its whim.[77] The object of experience cannot be regarded as a category or concept unless one holds that reason alone can

---

74 We must keep in mind Kant's distinction between the objects of appearance, which are the objects of inner sense that can be recognized and talked about, and the objects of experience, the phenomenal objects for which the employment of all categories is required. (Prol, 298: Prologue, 54).
In addition to both of these types of objects, Kant recognizes representations (*Vorstellungen*), which are the components the knower shapes into phenomenal objects. But we must not regard representations as the given, since they too are "phenomenal" in a loose sense of the word and not "noumenal"; that is, they are a part of conscious awareness and, as such, are already a product of the activity of the knower. (KrV, B317–324ff.: CpR, 276–281; Prol, 304: Prologue, 62).

75 KrV, B307ff., B310: CpR, 267–8, 272; Prol, 294–295: Prologue, 50.

76 KrV, B1, B433ff.: CpR, 41, 384ff.; Prol, 333–350: Prologue, 99–119.

77 KrV, Bxl: CpR, 34; Prol, 288: Prologue, 42. Here in his refutation of idealism Kant gives a very clear statement of the need for things in themselves with independence and resistance in

account for both reality and experience. This mistake leads to the antinomies. Similarly, the object of experience cannot be regarded as merely sensible unless one holds that the material component exhausts both reality and experience. This error leads to the chaos of the indifferent "truth" of veridical and illusory experience. Both views involve the denial of negation and thus destroy the separability essential for objective determination.

We must not conclude, however, that these components constitute all of conscious awareness.[78] This mistake is easily made since Kant often saves the word "experience" for cognitive experience, for the experience of objects in space and time fully ordered by the categories of the understanding. Kant's treatment is further complicated by the fact that he sometimes refers to the inner awareness of duty as an awareness of the noumenal, that is, as awareness of the free will of a noumenal being. He rarely makes this mistake, for he recognizes that even the awareness of oneself as a member of the intelligible world is only the awareness of one's noumenal self *as it appears* but not as it is in itself.[79] Nonetheless, this awareness of the appearance of the noumenal self is clearly not a phenomenal appearance in the strict sense of "phenomenal." This self-awareness cannot be ordered by the category of causality.

We need not elaborate these complexities here. What we must note is that conscious awareness, or experience in the commonsense usage of the term, is recognized by Kant. And this "experience" is far broader than cognitive experience (experience in the strict sense of *Erfahrung*). At the same time, this non-phenomenal experience is neither noumenal nor merely sensible, nor merely conceptual, though all of these factors are ingredient in it as they are in phenomenal experience.[80]

---

order to account for the independence of the sensible given from conceptual control. Cf. KpV, 6: CprR, 120.
Kant always describes sensation as the way in which the subject is *affected*. (KrV, B208, *passim*: CpR, 201, *passim*). See also Adickes, *Kant und das Ding an sich*.

78 See Note 74 supra.

79 GMS, 451: GMM, 111–12; KrV, B158, B334: CpR, 169, 287. Cf. Schrader, "The Thing in Itself in Kantian Philosophy," 28ff.

80 Kant is well aware of this broader range of "experience," and in fact he uses the term "*Erfahrung*" in this non-technical sense in several of his writings, including the first *Critique*, the *Anthropology*, the *Religion*, the *Grundlegung*, and several articles, especially the article on *Theorie und Praxis*, in which this usage occurs repeatedly. Cf. TP, 277, 284, 287: TaP, 43, 51, 53–4; RGV, 20, 63: Rel., 16–17, 56–57; Anth, 143: AN, 23–24. And in the first *Critique* we find, among others, the following important passage concerning the interaction of the moral and theoretical wills, that is, of the will of experience widely conceived as open both to causality and to freedom: "Pure reason, then, contains, not indeed in its speculative, but in a certain

(2) The second fundamental factor is also presupposed by our acceptance of the reality of synthetic *a priori* judgments. As a unity of truly divergent components in terms of a third thing, knowledge is in part the product of the knowing subject, an agent who also makes an essential contribution to experience.[81]

Since form and matter are held to be epistemologically distinct if knowledge is to be possible, and since they must be related for the fulfillment of this knowledge, it follows that there must be some agency to relate them. We have already seen that neither component functioning by itself can relate form to content without destroying the distinction between them. Neither can these components be related by an agency external to the knower. If we were to suppose the existence of an external knower who achieved the synthesis of these components on our behalf and presented them to us in a synthetic unity, we, as knowers, would receive these components in that unified manner that, by eliminating the possibility of error, makes knowledge impossible.

Kant's central idea is that the unity of knowledge must not precede the activity of the knower but rather must be the product of the knower's own agency. The knower must be both receptive of the material of intuition and productive of both the categories of the understanding and of their application to the material of intuition.[82] The knower must achieve knowledge through the employment of his or her own faculties. It must be the consequence of the blending of the conceptual and material components which apart from the knower's agency would remain separated and deficient for knowledge – the former being empty, and the latter being blind.

This is Kant's Copernican Revolution in metaphysics. It points to the necessity of spontaneity in the subject, of a creative force in the subject that is sufficient to determine objects. As subject, one does not create one's basic

---

practical employment, namely in the moral employment, principles of the *possibility of experience* (*Erfahrung*), namely, of such actions as, in accordance with moral precepts could (*könnten*) be encountered in the *history* of mankind... referring to the sensible world, viewed, however, as being an object of pure reason in its practical employment." (KrV, B835: CpR, 637. This translation includes my adaptations of Kemp Smith's text.) This is a clear recognition of interaction between the noumenal and phenomenal worlds, or the world of freedom and the world of necessity.

81 KrV, Bxvi, Bxxiii: CpR, 22, 25. The influence of the noumenal is also involved in the agency of the subject.

82 I do not want to leave the impression that it is a task of the knower to apply the forms of intuition, for intuition is already formed-matter, and the knower's agency has already been expressed at this state. Cf. Schrader, "The Transcendental Ideality and Empirical Reality of Kant's Space and Time."

concepts arbitrarily nor does one create the given material; yet one cannot have experience until one has produced by the spontaneity of one's own reason the forms of the understanding and achieved their embodiment in the given matter. The achievement of this combination is one's own. Its adequacy or inadequacy is, in part, one's own responsibility.[83]

The subject is not to be understood, however, simply as an individual devoid of all self-transcendence. A mere individual and idiosyncratic subject could not be the agent unifying form and matter in the achievement of knowledge. A purely subjective individual would have no enduring structure or character; such a being would lack the temporal, spatial, and conceptual continuity required for knowledge. Objectivity could have no meaning for such a purely subjective entity who had nothing in common with other knowing agents. Thus, in order to account for the experience and the knowledge which we do have, Kant introduces a "transcendental unity of apperception" which is common to all rational beings.[84] The spontaneity of the subject in producing the conceptual components of knowledge must be well-ordered and universal – an expression of reason.

On the other hand, we must not interpret the knowing agent simply as the unity common to all knowers. The subject cannot be merely the transcendental unity of apperception for such a being would then be reduced to a mere formal structure. Devoid of all sensible intuition, he or she would have no access to the material component of knowledge and would be unable to apply the universal categories of thought. The forms of universality can be made determinate only by a subject who, through intuition, is provided the content of sensibility which is unique for each subject.[85] Each is differentiated as a knower by the impress of sensibility upon him or her. Were each one not so differentiated, there would be no content by means of which his or her universality could be brought to determinate expression. And were sensibility not independent of one's manipulative powers, there would be no restraint upon one's fancy.

Furthermore, there is no real significance to a content that is not resistant to form. Hence the noumenal must be presupposed as the ground of sensibility such that the world of appearance that is formed by the agency of the knower is

---

83 KrV, A96ff., B136ff.: CpR, 129ff., 155ff. We see also that the Copernican knower fulfills the conditions set down for one who has rational as opposed to mere historical knowledge. The extent of his responsibility is, of course, quite restricted in this theoretical sphere. Here we are not speaking of what could properly be called moral responsibility. We do have technical responsibility, however, since the knower must think in certain ways if the knower is to acquire experience.

84 Ibid, B135, B143–5: ibid., 155, 160–61; Prol, 298ff.: Prologue, 56ff.

85 KrV, B146, B149: CpR, 162–163.

the appearance, not of the knower's fancy, but of the world of things in themselves.[86] The subject, either as sheer particularity or as mere universality, as wholly material or wholly formal, is unfit to serve in the capacity of knower. Such a subject could never escape the subjective chaos or the objective emptiness of these extremes.

Thus the concept of a subject adequate to our needs in the explanation of synthetic *a priori* knowledge must have characteristics both of universality and particularity. Nor can a subject be a mere passive unity of these characteristics. Rather, the subject must have a noumenal nature, capable of freedom and rationality; and must have a sensible nature capable of passively receiving sense data. In attaining synthetic *a priori* knowledge, the subject must be capable of synthesizing the universal and the particular, the abstract and the concrete. Thus, he or she must possess both the faculties of receptivity and of organization; that is, the resources and the creative power to provide for the characteristics of the experience that it is his or her task to produce.[87]

In summary, then, we find that the Kantian conception of philosophy is one which stresses rationality and its dedication to morality as the final end of humankind. We find that Kant's method of logic stresses the importance of individual, autonomous thought and points out the necessity of appeal to the human community in the successful employment of reason. The transcendental method is based upon human experience and seeks to explain its conditions. This experience, supplied by the human community, is the given experience for both the metaphysic of nature and the metaphysic of morals. In order to account for the possibility of this experience and in order to provide both science and morality with a sound intellectual foundation, Kant directs his thought to the key epistemological problem presented by experience – namely, to the possibility of synthetic *a priori* judgments.

Recognizing the synthetic *a priori* structure of experience, Kant sees that form and matter are both essential to it and must be accepted for what they are – heterogeneous components which must be united without the loss of their heterogeneity. The uniting of form and matter, which is the problem of schematism, is thus crucial in Kant's examination of the possibility of experience. By his own rational spontaneity, and equipped with both formal and material faculties, the subject achieves the union of form and matter in experience as a product of his own creative power.

---

86 KrV, B344–5, *passim*: CpR, 293, *passim*.
87 Ibid, B75: ibid, 93; Anth, 140: AN, 34–35; Log, 35–6: Logic, 546–7.

Just as we must focus our attention upon the relating of form and matter in the production of "cognitive experience" to understand Kant's theoretical philosophy, we must likewise attend to the relating of form and matter in the production of "moral experience" to understand Kant's moral philosophy. To understand Kant's aesthetics we must examine the relating of form and matter in "artistic experience." And to find the Kantian answer in all these areas of human life, we must use the Copernican Revolution as a clue and look for the solution to the problem of the relating of form and matter in the nature of the subject.

Man is that subject. Humans alone possess the rational and sensible faculties enabling them to unite form and matter in experience and knowledge. If we are to see the whole of Kant's thought with the many facets of "experience" in their proper relation to one another, we must probe mankind's moral nature – the most fundamental aspect of that nature. To understand the Philosophy of Experience we must, above all else, understand Kant's view of moral experience; we must understand the unity of form and matter in this, the most basic area of human life and the one in which reason finds its primary employment.

Thus the central problem of Kantian philosophy is to be found, as Kant himself says, in the question, "What is it to be human?" The unity of Kant's philosophy can only be found in his answer to this question. Mankind is the only bridge between the noumenal/intelligible world and the phenomenal/sensible world, between science, morality, and art. The Philosophy of Experience most nearly attains its goal under the cosmopolitan conception when, in striving to disclose mankind's role in relating form and matter in all areas of human life, it discloses the way in which human agency in all other areas culminates in the schematism of form and matter in morality.[88]

This is the background idea of the whole of Kant's philosophy which we must bear in mind if we would offer a systematic interpretation of Kant's ethics. In light of the whole of Kant's thought we must recognize the primacy of Kant's moral writings. In fidelity to the whole sweep of Kant's thought we must recognize that the right to interpret his writings on pure reason in the light of his ethical writings is at least as defensible as the reverse procedure.

We know that Kant's ethical theory must have material as well as formal components; we know that the moral task must consist in the relating of these components by the moral subject; we know that in order to provide both material and formal components in Kant's ethics there must be a doctrine of the good as the object of volition as well as a doctrine of duty. We know that

88 See Vaihinger, 8–9 for an excellent statement of Kant's basic anthropocentrism.

there can be no moral examples nor legalistic duties since the union of form and content cannot *confront* the moral subject but must be *produced* through his agency alone; we know that Kant's ethical concepts must be established transcendentally, and we know that his basic ethical concepts must be expressed in propositions which are synthetic *a priori*. These conclusions provide the soundest criteria for interpreting Kant's ethical writings, since they free the interpreter from slavish submission to frequently inconsistent texts while providing criteria of selection, evaluation, and interpretation which are grounded, not subjectively, but objectively in the system of Kantian thought as a whole.

Chapter II: The Copernican Revolution In Ethics: The Good Reexamined

1 The Primacy of the Moral Law in the Determination of the Good

Before Kant, most philosophers in the Greek and scholastic tradition believed that ethical inquiry should begin with the definition of the good and derive the moral law and the concept of obligation from that definition. But from his revolutionary point of view, Kant saw that this was precisely the source of

> all the confusions of philosophers concerning the supreme principle of morals. For they sought an object of the will in order to make it into the material and the foundation of a law; ... instead they should have looked for a law which directly determined the will a priori and only then sought the object suitable to it.[1]

In the "analytic" of the *Critique of Practical Reason* Kant demonstrates that all attempts first to define the good as the object of the will and to derive from it the moral law and duty make the good into a material concept, and that all material principles are incapable of grounding the supreme principle of morality.[2]

A few basic definitions will help clarify Kant's argument. First, we must understand what Kant means by a practical principle. "Practical principle" is a generic term referring to the class of all propositions which contain a general determination of the will.[3] The will is the power of a rational being to act in accord with its own idea of law rather than in mere conformity to law, whether it be a natural law or a legal system or institution.[4] This idea of law in terms of which the will acts is the principle of the will and therefore a practical principle. A being possessed of will does not simply respond to a stimulus in an act of willing; rather, such a being consciously projects an intention. This intention is again the practical principle. But practical principles may be of two kinds: either subjective, in which case the principle of volition is regarded by the subject as valid for itself alone, or objective, in which case the principle is regarded as

---

1 KpV, 64: CprR, 172–3.

2 Ibid., 41, 109: ibid., 152, 214. Kant's argument is not systematic; it comes in odd places and from many vantage points. Sometimes it is implicit and at other times repetitiously explicit. Nonetheless, the argument is capable of systematization.

3 Ibid., 19: ibid., 130.

4 GMS, 412: GMM, 80.

valid for all subjects. Subjective principles are called maxims whereas objective ones are called practical laws.[5]

We must also bear in mind Kant's distinction between "formal" and "material" as these terms relate to concepts and knowledge. Knowledge, or a concept, is material when it refers to some object; it is formal when it refers merely to the form of understanding and reason, that is, when it refers only to "the universal rules of thinking as such without regard to differences in the objects" of possible thought.[6] Thus, the presence or absence of a specific object determines whether or not concepts and knowledge are formal or material.

It follows analytically from these definitions that the traditional concept of the good is a material concept. A formal concept, by contrast, is one which makes no reference to an object. But the traditional concept of the good, defined prior to the moral law, is the concept of an object for which the will is to strive – for example, the pursuit of happiness, courage, temperance, justice or another virtue. Because of its reference to an object, the good is a material concept.

Kant's insistence that the moral law and duty can never be grounded on material concepts does not follow analytically, however, from these definitions. As Kant sees it, for the good to be a meaningful ethical concept, it must be related to the moral agent as the obligation of the agent to embody the good in the practical principle of his or her will.[7] But the good as a material concept cannot, Kant claims, be related to the will in this fashion. For if it is related to the will at all, then the good must be related to the will either empirically and contingently, and hence without obligation, or it will determine the will as the natural cause of whatever is willed, and hence the freedom of the will, and thereby the will itself, will be destroyed. Thus, the attempt to ground the principle of morality on a previously defined material concept of the good founders on this dilemma: either the good stands in no relation or in a contingent relation to the will, or the good itself has the power to determine the will to action and thereby destroys the will. In neither case can the moral law be derived from the good and, therefore, no relation of obligation can be effected between the good and the will.

Kant's support of this position is presented in his exposition of the theorems developed in the *Critique of Practical Reason*. Suppose, Kant argues, one defines

5 KpV, 19: CprR, 130; GMS, 401n: GMM, 699n.

6 GMS, 387: GMM, 55.

7 Kant takes for granted that moral obligation is categorical, i.e. necessary, inescapable obligation. And he also holds that obligation presupposes freedom of the will. We will assume these points for the present and hold that a sound moral theory must give an account of obligation on these terms.

the good as the object (material) of the faculty of desire – for example, the desire for wealth. The good then becomes an object whose reality is desired. As such the good stands in relation to the will[8] as that which the will desires. The practical principle of the will then expresses the desire of the will for the desired object, namely the good. But in this case, the practical principle can never be an objective practical law for all wills but only the subjective maxim of a particular will as it empirically encounters a desire within itself. The relation of the will to the good, therefore, is contingent because the decision of the will either to pursue or not pursue the good

> consists in the conception of an object and its relation to the subject, whereby the faculty of desire is determined to seek its realization. Such a relation to the subject is called pleasure in the reality of an object, and it [this pleasure] must be presupposed as the condition of the possibility of the determination of choice.[9]

But in defining an object as the good we cannot know a priori that it will be "associated with pleasure or displeasure or will be merely indifferent."[10] Thus a theory of ethics which defines the good in this fashion can offer no rational foundation for the relation of necessity between the good and the will, and hence cannot derive the concept of duty from the idea of the good.

Furthermore, the will that relates itself to the good on the basis of desire will be acting according to a principle which is merely a subjective maxim and not an objective moral law valid for all rational beings. Since the practical principle of the will is determined by the pleasure or aversion of the faculty of desire in regard to the good as its object, the practical principle is inevitably determined subjectively. There is no determinate object that can arouse the desire of even one person while likewise arousing the same desire in all persons or even in the same person at all times. Hence a practical principle cannot be an objective (universal) law if it is based on a choice determined by reference to pleasure or displeasure in regard to an object. The principle is *in fact* binding only on the will of the person who actually desires the good and who actually takes pleasure in its reality. Even so, it is only hypothetically binding on such a person as the maxim of a subject who happens to take a particular delight in a particular object at a given point in time. In such a theory the good is either unrelated to the will or is only contingently binding upon it.

---

8 For Kant the will is both practical reason and the faculty of desire (KpV, 9n: CprR, 123–124n).
9 KpV, 21: CprR, 132.
10 Idem: idem.

From this argument Kant deduces theorem I: "All practical principles which presuppose an object (material) of the faculty of desire as the determining ground of the will are without exception empirical and can furnish no practical laws."[11]

There were moralists prior to Kant who saw this difficulty and sought to avoid it by distinguishing between a higher and a lower faculty of desire on the basis of the origin of the pleasure entertained by the faculty of desire. Pleasures belonged to the lower faculty of desire if they originated in the senses and belonged to the higher faculty of desire if they arose from the understanding. These moralists argued that if the good as the object of the will were related to the will through the higher faculty of desire, that is by means of a pleasure of the understanding, then it could be related to the will as law.

Kant rejects this approach because the good is still related to the will contingently. The good is binding on the will only if in fact there is a felt desire on the part of the will to attain the reality of the good. And this desire will be present only if the faculty of desire, whether higher or lower, encounters within itself pleasure in the anticipation of the reality of the good. Thus the concept of duty cannot be derived from the definition of the good even when the good is the object of the understanding as the higher faculty of desire.

Nor is this the only problem. This distinction between higher and lower faculties of desire does not enable us to regard objects of the higher faculty of desire as laws. Whether an object of the will stems from the understanding, whether the good is defined in terms of sense or in terms of the understanding, or whether the good is defined rationally or empirically, the consequences are the same. If the only way the good can determine the choice of the will is by means of desire, then the principle of the will must be subjective and no practical law can result. Kant concludes,

> However dissimilar the conceptions of the objects, be they proper to the understanding or even to the reason instead of to the senses, the feeling of pleasure, by virtue of which they constitute the determining ground of the will (since it is the agreeableness and enjoyment which one expects from the object which impels the activity toward producing it) is always the same. This sameness lies not merely in the fact that all feelings of pleasure can be known only empirically, but even more in the fact that the feeling of pleasure always affects one and the same life-force which is manifested in the faculty of desire, and in this respect one determining ground can differ from any other only in degree.[12]

---

11 Ibid., 26; cf. 36: ibid., 132; cf. 148.

12 Ibid., 23: ibid., 134. John Stuart Mill's failure to heed this passage points graphically to the importance of the history of philosophy as a guide and measure for fruitful philosophical inquiry. By ignoring Kant's argument Mill advanced a position that Kant had already refuted. See Mill, *Utilitarianism*.

Since Kant calls the principle of choice based on the desire for that which is pleasant the principle of self-love or the principle of personal happiness, his second theorem follows: "All material practical principles are, as such, of one and the same kind and belong under the general principle of self-love or one's own happiness." The corollary also follows: "All material practical rules place the ground of the determination of the will in the lower faculty of desire, and if there were no purely formal laws of the will adequate to determine it, we could not admit [the existence of] any higher faculty of desire."[13]

Kant's first Theorem seems obvious enough. No one can responsibly argue that the good can be defined merely as the object of felt desire if one hopes to give meaning to moral obligation. But Kant's second Theorem and its corollary cut much more deeply since they strike down not only the claims of moralists like Hutcheson and Shaftesbury who ground the moral law on moral feeling directed toward the good, but also strike down the claims of Wolff, the Stoics and moralists who ground morality on the idea of perfection. The weakness in the argument of the first school of moralists, its empiricism, has already been examined. Because those of the second school base their theories on the rational idea of perfection, it would seem that by defining the good in this manner they would have avoided the difficulty the empiricists confront. The difficulty remains, however, for when the concept of perfection is used in its practical sense it does not refer to the perfection of a substance, whether of a particular substance or of being in general. When used in the practical sense, the idea of perfection refers to the sufficiency of an act or a being to a given end. The perfection of a knife, for example, is determined by its ability to cut. Until the end of cutting is given, however, one cannot give meaning to the practical concept of perfection in a knife. The idea of perfection, even though it is developed by reason, cannot determine or even guide the will to action unless ends are antecedently given by which perfection is to be judged. Hence we face once more the problem of relating the end to the will. Kant explains the dilemma:

> as an object which precedes and contains the ground of determination of the will ... is, if taken as the determining ground of the will, only empirical; it could thus serve for the Epicurean principle in the happiness theory but never as a pure rational principle of ethics

---

13 KpV, 22: CprR, 133. Here Kant does not distinguish the higher faculty of desire from the lower on the basis of desire but rather on the fact that the higher faculty of desire is determined by principles and not by desires. The truly higher faculty of desire is not determined by either sensible or intellectual desire but its desire is produced by and is only the consequence of a principle.

> and duty. Thus talents and their cultivation, because they contribute to the advantages of life, or the will of God, if agreement with it (without any practical principle independent of this idea) be taken as an object of the will, can be motives only by reason of the happiness expected from them.[14]

If the concept of perfection could be given practical significance apart from the antecedent determination of an end, then it might be possible to sustain a theory of ethics which defines the good as perfection. But perfection has no meaning as a practical concept unless it specifies the degree of sufficiency of an object or act or person to a given end. Hence, if the will is not already related to some end as its object, it cannot be judged by the norm of perfection (whether human or divine perfection). But if the will is already related to some object, then we face our original difficulty of relating the will to the object in a way that makes the object normative for the will. Thus far, however, we have found that the object is either irrelevant to the will or that it determines the principle of the will through natural desire with the consequence that the will's connection to the object is empirical, contingent and merely subjective.

But we may ask why the good, as the object of the will, must be related to the will by means of desire at all? Granting the soundness of the objection to relating the will and the good in this manner, it does not become convincing until it has been shown that when the good is defined as the object of will prior to the law, desire provides the only way of relating the good to the will.

Kant's answer is contained in Theorem III: "If a rational being can think of its maxims as practical universal laws, he can do so only by considering them as principles which contain the determining grounds of the will formally and not materially."[15] As Kant states and defends this theorem it is not clear that his argument moves beyond Theorems I and II. In his demonstration of it Kant says:

> The material of a practical principle is the object of the will. This object either is the determining ground of the will or it is not. [If it is not, then the object (the good) is irrelevant to the will.] If it is, the rule of the will is subject to an empirical condition (to the relation of the determining notion to feelings of pleasure or displeasure), and therefore it is not a practical law.[16]

Although Kant seems to be assuming the very point at issue, in fact he is not, since he bears in mind the nature of the will. We have noted previously that the

14 Ibid., 41: ibid., 151–152.

15 Ibid., 27: ibid., 138.

16 Idem: idem. The sentence in brackets is my explication of a tacit part of Kant's argument.

will is the faculty of a rational being to act in accord with *its own idea of law*, rather than in conformity with the laws of nature. That is, the will is itself "a kind of causality" and "freedom would then be the property this causality has of being able to work independently of *determination* by alien causes."[17] The will must be unconditioned, independent, capable of being the cause of actions without itself being the product of causes external to itself. In short, the will must be capable of responsible action. Its presence in a person must mark that person as a moral agent, as a being "whose actions can be *imputed* to him."[18]

If the will is related to an object in such a way that it is determined by that object, then the will is conditioned by that object. But the will cannot be free and responsible unless it is unconditioned, capable of acting apart from external determination by an object. Were it externally conditioned in this fashion, it would indeed be related by law and with necessity, but it would not be related to the will of a moral person. For in relating to the subject as its causal determinant, the good destroys the freedom and moral nature of the person. If on the other hand the will is related to the good as its object in such a way as to retain its power to act undetermined by that object, then the freedom and moral significance of the will as well as its relatedness to the good can be maintained.

Kant's understanding of the relation between the will and the good as its object is clear in part: the good does not condition the will. It does not reduce the will to an effect of external causation. But apart from this negative statement, what can be said about its relation to the will? If, prior to the determination of the moral law, the good is presented to the will as an object and yet is not made the causal determinant of the will, the good in no way binds or obligates the will. The relation between them is either nonexistent or, if present at all, is empirical and contingent. If the good so defined is to be related to the will at all, without destroying the freedom of the will, it can be related *only by the agency of the will itself*. That is, the will must freely elect the good as its object. But this election of the good as a previously defined object is contingent and empirical. The will may or may not elect this object. If the object appeals to the will, arouses in the will a desire for it realization, the will and the object are, in fact, related. But if the will does not happen to desire the object, then no relation obtains between them. Since the object is defined prior to the moral law, the moral law cannot serve to obligate the will to the object. There is simply

17 GMS, 446: GMM, 114; cf. KpV, 33: CprR, 144.

18 MS, 223: MOM, 378; cf. ibid., 227: ibid., 381–2; GMS, 44: GMM, 112; KpV, 96–97: CprR, 202–203.

no principle or law, or universal condition, which can be called upon to relate the will to this object so long as the will remains free and morally responsible.

Bearing in mind Kant's definition of the will[19] we see the force of his demonstration of Theorem III.[20] If the rational being thinks of its maxims as being voluntarily conditioned by a subjective relation between itself and the good as its object as a result of the attraction the object has for it, then it cannot think of its maxims as universal laws.[21] If the rational being seeks to act on maxims which are practical laws while preserving the unconditioned quality of its freedom, it must relate itself to an object by means of the practical principle itself which must determine the will formally and not materially. If in its practical principle the rational being has abstracted all consideration of the object and makes the mere form of universality itself the determining ground of the will, then the will is indeed determined but it is not conditioned. Its act is free and unconditioned because, by abstracting from all consideration of the object, the will disassociates itself from "every inducement that might arise for it [the object]."[22] When this is done, the will can be related to the object only by reference to the practical principle of the will itself, that is, by reference to its own idea of law which, through the universality of its form, transcends all conditions and, hence, can serve as the ground of the determination of the will without conditioning it.[23]

In summary, we see the force of Kant's insistence that to define the good prior to the law as an object of the will makes it impossible to relate it to the will except by desire. When we turn to Kant's positive view of freedom and the will, we can see the justification of the alternative he presents in Theorem III. When

19 An extended examination of the complex nature of the will will be offered in Chapter III.

20 And it is perhaps worthy of note that this examination of the will provides us with the demonstration of Theorem IV which, because it is presupposed in the demonstration of Theorem III, necessitated this detour into Kant's constructive theory. In light of our previous discussion, we can, without further examination, accept Theorem IV: "The autonomy [freedom] of the will is the sole principle of all moral laws and of the duties conforming to them; heteronomy of choice [conditioned choice], on the other hand, not only does not establish any obligation but is opposed to the principle of duty and to the morality of the will." (KpV, 33: CprR, 144).

The words in brackets are my additions. They are often used by Kant, however, as substitutes for the terms preceding them.

21 KpV, 34, 58, 62ff.: CprR, 145, 167, 171ff.

22 GMS, 402: GMM, 70; KpV, 34: CprR, 145.

23 Of course, Kant insists, and most of Kant's interpreters have ignored this point, "It is certainly undeniable that every volition must have an object and therefore a material; but the material cannot be supposed for this reason to be the determining ground and condition of the maxim." KpV, 34: CprR, 145; cf. ibid., 35: ibid., 146.

we consider the character of freedom, when we recognize that freedom presupposes unconditionedness, we see that an object can be related to the will with necessity only if it is related formally from the side of the law and not materially from the side of the object. The good as an object cannot be related to the will materially, that is, by reference to its nature as an object unless the good as an object conditions the will either (1) by forcing itself upon the will as the causal determinant of the will's action or (2) by happening to be of such a nature that the will is impelled by desire to determine itself to seek the attainment of the object. Now, if the object conditions the will in the first way, it destroys the will. Hence, no moral theory can take this course in relating the good to the will. If, on the other hand, the object conditions the will in the second way by virtue of the action of the will itself, then the relation of the good to the will is both contingent and subjective and obtains or not according to whether the will happens to desire or not desire the good as its object. But no moral theory preserving the freedom of the will can take this second way in relating the good to the will, since no moral law or obligation can be derived from such a relation. Since neither course can relate the good to the will in a manner which preserves the freedom of the agent while obligating him or her necessarily by the moral law, the hopelessness of this procedure in ethical thinking is apparent.

Thus Kant has succeeded in showing that when the good is defined prior to the moral law as the object of the will, the good is either (1) in an indifferent relation to the will, or (2) is related to the will contingently through a decision of the will that is based on the subjective conditions of desire, or (3) determines the will and thereby destroys its moral significance. In showing so much, Kant has demonstrated that the Greeks and Scholastics can never relate the good to the moral agent with the necessity of law and obligation. He has shown therefore the error of the method most commonly employed in moral philosophy: that moralists who begin by defining the good prior to the moral law can never endow their concept of the good with moral significance.

2 The Heterogeneity of the Good

Kant's argument against the classical tradition went even further. In defining the good prior to the moral law, the classical philosophers arrived at a homogeneous concept of the good, one that failed to distinguish between the moral and non-moral good. This had serious consequences for ethical theory because with a homogeneous concept of the good, happiness and virtue cannot be distinguished, freedom of the will is denied, and the experience of obligation is impossible. Because the good is defined prior to any consideration of the moral law, the good can be brought into effective relationship with the moral agent (allowing for the sake of argument that the conditions of moral agency are not destroyed) only by making the good itself compulsive for the moral agent. It must, therefore, be defined as the object of the agent's desire. But when this is done, the good becomes a homogeneous concept whose relation to the will can be measured by the agent's desire. Although such an ethical theory might begin with a distinction between what is desired and what *ought* to be desired, this distinction cannot be maintained. The good is related to the agent only by desire, and there is no distinction in the *faculty of desire* between *good* desires and *bad* desires.[24] Desires are not quelled simply because they are illicit in terms of this concept of the good for the only means whereby the good can influence the will is through the fact of desire or aversion itself. Hence, the independence of the good from desire, which is essential if the good is to be normative for desire, can be achieved only at the price of the irrelevancy of the good. Although perhaps not consciously intended by these philosophers, the good becomes a homogeneous concept which sanctions all desires or is merely silent.

The classical ethicists were aware of this problem to some extent, since their theories culminated in moral paradoxes which they were then hard pressed to explain. Socrates found that his theory led to the following paradoxes: a person would *prefer* to suffer injustice rather than to do it; that person would be *happier* than the one who was unjust with impunity; the unjust person, however fortunate, would be the most miserable of people while the just one, however mistreated, would be happy. The Epicureans were led to the paradox that the happy person is a virtuous one. And the Stoics shared with Socrates the paradox that even in misery the virtuous individual is happy.

Kant insists that these are not unresolvable paradoxes of the moral life. They are instead the reductio ad absurdum of ethical theories that assume a homogeneous concept of the good.[25] Nothing is more obvious, Kant thinks, than that we do not make a person good by making a person happy. Nor do we live in so blessed a world that we can fail to see individuals brought to ruin as a direct result of their fidelity to duty.[26] It is unfortunate, Kant adds, that philosophers so often strive "to overcome essential differences in principle, which can never be united, by seeking to translate them into a conflict of words and thus

---

24 KpV, 23: CprR, 134.

25 The controversy on this issue continues between defenders of Kant's position and those who argue for the adequacy of the classical position. See Friedman, "Virtue and Happiness: Kant and Three Critics."

26 KpV, 35ff., 127–128 *passim*: CprR, 146ff., 230 *passim*.

to devise an apparent unity of concepts with other terms."[27] Nothing can be gained but absurdity and the decay of all moral sensitivity from the habit of "digging up an identity between such extremely heterogeneous concepts as those of happiness and virtue."[28]

Glaucon, Callicles and Kant are right in thinking that it is silly to appeal to a person's *self-interest*, to a person's *desire for happiness*, in order, for example, to persuade that person to be blinded, castrated, and then buried alive in punishment for a crime he or she has committed.[29] Socrates can answer, of course, that one's self-interest and one's happiness are not to be understood merely in terms of bodily appetites and physical health. He can insist, rather, that they must be understood in terms of the health of the soul. But when Socrates does this he falls into an inconsistency. He predicates this distinction on a genuine heterogeneity in the concept of the good. He makes justice (or the moral law) the basic ethical principle in terms of which the good and happiness are defined. By this tack, Socrates reveals the genuine confusion in his ethical theory. When he says that one should seek justice as the health of the soul and suffer injury to the body rather than incur a disease of the soul, he identifies morality with the welfare of the soul and prudence with the welfare of the body. But Socrates then blurs this important distinction by saying that one can genuinely pursue one's happiness, his self-interest, by permitting injury and even destruction to one's body when the health of the soul cannot otherwise be maintained. Instead of sustaining his distinction between prudence and morality – distinguishing happiness form moral contentment – Socrates combines these two mental states under the term "happiness" and, as a result, comes into direct conflict with human experience.[30]

Unfortunately, it often happens that a person's refusal to violate the dictates of his or her conscience causes great personal misfortune. Such a person may be possessed of a certain self-respect through having been faithful to the moral law which is the law of his or her personality. But, Kant insists, "this comfort is not happiness, not even the smallest part of happiness; for no one would wish to have occasion for it, not even once in his life, or perhaps even would desire life itself in such circumstances."[31] Kant's insight comports better with moral experience than Socratic analysis.

27 Ibid., 111–12: ibid., 216.
28 Idem: idem; cf. ibid., 92, 127–128: ibid., 198, 230.
29 Plato, *Republic*, 1002 (Stephanus 361e); *Gorgias*, 827 (483b). See KpV, 37–38: CprR, 149.
30 KpV, 115ff.: CprR, 219ff.
31 KpV, 88: CprR, 194; cf. ibid., 7: ibid., 122.

One might argue that if the Socratic analysis were sound, if Socrates were genuinely happy in drinking the hemlock, why would not people so order society that great numbers of them could share this fate? If happiness were a simple concept referring to the mental state of a person whose action comports with a homogeneous concept of the good, why should people so overwhelmingly prefer a quiet death in bed to the martyr's death by execution? We cannot avoid the dilemma posed by the Socratic analysis of the good by arguing that although Socrates was not *positively* happy while drinking the hemlock, he would have been very unhappy had he avoided this draught by escape – an option that was apparently open to him. Socrates would not have been unhappy choosing the alternative of escape unless prior to his acceptance of the good as the object of his desires he had accepted the moral law not merely as the descriptive law of his desires but as the prescriptive law of what he should desire – and made his happiness and the satisfaction of his desires contingent upon the fulfillment of this law. As Kant states it,

> One must already value the importance of what we call duty, the respect for the moral law, and the immediate worth which a person obtains in his own eyes through obedience to it in order to feel satisfaction in the consciousness of his conformity to law or the bitter remorse which accompanies his awareness that he has transgressed it. Therefore, *this satisfaction or spiritual unrest cannot be felt prior to the knowledge of obligation, nor can it be made the basis of the latter.*[32]

And in a shorter essay, Kant states,

> Only the virtuous person, or one who is on his way to becoming so, is capable of this pure moral dissatisfaction (which does not stem from consequences of the action in question which are disadvantageous to him, but from the action's very opposition to the law). Accordingly, *the dissatisfaction is not the cause but the effect of the fact that he is virtuous*; and the motivation to be virtuous cannot be derived from this unhappiness (if one so wishes to call the pain resulting from such a misdeed).[33]

Socrates, consequently, could not claim to have done his duty (the good) because it made him happy nor that he was happy because he had done his duty without doing violence to everyday human experience. Similarly, the avoidance of mental discontentment could never be the motive for the fulfillment of duty, since there could be no mental discontentment at all were not the moral law respected antecedently and for its own sake.

---

32 Ibid., 38: ibid., 150. Italics are mine. Cf. ibid., 116ff: ibid., 220ff.

33 TP, 283n: TaP, 50n. Italics are mine.

When the principle of one's own action is a form of self-love – whether called prudence or happiness – the determinants of one's action are fundamentally different from actions determined according to duty. For example, the principle of happiness or self-love, or any homogeneous notion of the good, cannot account for such a common human experience as feeling delight in having won a prize while despising oneself for having cheated to do so. "For to have to say to himself, 'I am a worthless man, though I've filled my purse,' he must have a different criterion on judgment than if he approves of himself and says 'I am a prudent man, for I've enriched my treasure.'"[34] A philosopher who lumps these extremely disparate judgments together by saying "the person is simply unhappy" contributes only to confusion. "So distinct and sharp are the boundaries between morality and self-love that even the commonest eye cannot fail to distinguish whether a thing belongs to one or the other."[35]

The Socratic thesis – that to know the good is to do it – is clearly naïve. Socrates' philosophical position does not consider obligation and the apparent freedom of the will to rebel against that which it knows to be good. Instead he rejected such views as the mistaken opinion of the multitude.[36] From the assumption of the homogeneity of the good it follows, as we have seen, that virtue and happiness are identified and are realized together in the attainment of the good.[37] Since all human beings seek happiness, and since virtue and happiness are realized together, all human beings seek virtue; hence there can be no consciously intended motive or desire for evil action. On this view, with the good so defined as to comprise the greatest self-interest of the individual, only ignorance could lead one to act in opposition to the good. Therefore, Socrates concludes consistently and with the assurance consistency brings that a person who knows the good will do it.

Socrates' assumption regarding the good deceived him. While he held fast to this assumption, it was impossible for him to observe the facts of the moral situation which his theory needed to explain. He was thus not able to see the untenable consequences of his assumption because the assumption itself reduced all the evidence which could refute it to erroneous opinion. It is this characteristic of the assumption of the good's homogeneity, namely, that it blinds one to contravening evidence, which undoubtedly has accounted for its staying power.

---

34 KpV, 37: CprR, 149.

35 Ibid., 36: ibid, 147.

36 Plato, "Protagoras," 784–5.

37 Plato, "Republic," 989ff.

The classical ethical theorists were correct to regard the desired objects of self-love as good. But they were imperceptive in failing to see that the concept of the good is not unitary: rather, it has two aspects, the moral and the natural.[38] The ancients did much sound work in defining the natural concept of the good. Such programs for the harmonious realization of natural values as that recommended in the *Republic* are among the greatest achievements of thought. But a philosophical system must not seek simplicity at the cost of making impossible the very experience it is trying to articulate. Moral experience is far more complex than the account given of it by the classical tradition. A human is a being with many natural desires – for health, food, companionship, sex – all contributing to happiness. But a human is likewise a rational being capable of taking an interest in the enactments of his or her free moral nature which are often attained only at the expense of his or her natural desires.[39] The object of the human being's intention in this case is the moral good as distinct from and opposed to the natural good.

It is, thus, in the moment of moral decisions, such as those confronting Sir Thomas More and Martin Luther, that the confusions of classical philosophical analysis fall away. Moral individuals find themselves torn between that which they desire to do and that which they ought to do and ought also to desire to do. They do not behold the good as the homogeneous object of their faculty of desire. Instead, they frequently encounter the good as perplexingly and even disastrously heterogeneous such that they are unable to fulfill the moral good apart from the sacrifice of the natural good, or vice versa.[40]

The plausibility of assuming the homogeneity of the good vanishes when we look more closely at the moral situation. In this situation, we confront the good in the experience of *obligation*, not in the experience of simple *self-fulfillment*. In the moment of moral decision a human being not only knows the good, he or she knows two different goods. In the moment in which one recognizes the natural good as being one's personal advantage to pursue, one also recognizes the moral good as one's duty. The moral agent does not seek a Socratic or Stoic argument to prove either that the health of body and mind is of no consequence to him or her or that personal moral well-being is the condition of worthiness to have physical and intellectual well-being. The moral agent

38 KpV, 126–127: CprR, 229–230.

39 Ibid., 86–87: ibid., 193–4.

40 Ibid., 61–62: ibid., 170; GMS, 451: GMM, 111–12. To indicate this difference in kinds of good, Kant thinks it is wise to refer to the natural good as "*das Wohl*" and the moral good as "*das Gute*," to natural evil as "*das Übel*" and to moral evil as "*das Böse*." (KpV, 59–60: CprR, 168). See Chapter IV for a full discussion.

knows the first proposition to be false and the latter to be true; otherwise, he or she would never have experienced the temptation to reject the moral good. This awareness of duty testifies to the goodness of both the natural good as happiness and the moral good as the condition of a person's worthiness to attain happiness.

Moral agents must find the strength of will to do that which they know to be their duty (the moral good) even though they know that to do their duty may cost them their happiness and self-fulfillment, which they know to be good also. To be sure, the moral agents need to know the good, both in its moral and natural dimensions. As Kant viewed the matter, this problem of knowledge precedes the moment of moral decision which is a moment not of speculation but of action.[41] It is the knowledge or awareness of the good in its heterogeneity that poses the moral problem for the will. If this knowledge is not attained prior to the moment of decision, then the conditions for moral decision are not met. In confronting the good as heterogeneous, moral agents confront both the natural good as the object of desire and the moral law. In this encounter, the moral law does not tell them what they must do as a member of the natural world; it tells them what they ought to do as a self-legislating member of the intelligible world.[42] The moral law relates itself to the will "under the name of *obligation*"[43] and thereby reveals to the moral agent both that agent's duty and that agent's freedom "which, without the moral law, would have remained unknown to him."[44]

To recapitulate: We now see additional objections to the method of ethical inquiry which begins by defining the good prior to the moral law as the object of the will. We have seen that when the good is defined prior to the moral law, it becomes a homogeneous concept and is related to the will as the object of its desire. But if the good is the object of desire, the good is always sought. Virtue and happiness become identified. To the extent that one attains the good, that person will be both virtuous and happy. Since the good is naturally the object of the will, the will is not free; it merely does that which it believes to be the good. There are no moral problems; there is no awareness of conflicting goods, no

---

41 GMS, 405, 453–5: GMM, 72–3, 121–3. We note Kant's statement: "On the other hand, practical reason is not concerned with objects in order to know them but with its own capacity to make them real (according to knowledge of them)." (KpV, 89: CprR, 195).
42 KpV, 29–32: CprR, 140–143. We shall see in due course that Kant cannot account for moral experience by consigning the moral agent to the intelligible world for he must act in a phenomenal world extended and enriched beyond Kant's original dimensions. See Chapter III.
43 Ibid., 32: ibid., 143.
44 Ibid., 300: ibid., 142; cf. ibid., 4n: ibid., 119n; GMS, 459: GMM, 127.

awareness of temptation, no awareness of obligations, and no awareness of freedom. To know the good then becomes the critical problem in ethics since the good, by its very attractiveness, determines the will to strive after it once it is known.

On this view we seem to be living in the best of all possible worlds where all people strive after the good, whether with knowledge or in ignorance, and where those with knowledge strive to teach those in ignorance. But when we confront this theory with the facts of moral experience which a sound ethical theory must account for, we find that, far from explaining the facts of moral experience, this theory either gives rise to paradoxes and inconsistencies or explains away moral experience – the experience of duty – as the erroneous opinion of the multitude.

The crux of the issue is this: The good must be heterogeneous in order to account for humanity's awareness of obligation and freedom. But it is the moral law, as the *ratio cognoscendi* of freedom, which provides the principle of distinction between the two basic types of good that together constitute the good in its heterogeneity. That concept of the good, and evil as well, which is defined prior to the moral law is the concept of the natural good (*das Wohl/das Übel*), whereas that concept of good (or evil) which is defined subsequent to and by reference to the moral law is the concept of the moral good (*das Gute*). Unlike the natural good, the moral good can never be defined apart from the moral law. It must be the object of human striving; yet it must be related to the agent in such a way that the agent's freedom is not destroyed. Only the moral law can relate the good to the free moral agent without regard to what is desired or promises pleasure. Kant concludes, therefore, that the genuine moral paradox is this:

> that the concept of the good and evil is not defined prior to the moral law, to which, it would seem, the former would have to serve as foundation; rather the concept of the good and evil must be defined after and by means of the law.[45]

3 The Good as the Object of the Moral Law

Although Kant rejected the classical approach to ethics, he nonetheless recognized the responsibility of the ethicist to define the concept of the good. He recognized that the will must have an end, that "every volition must have an

45 KpV, 62–3: CprR, 171.

object"[46] for "since there are free actions, there must also be ends to which, as their objects, those actions are directed."[47] Kant's problem, therefore, was to find an object for the will which, while standing in a necessary relation to the will and serving as a guide to moral action, would not destroy the freedom of the moral agent. In order to preserve the agent's freedom while introducing an object as the guide to that agent's volition, Kant saw that the object of the will must be determined by the will itself rather than the will by the object. If the will did not determine the object it would be conditioned by the object and its freedom destroyed. Furthermore, Kant saw that the obligation of the will to the object must be *categorical*; the object must be one that the will necessarily determines for itself. If the object were conditional, the will's obligation would be subject to that which conditions the object. The will, then, must have an object of volition that is determined by the will, and it must be categorical so that the obligation of the will to that object is unconditional: it must be a categorical imperative.[48] But free will alone has the property of being unconditioned. It alone is undetermined and unqualified by anything external to it. Therefore, only the free will – the autonomous will – can be the unconditioned object of the will. And since free will is unconditioned and free only in relation to itself and not in relation to other free wills, which by virtue of their own freedom condition themselves in independence of outside wills, the only object that a particular will can determine for itself unconditionally is its own free willing. Now to this object – its own free willing – the will can be related without being conditioned or without having its freedom destroyed. In determining itself to this object the will determines itself merely to be free, that is, to be unconditioned.

Its unconditionality is maintained in the act of willing only if it wills according to the universality of law, thereby transcending the conditioning effects of subjective inclination. Willing according to law is ingredient, therefore, in the act of unconditional free willing. Thus free willing itself, the good will, is the sole unconditioned object to which the will can be related with necessity

---

46 Ibid., 34: ibid., 145.

47 MS, 385: MOM, 517. Consider also Kant's statement that "rational nature separates itself out from all other things by the fact that it sets itself an end. An end would thus be the matter of every good will." GMS, 437: GMM, 105; cf. ibid., 414–15: ibid., 81–2; MS, 379ff.: MOM, 512ff.; KrV, B835–6: CpR, 637–38; TP, 279: TaP, 46; RGV, 4–5: Rel, 4.

48 "But among these ends," Kant says, "there must also be some that are also (i.e. by their concept) duties. – For were there no such ends, then all ends would hold for practical reason only as means to other ends; and since there can be no action without an end, a *categorical* imperative would be impossible. This would do away with any doctrine of morals." (MS, 385: MOM, 517). The moral law must command "categorically because it is unconditioned." (KpV, 32: CprR, 143).

without destroying either the unconditionality of the object, or the unconditionality of the will, or the unconditionality of the will's relation to the object. Since moral obligation requires the unconditionality of both the will and the object in addition to the unconditionality of the relation between them, the good will is, therefore, the sole moral good, the sole object that can be given with necessity by the moral law.[49] As Kant states the argument: the moral good must be unconditionally good; the moral good must be the moral will itself projected as its own object since only the will, by virtue of its freedom, has the requisite unconditionality when projected as its own object.

> If something is to be, or is held to be, absolutely good or evil in all respects and without qualification [which is essential to the moral concept of the good], it could not be a thing, but only the manner of acting, i.e., it could be only the maxim of the will, and consequently the acting person himself as a good or evil man.[50]

We see, then, how Kant proceeds to define the good. He rejects the attempt to begin with the good as a previously defined object to which the will must be related. This method, he finds, can never relate the object (the good) to the will as an obligation. Such a concept of the good is merely related to the will irrelevantly, contingently, or compulsively, and is thus unable to account for the theoretical conditions of obligation – namely, for the freedom of the will and at the same time the necessitation of the good upon it. When so defined the good makes impossible the human experience of obligation in which duty is experienced in the tension between the natural and moral aspects of the good. Consequently, Kant, in keeping with his critical method, begins his ethical inquiry with an examination of the experience of obligation. By searching for the conditions of the possibility of this experience he discovers that the good must be heterogeneous and that the moral concept of the good, instead of being defined prior to the moral law, must be determined by that law and posed by it as the object of the will. As the object of the will, the moral good may indeed conflict with the natural good as the object of personal desire. The good is thus encountered in its heterogeneity. By following his original method of inquiry in ethics, Kant thus succeeds in determining the good in such a way that he can account for the moral experience from which he began.

---

49 KpV, 58, 60: CprR, 167, 169.

50 Ibid., 60: ibid., 169 (the clause in brackets is my addition). As Kant observes, morality "has not nature but freedom of choice for its object." (MS, 216: MOM, 371). Or again "for analysis finds that the principle of morality ... commands nothing more or less than precisely this autonomy." (GMS, 440: GMM, 1088, see also ibid., 446: ibid., 114).

Chapter III: Kant's Analysis Of The Will

1 The Theoretical Background and Importance of the *Religion*

Kant's *Religion*, we may say without exaggeration, compares in importance for the understanding of his ethics with his *Groundwork of the Metaphysic of Morals* and the second *Critique*. Kant's ethical statics, to borrow a term from physics, may be found in varying degrees of systematization in most of his post-critical works. Only in the *Religion*, however, do we find what might be called Kant's ethical dynamics. Kant had discussed the nature of the good, the character of imperatives, and the methodology of moral inquiry in his earlier works; in the *Religion* he addressed himself to the problem of evil – its nature, its origin, and the possibility of its eradication. In the process he raised questions which necessitate an understanding of the will in its full complexity and dynamic unity. We therefore find, in the *Religion*, in his struggle with the problem of evil, Kant's most explicit and systematic account of the will and of human freedom – an account which, in turn, clarifies his entire system of ethics.

Confronting the problem of evil, Kant was concerned, not with natural disasters and faulty natural faculties, but with the power of free beings to misuse their freedom. He sought a rational account of moral obligation while admitting as brute fact that human beings can disregard it. How is categorical obligation possible? Since a *categorical* relation is a necessary one and since obligation presupposes freedom, Kant had to show how necessity can be combined with freedom in a single relationship.

Kant thus set himself a task far more difficult than that undertaken by Plato and ethical naturalists on the one hand, or by Christian theologians and ethicists and religious non-naturalists on the other. Plato argued that the Good is necessary to the soul as a condition of its being because irrationality and injustice, in their disregard of the Good, destroy the soul. His demonstration depends, however, upon his assumption that the Good is homogeneous and the natural object of the soul's desire. Having made this assumption, Plato had to conclude that knowledge leads inevitably to virtue, that one who knows the Good will act accordingly, and that no one can intentionally be ignorant of the Good. This conclusion reduces the experience of moral obligation, which presupposes that one can knowingly reject the Good, to an illusion and fails to explain why the illusion should so commonly occur. The Christian tradition can account for the experience of obligation because it understands the awful power of freedom, that is, the human being's ability to rebel against the Good and its Creator. But it does not explain why human beings are necessarily or categorically obligated to obey God or seek the Good. The fact that humans can live and flourish in a state of rebellion shows that obedience to the Good is not a necessary condition of self-fulfillment, at least in this life; the obligation to God and God's commands remains merely hypothetical. It obligates only those who feel a prudential concern for the hereafter or who, out of purity of heart, prefer obedience to rebellion. Dissatisfied with Plato's cavalier rejection of human experience of moral obligation and with all Christian attempts to reduce moral obligation to a hypothetical imperative subservient to a Divine decree, Kant tried to explain categorical moral obligation in such a way as to make it consistent with the Christian insight into the dark and irrational depths of human nature and, simultaneously, with Platonic confidence that freedom and obligation are both ultimately grounded in reason.

Kant was aware that his earlier attempt in the *Groundwork* to explain how the categorical imperative is possible was a failure[1] because his comprehension of freedom and the will was still too fragmentary. In the *Groundwork* Kant defined the will as "the power of a being to act *in accordance with his idea* of laws"[2] and as the "kind of causality belonging to living beings so far as they are rational."[3] So defined, the will could be nothing other than practical reason, free in the negative sense that it is "able to work independently of *determination* by alien causes" and in the positive sense that it is autonomous, "in all its actions a law to itself."[4] According to these definitions, a free will and a will acting according to laws, that is, maxims capable of universalization, were one and the same. Kant therefore concluded, in a manner reminiscent of Plato, that the free will is the will acting according to moral laws.

But what of the will that rejects the moral law in its actions? This question exposes the incompleteness of Kant's early understanding of freedom. Such a will, Kant said in the *Groundwork*, is heteronomous; that is, the "will does not give itself the law, but the object (of desire) does so in virtue of its relation to the will."[5] If the object gives the will its laws, then the will acts in accordance with the laws of nature and hence is not free but a slave to its inclinations. The heteronomous will, inasmuch as its actions are not free, cannot be held responsible for its unlawful acts, cannot be guilty, and cannot, therefore, be will at all. Kant did not leave room for the introduction of desires into the will nor for the capacity of the will to act in opposition to the law when he defined the will

1 See Paton, *The Categorical Imperative*, 202–206.
2 GMS, 412: GMM, 80.
3 Ibid., 446: Ibid., 114.
4 Ibid., 447: Ibid., 114.
5 Ibid., 441, cf. 443–4: ibid., 108, cf. 111.

simply as practical reason. The intrusion of desire and opposition to the law must, however, be reckoned with if human experience of moral obligation in which the moral law confronts the human will as a categorical imperative is to be explained. Kant himself stated, without squaring his statement with his definition of the will, that the moral law is related to the human will as an imperative only because the will has the *power* and the *temptation* to reject the law.[6] Kant was on solid ground in arguing that freedom involves rationality. But in the *Groundwork*, he fails to see that the irrational is a mode of the rational, that heteronomy is a mode of free willing, and that the will must be defined in terms of desire as well as in terms of practical reason. He therefore fails to explain how the categorical imperative is possible.

Kant's advance toward the solution to this problem is clearly visible in the second *Critique*. In the first place, Kant now sees that the moral law is given as a *fact* of pure reason and is so firmly established that it can provide the foundation for a transcendental deduction of freedom. In an epigram of uncommon perspicuity he says that "though freedom is certainly the *ratio essendi* of the moral law, the latter is the *ratio cognoscendi* of freedom."[7] Man's freedom is a fact "which, without the moral law, would have remained unknown to him."[8] Kant thus finds that a rational account of the experience of obligation, in which the moral law is legislative for the human will, necessarily presupposes and therefore transcendentally justifies the concept of freedom.[9]

With this starting point firmly established, Kant, in the second place, clarifies his conception of freedom. He continues to hold, as he had in the *Groundwork*, that freedom must be understood positively as autonomy, as the capacity of the will (as practical reason) to act in accordance with universal law.[10] Kant now insists, however, that freedom in the negative sense – now called transcendental freedom – involves more than mere independence of the will from causal necessity in time and nature: transcendental freedom also involves absolute spontaneity.[11] And the will, possessed of freedom in this more

---

6 Ibid., 412–4: ibid., 80–81.

7 KpV, 4n: CprR, 119.

8 Ibid., 30: ibid., 142; cf. KU, 468: CoTJ, 142.

9 KpV, 16–7, cf. 29–31: CprR, 156, 157, cf. 141–143. Earlier Kant had vacillated on this point by seeking a transcendental deduction of the moral law (GMS, 419–20: GMM, 86ff.). Kant always insisted, however, that his theory of ethics was to provide a rational account of ordinary moral experience, not to create a new morality (GMS, 391–2: GMM, 60; KpV, 8n: CprR,. 123n).

10 KpV, 33: CprR, 144.

11 Ibid., 99, cf. 7–8, 29, 48 *passim*: ibid., 205, cf. 122, 140, 158 *passim*. The term "transcendental freedom" is apt in view of the deduction of that concept, even though Kant,

radical sense, also has the capacity to reject the law. When the will acts in terms of its sensuous desires, it is, as Kant put it, "pathologically affected" but not "pathologically determined – and thus still free."[12] When merely subjective interests are made the basis of action, heteronomy results; heteronomy, however, is now a mode of freedom.[13]

In the third place, Kant's advance in the second *Critique* may be seen in his recognition that the will which is categorically obligated is not the will of a rational being as such but of a rational and sensible being – a human being torn between the demands of its sensible and rational natures. Kant recognized this to a degree in the *Groundwork* when he distinguished between the holy will and the moral will, but he did not sustain this distinction by defining the moral will in terms of the human will. Instead, he persisted in defining the will and its relation to the law in a way that was supposed to be valid for all rational beings as such. Kant did not realize then that if the moral law "when applied to man ... does not borrow in the slightest from the acquaintance with him (in anthropology), but gives him laws *a priori* as a rational being"[14] it cannot confront humanity as the categorical imperative. Yet this confrontation is precisely Kant's

lapsing into an earlier viewpoint, occasionally refers to it as transcendent (ibid., 113: ibid., 209). It is transcendent if regarded as a theoretical concept. But the concept of freedom is as thoroughly deduced from the standpoint of moral experience as is the concept of causality from the standpoint of scientific experience (ibid., 34–34: ibid., 141–142).

12 Ibid., 30–31: ibid., 144.

13 Ibid., 33, cf. 98 *passim*: ibid., 145, cf. 204 *passim*. Kant says that when maxims of merely subjective validity are acted upon "the heteronomy of *Willkür* results" (ibid., 33: ibid.,145). The term "*Willkür*" could mean in this context either "choice" (as Beck translates it) or "the faculty of choice," that is, the will itself. There is no adequate way to determine either from the immediate context or from the second *Critique* as a whole what this particular usage of "*Willkür*" means or how it should be translated. At the time Kant was writing the second and third *Critiques* he had not settled upon a distinct technical meaning for either "*Wille*" or "*Willkür*" but used them almost interchangeably in certain contexts. The discovery and formulation of meanings for these terms was, moreover, one of Kant's foremost achievements in the *Religion* and in the *Metaphysic of Morals*. In light of the meanings given there we can quite easily discern both Kant's use and misuse of these terms as he groped for insight into the nature of the will without foreknowledge of his goal, and we can settle upon the correct interpretation of passages such as the one just quoted. In this passage "*Willkür*" must be translated as "the faculty of choice" or "the choosing will" or some reasonable equivalent. The evolving complexity of Kant's theory of the will is missed by English readers unless they can know when Kant is using "*Wille*" and when he is using "*Willkür*." The practice of translating "*Willkür*" by terms used to translate "*Wahl*" is, unfortunately, as prevalent among English translators as it is misleading. A notable exception is T.K. Abbott, who usually followed the practice of translating "*Willkür*" as the "elective will" and "*Wille*" either as "will" or "rational will."

14 GMS, 389, cf. 411–4, 424–5: GMM, 57, cf. 78–81, 92.

methodological starting point and the basis of his distinction between the moral will and the holy will. In the second *Critique* Kant faced the fact that if desires are to tempt the will, thereby transforming the moral law into a categorical imperative, they must have access to the will. The will, accordingly, is now defined both as practical reason and as the faculty of desire – a definition that is neither drawn from, nor applicable to, mere rational beings.[15] The will, under this modified definition, is caught between the commands of reason and the attractions of sensible inclinations; it is obligated but not compelled to subordinate itself as a faculty of desire to its own legislation as pure practical reason.

Partial answers, however, have a way of raising new problems in the place of those they resolve. Unable to sustain his new insights (excepting the first) with an adequately complex understanding of freedom, the will, and the role of desire in the determination of the will, Kant still occasionally qualified and contradicted many of the ideas he advanced previously, leaving parts of the second *Critique* in confusion bred of his indecision.

On the basis of his insight that heteronomy is a mode of freedom and that the will is both practical reason and the faculty of desire, Kant could account for the will's being torn between the moral law and its natural desires, between the attraction of the natural good and the awareness of the moral good. War "within the members" (which Plato had ascribed to ignorance) Kant, with St. Paul, ascribes to the human situation. There are incompatible goods competing for a human being's favor; hard choices must be made in terms of diverse standards of value; and virtue, if attained at all, is a victory over mighty odds.[16] But if the heteronomous will is free even as it rejects the moral law in favor of sensible inclinations, what then is the foundation of the categorical demand that the will obey the law? When Kant argues, as he did in the *Groundwork*, that by rejecting the law the moral agent ceases to be free and loses his or her personality, he could demonstrate that the law is an essential condition of personal existence and fulfillment. On this view the repudiation of the law involves the repudiation of oneself. But this view, as we have noted, makes the imputation of guilt impossible. Overcoming this difficulty in the second *Critique* by defining heteronomy as a mode of freedom, Kant faced the dismaying consequence that a

---

15 KpV, 9n, 20–25, 33, 55, 58, 60: CprR, 123–124n, 131–136, 144, 164, 167, 169; cf. KU, 443, *passim*: CoTJ, 109, *passim*. Kant knew from pre-critical days that all objects of the will are in some way related to desire. He disassociated himself from the "moral feeling" school of ethics by insisting that desire cannot determine the will inasmuch as such determination would destroy the will's freedom. To relate the will to desire seemed, therefore, both necessary and impossible.

16 KpV, 35–7, 110–3, 127, *passim*: CprR, 146–149, 215–217, 230 *passim*.

person is still a person in possession of freedom even if he or she rejects the law. Thus the law no longer appears to be related to the will as a condition of its being. The categorical imperative seems to resolve itself into a hypothetical one: if one wishes to be moral, one must obey the moral law; if, however, one is not dismayed by the disapprobation of the moral law and superior moral beings, one can still be a person and indulge one's subjective fancies. Unable to anticipate his own later discoveries, and unwilling to accept such a conclusion, Kant occasionally reverted in the second *Critique* to his earlier position and defined freedom as action determined solely by the moral law.[17]

The relation of pleasure and desire to the will was even more troubling to Kant. In the second *Critique* he never seemed fully clear about the status of the faculty of desire: sometimes he refers to it as an aspect of the will; at other times he refers to it as no more than a sensibly determined faculty of appetition.[18] He was similarly unsure regarding the role of pleasure in the moral determination of the will: he flatly contradicts himself by both affirming and denying that moral satisfaction can be a kind of pleasure and a determinant of the will as the faculty of desire.[19]

Despite his own uncertainty, Kant's insights that heteronomy is a mode of freedom, that the faculty of desire is an aspect of the will, and that moral satisfaction and dissatisfaction are legitimate moral incentives were essentially sound. And Kant was able, in large measure, to demonstrate their soundness by means of his extended examination in the *Religion* of the dynamic inner workings of the will and the character of its motivations. To this examination, interpreted in the light of its partial systematization in the *Metaphysic of Morals*, we must now turn.

2 Freedom

What does it mean to be a willing being, an individual, a person?[20] This question is central to the understanding of Kant's ethics. But in order to answer it one must understand the nature of freedom, the nature of the will and volition, and the nature of incentives. This question provides not merely a

17 Ibid., 78, 93–4: ibid., 186, 200.

18 Ibid., 62, 74, cf. 9n, 22–3, 34, 57, 75, 97ff.: ibid., 171, 182, cf. 123, 124, 133–134, 145, 166, 183ff.

19 Ibid., 73–4, 77, 79–80: ibid., 181–182, 185, 187; cf. KU, 209: CoAJ, 48.

20 It is the willing being, the individual person, who actually asks the three basic questions: What can I know? What ought I do? What may I hope?

unifying framework on which to string the diverse aspects of Kant's ethical thought. If answered fully, it secures Kant's methodological starting point in moral experience by showing how the categorical imperative is possible.

This question cannot be answered, however, until it is stripped of certain pretensions. The question does not concern the nature of "personality" in a purely rational being – assuming such a being could exist – nor are we asking what is the nature of the will as such. Kant's ethics, like his theory of cognition and his aesthetics, is grounded in and limited to human experience; it consists in the transcendental deduction of those concepts and relations which must be presupposed in order to give a rational account of moral obligation.[21] If we accept the limitations of Kant's method we must limit our inquiry to the nature of the human will and human personality. We will do well to start with a systematic statement of personality in terms of the concept of freedom which it presupposes, and then discuss the manifold relations of the human will.[22]

The moral law, according to Kant, reveals the fact and the meaning of human personality (*Persönlichkeit*). By telling us what we *ought* to do regardless of what our inclinations and desires may bid us do, the moral law forces us to become aware of ourselves as free agents rather than mere creatures of desire. We are not, like Buridan's ass, determined to act by our strongest desires or immobilized between two desires of equal strength. We are, rather, *willing* beings who, while acting according to desire, determine or choose for ourselves that which shall be irresistibly desirable. The moral law thus informs us, through the voice of categorical duty, of our control over and responsibility for our actions. Such responsibility is the mark of personality. "A person," as Kant puts it, "is a subject whose actions can be *imputed* to him."[23]

Freedom is necessarily presupposed by such accountability. In order to be responsible for one's actions, a person must be able to institute effects for which he or she can be legitimately singled out as the cause. But there is no way to restrict the extension of causal influence (and hence to give limit and meaning to personality) apart from the assumption that persons, as causes, are themselves free. If there were no free causes, we would have no rational justification

21 For a fuller discussion of Kant's method in ethics, see Chapter I.

22 The following systematic statement of Kant's conception of freedom is drawn from most of his post-critical writings. Of special importance are the chapter on "The Canon of Pure Reason" from the first *Critique*, Chapters II and III of the *Groundwork*, and the section on "The Critical Examination of the Analytic of Pure Practical Reason" from the second *Critique*. Most important are Book One of the *Religion* and the "Introduction" to the *Metaphysic of Morals*.

23 MS, 223, cf. 224, 227: MOM, 378, cf. 378, 381; cf. RGV, 25, 26n, 31, 44, 48–9: Rel. 20, 21n, 26, 40, 45.

for limiting responsibility to beings whom we designate as persons. The only truly responsible agent, if we deny that there are free causes, would be the entire universe extended in space to infinity and in time to the farthest reaches of the past. Responsibility cannot be personal unless it is found in free individuals who can act without being determined to action by external and antecedent causes. (By "external" I mean, of course, external to the *will*, not necessarily to the physical body of the individual.)

That freedom of the will involves the independence of the will from external influences has been generally recognized. It has not been so clearly seen that freedom also involves independence from all antecedent determination as well.[24] It has often been supposed, for example, that individuality, personality, and responsibility can be understood as the self-determination of beings in a non-mechanical but nonetheless deterministic universe. On this view, the responsible, free person is said to be determined by his or her own nature and by nothing alien to this nature. The person's action, it is argued, flows through and expresses the core of his or her being.

Kant saw through this subterfuge which he called the "freedom of the turnspit" and which we, in a more technologically advanced age, might call "the freedom of the thermostat."[25] Self-determination on this theory is not merely unfree; it is not even self-determination. Genuine self-determination does not consist in the determination of effects *through* the self; it requires rather the determination of effects *by* a self which is not determined by anything else – not even by its own prior nature or prior decisions. Self-determination is fully compatible with freedom; indeed, it presupposes freedom. When, however, self-determination is conceived to preclude any cause that cannot be accounted for by antecedent conditions, self-determination is a misnomer because it is incompatible with freedom. Such self-determination is actually self-predetermination and is therefore obviously not free.

Freedom and determinism, Kant insists, are fully compatible; the actions of moral beings are determined by the wills of those beings and express their characters.[26] But freedom and predeterminism are fundamentally incompati-

---

24 The meaning of antecedent includes prior acts of will. One who has become compulsively addicted to drugs, for example, may be determined by prior acts of will. In this case such a one has lost freedom. One who is merely tempted but can resist is still free from determination by prior acts of will.

25 KpV, 97, cf. 94ff.: CprR, 203, cf. 200.

26 Their compatibility is possible only because, according to Kant, a person stands in both the world of nature and in the intelligible world. This theory of two standpoints poses difficulties of its own which will be examined later in this chapter in Section 3.

ble. "What we wish to understand and never shall understand," Kant notes, "is how *predeterminism*, according to which voluntary (*willkürliche*) actions, as events, have their determining grounds *in antecedent time* (which, with what happened in it, is no longer within our power), can be consistent with freedom, according to which the act as well as its opposite must be within the power of the subject at the moment of its taking place."[27] A person capable of responsible action must be free in the transcendental meaning of the term. Freedom must secure that person both spatially and temporally from determination by all factors alien or antecedent to itself in the moment of action; it must endow the person with the power of his or her own decision. Freedom in the negative sense as independence from all alien and antecedent influences is like a moat surrounding the individual will, an insulation that leaves it free to act either according to the moral law (autonomously) or according to the inclinations that the will gives determining force (heteronomously). If a person is not free in this mode of radical independence and spontaneity, then, according to Kant, that person is not free at all, and his or her self-determination, responsibility, and moral identity are as illusory as his or her freedom.[28]

Transcendental freedom establishes the basis for moral individuality and endows the individual with many potentialities, the realization or rejection of which are left to the individual in the exercise of his or her freedom. Heteronomy (free action in violation of the moral law) and autonomy are the two primary modes of expressing transcendental freedom.

In every decision he or she makes, the individual must have an end, that is, must have some specific intention in the act of willing: in order to will, one must will *something*. Just as every volition must have an object, every object of volition must have material content; it must be sufficiently concrete and determinate to enable the individual to know what he or she is willing.[29] A person who only willed to be good, for example, would not have an object of volition

---

27 RGV, 49n: Rel, 45n. The objection that a subject who is free in this way can never be responsible for his or her actions will be considered in Section 3, following.

28 Kant does not deny that there are influences on the will and limitations on the expression of freedom. Moral instruction, temptation, disease, health, intelligence, and stupidity influence the will by increasing or decreasing or modifying its power of self-expression. Kant speaks, consequently, of the direct proportion between accountability and freedom (MS, 228: MOM, 382). Kant does deny, however, that such factors can *determine* the will without destroying it. If a person is free and responsible, then his or her freedom is unqualified and absolute, although the possibilities for its expression may vary considerably.

29 MS, 379–82, 384ff.: MOM, 512–15, 516ff.; cf. RGV, 4ff.: Rel, 4ff.; KpV, 34–5: CprR, 145–6.

until some specification was made of what that person intended in order to become good. But the desires and inclinations and contents of experience which provide the material for the object of volition do not determine the individual either in framing or in willing that object. As a transcendentally free being, the individual is determined neither by desires and inclinations nor by his or her own past character and habits. Individuals themselves propose their objects of volition and give them determinant content by freely selecting from, and arranging, the contents of experience. The structure or form of the object of volition, that is, the principle that guides the individual in the determination of the content of that object, is called by Kant the maxim of choice. Selection of the maxim and determination of the object of volition in terms of it are aspects of individual self-determination. If in an act of volition the individual merely accepts his or her strongest desire as the basis for action, he or she acts on the maxim of willing to do that which he or she most strongly desires to do. Such individuals think of themselves passively as if they were determined by laws other than those of their own choosing; they act as if they were determined by the same laws of nature that determine the behavior of animals. If an individual acts in terms of a law compelled by the forces of nature, by forces other than his or her own, the action is heteronomous. But the decision to act heteronomously is nonetheless the individual's own decision. The adoption of the heteronomous maxim is an expression of transcendental freedom, the actualization of one of its potentialities.

The actualization of heteronomy is not, however, a *fulfilling* realization of transcendental freedom; on the contrary, heteronomy involves its abnegation. The individual in adopting a heteronomous maxim freely renounces his or her power as a free being to act independently of natural desires. Such individuals freely choose to act just the way they would act if they had no such freedom at all. Heteronomy is thus one but not the only possible mode of free expression. Were it the only potential mode of expression, transcendental freedom would be hollow and meaningless, for the positive realization of spontaneous action in independence of natural determination would not be possible. Transcendental freedom would involve no more than the independence and power willfully to act as if there were no such independence and power. Choice and freedom would be defined so as to preclude their possible fulfillment. The potentiality of freedom would be identical with the potentiality of life for a person who could do nothing but choose between alternative means of suicide – in much the same way that an animal has some limited capacity to decide how to satisfy a controlling, overpowering appetite.

The transcendentally free individual, always potentially heteronomous, is likewise potentially autonomous, and need not abnegate his or her freedom by heteronomous willing, but is able to affirm in volition his or her independent and spontaneous nature. While influenced by desires and inclinations, the transcendentally free individual can positively maintain unconditional and continuing independence from them by willing in accordance with the demands of universal law. Because desires and habits are ineluctably subjective and particular, they can never be viewed as the determinants of a universal maxim or of an object of volition based on such a maxim. By adopting a maxim which has been framed out of concern for its universal validity, that is, as a law of volition for all willing beings such as oneself, the very universality of an individual's maxim establishes his or her transcendence of and independence from determination by any specific desire.[30] The individual continues to be influenced by desires and inclinations and must draw upon them to give content to his or her object of volition. But the content of the object is determined by the universal maxim which guides the will in the evaluation, selection, and finally free adoption of the contents of sensibility. The maxim, therefore, determines the presence and composition of desires and inclinations in the object of volition; neither the object nor the maxim is determined by desires and inclinations. Any object willed on the basis of a universal maxim demands the approbation of all persons who express their freedom positively and not merely the approbation of those beings, animals or men, whose desires may be gratified by the object.[31] When an individual so wills that the maxim of his or her act is in accord with the universality of law, he or she is then autonomous, that is, acting according to the law of his or her own free nature.

To say that individuals who reject maxims based upon the strength of subjective desires in order to act on universal maxims act in terms of a law of their own nature seems at first glance an odd claim. Are not natural desires or culturally developed habits equally a part of an individual's nature? Indeed, Kant would insist, sensuous desires and inclinations may and do influence one's maxims and contribute to the content of the object of one's volitions. Desires may be constituted in objects chosen primarily on the

---

30 The universality of the act establishes its independence from sensibility, for desires are always particular and specific.

31 An object determined by the will on the basis of a universal maxim and thus claiming universal approbation by all human beings is morally good. The morally good, according to Kant, is an object which, like the object of experience, is determined in part by the subject as a moral agent. The morally good is therefore either the good will itself or the concrete expression of good willing, i.e. the concrete object of volition of a good will, as discussed in the previous chapter.

basis of universal maxims. When a person wills in accordance with a universal maxim, the object may still incorporate sensuous inclinations though in a subordinate mode. In risking one's life to save a child for duty's sake, for example, one may nonetheless satisfy other desires without those desires being the determining ground of his or her decision. Desires and inclinations cannot provide the determining principle of volition for an individual who would assert his or her individuality rather than abnegate it. One's nature as a person, as a responsible individual, is grounded in one's freedom. Only one's nature as an animal, a turnspit, or a thermostat can be positively expressed by maxims asserting nothing more than the decision to be determined by one's strongest desires. One's free and responsible nature is not positively expressed in one's free acts unless the maxims of those acts, by virtue of their conformity to universal law, transcend all particular desires and inclinations and assert one's actualized power to act in independence from them. By adopting maxims in accordance with universal law, individuals express positively the unconditionedness of their will; they take as their object of volition the concrete realization of their unconditioned free willing – that is, individuals will the realization of themselves as free beings. In this sense the law in accordance with which one wills is the law of one's nature.

We can now observe the thorough interpenetration of reason and freedom. Rationality is involved in both the heteronomous and the autonomous modes of free expression. It is not merely from impulse that an individual acts from impulse. Even heteronomous action involves the use of reason, independent from inclinations, to determine maxims that negate both freedom and rationality by following inclinations. Autonomous action, in turn, expresses the universality of reason which is the sole means whereby the will can positively assert its creative independence. Both heteronomy and autonomy are modes of rationality just as both are modes of freedom; in essence, Kant holds, they are spontaneity itself. Freedom to act heteronomously by freely negating our freedom is *actual* in the makeup of any person as is the potentiality to act autonomously in the fulfillment of freedom.

This aspect of Kant's though is easily overlooked since he frequently discusses reason as the canon for the exercise of spontaneity. So considered, reason is merely the structure and form of the sound use of our faculties in logic, science, moral conduct, aesthetic creation, and matters of taste; reason, so regarded, appears static. But reason is dynamic in all its functions, in understanding as imagination and judgment, in volition as will and judgment, and in artistic creation and appreciation as genius, taste and judgment. In all these activities, reason functions as *spontaneity*, the inscrutable power of the mind, of the will, and of genius.[32] Reason, in Kant's philosophy, is essentially free; freedom is essentially rational; and both consist ultimately in spontaneity.[33]

Inasmuch as spontaneity constitutes the power of both freedom and reason, heteronomy and irrationality no less than autonomy and rationality are possible modes of their expression; heteronomy must not be reduced to complete determination by natural causality, nor should irrationality be confused with the non-rational. The validity of this insight will become clear when we examine Kant's treatment of the problem of evil. (The rational in the generic sense in which Kant often uses it includes both the rational in the honorific sense and the irrational, just as freedom in its transcendental meaning includes both autonomy and heteronomy.) Heteronomous and irrational actions involve the denial and misuse of the power of spontaneity, the failure to actualize its potentialities and, therefore, the diminution and even the destruction of the person as a spontaneous being. By the use of drugs or alcohol to the point of addiction, for example, the person may find great pleasure and satisfaction but gradually experience the loss of self as a person capable of acting independently from the desires resulting from his or her addiction. By rejecting through irrationality and heteronomy the realization of that power which enables one to be oneself, the individual denies himself or herself.[34] The moral law, which

---

32 KrV, A97–8, B129–33, B180–1, B562: CpR, 130–131, 151–153, 183, 465; GMS, 389, 412, 440, 452, 463: GMM, 57, 80, 108, 120, 130–131; KpV, 7–8, 29, 48, 67–8, 98–101: CprR, 122, 140, 158, 176, 204–206; MS, 378: MOM, 511; RGV, 23–4, 44, 49n, 143: Rel. 19, 40, 45n, 134; KU, 197, 294, 307ff., 317ff., 326 *passim*: CoAJ, 39, 152, 168ff., 180ff., 192 *passim*. Germane to this point is Kant's division of knowledge into rational and historical modes, the former being creative and active, the latter being slavish and passive (KrV, B864: CpR, 656).
33 One could argue, I believe, that spontaneity is the *ontological* foundation of both rationality and freedom in Kant's philosophy. But the elaboration and defense of this point is not necessary to this discussion.
According to Stanley Rosen, Kant's defense of *moral* freedom in terms of spontaneity of the will opens a Pandora's box that in time made possible the postmodernist celebration of an extreme freedom that must, logically, include the freedom to accept or reject the Copernican revolution. Spontaneity is the ungrounded ground of the transcendental ego. What this means, Rosen claims, is that "we are free to accept or to reject the worlds of knowledge and morality as 'defined' by Kant. As a consequence, these worlds are radically contingent. We are free to posit chaos as the primeval condition." As Rosen views the problem, Kant's spontaneous will prepares the ground for the transformation of philosophy into hermeneutics. See Rosen, 24–27.
34 The self-rejection of the individual is, from the standpoint of his or her theoretical faculties, his or her irrationality, and from the standpoint of his or her moral nature, his or her heteronomy. Since reason and freedom have a common essence in spontaneity, however, it is

demands that the individual act according to a maxim that is capable of universalization, is a law that defines the conditions for the fulfillment of personality, just as the law of non-contradiction and the rules of sound understanding define the conditions for the fulfillment of mind. The moral law is a normative law for the will of an individual, just as the law of non-contradiction is normative for the use of an individual's mind.

Kant's theoretical advance beyond Plato and other predecessors in the understanding of freedom is now apparent. Like Kant, Plato identified freedom and rationality. Unlike Kant, however, Plato understood reason only in its fulfilled meaning. Anything that was not, Plato argued, in accord with the fulfillment of reason as a canon, as the static form of the good, was non-rational, determined either by non-rational eros or non-rational spirit or blind necessity, but not by the misuse of reason itself. For a misuse of reason would imply that irrationality, the boundless and the dark forces of necessity, could be found within reason itself – a thought which Plato could not abide. Thus, having identified freedom with rationality and having a conception of reason that excluded the irrational and non-rational, Plato was limited to a conception of freedom as rational freedom alone. In consequence, ignorance, whether moral or intellectual, became for Plato a mode of the non-rational and the non-free, and guilt and culpable irrationality were simply not possible. Kant, recognizing what he took to be the actuality of both, defined freedom and reason as spontaneity and pointed to rationality and autonomy as the fulfilled mode and to irrationality and heteronomy as the deficient mode of its expression.

Recognizing that any rejection of reason is irrational but, nonetheless, still a mode of the rational (because that which violates or rejects the laws of reason must be subject to them and hence rational in its inclusive meaning), Kant discovered that the moral law is a necessary part of the internal structure of human personality. As such, the moral law is the descriptive condition for personal self-fulfillment without any reference to obligation for pure rational beings or holy wills. But it becomes the categorical imperative for rational-sensible beings who are tempted to reject it.

A person is not *obligated* to be *actually* transcendentally free and *potentially* either autonomous or heteronomous. Either one's given nature as a free being includes these factors, or one is not a person, a being whose actions can be imputed to that being. To speak in the language of the *Groundwork* a person

---

just as correct to speak of the heteronomous uses of the mind and the irrational expressions of the will.

is not obligated to be a member and ruler in a kingdom of ends. Either one is both member and ruler or one is not a person. Obligation enters as a relation between the subject and the ruler, as the duty of the subject to obey itself as ruler when as subject it is tempted to disobey. Transcendentally free human beings, if tempted by objects of desire to abnegate their freedom in the expression of it, are categorically obligated to subordinate their desires to a rationally formulated universal maxim in order to actualize their free nature. One is obligated to be autonomous, to be the spontaneous individual one is, and to avoid self-rejection in heteronomy. And because personality is diminished as the law of one's nature and the condition of its fulfillment is denied, the law still has an inescapable authority over a person. One has the freedom to reject actions in accordance with the law but one cannot escape the law's condemnation or its punishment in the impairment or even destruction of one's personality. The imperative issuing from the moral law is therefore categorical. Without appeal to divine decree or contingent facts of desire, Kant's theory thus provides a theoretical but non-theological foundation in the very nature of free volition and personality for the moral law and for its power to obligate categorically.

3 The Human Will

Though Kant's conception of freedom clarifies the nature of personality and moral obligation, its full interpretive power does not become apparent until it is considered in the context of his analysis of the human will in moral struggle. According to Kant the will is a unitary faculty. But, like reason and the understanding, it is subject to division into "parts" for the purpose of analysis. These parts, to which Kant refers by the terms "*Willkür*," "*Wille*," and "*Gesinnung*" are aspects or specific functions of this essentially unified faculty of volition.[35]

35 Since Kant gives the terms "*Willkür*" and "*Wille*" technical meanings not recognized in ordinary German usage, and since there are no English equivalents for these terms, I shall adapt them to English usage without translating them. The term "*Gesinnung*" is adequately translated by the English term "disposition"; the latter is as imprecise in English as the former is in German, but Kant's technical meaning can be derived, as is true of "*Willkür*" and "*Wille*", from his usage. I shall use the English term "will" to refer to human volition as a unified function including *Willkür, Wille* and disposition. Kant occasionally uses "*Wille*" in this sense, which is ordinary German usage.

i. Willkür

When Kant refers to the will in its familiar aspect as the power to choose between alternatives, he calls it *Willkür.* As such, it is a faculty of desire, for Kant held that the *Willkür* is determined according to the strength of the pleasures or displeasures it anticipates in connection with the alternatives open to it.[36] But the human *Willkür* is not an animal *Willkür,* an *arbitrium brutum.* The animal *Willkür,* like an iron filing drawn to the strongest magnet, is directly determined by the strongest impulse. The human *Willkür* is influenced but not wholly determined by impulses: its actions are always determined according to the strongest impulse, but only after the *Willkür* itself has made the decision by which the strongest impulse is determined. Thus the human *Willkür* determines itself and is free, an *arbitrium liberum.* "The freedom of the *Willkür,*" Kant held, "is of a wholly unique nature in that an incentive can determine the *Willkür* to an action *only so far as the individual has incorporated it into his maxim* (has made it the general rule in accordance with which he will conduct himself)."[37] No impulse or desire can be a determining incentive for the *Willkür* until the *Willkür* chooses to make it so. The irresistible strength of the incentive that determines the action of the *Willkür* (when the latter is viewed psychologically) derives from the decision of the *Willkür* (viewed morally) to give it determining strength. Unless this power to choose its determining incentives is attributed to the *Willkür,* it cannot be both free and yet under the influence of desires and incentives: "Only thus," Kant argued, "can an incentive, whatever it may be, coexist with the absolute spontaneity of the *Willkür* (i.e., freedom)."[38] We know that sensible incentives and absolute freedom coexist in the human *Willkür* for they are co-present in the experience of obligation from which our awareness of *Willkür* arises. The moral law, as Kant states it, "informs us of the independence

---

36 MS, 399, cf. 213: MOM, 528, cf. 374–375; RGV, 30–31: Rel, 26. Because *Willkür* acts in accordance with the strongest desire, Kant insists that whatever is good must be in some way the object of desire and that "the highest ground of morality must not simply be inferred from the pleasant; it must itself be pleasing in the highest degree." (Letter to Marcus Herz, 1773: Br (AA10), 145: Corr, 140). See also GMS, 460: GMM, 128: "It is admittedly necessary that reason should have the power of *infusing a feeling of pleasure* or satisfaction in the fulfillment of duty, and consequently that it should possess a kind of causality by which it can determine sensibility in accordance with rational principles."

37 RGV, 23–4: Rel, 19; cf. MS, 213–4: MOM, 374–5. For a thoughtful discussion of the philological issues in Kant's distinction between *Wille* and *Willkür*, see Meerbote, "*Wille* and *Willkür* in Kant's Theory of Action."

38 RGV, 24, cf. 49n: Rel, 19, cf. 45n; MS, 213–4: MOM, 374–5.

of our *Willkür* from determination by all other incentives (of our freedom) and at the same time of the accountability of all our actions."[39]

The *Willkür* is thus the core of personality and responsibility. Just as a human, the being who experiences moral obligation, must stand in two worlds – the natural and the moral – in order to experience as obligation the conflict between them, the *Willkür* must be found in both realms as well. The human being, as both a natural and a moral being, has *Willkür*. The *Willkür* of a human being as a natural being is the ground of human action and human virtue as phenomena (*virtus phaenomenon*). The *Willkür* of a human being as a moral being is the ground of the adoption of maxims on which action is based and the source of intelligible virtue (*virtus noumenon*).[40] The distinction that Kant draws between events and acts is this: an event is that which occurs according to determination by causal laws; an act, or deed, has as its author a free cause (*causa libera*). In moral conduct, the individual is responsible for his or her actions because they are the effects of the individual as *causa libera*. The individual's actions in the phenomenal world which are contrary to the demands of the moral law are actions of his or her *Willkür* and therefore attributable to the individual as vices, including evil as an extreme instance. Similarly the actions of the individual's *Willkür* which accord with the demands of the moral law are attributable to him or her as virtues. But the motives behind one's phenomenal acts, that is, the maxims upon which they are based, can never be observed by others and are only sometimes apparent to oneself in inner sense.[41] Yet the actions which an individual's *Willkür* performs in the phenomenal world issue from the maxims of the self-same *Willkür* in the intelligible world. Otherwise they could have no moral significance, for the individual could not be held accountable for them.[42] The *Willkür* – which is the expression of a human being's transcendental freedom, his or her ultimate spontaneity – is thus, like that human being itself, inextricably involved in both the phenomenal and noumenal orders.

---

39 RGV, 26n, cf. 49n; Rel, 21n, cf. 45n.

40 RGV, 14, 31–2, 47 *passim*: Rel 13, 26–7, 43, *passim*; cf. MS, 226, 383, *passim*: MOM, 380–1, 515, *passim*.

41 RGV, 20: Rel, p. 16. Later I shall refer to motives, maxims, and moral awareness as moral phenomena.

42 Ibid, 31, *passim*: ibid, 26, *passim*; cf. MS, 226, *passim*: MOM, 380, *passim*.

ii. The Problem of Two Standpoints

We must now turn to a problem which, though of interest to anyone concerned with the relation of ethics to science, is also a fundamental metaphysical problem for Kant's ethics. In order to resolve the Third Antinomy Kant decided, in the first *Critique*, to bifurcate reality into the phenomenal world of appearances and the noumenal world of things in themselves. All events in the phenomenal order, he said, are necessarily related in terms of the category of causality and are in principle fully predictable. In the noumenal order, on the other hand, free causes can express themselves; that is, events may take place in the absence of any antecedent causal determinants. Scientific experience and knowledge pertain to the phenomenal world; moral experience and knowledge pertain to the noumenal. Kant thus asserted that all of the phenomenal actions of humans are fully predictable in principle, and, were human knowledge sufficient, would be predicted.[43] But he insisted no less strenuously that a human being's moral acts are free and not predetermined, hence unpredictable in principle.[44]

Kant could never fully accept, however, the bifurcation of human experience required by his "two standpoints theory." Although he asserted that the two realms exist "independently of one another and without interfering with each other,"[45] he found it impossible to speak of moral problems without presupposing their necessary interaction.

The experience of moral obligation is a prime example of this interaction. If the same human being (and, therefore, the same *Willkür*) were not both moral and natural, existing fully and simultaneously in both realms, moral experience would be impossible. Humans would either have purely holy wills in which no moral error would be possible or would be directed entirely by natural causes in which event moral responsibility would be impossible. Moral experience presupposes the capacity of the moral self in the noumenal world to reorder the material, phenomenal world according to the demands of the moral law. According to Kant, the moral individual in the noumenal world is obligated by the moral law as the categorical imperative expressed in universalizable maxims: (a) to seek the reordering of the sensible world as it would be ordered if the categorical imperative were a constituent case in the phenomenal order. Thus the individual in the noumenal world would seek in reordering the sensible world to reorder that world in terms of the idea of the highest good (which requires the union of

---

43 KrV, B581; CpR, 476.

44 RGV, 49, *passim*; Rel, 45, *passim*.

45 KrV, B585: CpR, 479; cf. KpV, 104–5: CprR, 209–10.

the two worlds); (b) specifically, to will as a noumenal being to seek the happiness of other human beings in the phenomenal world; (c) to so act in the phenomenal world as not to contribute to the moral downfall of others as noumenal beings; and (d) to rear his or her children, after their physical procreation in the phenomenal world, so that their moral natures are fulfilled in the noumenal world, etc. Further examples could be given almost ad infinitum.[46]

Unless one assumes that a pre-established harmony coordinates the phenomenal and noumenal worlds, the "two standpoints theory" fails to support the facts of everyday life. If we presuppose that such a harmony does obtain, there is nothing incredible, for example, if whenever a murderer in the noumenal order freely wills to kill a victim, a gun in the phenomenal order is independently predetermined to go off in that person's hand. But while the interactions between the two orders would no longer seem incredible, nothing can lend credibility to the presupposition itself! And Kant, in discussing Leibniz, clearly rejects pre-established harmony as an ad hoc solution.[47]

Kant attempted to resolve the problem of interaction between the two worlds without relying on an assumption of pre-established harmony. He did so by holding that the noumenal world is timeless and therefore that decisions made therein (having no causal antecedents) can be regarded regulatively as causes of temporal sequences in the phenomenal world.[48] But the results of this attempt lead to disastrous conclusions. In the first place, if the series of phenomenal events is in no way altered by the intrusion of noumenal free causes, the latter are clearly ineffectual and superfluous. As long as the acts of moral volition cannot alter the determination of any events involving human behavior in the phenomenal world, all categorical demands that they do so are in vain. Second, Kant erred either in designating the moral realm as the noumenal realm or in denying that the noumenal realm is temporal, for moral volition is ineluctably temporal. The will is tempted in time, decides in time, and, depending on its decision, feels guilty or morally satisfied in time. The

46 See ibid., B830–2, B835ff.: ibid., 633–634, 637ff.; GMS, 407–8, 413, 438–9: GMM, 75, 81, 106; KpV, 32–34, 43, 56ff., 67–8, 72–4, 77, 83ff., 105, 110ff.: CprR, 144, 154, 165ff., 175–176, 180–182, 185, 190ff., 210, 215ff.; KU, 172, 173, 175–6, 195: CoAJ, 9, 10, 13–14, 37; KU, 368, 431–2, 435, 443, 446, 468: CoTJ, 14, 94–96, 99, 109, 113, 142; RGV, 6,7, 14, 31, 32–3, 39n, 46–8, 70–1, 74, 76–7, 85, 96–7, 107–8, 139, 160, 170–1 *passim*: Rel. 6, 7, 13, 17, 26, 28–9, 34n, 42–45, 65, 69, 71, 81, 88, 98, 130, 148, 158 *passim*; MS, 214–8, 226–8, 280–1, 382n, 391–4, 397, 400: MOM, 370–3, 380–2, 429–30, 514n, 522–4, 526–7, 529.

47 KrV, B839: CpR, 293.

48 KrV, B577, B581ff.: CpR, 474, 476ff.; KpV, 44ff.: CprR, 154ff.

pilgrim's and the rake's progress are, as the word "progress" indicates, thoroughly temporal adventures. In the *Religion* no less than in the *Groundwork* and second *Critique*, Kant again and again refers in temporal terms to the problems of moral volition, improvement, and decline. When Kant tried to conceive of moral experience apart from time, he was so deeply involved in the highly abstract problems of the Third Antinomy (or in remaining consistent with his solution to them) that he ignored the plain facts of moral experience of which he himself on most occasions was acutely aware.

If we are to understand Kant's ethics and, specifically, his theory of the will as developed in the *Religion*, we must recognize that interaction between the phenomenal and noumenal worlds is required – even though Kant himself has denied that such interaction is possible. We cannot conclude our discussion of this problem by saying, as Paton said, "Kant never properly faces this difficulty."[49] We have to face this difficulty precisely because Kant did not do so and because his ethical theory remains logically and factually impaired until we do.

Some scholars apparently fail to see any problem with Kant's support of a deterministic phenomenal world and a noumenal world of freedom between which there is no interaction. In his fine introduction of Kant's *Religion within the Boundaries of Mere Reason*, Robert M. Adams writes that for Kant "any experience that is possible for us must be structured by certain fundamental concepts such as those of substance and cause, and by space and time as 'forms of intuition' within which objects of sensation can be represented" and specifically, "that space and time definitely do not characterize things as they are in themselves."[50] Adams cites several texts to support this interpretation.

Unfortunately, however, were his interpretation accepted as a defining aspect of Kant's moral theory, we would reduce Kant's position to an absurdity. On Adams' view moral action becomes a mystery. The free noumenal person decides to commit murder. Remarkably, the gun the person freely fires in the noumenal world is causally determined to fire in the phenomenal world as the act of a being who presumably has no experiential knowledge of himself or herself as a free noumenal being. This view flatly rejects our common moral experience and fails to preserve the moral experience of ordinary folk, which is the foundation of Kant's ethics. I shall argue that Kant must introduce a moral phenomenal world in which free acts are possible, in addition to a phenomenal world structured by causality, space and time. One must admit this broader

---

49 For an excellent statement of the difficulty, without however any suggestion as to its resolution, see Paton, *The Categorical Imperative*, 277.
50 Adams, ix.

conception of experience in order for human beings to act freely in space and time. Fortunately, there are many texts in which Kant supports this position, the most important and least ambiguous of which, perhaps, is the following:

> Pure reason, then, contains, not indeed in its speculative employment, but in that practical employment which is also moral, principles of the *possibility of experience*, namely, of such actions as, in accordance with moral precepts, *might* be met with in the *history* of mankind. For since reason commands that such actions should take place, it must be possible for them to take place. Consequently, a special kind of systematic unity, namely the moral, must likewise be possible.[51]

Accordingly, Kant writes,

> I entitle the world a *moral world*, in so far as it may be in accordance with all moral laws; and this is what by means of the freedom of a rational being it *can be*, and what according to the necessary laws of morality it *ought to be* ... [T]his world is so far thought as an intelligible world only. To this extent, therefore, it is a mere idea, though at the same time a practical idea, which really can have, as it also ought to have, an influence upon the sensible world, to bring that world, so far as may be possible, into conformity with the idea. The idea of a moral world has, therefore, objective reality, not as referring to an object of an intelligible intuition ... but as referring to the sensible world, viewed however as being an object of pure reason in its practical employment.[52]

Kant has no intention of forfeiting the basic experience of morality for freedom as a fact of pure reason. He does not assert our freedom in order to deny the possible exercise of that freedom within experience – experience that, as Kant himself says, might be met with in the history of humankind. This is why I have argued from the outset that Kant's specific quotations must be judged in the context of the whole of his philosophy to arrive at an interpretation that preserves his views as complete and whole as possible.

Indeed, we have already done so to this extent: we have seen that Kant's ethics necessarily involves the proposition that the human will (particularly as *Willkür*) exists in time and acts in both the phenomenal and noumenal worlds. But the difficulty of incorporating this conclusion into the remainder of Kant's thought without contradiction and without destruction of any of the essential characteristics of his critical philosophy must be faced. Kant explicitly called upon his readers to assist him as co-workers . He knew that there were contradictions in his writings, but he was confident that they could be resolved by

---

51 KrV, A807/B835: CpR, 637. Emphases are Kant's.
52 Ibid., A808/B836: ibid., 637. Emphases are Kant's.

readers who mastered his position in its entirety. Kant also believed that we can often understand an author better than he has understood himself.[53] These statements define, I believe, an obligation imposed on those who interpret Kant's views. Although the problem, considered for itself, calls for a prolonged investigation, a suggestion of its possible resolution will, I believe, suffice to remove it as an obstacle to our further examination of the will.

First, we must revise some of Kant's views in the first and second *Critiques* in light of his views in the third. Kant's early confidence that in principle science can predict all human activity is absent from the third *Critique*. Aware of the implications of humankind's purposeful activity in art and morality, Kant conceived of the principle of finality on the analogy of such activities and regarded nature in terms of this principle as a work of art.[54] He argued that scientific investigation is dependent upon this principle for three reasons:

(a) Scientific method rests on assumptions which regard nature as an artist or work of art; Occam's razor and the saying "nature takes the shortest route" are examples.[55] This assumption is necessary to guide empirical observation and formulation of hypotheses.
(b) The natural sciences, while achieving islands of determinately ordered experience, have no means for uniting their knowledge into an overall system of nature apart from the use of the principle of finality.[56]
(c) Most important for our investigation, Kant denied that science would ever produce a Newton "to make intelligible to us even the genesis of a blade of grass from natural laws that no design has ordered."[57] In Kant's view, natural laws, having no reference to desire or intention, cannot account for the possibility of organic phenomena in which teleological relations of causes to effects are necessarily involved.[58] Much less, he believed, can natural causation account for the prediction of organic behavior.

---

53 KrV, Axx-xxii, Bxliii; B384–5, cf. B861–2: CpR, 14, 37; 319, cf. 654; KpV, 10: CprR, 124–125.

54 KU, 375–6, 383–4: CoTJ, 24, 34.

55 Ibid., 373 *passim*: ibid., 21 *passim*. See also the First Introduction to the *Critique of Judgment*, Sections IV, V, X EEKU (AA20). Unfortunately, this important work, which Kant abandoned only because of its excessive length, had not been translated into English as part of earlier translations of the *Critique of Judgment*.

56 See Section IX, EEKU (AA20) and CoPJ.

57 KU, 400: CoTJ, 54. This assumption would be questioned or denied by many scientists today. But it is not at all clear that they consistently avoid using this assumption surreptitiously.

58 Ibid., 389–95; 409, 410, 421, 422: ibid., 40–47, 66, 67, 81, 82; and Section IV of EEKU and CoPJ.

The extension of scientific inquiry to organic nature and to the human being as an organic and purposive being, Kant held, requires the adoption by scientists of the principle of finality. Through the use of this teleological principle, scientists may extend the use of the principle of natural causality and may aspire to predictive knowledge of organic life in terms of these principles. But there is no guarantee of success; furthermore, the principle of finality (unlike that of natural causality) is only a regulative principle for reflective judgment and cannot provide determinate knowledge. It is an objective principle, for its use is necessary to the acquisition of knowledge of organic nature and the unification of the sciences. But finality is constitutive and provides determinate knowledge of nature only when employed from the moral standpoint. There it is used constitutively, in connection with the moral argument, to regard nature as ultimately rational and directed toward the fulfillment of the moral aims of men.[59]

The unjustified metaphysical assumption that science can predict the course of human affairs in principle if not in practice – which Kant took for granted in the first and second *Critiques* – is thus rejected in the third *Critique*. In addition, Kant's belief that science requires the use of the principle of finality in order to extend its investigations to organic nature and to humanity has the consequence of leaving room in the phenomenal world for the effects of free causes.[60] Finality, which interprets nature in terms of intentions and goals, is a regulative, reflective principle when used at the behest of science. And, as a reflective principle, it does not conflict with either a reflective or even a determinate employment of the idea of freedom: Both principles may be used to interpret the same action. Kant does not deny that explanation in terms of natural causality is the continuing aim of science and the only knowledge of nature in the true sense of the term.[61] But he does deny that this aim can be attained without the employment of reflective, non-determinate principles. This late development in his thinking must not be overlooked.

Second, Kant's conception of the phenomenal and noumenal realms must be revised to account for the existence of the moral will in time and for its capacity to act in the phenomenal order. In the first *Critique*, Kant introduced the distinction between phenomena and noumena for two reasons: (a) he wanted to

59 KU, 457–8: CoTJ, 127–8.
60 But today most biologists and cosmologists deny the need for the principle of finality to sustain their research and the attainment of knowledge. But Kant would note with interest that often they use purposive language in describing their work. Edward O. Wilson's comment that "the organism is only DNA's way of making more DNA" (Wilson, 3) is the classic example of reliance on a teleological principle by a scientist who denies any such intention.
61 KU, 386–8: CoTJ, 36–9. See RGV, 71n: Rel, 65n.

emphasize the fact that the mind is passive in sensation and that knowledge resulting from the articulation of the data of sensibility by the categories of the understanding is merely knowledge of the appearance of reality; (b) he wanted to resolve the Third Antinomy by establishing independent orders for freedom and natural causality. The former insistence upon the finitude of human knowledge and its dependence on the knower is an essential – perhaps *the* essential – tenet of Kant's philosophy. The latter insistence upon separate realms for the employment of free and natural causation is not essential and is even inimical to Kant's thought. It is unnecessary because the third *Critique* suggests an alternative solution to the Third Antinomy on the basis of the limitations of natural causality and the regulative employment of finality. It is inimical because moral experience involves, as we have seen, the temporal awareness of duty and the involvement of the moral agent in the phenomenal world.

In the first *Critique*, Kant defined noumena as things-in-themselves, as objects of non-sensible intuition, and he denied that human beings were capable of non-sensible intuition. Moreover, he defined phenomena as objects of appearance which are known by applying the categories of the understanding to sensible intuition.[62] In terms of these definitions there is obviously no place for moral experience in either realm. The noumenal realm is closed to all human experience through the lack of intellectual intuition, and the phenomenal realm is limited to experience conceptualized by the categories of the understanding. We cannot object to Kant's insistence on sensible intuition, on the perceptual, as a condition for knowledge: Kant has amply described the dangers of superstition and fanaticism which accompany merely conceptual flights into the transcendent.[63] We must question, however, his assumption that everything given in sensibility, in the matrices of space and time, has to be conceptualized by categories of the understanding. Kant did not err in his definition of the noumenal; he erred, rather, in placing arbitrary and uncritical limits on the phenomenal, for they forced him mistakenly and contradictorily to locate moral experience in the noumenal realm.

Kant's method, as developed in Chapter I, was not to ask if the actual experience of human beings is possible but rather to ask how it is possible, i.e. what must be presupposed to account for its possibility. Kant insisted that he was not inventing moral experience but merely offering a rigorous account our moral experience. The experience of moral obligation – which Kant called the one fact of pure reason – occurs in time, in inner sense, and therefore involves sensible intuition. Any principle or concept which must necessarily be presup-

62 KrV, B305–8, B310ff.: CpR, 265–267, 271ff.
63 Ibid., B292ff., B303: ibid., 257ff., 264.

posed in order to give determinate structure to this experience has, by virtue of that necessity, its own transcendental justification. Thus the experience of duty provides the basis for the transcendental deduction of freedom and the transcendental analysis of the will. We have no reason to say that this knowledge stems from an intellectual intuition of noumena. Kant rightly insists in the *Religion*, as in most of his ethical writings, that we know ourselves morally only as we appear to ourselves, that we can never know the secret motives of the heart or the character of our dispositions except by indirect reasoning from our moral actions.[64] Our knowledge of freedom, the will, and ourselves as moral beings would seem, consequently, to be a knowledge of moral phenomena and a part of our knowledge of the phenomenal realm as a whole. By broadening the conception of the phenomenal world to include all aspects of human experience – the moral, aesthetic, and organic, no less than the theoretical[65] – we pose many tasks for Kant's interpreters, but no insurmountable problems for Kant's system. What we must do is to realign his theory of phenomena and noumena to fit his actual practice developing his philosophy.

In light of the above discussion, we need not be troubled by Kant's insistence on the presence of *Willkür* in both the phenomenal and noumenal orders. We recognize the temporal nature of *Willkür*[66] and its presence in both moral and theoretical dimensions of the phenomenal world. *Willkür* can be regarded from a theoretical standpoint as a theoretical phenomenon or from a moral standpoint as a moral phenomenon. Because these orders are not mutually exclusive, the ultimate unity of the will, which is essential to morality, is not impaired.

This interpretation is required by Kant's ethical position and reflects the direction taken by Kant in his later writings. It is noteworthy that in the *Religion*

64 RGV, 51, *passim*, cf. 20, 47–8: Rel 46, *passim*, cf. 16, 42–3.

65 It may be wondered why religious experience is not included. Although Kant recognized the autonomy of moral and aesthetic experience and the knowledge of organic nature (hence our extension of the concept of the phenomenal to include this wider range of experience) he refused to admit that religious experience is a genuine, autonomous aspect of human experience. The reasons are these: (a) Kant found nothing in religious experience as such to restrain the fanatical and superstitious tendencies of religious imagination. The concepts of religion would seem to be blind, empty, and often perverse without the restraining correction of moral principles. And, as Greene points out, (b) Kant was far too rationally inclined to believe that truth might be essentially historical and dependent for its discovery on non-rational revelation. One of many clear instances in the *Religion* of Kant's refusal to recognize the legitimacy of religious data that can be supported by neither theoretical nor moral experience is found on RGV, 53: Rel, 48.

66 This is not to say that there is a temporal origin, i.e. an antecedent determination, of the acts of *Willkür*. But these acts all take place freely in a temporal continuum. See RGV, 39: Rel, 35.

Kant put no stock in his earlier technical distinction between phenomena and noumena; he remarks, with some suggestion of impatience, that "these expressions [phenomena and noumena] are used only because of the schools."[67] In order to follow Kant's usage in the *Religion*, we shall have to continue to speak occasionally of the phenomenal and noumenal actions of the *Willkür*, but we must bear in mind that, strictly speaking, all so-called noumenal acts should be regarded as morally phenomenal acts of inner sense which are not publicly observable, and that the noumenal realm should be regarded as the locus of the will only when it is considered as transcending human knowledge as a thing-in-itself.

iii. Wille

In our discussion of the human will, to which we now return, we have considered the will merely in terms of its radical capacity of free choice – that is, as *Willkür*. The analysis of the will in terms of this single aspect is by no means complete. The moral law awakens *Willkür* to its transcendental freedom, to its power to act as a free faculty of desire. But the moral law is not the *Willkür*: it is not the transcendental freedom to act autonomously or heteronomously. The moral law expresses, rather, the rational conditions for the existence and realization of transcendental freedom and confronts *Willkür* with these conditions in the form of the categorical imperative. Kant makes room in the will for the presence of the moral law by introducing the concept of *Wille* which refers to the purely rational aspect of the will. *Wille* is as much a part of the will as *Willkür*, for without it there could be no rational structure for freedom, no experience of obligation, and hence no awareness of the power of volition.

Unlike *Willkür*, however, *Wille* does not make decisions or adopt maxims; it does not act. Rather it is the source of a strong and ever present incentive in *Willkür*, and, if strong enough to be adopted by *Willkür* into the maxim of its choice, *Wille* "can determine the *Willkür*" and then "it is instead practical reason itself."[68] *Wille* expresses the possibility of autonomy which is presupposed by transcendental freedom. The *Wille* represents the will's own demand for self-fulfillment by commanding *Willkür*, that aspect of the will which can either fulfill or abnegate its freedom, to actualize its free nature by willing autonomously in accordance with the law. *Wille* defines the principle on which all

67 Ibid., 14: ibid., 13.

68 MS, 213: MOM, 375. I have substituted Kant's terms "*Wille*" and "*Willkür*" respectively for Gregor's "will" and "choice" in order to preserve Kant's important technical distinction between the two.

decisions should be made; it is rationality or reason itself as it is directed toward action.

The most important difference between *Wille* and *Willkür* is apparent here. Whereas *Willkür* is free to actualize either the autonomous or heteronomous potentialities of transcendental freedom, *Wille* is not free at all. *Wille* is rather the law of freedom, the normative aspect of the will, which as a norm is neither free nor unfree. Having no freedom of action, *Wille* is under no constraint or pressure. It exerts, instead, the pressure of its own normative rational nature upon *Willkür*.[69]

In order to influence *Willkür*, which is a faculty of desire, *Wille* must be able to arouse desires or aversions in *Willkür*. The feeling which can be aroused by *Wille* is called moral feeling and consists in the "simple respect for the moral law."[70] The presence of *Wille* in the will, and specifically in relation to *Willkür*, constitutes what Kant calls the predisposition of the will to personality. This predisposition "is the capacity for respect for the moral law as in itself a sufficient incentive of the *Willkür*."[71] This predisposition is appropriately named because personality involves freedom and because the capacity to be motivated to action simply by the universality of one's maxim, i.e., by its accordance with the moral law, is a necessary condition for the actual possession of transcendental freedom and the potentiality of autonomy. The capacity to act merely according to the demands of the moral law without regard to the motive of such action is a capacity shared by trained animals. But the capacity to act from the incentive of universal law, and thereby to transcend determination by particular inclinations and habits, is a capacity enjoyed only by free, responsible beings; it is the capacity to act from the incentive of willing the fulfillment of one's own nature as a person. "The moral law," said Kant, "with the respect which is inseparable from it ... is personality itself (the idea of humanity considered quite intellectually)."[72]

The determination of *Willkür* by *Wille* can occur in varying degrees, with the general provision that nothing determines *Willkür* unless *Willkür chooses* to be so determined. The natural predisposition to personality (the capacity of the *Willkür* to make the law a sufficient incentive for action) can be fulfilled "only when the *Willkür* incorporates such moral feeling into its maxim."[73]

---

69 Ibid., 226: ibid., 380.

70 RGV, 27, cf. 30, 36, 46–8 *passim*: Rel, 23, cf. 26, 31, 42–44, *passim*.

71 Ibid., 27: ibid., 22–3. In this regard *Wille* functions much as Aristotle's god, that is, as an unmoved mover.

72 RGV, 28: Rel, 23.

73 Ibid., 27, cf. 21, 23–4: Rel, 23, cf. 17, 19; MS, 213: MOM, 374–5.

Nonetheless, the *Willkür* can never be totally devoid of moral feeling for then it would cease to be itself. If *Willkür* did not make the moral law (*Wille*, as the rational structure of its own nature) a determinant of action at least to the extent of feeling duty-bound, that is, categorically obligated to do so, whether that obligation were fulfilled in action or not, the *Willkür* would cease to be transcendentally free. "No human being," Kant argued, "is entirely without moral feeling, for were he completely lacking in receptivity to it he would be morally dead; and if (to speak in medical terms) the moral vital force could no longer excite this feeling, then humanity would dissolve (by chemical laws, as it were) into mere animality."[74] To this minimal extent *Wille* necessarily determines *Willkür*. Although the agency of determination is on the side of *Willkür*, when for purposes of analysis these aspects of volition are separated, the necessity of this determination derives from the dependence of *Willkür* on *Wille*. This dependence, as we have seen, is grounded in the inseparability of freedom and rationality. A *Willkür* totally unresponsive to *Wille* would be a freedom totally dirempted from rationality. Of such a freedom we have neither experience nor knowledge. As Kant put it: "To conceive of oneself as a freely acting being and yet as exempt from the law which is appropriate to such a being (the moral law) would be tantamount to conceiving of a cause operating without any laws whatsoever (for determination according to natural laws is excluded by the fact of freedom); this is a self-contradiction."[75]

iv. Moral Feeling

Since moral feeling is not merely an incentive for *Willkür* but expresses, in addition, the *Wille*'s relation to *Willkür*, its delineation and careful examination constitute an essential part of Kant's analysis of the will. Moral feeling can be experienced in a variety of pleasant or unpleasant ways: (a) it can be painful frustration when respect for the law demands the rejection of the objects of sensible desires; (b) it can be the painful feeling of moral dissatisfaction when it forces the *Willkür* to reflect upon its past betrayals or present temptations to betray its own free nature through heteronomous action; (c) it can be the pleasant feeling of moral satisfaction in having affirmed one's freedom through

---

74 MS, 400: MOM, 529. Kant writes: "The incentive which consists in respect for the moral law we have never been able to lose, and were such a thing possible, we could never get it again." Cf. RGV, 35: Rel, 30.
75 RGV, 35: Rel, 30.

autonomous action; or (d) it can be the pleasant and painful experience of the sublimity of personality, the experience of the power of the human will to assert its rational independence from the forces of sensibility even at the cost of happiness or of life itself.[76]

It is easier to describe how moral feeling can be experienced by the will than precisely to specify how it is to be distinguished from all other feelings. It would seem possible, for instance, to distinguish moral feeling from non-moral feelings by noting that the former, unlike the latter, does not *affect* the *Willkür* but is *effected* by it. In a sense, however, this can be said for all feelings if the *Willkür* is regarded from both theoretical (psychological) and moral standpoints. If the *Willkür* is regarded from the former standpoint, it is thought to be *affected* by its strongest desire. Regarded from the latter, it is thought to *effect* its strongest desire as its act of free volition. All desires and feelings would seem to be alike, therefore, in their relation to *Willkür*: from one standpoint all seem to affect the *Willkür*; from the other, the moral standpoint, all are effected by it.

But the foregoing observations, while sound, are superficial. For despite the observed similarities in the relation of moral feeling and non-moral feeling to *Willkür*, there are also radical differences: whereas the non-moral feelings of sensible desire influence the *Willkür* to varying degrees both before and after *Willkür* chooses its determining incentive, the moral feeling of respect for the law is not originally an incentive at all. Respect for the moral law is a feeling that is aroused in the *Willkür* only when it recognizes the law as a condition of its own being and the necessary standard of judgment in all its decisions. The *Willkür* first recognizes and accepts the law in this sense and only thereafter effects this feeling of respect in the process of expressing its free nature. Viewed phenomenally, this feeling effected by *Willkür* may then appear to affect *Willkür* in determining its choice. But this feeling never appears at all except as an effect of the *Willkür*.[77]

---

76 KpV, 71–89: CprR, 180–195; KU and CoAJ, Sections 27, 28, 29; RGV, 50, *passim*: Rel, 45, *passim*. See Chapter IX for a fuller examination of moral feeling.

77 It is apt to be misleading to say that the feeling of respect is an effect of *Willkür*; it is sounder perhaps to say that this feeling is an effect of the will as a whole. Moral feeling involves the dynamic unity of the parts of the will and is as much the effect of *Wille* as of *Willkür*. When the examination of *Wille* is extended, *Wille* is seen to be merely the internal rational conditions of the existence of *Willkür*. Hence, when Kant says that *Wille* determines *Willkür* through moral feeling, he is saying that *Willkür* determines itself according to its rational nature. And when Kant denies that *Wille* can determine *Willkür* unless the latter freely accepts such determination, he is merely following the line of his analysis of the will, in terms of which the radically self-determining aspect of will, the choosing will, is called *Willkür*. These complications are not theoretical difficulties. No analysis of a dynamic unitary function into

The distinction between moral feeling and sensible desires can be seen more clearly perhaps by means of an example. Suppose a person obeys the moral law in situation A in which such action is profitable to that person in terms of happiness, gratification of desire, etc. If we are asked to explain why the person obeys the law we can say, from a theoretical perspective, he or she is motivated to this action by desires. Although this explanation is by no means complete or exhaustive[78] it has considerable plausibility. Here the *Willkür* is viewed as if it were determined by sensible desires (pathological desires, as Kant curiously calls them) which *affect* and influence its behavior.

But now let us suppose (ruling out, by hypothesis, all prudential concern for the hereafter) that the individual obeys the moral law in situation B, in which his or her action causes him or her much suffering, loss of property, happiness, and perhaps the loss of life itself. The interpretation of the individual's action in this situation reveals concretely the difference between moral and pathological pleasure. From the theoretical perspective – in which all pleasures are assumed to be of the same sort (pathological, in Kantian terms) – we explain the individual's action by saying that he or she obeyed the moral law because he or she was happy doing so or feared a guilty conscience if he or she did not. Here moral feeling is treated as if it were like other sensible feelings, as if – prior to the decision of *Willkür* to make it so – it were a natural desire or incentive of the will. It is said that one is determined *by desire* to obey the law in situation B, the situation harmful to one's sensible interests, just as one was in situation A. This explanation, too, has an initial plausibility. But, as Kant saw quite clearly, it is one of the world's oldest and most popular examples of circular reasoning.

In situation A, the person has grounds for desiring to obey the law. We can point to the happiness and prosperity that come with such obedience. In situa-

---

stasic parts can be immune from distortion. But distortion can be held to a safe minimum as long as one does not hypostatize or concretize the isolated abstractions. To pretend that *Wille* and *Willkür* are perfectly discrete and separate parts of the will involves precisely such erroneous hypostatization. Some flexibility of usage is required to convey Kant's analysis with precision.

78 From a moral perspective Kant would supplement this explanation by saying that as long as the agent is a responsible person, he or she has to will that some desire have determining strength. And he would observe that since the demands of the moral law and of self-interest coincided in situation A, it is possible that a moral incentive was also involved. But Kant would regard the judgment as theoretically sound because it was made within the limits of theoretical presuppositions and did not have to borrow surreptitiously from moral ones. Finally, since such an explanation involves no trace of prediction, it poses no difficulties for the moral presupposition of freedom.

tion B, however, no ground other than the individual's desire to obey the law itself can be brought forward to explain his or her action. It is explained that the person desires to obey the law because he or she desires to obey the law. This circularity is obscured in the statement that the agent obeys the law because of "fear of a guilty conscience." But the fear of a guilty conscience only derives from the prior recognition of the authority of the moral law, and the law instills the resulting desire to obey it. We cannot argue that the person recognized the authority of the moral law and made obedience to it the condition of his or her happiness because afraid of a guilty conscience. The person would have had no conscience – clear or guilty – until after he or she recognized the law. An amoral person does not become moral for fear of having a guilty conscience. Such fear follows from but can never precede one's being moral.[79]

The difference between pathological pleasure and moral pleasure is thus a difference in kind. But the difference cannot be observed from the theoretical (psychological) standpoint, from which all pleasures and incentives appear alike as influences which affect and ultimately determine *Willkür*. The individual who feels respect for the moral law appears to the theoretical observer simply as one of those rare persons who, as a matter of fact, likes to do his or her duty. The difference between moral and pathological feeling cannot be observed on this level because the free moral power of *Willkür* is not a theoretical phenomenon. From the moral phenomenal standpoint, however, the difference between, no less than the similarity of, these kinds of pleasure is observable. From the moral phenomenal standpoint of inner sense we observe: (a) the recognition by *Willkür* of its own rational nature and the emergence of moral feeling which accompanies it; (b) the fact that the *Willkür* is passively affected by a vast array of desires and is sorely tempted to renounce its power of self-determination to the most alluring of them; and (c) the decision of *Willkür* which potentiates one of these influences, either the moral or the pathological, to determining force (thus accounting for the appearance of the dynamics of choice from the theoretical perspective). Passing over the similarity of these pleasures, we find that the basis of their difference lies in their mode of origination within *Willkür*. Pathological pleasure originates in the sensible nature of the human will, in *Willkür* as the merely passive recipient of sensuous influences (which can never be deter-

---

79 The attempt to persuade an amoral being to be moral by threatening him or her with a guilty conscience or tempting him or her with a clear one is as foolish as the attempt to use reason to persuade a non-rational being to be rational. To be sure, both procedures are often effective when dealing with immoral or irrational beings respectively, for only a moral being (in the generic sense) can be immoral, just as only a rational being (in the generic sense) can be irrational.

minants of *Willkür* without its active cooperation but which, regardless of its action, never cease to be influences). Moral pleasure, in contradistinction, originates in the rational nature of the human will, in *Willkür* as the active, self-originating, spontaneous (hence, rational) aspect of the will.[80]

By establishing the difference between these kinds of pleasure through his prolonged analysis of the human will, Kant realized a theoretical ambition of long standing.[81] On the basis of this distinction, Kant could admit that the moral law issues in a sensible delight and thereby has a practical influence in the sensible world without jeopardizing the rational foundation of obligation and transforming his ethics into an empirically derived one of the kind advocated by the "moral sense" theorists. He was concerned never to confuse these kinds of pleasure because the foundation of his ethics, in the experience of obligation, depends on their clear distinction,[82] and their confusion, he held, leads to "the euthanasia (easy death) of all morals."[83] Although Kant offered many clear statements of the nature of moral feeling prior to Book One of the *Religion*, he rightly said, "In another place (the Berlinischen Monatsschrift) I have, I think, reduced the distinction between *pathological* pleasure and *moral* pleasure to its simplest terms."[84] Kant's other statements on this matter cannot be fully understood apart from his careful analysis of the various structures and functions of the human will upon which the distinction between moral and pathological pleasure depends.[85]

---

80 My position is not universally shared. For a different view of the agency of *Willkür* see Lauener, 132–133. Lauener comments on my view of the *Willkür*, stating that I argue that *Willkür* must belong to both the noumenal and phenomenal spheres. I don't argue that it belongs to the theoretical phenomenal sphere, but only that the phenomenal sphere must be enlarged to include moral phenomena and *Willkür* definitely exists in that moral phenomenal sphere as well as in the noumenal sphere as a thing-in-itself about which we know nothing more than that it exists. Lauener's position depends on his having failed to notice what I consider an essential enlargement of the phenomenal sphere in order to give coherence to Kant's ethics.

81 See note 36 supra.

82 KpV, 36, 37, 112, 127, *passim*: CprR, 147, 149, 216, 230, *passim*.

83 MS, 378: MOM, 511.

84 Idem: idem. In the Preface to the *Metaphysic of Morals* Kant referred to his article in the *Berlinische Monatsschrift* on the subject of radical evil in human nature. He later published this article as Book One of the *Religion*.

85 Furthermore, on the basis of his clarifying analysis of the will in the *Religion* one can decide which of Kant's conflicting statements in the second *Critique* on the nature of moral feeling are sound. For what I consider to be Kant's finest statement concerning moral feeling, a statement published after Book One of the *Religion* and in the light of it, see TP, 283–4: TaP, 50–1.

There is one more issue to be addressed. Once moral feeling is present in *Willkür*, then *Willkür* (viewed psychologically) is determined by it. But what incentive, we may be tempted to ask, can prompt *Willkür* to recognize the authority of the law in the first place? Our question, however, is mistakenly raised. In asking this question, we are looking for the antecedent conditions from which *Willkür*'s free acceptance of the law must follow. But if such conditions could be found, then *Willkür* would not be free, since freedom involves the capacity to act independently of such conditions. When we look for such conditions, Kant argued, we reveal our failure to comprehend the nature of freedom, that is, we fail "to comprehend its *incomprehensibility*."[86] For the scientifically inclined, the incomprehensibility of freedom is usually enough to warrant its peremptory dismissal.[87] But Kant refuses to dismiss one of the necessary presuppositions of humanity's moral experience merely because that presupposition is incomprehensible. Kant was far too empirical and skeptical to accept the metaphysical position that the universe is necessarily and exhaustively comprehensible. He left to dogmatic rationalists like Wolff and, surprisingly, to many of the reductionist, positivist scientists the promethean metaphysic in terms of which one rejects as illusory all that one cannot comprehend. Kant's awareness of the finite limitations of human knowledge was built into his philosophy in the concept of the thing-in-itself.

v. The Origin of Evil

From the inscrutable depths of freedom, which Kant will neither dismiss nor pretend to understand, issue the moral qualities of the will, both good and

---

86 GMS, 463: GMM, 131; cf. KpV, 96–7: CprR, 202; RGV, 21n, 25, 39, 40, 43, 50, *passim*: Rel. 17n, 20, 35, 36, 38, 45, *passim*; MS, 380n: MOM, 512n. In his discussion of the incomprehensibility of freedom (Rel, iv), Greene seems to overlook the fact that it is logically necessary that freedom be incomprehensible; its incomprehensibility does not follow from Kant's disastrous "two standpoints theory." If freedom and predetermination are incompatible (and Kant holds that they are), and if explanation consists in specifying the set of conditions from which an act or event necessarily follows (and this is the only kind of explanation which Kant refers to), then since such explanation involves predetermination, such explanation cannot be offered for freedom. This obstacle to the comprehension of freedom can be removed if freedom is defined in such a way that it is compatible with predeterminism. But when freedom is so defined, Kant insisted, it is not explained but is explained away. See Section 2 supra.

87 MS, 378: MOM, 511.

evil.[88] "Man *himself*," Kant says, "must make or have made himself into whatever, in a moral sense, whether good or evil, he is or is to become. Either condition must be an effect of his *Willkür*; for otherwise he could not be held responsible for it and could therefore be *morally* neither good nor evil."[89] The moral quality of the will is completely self-acquired. No matter how bountifully or stepmotherly a human being is treated by nature, his or her opportunities are basically the same as those of all other human beings in the development and expression of their moral personality. Until by one's own free action one acquires a good or evil will, one is innocent; thereafter, one is still free to be different from what one has been. Hence, every

> action (whether good or evil) must be regarded as though the individual had fallen into it directly from a state of innocence. For whatever natural causes may have been influencing him, and whether these causes were to be found within him or outside him, his action is yet free and determined by none of these causes.[90]

There is no original sin and no original goodness in human beings except in the sense that sins and virtues *originate* in their free *Willkür*.

If there is no original evil in a human being until that person originates it, how does one happen to become corrupted? The human *Willkür*, on Kant's analysis, comes to self-awareness in relation to *Wille*, the voice of its rational nature, which instills in *Willkür* respect for the moral law as a part of *Willkür*'s self-recognition. Possessed of moral feeling, and in a state of innocence, why should *Willkür* ever choose to be evil? What is the occasion or condition of its choosing an evil maxim? It cannot be found in a defective or morally corrupt *Wille*. The presence of an inviolate *Wille* is a necessary presupposition of the existence of free choice: the universality of law (as noted earlier) is the necessary condition for the expression of freedom. Were this law itself corrupted, the necessary conditions of freedom, and hence of good or evil, would not be present.[91]

---

88 See Michalson, "The Inscrutability of Moral Evil in Kant." Michalson at first locates evil simply in a maxim (247). Later he clarifies his view by locating evil in the act of a will which formulates the maxim (250). Citing me at several points, he writes, "... as one commentator has aptly framed the issue, for Kant 'it is logically necessary that freedom be incomprehensible.'" Michalson continues with the observation, "An implicit yet clear corollary of this observation is the claim that moral evil is finally inscrutable" (265). It is inscrutable in the "hard" sense – simply beyond our ken.

89 RGV, 44, cf. 31, 43, 59n: Rel, 40, cf. 26, 38, 52.

90 Ibid., 41, cf. 21: ibid., 36, cf. 17.

91 RGV, 35, *passim*: Rel, 30–31, *passim*.

Many moralists and theologians have sought the condition or occasion of evil in humanity's sensible nature. Kant, however, explicitly rejects this position and argues that humanity's sensible nature, neither evil in itself nor the occasion of evil, is good and worthy of fulfillment:[92]

---

92 Kant has been signally unsuccessful in getting the attention of his readers on this point (though he made it often enough and with sufficient eloquence). Convinced that Kant's ethics is a formalistic ethic of duty and virtue alone, many critics have refused to accept as "Kantian," or have regarded as anomalous and inconsistent, all of Kant's doctrines and texts which insist upon the goodness of happiness and express a concern for its fulfillment. (See Chapter II, Section 2, page 56ff. supra and the discussion of Erich Adickes' attempt, summarized in the Preface to the Second Edition of the *Religion* (lxii ff.), to find an alleged repudiation by Kant of his own moral argument.)
Kant encountered this critical reaction in his own lifetime. In his essay "Theory and Practice" (TP: TaP), Kant noted that a respected contemporary, Garve, interpreted him to hold that "even where there is no question of duty, and he will not contradict duty, the virtuous man should still take no regard for happiness" (TP, 281: TaP, 48). Having clearly stated in the second *Critique* (and elsewhere) that "Pure practical reason does not require that we should renounce the claims to happiness" (KpV, 93: CprR, 199), Kant added in "Theory and Practice" with some show of emotion, "These objections are not misunderstandings... Their possibility must remain a mystery, unless such phenomena are adequately explained by the human tendency to follow one's own accustomed thought patterns even in the judgment of strange views, and to carry over the former into the latter" (TP, 281–2: TaP, 48–9). It is easy enough to find isolated passages in Kant's writings where he speaks as if the moral good were the only good. Such passages are relatively few, however, and passages which insist upon the goodness of happiness are far more numerous.
Aside from textual proofs alone, which can never be decisive in themselves apart from their relation to the theory as a whole, Kant's ethical position requires the existence of two basically different kinds of goodness – moral goodness and natural (*physische*) goodness: (1) The experience of obligation occurs when the moral individual confronts genuine, but conflicting values. Kant took issue with Stoic and Epicurean ethicists for trying to collapse the difference between virtue and happiness, thereby denying the distinct goodness of one or the other. (2) He recognized that the material of moral volition must be determined by the formal principle of the law in relation to the content of a human's sensuous nature; hence the direct duty to seek the happiness of others and the indirect obligation to seek one's own. (3) He offered a moral theory of punishment which presupposes non-moral values with which to reward and penalize. (4) In each of the *Critiques* and in most of his ethical writings, Kant argued that the moral purpose of creation and humankind's ultimate object of moral volition consists in seeking the highest good – the realization of virtue and happiness in proper proportion to one another. The close theoretical bond of happiness and virtue in Kant's ethics (which follows from the close bond of humanity's rational and sensible natures) is reflected in Kant's definition of virtue as the worthiness to be happy, and in his phrasing of the categorical imperative as the duty to "*Do that through which thou becomest worthy to be happy*" (KrV, B 836–7: CpR, 638). See ibid., B834ff.: ibid, 636ff.; GMS, 393, 415, 442: GMM, 61, 83, 109; KpV, 36–7, 76–7, 83, 92ff., 110ff.: CprR, 130, 148–9, 184, 190, 198ff., 215ff.; KU, 448: CoTJ, 114ff.; RGV, 5ff.,

> Natural inclinations, *considered in themselves*, are *good*, that is, not a matter of reproach, and it is not only futile to want to extirpate them but to do so would also be harmful and blameworthy. Rather, let them be tamed and instead of clashing with one another they can be brought into harmony in a wholeness which is called happiness.[93]

The goodness of humankind's sensible nature is essential, moreover, to the expression of virtue, for it provides the content for the moral object of volition. Furthermore, the attribution of evil to humankind's sensuous nature rests on the assumption that humans can be moved to action by their senses alone – without their willful cooperation – and thus reduces human nature to an animal level on which evil is impossible.[94] The Stoics, Kant observed, located the cause of evil in human carelessness, in human neglect to combat the sensible inclinations. But he added, "this neglect is itself contrary to duty (a transgression) and no mere lapse of nature."[95] Genuine evil consists in one's failure to withstand those inclinations when they tempt one to transgress.

Willkür is confronted by the demands of its own rational nature, present in *Wille*, and by the demands of its sensuous nature, present in its natural desires and inclinations. *Willkür* is not torn between good and evil but rather confronts two basically different kinds of good. And while immediately tempted to act upon its natural desires and inclinations, *Willkür* recognizes the categorical obligation to assert its own personality in the determination of its actions, and therefore to act in accordance with the universal demands of the moral law.

All men, whether good or evil, have within them the good incentives of happiness and of virtue. The difference between good and evil people depends upon the order of subordination within their wills of the moral and natural incentives. Evil persons are those who freely decide to subordinate the demands of the law to the demands of their sensible nature.[96] By expressing no more of

---

23–4n, 34–5, 58, *passim*: Rel. 4ff., 18n, 19n, 30, 51, *passim*; MS, 385ff.: MOM, 516ff.; TP, 278–89: TaP, 45–6.
Many of Kant's readers (like Schopenhauer, who was influential in establishing this popular misinterpretation) have accepted the *Groundwork* (which offers only the formalistic foundation for Kant's ethics) as Kant's authoritative and complete work on ethics. They have ignored or rejected as mistaken those parts of the first and second *Critiques*, the *Religion* and the *Metaphysic of Morals* which deal with the material component of Kant's ethics; and some of them have then criticized Kant for his failure to recognize the legitimate place of happiness in the moral life. See Schopenhauer, 50–51.

93 RGV, 58: Rel, 51.

94 Ibid., 34–5, cf. 26–32: ibid., 30, cf. 22–27.

95 Ibid., 59: ibid., 51–2.

96 Ibid., 36ff.: ibid., 31ff.

one's personality than is expressed in its abnegation, one fails as a free person and is evil. The good person, conversely, subordinates the natural incentives to the moral incentive and thus positively expresses in action his or her power as a free being. Thus the ground of evil is found in a person's tendency or *disposition* to will the rejection of himself or herself as a self-determining personality, as a free being, for the sake of himself or herself as a creature of nature.[97]

vi. Disposition

With the introduction of the concept of the disposition (*Gesinnung*), the analysis of human volition takes on still greater complexity. The development of this concept in Kant's *Religion* is, perhaps, the most important single contribution of the *Religion* to Kant's ethical theory, for by means of it he accounts for continuity and responsibility in the free exercise of *Willkür* and for the possibility of ambivalent volition, as well as the basis for its complex assessment. In defining the disposition, Kant says, "The disposition, i.e., the ultimate subjective ground of the adoption of maxims, can be one only and applies universally to the whole use of freedom."[98] And since each individual is morally responsible for his or her disposition, the disposition itself must be freely adopted by his or her *Willkür*. As the ultimate subjective ground of decision, the disposition is a fundamental maxim influencing or directing the adoption of the particular maxims on which individual decisions are based. In discussing evil in human beings, for example, Kant refers to the disposition as "a maxim of all particular morally-evil maxims" and points out that it is not observable but can be only inferred from the maxims of particular actions which are observable:

> In order then to call a man evil, it would have to be possible *a priori* to infer from several evil acts done with a consciousness of their evil, or from one such act, an underlying evil

---

97 Ibid., 57, 83, *passim*: ibid., 51, 78, *passim*. A human being's proper aim is the fulfillment of himself or herself in both aspects, though the fulfillment for the moral is a necessary condition of the personal fulfillment of the natural. The moral fulfillment is fundamental to the individual while the natural, though to be desired, is not. Thus Kant writes in "Theory and Practice" (TP, 283n: TaP, 50n), "Happiness contains all (but not more than) that which nature provides us; virtue, however, contains that which no one other than the person himself can give or take from himself."

98 RGV, 25, cf. 70n: Rel, 20, cf. 64n. Unfortunately, Kant was never systematic in his discussion of disposition; hence, we must fit together a picture from widely separated passages.

> maxim; and further, from this maxim to infer the presence in the agent of an underlying common ground, itself a maxim, of all particular morally-evil maxims.[99]

The disposition is this underlying common ground. In discussing the return of the *Willkür* from evil to good, Kant speaks of the revolution that takes place in the disposition which consists in "going over to the *maxim* of the holiness of the disposition."[100] But, he notes, the "man who adopts this purity into his maxim is indeed not yet holy by reason of this act (for there is a great gap between the maxim and the deed)."[101] This is to say, there is a difference between the dispositional act of *Willkür* and its particular acts that may, if the dispositional act is firm, follow from it.

The nature of the disposition is further clarified by Kant's discussion of the two kinds of action that *Willkür* performs. "The term 'act,'" he writes,

> can apply in general to that exercise of freedom whereby the supreme maxim (in harmony with the law or contrary to it) is adopted by the *Willkür* [the dispositional act], but also to the exercise of freedom whereby the actions themselves (considered materially, i.e., with reference to the objects of *Willkür* [the specific acts]) are performed in accordance with that maxim.[102]

The dispositional act involves the decision of the *Willkür* to subordinate either its sensible nature to its moral nature or its moral nature to its sensible nature; that is, the dispositional act determines the basic orientation and motivation of *Willkür*. It determines whether the specific actions of *Willkür* are to stem from a virtuous respect for the law (and hence are to be done for the sake of the law) or whether they are to stem from subjective interests (and hence conform to the law only when there is a coincidence of moral and subjective interests). The dispositional act concerns the willing or the rejecting of the spirit of the moral law and establishes the moral quality of the specific acts of *Willkür*, the underlying intentional ground of all its specific acts and therefore its nature or empirical character.[103] The specific acts of *Willkür*, on the other hand, do not establish the motive of action but are largely the products of the motivational force of the dispositional act. As concrete expressions of the dispositional motive, they may express that motive accurately or with a distortion resulting from the influence of intervening

---

99 Ibid., 20; cf. 37, 38–9, 71: ibid., 16; cf. 32, 34, 65.

100 Ibid., 47: ibid., 43. Italics are mine. A change of disposition, according to Kant, involves a "change of heart," not a "change of practices."

101 Ibid., 46, cf. 47: ibid., 42, cf. 43.

102 Ibid., 31: ibid., 26.

103 Ibid., 32, 47, 47, cf. 20: ibid., 27, 42, 43, cf. 16 *passim*; cf. MS, 226ff.: MOM, 380ff.

forces within the *Willkür* (as we shall consider later). But they can never fail entirely to reflect their dispositional ground inasmuch as their occurrence depends primarily upon the potentiating dispositional act. In its specific acts, the *Willkür* wills or refuses to will in accordance with the demands of the moral law; these acts reveal the decision of the *Willkür* regarding the letter, rather than the spirit, of the law, and establish the *legality* of the acts of *Willkür*. Although the dispositional act can be intuited only by an omniscient being and merely inferred (and with considerable inaccuracy) by human beings, the specific acts of *Willkür* are observable either in inner or outer sense. To the extent that the dispositional act can be grasped by inference, it is part of moral experience. But beyond that, it is a noumenal thing-in-itself. The specific acts of *Willkür*, however, are all aspects of the morally phenomenal order, and when the intentions of these acts are carried out, some of them can be experienced as theoretical phenomena. The dispositional act establishes the intelligible or noumenal character of the *Willkür*, whereas the specific acts establish its morally phenomenal character.[104]

The disposition is thus the enduring aspect of *Willkür*; it is *Willkür* considered in terms of the continuity and fullness of its free expression. It is the enduring pattern of intention that can be inferred from the many discrete acts of *Willkür* and reveals their ultimate motive.[105] To use a military analogy, the disposition is the strategic *Willkür*, as opposed to the tactical *Willkür* of specific actions. Since *Willkür* is free, its dispositional aspect is alterable from one moment to the next. In each moment, *Willkür* is not predetermined by what it was. On the other hand, and this point is frequently overlooked, *Willkür* is not undetermined nor indetermined. Freedom is itself a mode of causality with its own law.[106] The acts of the moral individual are *determined* by what the individual himself or herself *is*. Admittedly, Kant refused to deny the spontaneous agency of the individual; he refused to fossilize him or her in a predeterministic scheme which makes an individual only the expression of what he or she was, or more accurately, the expression of what *he* or *she* never was but only of what *nature* was and continues to be. As a moral agent, one is responsible for

104 RGV, 32, 47, 47: Rel. 27, 42, 43. See also Michalson's discussion of the function of the disposition in Kant's doctrine of radical evil.
105 RGV, 71: Rel, 65. Although the disposition cannot be divided into temporal parts and is not in the scientifically determinate temporal order (since it cannot be intuited in time and since it is the maxim of the complete free expression of *Willkür*), it has nonetheless the temporal properties of endurance and change. (RGV, 71, cf. 39, 47–8, 50–1, 66, 73–4, *passim*: Rel, 65, cf. 34, 43, 46, 60, 68, 69, *passim*).
106 Ibid., 35, 49n: ibid., 30, 45n; cf. KpV, 66ff.: CprR, 175ff.; GMS, 412ff.: GMM, 80ff. See also Section 2 supra.

one's actions because one is the author of them and because they express what one is. But we must not suppose, Kant insists, that what a person *is* (and therefore what is within that person's power and for which he or she is responsible) is expressed exhaustively in each discrete act of volition. Kant knew that we discover what we are not merely by observing our many discrete actions[107] but by inferring from them the quality of our disposition or moral character.[108] Our disposition reveals much more about what we are than our individual actions taken in isolation or in aggregate. The disposition is not the compulsive carry-over of our past nature into our present nature but the indication of our true and full nature freely, though not always consciously, willed in every present moment. It is the endurance or perseverance of our intentional, volitional commitment. Through a free and hence precarious continuity, the disposition is a *de facto* continuity in volition, a continuity whose existence does not cease merely because it is unsupported by predeterministic forces.

Continuity in disposition is essential to moral self-identity. Our moral self-consciousness would be fractured and dissipated into isolated intentions and actions if we did not relate them to one another by reference to their common ground of intention in disposition. Specific acts of *Willkür* have in themselves no direct interrelation. Each is a free decision of *Willkür* and none is the cause of another. The establishment of a *moral* (intentional, motivational, and not merely legal) relation between our actions depends upon viewing them as expressing, more or less accurately, the dispositional act of which we are not directly aware.

This extended-present nature of *Willkür* (what it is in its full being as disposition, and not merely what it is in specific actions) is thus, on Kant's view, the ground of moral responsibility. The *Willkür* acts on the basis of what it freely chooses to be, and because it freely asserts its fuller being in disposition, in addition to the part of its being which is asserted in specific moral choices, it is an enduring moral self. As such it is responsible for its actions despite the non-predictable spontaneity of its freedom.[109]

This complex analysis of *Willkür* as both an aspect of dispositional volition and an aspect of individual volition also enabled Kant to resolve another problem confronting his theory. Having admitted that both moral and sensuous incentives are good and that moral evil consists merely in the decision to

---

107 Several of these can occur simultaneously as subsequent discussion will indicate.

108 See Anth, 286ff.: AN, 186ff.

109 The criticism that Kant's theory of freedom precludes the responsibility of the moral agent has usually been directed against an oversimplified conception of Kant's theory that omits all reference to the dispositional aspect of the free will. See C.D. Broad, "Determinism, Indeterminism, and Libertarianism."

subordinate the former incentive to the latter, while moral goodness consists of the subordination of the latter to the former, he was left with a rigoristic (he used the term with pride) conception of the will. Although there is always a mixture of incentives in the *Willkür*, the *Willkür* must reflect one to which all others are subordinated: only one of these basic incentives can be made the determining foundation of action. Kant therefore concluded that there can be no middle ground of moral indifference: either the will is good or it is evil. But Kant had to admit that in everyday life we find people of gray morality (and in all shades from light to dark) without ever finding the whites and blacks demanded by his rigoristic theory.[110] Kant resolved these problems by arguing that these judgments are made from two different moral standpoints. Our everyday judgments are made on the basis of empirical observation and concern the moral phenomenal virtue of the will and the legality of its actions. We can only conjecture about the motives behind the actions of others, and we can never be sure of the motives behind our own, although introspectively we can be aware of some of them. On the level of mere observation, then, we judge the will on the basis of its specific actions, and we conclude that most if not all wills are both good and evil. Had we the omniscience of a divine judge, however, to observe the dispositional act, the basic intention which is the ultimate motive behind all specific acts, this judgment would be altered. The disposition would be found to be either good or evil and its moral quality only more or less distorted by the specific acts which follow from it when the *Willkür* applies its dispositional intention in concrete moral situations. From the standpoint of such an omniscient judge, we would judge the noumenal nature of the will and the morality of its actions; we would observe that the dispositional act – which is the adoption of the maxim of the entire exercise of freedom – was one in which the intention to subordinate the law to the senses, or the reverse, was present. From this viewpoint, the will would thus be judged either good or evil.[111]

In addition to providing the continuity essential to moral self-identity and the basis for two distinct judgments of the quality of the will, Kant's analysis of *Willkür* into its enduring dispositional act and its immediate specific acts provides the foundation for the interpretation of the complexity and ambivalence of volition. That his analysis of the will enables him to interpret the full range of human volition is best demonstrated by his examination of the stages in the

110 RGV, 22–5, 36: Rel, 17–20, 31; cf. MS, 384–5, 390: MOM, 516–7, 521.
111 RGV, 25, 39n, 46–7, 51, 71–6, *passim*: Rel. 20, 34n, 42, 46, 65–71, *passim*; cf. MS, 226: MOM, 380.

decline of moral goodness in volition.[112] This discussion divides itself naturally into two main parts: the discussion of the declining quality of the will while the *Willkür* remains good in its dispositional aspect, followed by the discussion of the will's further decline after *Willkür* has become evil in disposition. The discussion thus derives its basic structure from Kant's rigoristic account of the moral quality of disposition as either good or evil, while within this structure the relative proportion of good to evil in specific acts and in the relation of specific acts to the disposition itself can be viewed in terms of a continuum.

vii. The Decline of Personhood

The optimum stage of volition is one in which there is the closest approximation in the concrete acts of *Willkür* to the purity and goodness of its dispositional act. This is the stage of volition in which *Willkür* acts both in accordance with and for the sake of the moral law. In its dispositional act, *Willkür* here wills to subordinate all inclinations and sensuous desires to the demands of the moral law; that is, *Willkür* wills to meet the conditions for the fulfillment of itself as a free being. Furthermore, this dispositional intention, which establishes the morality of *Willkür*, provides the motivational force for its specific concrete actions. They, in turn, express transparently the intention of the disposition through their legality, through their conformity to the demands of the moral law. In this stage, reason is fully practical, as *Wille* arouses moral feeling in *Willkür.*

Even at this stage of the most complete realization of autonomy, however, there may be some difference between the intention of the disposition and its expression in concrete volition. This difference, which may involve a deviation from the demands of the law, does not necessarily imply any moral inferiority on the part of the will. Kant recognized two legitimate grounds for deviation from the demands of the law. First, in any specific volition, *Willkür* must adapt the essentially timeless intention of its disposition to the conditions of temporal (and sometimes spatial) realization. Distortion inevitably results, and its inevitability precludes its being imputed to *Willkür.*[113] Second, in any act of volition,

---

112 See RGV, 29–30, 36–9: Rel. 24–5, 31–34. In order to give systematic completeness to Kant's analysis of the decline of moral quality of the will, we shall begin our discussion with the examination of the fully autonomous will. Kant did not consider this stage in connection with the subsequent stages because his discussion occurs in the context of an inquiry into the propensity to evil; hence he began with the first stage of evil, the stage just inferior to complete autonomy.

113 Ibid., 67n: ibid., 61n.

judgment is required in order to determine the specific demands of the universal law. Such judgment may err through inexperience, and unless *Willkür* ought to have gained the requisite experience prior to the action in question, the errors in judgment due to inexperience cannot be imputed to *Willkür.*[114] No deviation of motives from the strict demand of the law is permitted, however, for motives are fully within the power of *Willkür.* If the will is fully autonomous the basic dispositional motive will be faithfully revealed in each specific act.

The first stage in the decline of autonomous volition is occasioned by that capacity for evil which Kant called the "weakness" or "frailty" of human nature. At this level, the dispositional act is steadfastly good, although *Willkür* does not succeed in expressing its dispositional motive without distortion and ambivalence. Here the plaint of St. Paul, "What I would do, that I do not" becomes relevant. Although the will has adopted the good as a dispositional maxim, this maxim is not followed in the specific acts of *Willkür.* Out of weakness *Willkür* abandons the difficult course of willing the law of its rational nature and freely gives its strongest momentary desires mastery over its actions.

At first glance, this may seem to be a clear case of abject heteronomy. The specific act following inclinations is neither in accordance with the moral law nor done for its sake. Here, however, as Kant subtly and correctly observes, more than one act is involved.[115] *What Willkür would do* in terms of its dispositional intention – which it positively expresses in the lawful act of self-condemnation – *it does not do* in the specific act in which the domination of particular pathological incentives is willed. The same *Willkür* that wills immorally to betray the demands of the law in a specific act wills morally in disposition, in the very same act, to condemn itself for so willing.[116] St. Paul, and any individual at this moral level, is so virtuous that he cannot even enjoy his vice. The voice of *Wille,* still expressing the dispositional intention, is willed so strongly by *Willkür* that *Wille* cautions the *Willkür* prior to the act, palls its enjoyment in the midst of the act, and condemns it subsequent to the act. All these expressions of *Wille* are also specific aspects of the *Willkür* and in them the dispositional act is faithfully and autonomously expressed. The goodness of the weak will is revealed (when one thinks of the great moral suffering in comparison with the minimal satisfac-

---

114 Ibid., 188n: ibid., 176–7n.

115 RGV, 29–30: Rel, 25.

116 One can regard the decision of *Willkür* at any moment of action either as a complex single act or as a group of simultaneous but individual acts. I think the former description is both simpler and closer to the facts. I do not think our simultaneous acts of volition are normally sufficiently examined and analyzed to be regarded as an aggregate of individually considered decisions.

tion of the illegal desires) by the continuing prominence and even dominance of *Wille*. When, for example, Major Barbara quickens the conscience of Bill Walker, she rightly concludes that his redemption has begun. As Kant put it: "Only the virtuous person, or one on his way to becoming so, is capable of this pure moral dissatisfaction (which [stems] from the action's very opposition to the law)."[117] Because the strength of the disposition is judged in temptation, *Willkür* on this level acquires a very clear picture of the strength and weakness of its disposition and its own power to express it faithfully.[118] There is no confusion of motives in this *Willkür*. The clarity of its moral awareness is another mark of its essential autonomy.

The next lower stage in moral volition, that of the impurity of the will, is occasioned by the capacity for evil stemming from the failure of *Willkür* to distinguish between moral and non-moral motives in action. At this level the *Willkür* may adopt a good maxim and intend to observe the demands of the law; it may act "with good intent and under the maxims of the good."[119] But in neglecting to make its dispositional maxim, to act for the sake of the law, the "*all-sufficient*" motive of action, *Willkür* fails to live up to the full demands of the law. At this level *Willkür* usually acts according to the demands of the moral law but the motive power of its volition does not stem from its respect for the law of its own freedom. Its lawful actions are motivated rather by the happy coincidence, never rare in civilized society, of a combination of moral and non-moral incentives. Viewed externally, the impure will may seem morally superior to the weak will; the impure will acts legally and *what it would do, it does*. The hell-fearing catechumen and the self-satisfied tradesman usually appear more righteous than the sinners in whose ranks are found the saints. The legality of its specific actions and the goodness of its dispositional intent belie the moral deficiency of the impure will. Whereas the weak-willed individual is strengthened by the knowledge of his or her weakness and purified by the *Wille* that condemns his or her vice, the impure individual is dying the quiet death (euthanasia) of morality through confusion of moral and non-moral incentives. The impure *Willkür* does not even know that it *observes* the law without ever *obeying* it. The correcting voice of *Wille* is virtually silent, though uncorrupted, for the law is not violated. The disposition, whose strength grows

---

117 TP, 283n: TaP, 50n.
118 RGV, 28, cf. 29: Rel, 23, cf. 24. See ibid., 36–8 and ibid., 32–33 for a further discussion of this stage of volition. Page 32 of this later material must be used with caution, however, because Kant confuses there the impurity of the will with its wickedness. The various strands of the discussion must be carefully separated.
119 Ibid., 29: ibid., 24.

and is measured in moral struggle against conflicting motives, wastes away. It is not rejected through evil intent; it atrophies from disuse.

Autonomy and moral goodness decline to a vanishing point in impure volition. Subsequent decline in moral quality involves the radical shift of the disposition itself from good to evil. No longer indiscriminate about motive, *Willkür* now deliberately subordinates its moral incentive to its non-moral ones. Its specific actions may be either legal or illegal, depending upon what *Willkür* must do in order to express its evil dispositional intent. Wickedness can be pursued single-mindedly or haphazardly. Single-minded pursuit of wickedness may require the wicked person scrupulously to observe all proprieties and display the external signs of moral goodness. As Thrasymachus and Callicles knew, the successful scoundrel must have a reputation for moral goodness; the exploiter of the public must be renowned for philanthropy.[120] Despite the apparent variety in the specific acts of the wicked *Willkür*, however, all of them issue from the evil disposition. The change in disposition from good to evil may not be fully recognized (and perhaps can never be fully recognized) by the wicked individual himself or herself. The clarity of such recognition may vary from time to time within the individual and between different individuals. A person who, in reflecting on an immoral act in his or her past, says "I am glad I had that experience before I recognized how wrong it was," is conscious of his or her ambivalent wickedness. Such a person tacitly admits to having preferred moral ignorance when knowledge would have forced him or her openly to reject the law or, abiding by the law, to forego the object of desire. Such a person thus prefers the evil order in the subordination of incentives, although his or her practical reason is still too strong for the person openly to reveal his or her evil disposition. For such an individual, says Kant, "who despite a corrupted heart (disposition) yet possesses a good *Wille*, there remains hope of a return to the good."[121]

The presence and expression of the uncorrupted *Wille* in the acts of the wicked *Willkür* is clearly evident in the life of St. Augustine. Unlike St. Paul, who merely suffered the weakness of an otherwise good will, St. Augustine plunged to the depths of wickedness crying, "Lord, save me! But not now!" The ambivalence of the wicked *Willkür* is apparent: the *Wille*, incorruptible so long as the *Willkür* retains its self-awareness as a free being, is expressed in the *Willkür*'s specific plea, "Lord, save me!"; simultaneously, the evil dispositional act is expressed in the *Willkür*'s more forceful objection, "But not now!" Thus *Wille*

---

120 The ambivalent expression of evil thus renders uncertain the moral judgment of humans and, as Kant said, "constitutes the foul taint in our race." RGV, 38: Rel, 34.

121 RGV, 44: Rel, 39. Kant's use here of "*Wille*" rather than "*Willkür*" is noteworthy.

preserves the moral feeling in specific acts after it's authority has been repudiated by the disposition. The dispositional act is wicked, and the specific acts express faithfully its evil intent; co-present with them, nonetheless, are specific morally good acts which express a subdued but audible conscience. Although wicked persons can enjoy their vices because their disposition favors them, they cannot forget completely that the law that they are rejecting is the condition of their own personal self-realization. In the midst of increasing animality, *Wille* keeps alive in the *Willkür* the last vestige of personal realization.[122]

There is no stage in the decline of the moral volition beyond that of wickedness. Kant denied that the deliberate rejection of the law itself is possible for human beings. Not even a wicked person wills evil for the sake of evil. His or her evil consists in willing to ignore the moral law and to oppose its demands when it interferes with his or her non-moral incentives. The wicked person's evil consists in abandonment of the conditions of free personal fulfillment in favor of the adoption of the conditions of fulfillment as a natural creature of desire.[123] This represents the ultimate point in the abnegation of personality. In wickedness, the only *personal* assertion consists in *Willkür*'s free resignation of its power of self-determination in the adoption of natural, non-moral incentives, and in its awareness through *Wille* of what it is doing. Once *Wille* is completely silent, the free *Willkür* loses its freedom altogether and becomes mere animal "*Willkür*"; the weakness of personality is finally replaced by mere animality, by the animal-like surrender to whatever inclinations are strongest at the moment.[124]

---

122 This is a position shared by Michalson, 250–251. He sees this view as a corrective to Emil Fackenheim's position in his essay, "Kant and Radical Evil."

123 RGV, 34–7: Rel, 30–32. Kant, unlike Plato, recognized that human beings can will evil intentionally. But Kant agrees with Plato by denying that humans will evil for its own sake. Both assertions can be made with consistency by Kant because he recognizes the heterogeneity of the good and hence can designate the natural good as the object of volition of the wicked will which is fully conscious that willing that object is morally wrong.

124 MS, 400: MOM, 529. Allen Wood takes issue with my criticism of Kant's doctrine of evil. But Wood has misconstrued my position on this issue. That individuals may choose to rebel against the moral law for the sake of rebellion does not commit me or Kant to the assumption that individuals have a natural impulse to evil, and that, in consequence, human beings cannot be held morally responsible for such evil. Nowhere have I argued that human beings have an original or inborn need to do evil. To the contrary, I have consistently maintained with Kant that a human being can *freely* choose to do evil, which is why *strong* as well as weak personalities can choose to disregard the moral law. Wood, *Kant's Moral Religion*, 212–213. I find no fallacy in recognizing that the violation of the moral law does contradict Kant's view that no one can reject the law.
In his *Idealism and Freedom*, Henry Allison presents this issue of diabolical evil with clarity. He takes issue with my position on the ground that Kant's denial of diabolical will is an *a priori*

In this review of the decline of volition, we have observed the concomitant diminution of virtue and personal power. In this parallel movement we have an intuitively clear answer to the question, How is the categorical imperative possible?[125] The necessity of the conformity to law as a condition for the expression of freedom is graphically expressed. The will, always transcendentally free to reject the moral law, can never escape its jurisdiction and punishment. The will escapes the law only in the sense that a prisoner who is shot to death going over the wall of a prison can be said to have escaped. The categorical imperative is inescapable because its violation, according to Kant, diminishes or even destroys the personality of the violator. Since freedom is a power whose fulfillment depends upon the structure of rationality, its irrational misuse results in impotence. Thus the categorical imperative, grounded in freedom, is necessary. The question "How is the categorical imperative possible?" is thus answered.

To assert, then, as is often done in literature and in the popular imagination, that there can be devilish beings who defiantly and powerfully reject the moral law itself presupposes a conception of freedom which, according to Kant, is hopelessly transcendent and without foundation in human experience. In human experience, he insists, our knowledge of freedom is revealed exclusively by the moral law and its realization depends upon the incorporation of that law in volition.

Allen Wood questions my contention that "in Kant's view an evil man must be a weak personality."[126] I do not know what is puzzling about this contention,

---

claim that to be accountable, wether for good or evil, "it is necessary to recognize the validity of the moral law" (176). But as I have argued, Kant here rules out *a priori* the factual evidence that contravenes his theory. (See also Chapter 8, 158, in Allison's *Kant's Theory of Freedom*.)

125 When Kant asked, "How is the categorical imperative possible" (GMS, 417, 453ff.: GMM, 84, 121ff.), he might have been asking any or all of three different questions. He could have been asking (1) How can reason be practical by issuing such an imperative? or (2) Why is the moral law a categorical imperative for the human will? or (3) Why is the moral law bound to the will with necessity? The first question (though Kant asked it) is mistakenly asked because the starting point of his ethics (see Section 1 supra) is found in the experience of obligation in which reason is practical and any further explanation of how it is practical requires an impossibility – the explanation of freedom. The second question is properly asked but readily answered; the moral law is an imperative for human beings merely because the human will is both rational and sensible and is tempted to subordinate the moral law to non-moral incentives. The third question is the important and difficult one whose answer requires that one explain why the judgment which expresses the necessary obligation of the will to an act is synthetic a priori (ibid., 419ff., 426: ibid., 87ff., 94). The answer is found in the analysis of the concept of freedom which is, in this instance, the third thing "X" in terms of which the proposition expressing the synthetic relation of the concept of the will to the concept of the moral law is found to be transcendentally analytic – hence, a successfully deduced synthetic *a priori* judgment.

126 Wood, *Kant's Moral Religion*, 213.

since Kant describes the decline in freedom and personality as one moves from full autonomy through weakness and impurity to heteronomy in the degrees of wickedness. The degrees of freedom, and hence personality, are concomitantly reduced with each move away from obedience to the moral law. Kant draws the line at devilishness because once a being repudiates the moral law itself, its freedom and responsibility seek to exist. Devilishness (or absolute evil) is impossible, according to Kant, because it requires repudiation of the law itself, which is impossible. This is impossible because the law is the foundation or ratio essendi of one's freedom and also the source of our awareness of our freedom.

Kant demonstrated the categorical nature of moral obligation by showing it was essential to the fulfillment of freedom and the expression of personal responsibility. If Kant had argued that one may be free and a fulfilled personality without respect for the moral law, he would have reduced the categorical imperative to an hypothetical imperative: if you want to be a free and fulfilled person, you must obey the moral law. Kant did better than that: he argued that the moral law defined a categorical obligation, for it alone makes possible our existence as free personalities. If we fail to respect or even to recognize the law as requiring the subordination of our inclinations to it, then we lose the capacity of free personal responsibility and even the awareness of our nature as free beings.

Hence, speculation about devilish beings is transcendent superstition; since, according to Kant, the most evil mode of free expression is wickedness, devils must be responsibly portrayed in the weakness of wickedness.[127] The Satan of "Paradise Lost" is an example of transcendent evil of the sort Kant believes is illusory. He is asserted to be powerfully free without any indication as to the source of a freedom that is unrelated to the conditions of lawfulness. Such an image beckons to humans with its romantic illusions about the grandeur and heroism of wickedness. Milton's Satan, towering in his solitary, defiant rage, consumed by a

---

127 Other scholars have grappled with this problem in Kant's treatment of evil. See, for example, Anderson-Gold, "Kant's Rejection of Devilishness: The Limits of Human Volition." Anderson-Gold's solution is to view evil, including diabolical evil, as a cultural phenomenon. Extraordinary vices can develop, she argues, because of self-love operating within a competitive social context. Anderson-Gold claims that my discussion of the problem, which was first developed in my essay "The Ethical Significance of Kant's *Religion*" (1960), seriously distorts Kant's concept of moral evil. I see no way, however, to preserve Kant's meaning on Anderson-Gold's terms. The reality is that evil can be freely chosen for its own sake. While many forms of evil can be viewed as a corruption of the predisposition to humanity, as entailed by Anderson-Gold's concept of "vices of culture" and exemplified by rationally motivated crimes of property (robbery, embezzlement, etc.), the massive evil of a Hitler or a Stalin cannot be included in such a classification without trivializing the notion of evil. For further discussion of this issue, see my essay "Kant at Auschwitz" in the Appendix.

hatred of everything God-like save God-like power, differs in kind from the one whom Goethe calls Mephistopheles, the obsequious, knavish seducer of old men and young girls. Faithful (whether or not intentionally) to Kant's analysis of extreme wickedness as a weakness in personality, Goethe, in Part I of *Faust*, portrays the devil as one who serves the moral purposes of God by trying the dispositions of men, quickening them to their moral destiny or encouraging them to damn themselves. Sometimes, out of human compassion, Mephistopheles even feels sorry for men and their sorry lot. And, shameless, he appreciates the fact that God, whom he affectionately calls "*Der Alte*," condescends to speak with him. Goethe's Mephistopheles, though less imaginatively drawn than Satan and far less attractive, has the weakness of personality required by Kant's analysis.

I have attempted to make clear these relationships in the following diagram. Reading from left to right, we observe the struggle of the human will toward the realization of its full power as a responsible person. Reading from the right to left we observe the gradual decline and final loss by the will of its personality.[128]

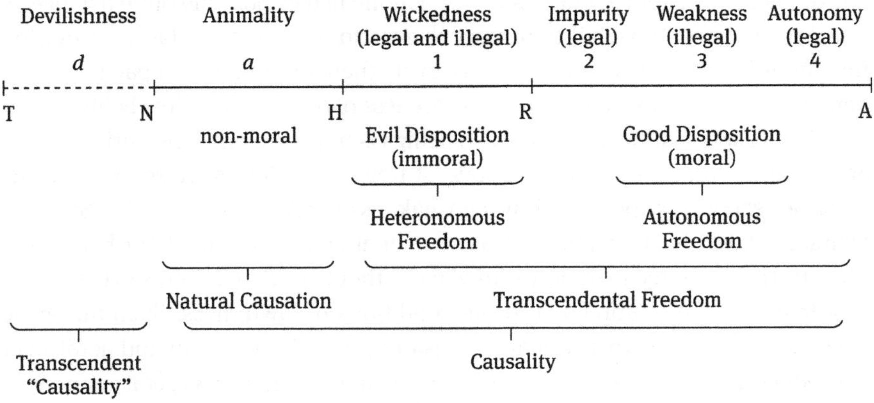

The diagram is largely self-explanatory. Line HRA represents the constant presence of transcendental freedom with its basic modes of potential expression – autonomy and heteronomy. It is constant because it is the *sine qua non* of responsibility and personality.

Specific positions on this line represent the degree to which the positive expression of transcendental freedom (autonomy) has been attained. The points on this line are read in an ascending scale from left to right, or a descending scale from right to left.

128 I note with thanks the suggestions on the design of this diagram by the late Professor Klaus Hartmann of the University of Tübingen.

Point H represents the minimal limit in the realization of freedom beyond which freedom ceases and natural causality begins. Point A represents the maximal limit. Point R represents the point of revolution in the disposition where its quality changes from being morally evil to morally good.

Line HR represents the heteronomous expression of freedom by the *Willkür* with an evil disposition. This line represents the minimal realization of autonomy even though *Willkür* is heteronomous: autonomy is minimally present here in the form of *Wille* which confronts *Willkür* with the actual possibility of autonomous volition. The specific acts of the heteronomous *Willkür* are read at point 1 and are evil. The designation in parentheses, which indicates the predominant relation of the specific acts to the demands of the law, shows that acts done in wickedness may be either legal or illegal; they vary widely depending upon the non-moral interests of the evil disposition.

Line RA represents the autonomous expression of the *Willkür* with a good disposition, from its minimal realization of autonomy at point R to its maximal realization at Point A. The presence of the good disposition sustains the judgment of any expression of *Willkür* on this line as moral rather than immoral and as autonomous to some degree. Point 2 represents a partial realization of personality in specific acts which are predominantly legal: there is no testing here of the disposition because of the impurity of the motives and the negligible activity of Wille due to the predominant legality of actions. Point 3 represents the confirmation in moral conflict of the autonomous nature of the disposition. *Wille* becomes strong and purifies the motives of *Willkür* so that moral self-awareness and critical self-judgment together with consequent fulfillment of personality follow. The typical specific act of the weak will is illegal, though a mixture of legal and illegal acts can occur. Point 4 represents *Willkür*'s achievement of mastery over its momentary inclinations so that the good dispositional intent is transparently reflected in specific actions. Specific actions are predominantly legal.

Point *a* on line NH represents action of *Willkür* after *Wille* has ceased to function and *Willkür* has become a mere animal *Willkür* causally determined by its incentives.

Point d on line TN represents the expression of a transcendent, merely conceptual, idea of a devilish freedom with personal power apart from any conception of law.

The rigorism of Kant's analysis is represented in the division of the exercise of freedom into autonomous (good) and heteronomous (evil) sections, line HR and line RA. And the common sense judgment of the mixture of good and evil in humans and the opinion that human beings are better or worse than one another to different degrees is represented in the numbered positions showing the greater or lesser realization of autonomy.

4 The Contribution of the *Religion* to Ethics

The contribution of Kant's *Religion* to his theory of ethics should now be apparent. My assertion that the *Religion* compares in importance for Kant's ethics with the *Groundwork* and the second *Critique* – which, coming at the beginning of this chapter, may have seemed exaggerated – is, I believe, accurate. The rationale of Kant's ethics turns on the interrelation of freedom, rationality and sensibility. Yet prior to the *Religion* Kant offered virtually no analysis of the human will which provides the foundation for the interrelation of these factors. He merely defined the will as practical reason and as the faculty of desire, without showing how these diverse conceptions can be united in a single faculty of volition. Without the establishment of the unity of these conceptions, however, no account can be given of the experience of obligation on which Kant's ethics is grounded. In the second *Critique*, Kant argued that the will is either heteronomous or autonomous. In the common moral experience of guilt, however, the will is obviously both – heteronomous in the acquisition of guilt and autonomous in the recognition and acceptance of it. The conception of the will prior to its development in the *Religion* was insufficiently complex to account for this experience. In all the *Critiques* Kant argued that a human being is obligated to seek the realization of both happiness and virtue; nevertheless, the *Religion* presents his earliest sustained account of a faculty of volition capable of willing these heterogeneous elements.

The capital importance of the *Religion* to Kant's ethics consists in the fact that the *Religion* offers us his only sustained analysis of the human will – an analysis which resolves several of these problems and removes many of the superficialities in his earlier statements. *Willkür* is analyzed in the *Religion* as a unitary faculty in which the forces of sensibility and rationality have a common meeting place. It thus provides the basis for an understanding of the experience of obligation as the constraint of the law upon a will tempted to reject it. Through the development of the important dispositional aspect of *Willkür*, moreover, Kant provides a theoretical account of the duplicity and ambivalence of human volition, a foundation for enduring moral character, and a basis for the rigoristic judgment of the will in terms of its entire exercise of freedom. Kant also now provides a dramatic confirmation of his conception of the categorical imperative by showing, in his analysis of the stages of evil volition, the concomitant decline of virtue and power.[129] All this amply assures the *Religion* a

129 Kant's demonstration of the decline of virtue and freedom as one moves from autonomy through stages to heteronomy and wickedness demonstrates the categorical nature of the

place of major importance in Kant's ethics. Kant's ethics cannot be understood apart from the position he developed in the *Religion*. It is only there that we find an exposition of the will as a dynamic unity of *Wille*, *Willkür* and *Gesinnung*.[130]

---

moral imperative. If one could maintain one's freedom and personality despite one's moral failure, the categorical imperative would be reduced to a hypothetical imperative holding only that *if* one wishes to be moral one should act in accordance with the moral law. But one is still fully free to do otherwise. Kant intends more than this. He holds that one's duty is categorical because any failure to act in accordance with duty results in the diminution of or loss of one's personality and hence of one's self as a full being.

130 The *Religion* is also important for its contribution to ethics in general. One aspect of this contribution consists, paradoxically, in the fact that the *Religion*, while purportedly strengthening Kant's conception of freedom, exposes possible flaws in two quite independent ways. The first turns on Kant's rejection of devilish volition as an illusion, the second on his handling of the problem of forgiveness. These issues shall be discussed in Chapter X.

Chapter IV: The Moral Good And The Natural Good

1 Terminological Problems

As Chapter II showed, the heterogeneity of the good – its division into the moral good, as virtue, and the natural good, as happiness – is central to Kant's ethics. In order to clarify and sustain this division, Kant was compelled to specify the valuational characteristics of each kind of good and their relation to one another. But in trying to analyze the good in its heterogeneity Kant faced a terminological difficulty. He could no longer speak simply of "the good" without speaking ambiguously. To avoid this ambiguity Kant decided to refer to the moral good by the term "*das Gute,*" and to the natural good by the term "*das Wohl,*" to moral evil by the term "*das Böse*" and to natural evil by the term "*das Übel.*"[1] This attempt at linguistic reform was not successful, however, for at least two reasons. First, Kant did not carry his reform of the language far enough. And second, Kant seriously underestimated and quickly fell victim to the power of common usage. The force of linguistic habit, both personal and social, and the wisdom inherent in common usage opposed the adoption of his terminology.

First, Kant failed consistently to develop and use a third term to refer to the quality of goodness common to both *das Gute* and *das Wohl.* At times he uses the term "*Wert*" to refer to both[2], and the natural good and the moral good are thus both said to have value. But Kant does not hold to the term "*Wert*" as the basic generic term for expressing what the derivative goods have in common. Instead, he follows the common linguistic practice and uses "*gut*" or "*das Gute*" to refer to the good both in the specifically moral sense and as a bridging concept for goodness in its inclusive sense. When speaking, for example, of the union of happiness and virtue in the concept of the highest good, Kant uses the phrase "*das höchste Gut.*"[3]

Second, Kant neglected to use the other concepts consistently. After pointing out that only the will is good or bad in the sense of "*gut*" or "*böse*" and that pleasure and pain are good or bad only in the sense of "*wohl*" or "*übel,*" Kant goes on to say, "Whoever submits to a surgical operation feels it without doubt

1 KpV, 59: CpR, 168.

2 See, for example, GMS, 435: GMM, 102.

3 KpV, 110: CprR, 214; cf. ibid., 61ff.: ibid., 170ff.

as an ill (*übel*), but by reason he and everyone else will describe it as good (*gut*)."[4] Again, when a practical joker is finally caught and given a beating, the beating is indeed an ill (*übel*); but it must also be regarded as a good in itself (*an sich gut*) even if nothing constructive follows from it.[5] In these two examples Kant obviously departs from his own terminological distinction. The will is not made good by means of a surgical operation; an operation, though ill (*übel*), may also be naturally good (*wohl*), but it can never be morally good (*gut*) since it does not concern the will but merely the physical well-being of the patient. Similarly, the beating which is administered to the joker is certainly not morally good. The will of the person giving the beating may be morally good, and the will of the beaten person may also be morally good if that person accepts the beating as a just reward. But the beating *itself* can be good in the moral sense only if we hold that it is a means whereby the moral good is attained and, therefore, that it is extrinsically *gut*.

This is not, however, what Kant appears to be saying here. He explicitly states that the beating is also good in itself (*an sich gut*). Consequently, in this instance he is speaking of the good in the sense of the highest good as the object of pure practical reason. He regards the beating as an embodiment of the demand of pure practical reason that happiness be distributed in proportion to virtue, the worthiness to be happy.[6] Although we can and must admit that the concept of the highest good as a union of happiness and virtue is a necessary extension of the moral good required by pure practical reason, we must note that this concept involves a concern for the natural good (*das Wohl*) as well as for the moral good (*das Gute*). This concept involves the application of the moral good as the object of pure practical reason to the sensible conditions of humanity and not simply to the conditions of rational willing as such. Kant's verbal ambiguity is undeniable.

There is, indeed, some consistency in Kant's usage in both of these examples. But this consistency either does not follow Kant's proposed usage, or it runs counter to his insistence on the heterogeneity of the good. For example, the term "*gut*" refers even here to what is intrinsically or finally good, whereas the term "*übel*" refers to something that is immediately bad in terms of physical well-being. But the term "*übel*" may also refer to something that is also good (*gut*) as the means either to future well-being or to a morally good state of affairs. When a physical ailment (*Übel*) becomes the occasion for a response that

---

4 Ibid., 61: ibid., 170.

5 Idem: idem.

6 Ibid., 110: ibid., 215. See Chapters V, VI and VII for an extended examination of the concept of the highest good.

leads to physical well-being (*Wohl*), as in the example of the medical operation, Kant calls it "*gut*" because it is a means to health or happiness which is presumably intrinsically or finally good (*gut*). Although this pattern of usage accords with Kant's insistence on the heterogeneity of the good, following which both the natural good and the moral good must have intrinsic value, the claim that health or happiness is intrinsically good runs counter to Kant's statement that only the will (the moral good) is of intrinsic worth.[7] We must therefore either reject or reinterpret such statements. We must either insist on the intrinsic goodness of the natural good or we must say that an operation is *gut* because it is a means to the attainment of the good will! Neither view accords with Kant's position.

If we submit Kant's writing to close textual analysis, we find that consistency of usage is limited to highly restricted textual contexts. And in any one context several alternative interpretations are possible. If we presume a consistent pattern of usage, interpretation drawn from this usage may run counter to Kant's central doctrines. If, on the other hand, we insist on Kant's distinction between "*gut*" and "*wohl*" we find ourselves unable to find a consistent pattern of usage. And if we start with a consistent pattern of usage which accords well with Kant's central doctrines we discover that it runs counter to the "*gut-wohl*" distinction.

Any attempt therefore to derive a definitive understanding of the nature of the good – as either the moral good, or the natural good, or the highest good – from a simple reliance on the Kantian text is pointless. Kant's initial distinction between *das Gute* and *das Wohl* was never adequately developed nor consistently followed. Hence, in order to understand the meaning of the good in its heterogeneity, we will begin with our own terms (all used by Kant, of course) – the moral good, the natural good, and the highest good – and find meanings for them which, with reasonable interpretation, will fit consistently into nearly all textual contexts and comport with the central doctrines of his ethical theory as a whole.

This procedure is indeed supported by Kant himself. In the *Anthropologie*, Kant finds there are two kinds of good contained within the highest good (*höchste Gut*), the physical and the moral good. He says, "*Die beiden Arten des Gutes [sind] das physische und moralische.*"[8] The physical good is found to be happiness and the moral good is found to be virtue. Together they constitute the highest good as the moral-physical good (*das höchste moralisch-physische Gut*).[9]

---

7 GMS, 434–435: GMM, 102.
8 Anth, 276–7: AN, 178.
9 Idem: idem.

I have deviated from Kant's terminology only to the extent of substituting the term "natural" for the term "physical." This alteration seems justified since, for Kant, happiness refers to the satisfaction of all desires, mental and spiritual as well as physical. Hence, to refer to happiness as the "physical good" seems mistakenly to restrict its meaning.

2 The Intrinsic Goodness of Both the Natural Good and the Moral Good

In specifying the valuational properties of the moral good and the natural good on this basis, let us turn first to the concept of the moral good. While it cannot be considered in complete isolation from the natural good and the highest good, an attempt must be made to reveal its unique characteristics. We must bear in mind that the moral good, as the object posed for the will by the moral law, is the good will itself. Since the quality of goodness of the moral good must be grounded in the nature of the object that is morally good, we must determine the essential characteristics of the moral good by considering the essential characteristics of the will as that object. As we noted in Chapter II, Kant asserts that the will is free and unconditioned and that it is the only thing that is free and unconditioned.[10] It is precisely because the will alone, by virtue of its freedom, is unconditioned that it alone can be the unconditioned object posed for the will by the moral law.[11]

Morality, as discussed in Chapter II, must have reference to an end, but the end to which the will is related must be related to the will as a duty, as an unconditioned obligation. The only object, however, to which the will can be related in an unconditioned manner is an object which is itself unconditioned. Since freedom alone has the quality of unconditionedness, freedom itself, or the will as the faculty of freedom, is the only object which can be posed by the moral law as the unconditioned object of the will. The free will alone can be the object given with *a priori* necessity by the moral law because, by virtue of its freedom, the will can determine the exercise of its own freedom while still

---

10 KpV, 97–101: CprR, 203–206; GMS, 412–3, cf. 446ff.: GMM, 80, cf. 114ff.

11 We must not overlook Kant's two uses of "*Wille*". Narrowly used, "*Wille*" refers to that aspect of will ("*Wille*" in the general sense) that is practical reason itself. In this narrow sense, *Wille* is the moral law presented as categorical imperative to the will as *Willkür*. In its broader usage, "*Wille*" encompasses the formal, functional unity of both *Wille* and *Willkür*; thus when *Willkür* expresses in free action the law of *Wille*, the dynamic unity of volition (*Wille* and *Willkür* taken together) is referred to as "*der gute Wille*." See Chapter III, Section 3, "The Human Will."

remaining free. The will (as *Willkür*) is not conditioned or qualified by being determined by the moral law (*Wille*) to seek itself as its object because that to which it is determined by the law is unconditionedness itself – autonomy as the fulfilled mode of freedom. Since the moral good is the good will, and since the will alone is free and unconditioned, Kant insists that "it is impossible to conceive of anything at all in the world, or even out of it, which can be taken as good without qualification (*gut ohne Einschränkung*) except a *good will*."[12] Similarly there is nothing which is evil without qualification except an evil will.

The quality of moral goodness is derived directly from the character of the will itself. In this passage Kant uses the term "*gut*" in the broad sense, meaning any kind of good, and he says that good in this general sense is never good *without qualification* unless it is the good of the good will. One cannot interpret Kant to be saying simply that "*gut*" in the narrow, moral meaning of the term can be found nowhere but in the good will. On this interpretation, Kant's thought would be reduced to an absurd tautology. Since for Kant the good will is the only moral good, it is obvious that we cannot conceive of the moral good anywhere other than in the good will. And since the will must be free, and in being free must be without qualification, it is tautological to say that the moral good is morally good without qualification.

We must therefore suppose that the words "without qualification" do not refer to the *moral* good but to the concept of good *in general*. By these words "without qualification" Kant points to the essential characteristic in terms of which the *moral* good is to be distinguished from the *natural* good. A qualified good or a good subject to qualification cannot be morally good. Unlike natural good or evil, moral good or evil is without qualification since it refers to the quality of a free and therefore unqualified being. Because freedom, by definition, is qualified by nothing beyond itself, neither is the good or evil which is expressed in its exercise.

The meaning of moral goodness is made additionally clear by Kant's further characterization of the quality of the goodness of the good will. "A good will," he says, "is not good because of what it effects or accomplishes – because of its fitness for attaining some proposed end; it is good through its willing alone."[13] The will, of course, has an object, and strains "every means so far as they are in its control" to attain the object it necessarily sets for itself.[14] But the attainment

---

12 GMS, 393: GMM, 61. I have inserted Kant's terminology parenthetically into Paton's translation.
13 Ibid., 394: ibid., 62.
14 Idem: idem.

of the objects toward which it strives is not completely under its control as an expression of its freedom. As a consequence, the attainment or lack of attainment of the object cannot alter the quality of the free will. The quality of the will is determined, therefore, only by the nature of the willing itself – by the straining of every effort in a manner consistent with the law of our free nature. When the will is judged from the standpoint of the moral concept of the good (defined by the moral law), it is judged on the basis of its striving alone and is either good or evil without condition or qualification.

This interpretation of the moral good, which comports well with Kant's doctrines of the will and of freedom, is supported by a multitude of texts. Kant employs many different phrases in order to highlight the same essential characteristic of the moral good. In addition to speaking of the moral good as a good without qualification (*ohne Einschränkung*)[15], Kant says it is held to be good in itself and unconditionally (*an sich und unbedingt gut*);[16] it is absolutely good (*schlechterdings gut* or *schlechthin gut*);[17] it is immediately good (*unmittelbar Gut*),[18] not good merely as the means to something else.

The absolute, unconditioned, immediate, and unqualified character of the moral good results from the fact that the will is free and by virtue of its freedom is set apart as that which has an inner, intrinsic value (*innern Wert*).[19] And since its freedom is an internal property of the will, its inner worth is completely inner. The moral good can never be an externally related good, for freedom presupposes unconditionedness.

We see, then, that the good will is the sole moral good and that its goodness is a completely self-contained inner goodness, a goodness that is immediate, unconditioned, and without qualification.

But contrary to claims of many interpreters of Kant, the good will is not "the sole and complete good."[20] There are also all the non-moral goods – intelligence, sober reflection, wit, social intercourse, power, wealth, honor, health, and, in summary, happiness as the fulfillment of all the needs of finite sensuous yet rational beings. It may seem at first to be a mistake to lump together all the talents of the mind and body as well as the enjoyments of the senses under the natural good as happiness. Kant at times does speak of happiness simply as the

---

15 Ibid., 393: ibid., 62.
16 TP, 282: TaP, 49.
17 GMS, 426: GMM, 93.
18 KpV, 59: CprR, 168.
19 GMS, 435: GMM, 102.
20 Ibid., 396, cf. 393ff.: ibid., 64, cf. 61ff.; KrV, B841: CpR, 640; KpV, 60ff., 100ff: CprR, 170ff., 214ff; Anth, 276ff.: AN, 176ff.; TP, 278ff.: TaP, 45ff.

fulfillment of this or that desire. But the natural good does not refer to happiness in this limited sense. It refers rather to the idea of happiness which encompasses the totality of inclinations. The natural good, as the idea of happiness, refers to "an absolute whole, a maximum of well-being in [one's] present, and in every future, state."[21] When the natural good as happiness is regarded in this manner, it is not the simple fulfillment of presently felt desires (for which the word "satisfaction" is more appropriate) but rather the rationally directed, albeit sensibly motivated, concern for the total fulfillment of humanity's sensible nature.

Under the idea of the natural good, maxims of prudence are determined by reason in regard to the totality of sensible needs and inclinations. Prudence consists in the skill shown "in the choice of means to one's own greatest well-being."[22] In this context prudence is not merely an individual's skill in manipulating others so that they contribute to one's own ends. It also involves "sagacity in combining all these ends to [one's] own lasting advantage."[23] Prudence thus involves the exercise of reason not merely in fashioning the techniques for attaining ends, but also in producing a harmonization of these ends. In this employment, reason is responsive to all the desires and inclinations of the person and attempts a systematization of them which will then become a new object of desire. In this employment the ultimate determination of the maxims of prudence comes from the sensible needs and desires of the individual. By forcing the faculty of desire to consider all its desires and needs at once, reason relates the many specific desires to one another in such a fashion that the resulting pattern of desires becomes more desirable than any single desire by itself.

When we refer to the natural good as happiness and attempt to group all the talents of mind and body and all the delights of the senses under it, we are referring to happiness as the idea of total well-being. Kant has this meaning of happiness and the natural good in mind when he regards all non-moral goods as included within the concept of the natural good.[24]

These natural goods are genuine goods. But beyond this it is very difficult to determine their valuational properties. Speaking negatively, they are not merely derivative or extrinsic values as means to the moral good. These goods can, nevertheless, assist the moral will. For example, wealth can lessen the temptation to steal just as abject poverty can intensify it. But we cannot say with

21 GMS, 418, cf. 399, 415: GMM, 85, cf. 67, 83; see also KrV, B834: CpR, 636.
22 GMS, 416: GMM, 83.
23 Ibid., 416n.: ibid., 83n; KpV, 61–62: CprR, 170.
24 For further discussion of the issues closely related to this, see Section 3.

precision that these natural goods are thereby extrinsically good in the moral sense of good. The moral goodness of the will is to be judged only with regard to the exercise of its freedom, and hence it is only by hypothesis that these natural goods can be regarded as means to the attainment of the good will.[25] Furthermore, the freedom of the will may itself be limited by extreme temptation. Even a wealthy individual may be tempted to commit evil given the right inducements. As a consequence, the virtue of the will, which depends on the actual freedom and capacity of a particular will, must be judged in light of the presence or absence of such temptation. "The degree to which an action *can be imputed* (*imputabilitas*)," Kant holds,

> has to be assessed by the magnitude of the obstacles that had to be overcome. – The greater the natural obstacles (of sensibility) and the less the moral obstacle (of duty), so much more the merit is to be accounted for a *good deed*. ... On the other hand, the less the natural obstacles and the greater the obstacle from the grounds of duty, so much the more is a transgression to be imputed.[26]

Kant concludes: "The degree of responsibility depends upon the degree of freedom."[27] The influence of the presence or absence of natural goods on the attainment of a good will is therefore cancelled out in the estimation of the quality of the will's actions. Natural goods may make the moral task easier or harder, but they cannot either increase or reduce the moral quality of the will. If they make a virtuous act easier to perform, then the will that performs it shows less moral worth in so doing than it would have shown without the assistance of the natural. Likewise if natural goods make a virtuous act more difficult and the will fails to perform it, then the evil of the will is reduced by the presence of the natural hindrances. Moral worth is judged solely on the basis of the will's exercise of its actual freedom. Hence, the influence of natural goods is cancelled out in assessing the will's moral worth.

We thus face a serious difficulty in our attempt to specify the valuational characteristics of natural goodness. We cannot say that the natural good is good

---

25 KpV, 93–4: CprR, 199–200; cf. GMS, 393, 399: GMM, 61, 67; MS, 388: MOM, 519–20.
26 MS, 228: MOM, 382.
27 VüE, 75, cf. 249: LoE, 62 (my italics), cf. 197. In 1924 Professor Paul Menzer published *Eine Vorlesung Kants über Ethik*. Menzer's text is based on a manuscript by Th. Fr. Brauer written down in 1779 by Brauer and copied by him for the complete manuscript bound together in 1780–81. Professor Menzer included in his translation notes by Theophilus Kutzner and by Ch. C. Mrongovius. The Menzer text was translated in its entirely by Louis Infield in 1930 and published as *Lectures on Ethics by Immanuel Kant*. A more recent and comprehensive translation is *Lectures on Ethics*, tr. Peter Heath and J.B. Schneewind.

as a means to the attainment of the moral good. Kant insists on comparing the moral good with the natural good: "the first is good in itself, but the second is in no way."[28] This statement, though expressed in an essay in which Kant emphasizes the importance and value of happiness and the moral legitimacy of one's concern for one's own happiness,[29] flatly rejects the notion that there is any intrinsic value at all in the natural good itself. But if the natural good is not a means to the moral good, and if the natural good is not good in itself, and if the moral good is not the only good, Kant's theory falls into serious contradiction. This contradiction consists in his having asserted the value of the natural good while at the same time having denied that it could have value either in itself or as a means to the moral good. In order to understand Kant's theory of the good, we must again forego the temptation to seize upon isolated passages. Rather, we focus on a group of representative passages to find an idea of the whole that will make consistent sense of Kant's position.

In the *Groundwork* Kant does not usually make so strong a statement as the one just cited from "*Theorie und Praxis*." In the former work, after explaining that the good will alone is good without qualification, Kant says that the natural good has "no inner unconditioned worth (*keinen innern unbedingten Wert*)"[30] whereas the good will "would still shine like a jewel for its own sake as something which *has its full value in itself*."[31] In the juxtaposition of these two important passages we find a clue. In the first quotation, Kant does not say that the natural good has no inner or intrinsic worth. He says rather that it has no inner *unconditioned* worth. It might yet have an intrinsic worth which was, however, subject to being conditioned by factors external to itself. In the second quotation, Kant does not say merely that the good will has its value in itself. He says that the good will has its *full* value in itself. In these passages Kant focuses on the unconditioned character of moral goodness, on the completeness and absoluteness of its value in itself, while at the very same time he focuses on the conditioned character of the natural good and on the lack of absoluteness of its value in itself. The difference between the moral good and the natural good is not the difference between intrinsic and extrinsic goods, but rather the difference between absolute and relational goods.

28 TP, 282: TaP, 49. I have revised Ashton's translation. The German reads, "*die erste ist an sich, selbst gut, die zweite keineswegs*." This statement is, to my knowledge, the most extreme Kant made on this issue.
29 TP, 278–9ff.: TaP, 45–6ff.
30 GMS, 393–4: GMM, 61.
31 Ibid., 394: ibid., 62. My italics. In the German the italicized phrase reads: "*seinen vollen Wert in sich selbst hat*."

This is the solution Kant offers in his distinction between goods which have a price and the one good which has a dignity beyond price. Consider, for example, this passage:

> In the kingdom of ends everything has either a *price* [*Preis*] or a *dignity* [*Würde*]. If it has a price, something else can be put in its place as an *equivalent*; if it is exalted above all price and so admits of no equivalent, then it has a dignity. What is relative to universal human inclinations and needs has a *market price;* what, even without presupposing a need, accords with a certain taste – that is, with satisfaction in the mere purposeless play of our mental powers – has a *fancy price* (*Affektionspreis*) but that which constitutes the sole condition under which anything can be an end in itself has not merely a relative value [*einen relativen Werth*] – that is, a price – but has an intrinsic value [*einen innern Werth*] that is, *dignity.*[32]

What does Kant mean by saying that the moral good has *einen innern Wert*? And what are the implications of the meaning which he assigns to the natural good? We must be wary of the English phrase "intrinsic worth" which is used to translate "*innern Wert.*" An "*innern Wert*" is surely what we would call an intrinsic good. But the phrase "*innern Wert*" may carry an additional meaning. When Kant contrasts the moral good with the natural good, he contrasts the good that has *einen innern Wert* with the good that has *einen relativen Wert*. This suggests that when he speaks of the moral good as having *innern Wert* he is pointing to its absolute worth and not merely to its intrinsic worth.

At times Kant speaks of the absolute worth of the will in terms which defy misunderstanding. In the paragraph following his discussion of the jewel-like properties of the will, he refers to "*dieser Idee von dem absoluten Werthe des blossen Willens.*"[33] We are surely justified in concluding that it is the absolute quality of the goodness of the will, rather than the mere inwardness of its goodness, that Kant is emphasizing in contrasting dignity with price. He is concerned, not with the mere inner intrinsic character of the moral good, but rather with its exhaustively or absolutely intrinsic character as having its full value, its unconditioned value, in itself.

In the first *Critique* Kant discusses the ambiguity of the term "absolute" and distinguishes that which is absolute from that which is merely inner or intrinsic in a manner that is instructive for the present discussion. Concerning transcendental ideas, Kant observes,

---

32 Ibid., 434–435: ibid., 102. Paton provides the German only for "fancy price"; I have added the others.

33 Ibid., 394: ibid., 62.

> The word "*absolute*" (*absolut*) is one of the few words which in their original meaning were adapted to a concept that no other word in the same language exactly suits. Consequently, its loss, or what amounts to the same thing, looseness in its employment, must carry with it the loss of the concept itself .... The word "absolute" is now often used merely to indicate that something is true of a thing considered *in itself* and therefore of its *inward* nature. In this sense the *absolutely possible* would mean that which in itself (*interne*) is possible – which is, in fact, the *least* that can be said of an object. On the other hand, the word is also sometimes used to indicate that something is valid in all respects, without limitation, e.g. absolute despotism, and in this sense the *absolutely possible* would mean what is *in every relation* (in all respects) *possible* – which is the *most* that can be said of the possibility of a thing. Now frequently we find these two meanings combined. But in most cases the meanings are infinitely far apart .... It is, then, in this wider sense that I shall use the word "absolute."[34]

By distinguishing, for example, that which is valid in itself (intrinsically valid) from that which is absolutely valid, and by pointing out that something could be valid in the former sense without being valid in the latter, although it might be valid in both senses, Kant's analysis parallels the distinction which he is trying to make between the moral good and the natural good.

That which has a price has value in itself but not in all possible respects or contexts; that which has a dignity has an absolute value. The character of the goodness of the natural good and the moral good is not fully specified even when we admit that both are intrinsically good. We are saying that the former is merely good in itself, whereas we are saying the latter is absolutely good in itself, in every respect, and without limitation or qualification. The natural good and the moral good are both intrinsically good; nevertheless, the character of their goodness is "infinitely far apart."

Since the difference between the goodness of the moral good and that of the natural good is in no way confused by our attributing goodness to each, there is no reason for denying the intrinsic goodness of each. It is no easier to confuse the value of dignity with that of price, even after the intrinsic goodness of both is acknowledged, than it is to confuse the two meanings of possibility after having admitted that both varieties are inner or intrinsic to a possible object.

The way Kant applies his distinction between dignity and price lends additional support to this interpretation of the valuational properties of the natural good and the moral good. All natural goods, among them skills, wit, humor, luxuries, shelter, etc., have fancy or market prices since bartering can take place in this area. Exchange can be carried on on the basis of desires and needs.[35]

---

34 KrV, B381–82: CpR, 317–18.
35 KpV, 23: CprR, 134.

Hence, losses can be compensated. If one were to break a beautiful piece of Meissen china, one could go to Dresden for a substitute. While substitution is possible among objects of desire, the same is not true of moral beings and their decisions and actions. There is only one object of the moral law and that is the moral good as virtue. If one is in default of one's duty and performs bad acts, that person cannot make up for the loss of value. "[N]ature and art alike contain nothing to put in their place; for their own worth consists ... not in the advantage or profit they produce, but in the attitudes of mind – that is, in the maxims of the will."[36] When the will performs its duty and fulfills the law, its actions

> exhibit the will which performs them as an object of immediate reverence .... This assessment reveals as dignity the value of such a mental attitude and puts it infinitely above all price, with which it cannot be brought into reckoning or comparison without, as it were, a profanation of its sanctity.[37]

There is only one moral good and that is the will as virtuous action, or considered as the vital enduring origin of virtuous action. Since virtue or moral goodness alone can be its object, nothing can redeem the loss of moral goodness in a bad act. But since the natural good as happiness may have many different objects, if one object is taken away, another object, equally satisfying, may be put in its place, and the loss to happiness can thus be restored. True, a given natural good might have a value surpassing that of all others so that no other object could be substituted for it without the loss of happiness. Such an object would then be invaluable from the natural standpoint and have no market equivalent. But it would nevertheless have a price if its pursuit and attainment conflicted with duty.

For example, we find no natural substitute for Job's lost children. Although they constituted a part of his happiness, and therefore his natural good, they were also moral beings having a dignity beyond price. Nevertheless Job would not trade his virtue for the preservation of his children, though in the Book of Job they were taken from him without his having any decision in the matter. This admittedly extreme case clearly illustrates Kant's point. On strictly Kantian terms, Job's virtue could not have been defined apart from the consideration of the welfare of his children as ends in themselves. But if we consider Job's loss as the writer of Job himself interprets it, Job was not responsible for the loss of his children and, hence, they function primarily as natural goods, along with health

36 GMS, 435: GMM, 102.
37 Ibid., 435: ibid., 103.

and even cattle. The episode is thus apposite to Kant's argument. Having asserted the incomparable value of the moral good, Kant then asks,

> What is it then that entitles a morally good attitude of mind – or virtue – to make claims so high? It is nothing less than the *share* which it affords to a rational being *in the making of universal law*, and which therefore fits him to be a member in a possible kingdom of ends. For this he was already marked out in virtue of his own proper nature as an end in himself and consequently as a maker of laws in the kingdom of ends – as free in respect of all laws of nature, obeying only those laws which he makes himself and in virtue of which his maxims can have their part in the making of universal law (to which he at the same time subjects himself). For nothing can have a value [*Werth*] other than that determined for it by the law. But the law-making which determines all value must for this reason have a dignity – that is, an unconditioned and incomparable worth – for the appreciation of which, as necessarily given by a rational being, the word *reverence* [*Achtung*] is the only becoming expression. *Autonomy* is therefore the ground of the dignity of human nature and of every rational nature.[38]

Here we see again that the value which Kant assigns to the good will as the moral good is based upon the fact of the will's freedom.

> ... [I]n morals the proper worth of an absolutely good will [*eines schlechterdings guten Willens*], a worth elevated above all price, lies precisely in this – that the principle of action is free from all influence by contingent grounds, the only kind that experience can supply.[39]

Kant's point here is not that goodness can inhere only in the will. Rather, his point is that only the good will, because it alone has freedom, can have a goodness which is absolute – beyond all comparison, exchange or qualification. As the unique expression of freedom alone, the moral good has no possible substitute and therefore no price. And because of the unconditioned nature of freedom, the moral good cannot be either enhanced or corrupted by anything beyond itself. Hence it can never be qualified in such a way as to make comparison possible between it and natural goods.

It is freedom rather than the moral law (the abstract formulation of the conditions required for the fulfillment of freedom, i.e., the law of freedom) that finally accounts for the unconditional goodness of the will. Kant does at times say that the moral law alone is worthy of reverence or respect (*Achtung*) and not

38 Ibid., 435–436: ibid., 103. I have inserted Kant's phrases parenthetically into Paton's translation.
39 Ibid., 426: ibid., 93. I have inserted Kant's words parenthetically into Paton's translation.

the will of the moral person. "This respect which we have for a person [is] really for the law which his example holds before us."[40] But here Kant merely fails to complete his argument. The feeling of respect (or aversion) which we have for a person may really be for the law which the person reveals, whether in virtue or in vice. But we respect the law, in turn, only because the law, as the law of freedom, reveals to us the freedom of the individual, his or her autonomy, which is the true ground of his or her dignity. Kant is on occasion very explicit: "Since this law, however, is in itself positive, being the form of an intellectual causality, i.e. the form of freedom, it is at the same time an object of respect."[41] Kant here completes the line of reasoning in a fashion paralleling his discussion of dignity in the *Groundwork*; here his statement is unambiguous; it is the freedom, the autonomy of the will, which is the source of its unconditioned goodness.

Bearing in mind that the moral good derives its valuational property from freedom, it is clear that it is the unconditionedness, that absoluteness of the moral good rather than merely its intrinsic, inner quality, that distinguishes it from the natural good. When this is understood, we can attribute to the natural good an intrinsic goodness (though indeed a relative and conditioned goodness) while still maintaining the distinction between it and the moral good. Thus we can accept without contradiction Kant's insistence that the moral good is not the sole good as well as his insistence that the natural good is not good as a means to the moral good.

3 Particular Natural Goods and the Natural Good

Our interpretation of the natural good as an intrinsic, relational good poses difficulties which must be considered and, if possible, removed. Outstanding among them is Kant's assertion that "all the objects of inclination have only a conditioned value [*einen bedingten Werth*]; for if there were not these inclinations and the needs grounded on them, their object would be valueless."[42] Here it seems that our interpretation must founder. But it is precisely at this point that it gains additional support, and we are given a second clue to the solution of the problem.

The value of any particular object of inclination is subject to annihilation as a result of the variability of desire and is, therefore, only contingently valuable.

---

40 KpV, 78: CprR, 185.
41 Ibid., 73, cf. 74, 86ff.: ibid., 181, cf. 182, 193ff.
42 GMS, 428: GMM, 95. I have inserted Kant's phrase parenthetically into Paton's translation.

But there are always sensible inclinations and desires and therefore always some objects of desire which are valued. Although specific natural goods may cease to be of value, the natural good in general – as the general fulfillment of the needs and inclinations of finite rational sensible beings, without regard to the particular objects which constitute this fulfillment at any particular moment – is always of value. For it happens that reason, and hence the law itself,[43] *must* admit to the necessity of inclinations and the needs which are grounded on them even if no particular specific objects are necessarily desired at all times. Reason and the law must therefore admit the ever-present value of the natural good in general, as well as the transient value of some particular natural goods which constitute the natural good at any given moment. In support of the necessary value of the natural good in general, Kant writes,

> Certainly our weal and woe are very important in the estimation of our *practical reason*; and, as far as our nature as sensible beings is concerned, our happiness is the only thing of importance .... Man is a being of needs, so far as he belongs to the world of sense, and to this extent his *reason* certainly has an *inescapable responsibility* from the side of his sensuous nature to attend to its interest and to form practical maxims with a view to the happiness of this and, where possible, of a future life.[44]

Were Kant to overlook the inescapable presence of the sensuous needs and inclinations of human beings, he would be obligated to drop his concept of the assertoric and the categorical imperatives. In presenting the rational grounds for the assertoric imperative Kant says,

> There is, however, *one* end that can be presupposed as actual in all rational beings (so far as they are dependent beings to whom imperatives apply); and thus there is one purpose which they not only *can* have, but which we can assume with certainty that they all *do* have by a natural necessity – the purpose namely, of *happiness* ... a purpose which we can presuppose *a priori* and with certainty to be present in every man because it belongs to his very being.[45]

Had Kant failed to acknowledge the sensuous component of humans as an essential part of their being, he would have had to reject the concept of duty (or imperative) altogether. It is only because humans are rational beings who are *also* sensible beings under the constraint of inclinations that the moral law

---

43 At this point we must bear in mind the fourth sentence in the long quotation on page 15, supra: "For nothing can have value other than that determined for it by the law." In the pages following we will try to sustain our interpretation in light of this sentence.

44 KpV, 61, cf. 61ff.: CprR, 170 (my italics), cf. 170ff.

45 GMS, 415–416: GMM, 83.

confronts them as an obligation, as duty, rather than as the descriptive law of their behavior.[46] If Kant had denied the presence of inclination and hence of the natural good in general (and some non-specific particular natural goods), he would have denied the experience of obligation, a necessary condition of moral experience.

We have not shown, however, that the law has grounded the value of the natural good. We have shown that the legitimacy of the inclinations and the needs that arise from them is established independently of the law, since the concept of duty vanishes unless the value of the natural good is posited. To this extent Kant must acknowledge a correction to or a reinterpretation of his statement that "nothing can have a value other than that determined for it by the law."[47] He need not deny (and we shall see later, he correctly insists) that the law does qualify the value of any object and even of the natural good in general. But he must admit that there can be value besides that which is determined by the law. Kant must admit the value of the natural good *in independence of* the determination of this value by the law because moral experience itself, no less than anthropological observation, points to the presence in human beings of a sensible as well as a rational nature. The objects of inclination are therefore never valueless because sensible needs and the inclinations on which their value is grounded are always present. By viewing the natural good not merely in terms of this or that specific natural good, that is, in connection with specific contingent and variable objects of inclination, but also in general, in connection with humans as sensible beings, we see that the natural good as happiness, that is, as fulfillment of humanity's sensible nature, is of genuine, intrinsic worth since "it belongs to [humanity's] very being."[48]

Since the sensible nature of a human being is essential even though it does not exhaust human nature, it is still true that the natural good is both an intrinsic and a relative and conditioned good. In due course, we must try to make clear in what ways the value of happiness can be conditioned. We must recognize that the value of happiness does not vanish in the presence of virtue, but that both virtue and happiness are good in themselves and that "they strongly limit and check each other in the same subject."[49]

If we were to deny this, we would be at a loss to explain why, according to Kant, we are morally obligated to seek the happiness of others as well as our

---

46 Ibid., 412: ibid., 80; KpV, 32, 83: CprR, 143, 190.

47 GMS, 436: GMM, 103. (See 121–22 of this chapter supra.)

48 Ibid., 415–6: ibid., 83.

49 KpV, 112, cf. 93; CprR, 217, cf. 199.

own perfection.[50] And if the intrinsic goodness of the natural good is denied, we cannot explain Kant's insistence that we are permitted to seek our own happiness. Kant maintains that to say that "even where there is no question of duty and he will not contradict duty, the virtuous man should take no regard of happiness ... contradicts my position completely."[51] Indeed he insists that we do not have a determinate duty to pursue the happiness of others. As he puts it, "a maxim of promoting others' happiness at the sacrifice of one's own happiness, one's true needs, would conflict with itself if it were made a universal law."[52] One's duty to seek the happiness of others is qualified and made indeterminate by the fact that one has the right to consider also one's own happiness since one is also obligated to treat oneself as an end in itself. It is only because a person will naturally pursue his or her own happiness as a descriptive law of behavior that Kant denies that one has a duty to pursue one's own happiness:

> What everyone already wants unavoidably, of his own accord, does not come under the concept of *duty*, which is a *constraint* to an end adopted reluctantly. Hence it is self-contradictory to say that he is *under obligation* to promote his own happiness with all his powers.[53]

Kant recognizes the legitimate claims of happiness. As long as humans are sensible beings as well as rational ones, the natural good, as happiness, cannot fail to have intrinsic value.[54] But this does not commit Kant to a view that the intrinsic worth of the natural good is absolute, unconditioned, or unqualified. Nor is he committed to the view that the worth of the natural good is only of intrinsic worth. Since he clearly insists on the relativity of the natural good, we must now consider the manner and extent of its relativity.

We have already noted that the natural good is relative to the sensible nature of humankind and that apart from this relation the natural good is indeed without value. But this is not a significant aspect of its relativity because the sensible part of human nature is essential both to humanity and to morality.

---

50 MS, 385ff.: MOM, 516ff.

51 TP, 281: TaP, 48. This is my modification of Ashton's translation.

52 MS, 393: MOM, 524.

53 MS, 386: MOM, 517. See also KpV, 36–7: CprR, 148.

54 In arguing the case for the intrinsic value of the natural good in light of Kant's ethical theory, we have failed to mention one of the strongest arguments, namely, that unless the intrinsic worth of happiness is presupposed there can never be an application of the moral law. For a consideration of this crucial argument see Chapter VI.

Indeed, moral good is also of "relative" worth in this narrow sense. That is, apart from an individual's being a free, rational being as well as a sensible being, there could be no such thing as moral goodness. When the natural good is regarded simply as happiness, that is, as the fulfillment of a human being's sensible nature, and when that sensible nature is seen to be an essential part of human nature and a necessary component of moral experience, it is clear that the natural good is no more relative than the moral good. The value of both depends upon their relation to the nature of a human being; both are grounded there. For this reason we have insisted that Kant's theory ascribes intrinsic worth both to the natural good and the moral good.

If we consider particular natural goods, however, instead of the natural good as the total fulfillment of a human being's sensible nature,[55] we see that natural goods as the objects of inclination and desire are indeed relative in ways in which the particular moral goods, i.e. moral acts, are not.

The moral good is the good will itself posed as its own object. Particular moral goods are simply the acts of will. An act of willing is the exercise of volition. It is determined solely by free willing and is a deliberate expression of the will alone. The will, consequently is inseparable from its acts. That is, the moral quality of the will is revealed in its acts. As expressions of the will alone, the acts of the will cannot be good or bad, except as the will itself is good or bad. The moral act is not some sensible, concrete act apart from the intention. It is true that in most cases there is a sensible act which is the manifestation of the pure act of willing. But this act can be regarded as a sensible manifestation of willing only in a rough and ready manner since it is the consequence of natural factors in addition to the act of willing. Strictly speaking, only the act of willing itself is the moral good.[56] Therefore, no separation can be made between the moral act and the moral will, or between particular moral goods and the moral good. The moral good is the expression of the rational aspect of humanity and is involved in every act of volition. Hence it is illogical to argue that the rational part of a human being's nature is of intrinsic moral worth but that particular acts of will are only good as a means to this rational nature, for each and every act of volition is an expression of humankind's rational nature.

---

55 This distinction between the natural good as happiness and particular natural goods as contingent objects of inclination is an important one. If it is accepted most of the apparent contradictions in the text are resolved.

56 KpV, 151: CprR, 249. Strictly speaking there is morality of intention and willing (moral action) and legality of phenomenal actions, though for Kant there is as a rule some connection between the willing of an intention and phenomenal action.

A very different situation prevails with regard to the relation of particular natural goods to the natural good. In moments of realization, objects of inclination and desire make up the individual's happiness. The happiness of a lifetime is a complex of millions of such moments of fulfillment in which specific objects of desire were enjoyed. But no particular object which contributes to the attainment of happiness is specifically essential to its attainment and, consequently, no particular object is inseparably grounded in humankind's sensible nature. A particular object is valuable only so long as it continues to be desired, that is, only so long as it is considered essential to the attainment of happiness. Happiness, by virtue of its generality, is always desired and never ceases to have value. But any particular object can cease to be desired, and, hence, its value is contingent and relative to the fact of being desired. Particular objects of desire have value only when they are necessary components of happiness as the enjoyment of fulfilled desires. Particular objects are, therefore, good merely as means to happiness.

4 Particular Natural Goods as Extrinsic, Relational Goods

Kant correctly insists that the worth of particular objects of desire is merely relative to the fact of their being desired.[57] And their being desired in turn depends upon their being regarded as means to the attainment of sensible well-being or happiness which, as the natural good, has intrinsic worth. Particular natural goods are relative, extrinsic, and conditioned goods. Their value cannot be determined apart from the context in which they are found. In order to determine the valuational properties of these goods, an examination must therefore be made of the contexts in which their value may be qualified.

Among the many contexts in which these natural goods may be found, at least three fundamentally qualify or alter particular natural goods. First, particular natural goods are subject to qualification in the personal context – that is, in the context of individual faculties of desire. In this context, particular natural goods fluctuate constantly accordingly as a person's desires increase and wane, as new objects are found and old ones discarded. On the scale of their attractiveness to the particular individual, on the scale, that is, of felt desire, particular natural goods have values that can be strictly compared. Here

57 GMS, 427: GMM, 95.

> ... two opposite courses of action may both be conditionally good [*bedingterweise gut*], though one is better than the other (which would then be called comparatively bad [*komparativ-böse*]). They do not differ *in kind, merely in degree.*[58]

Such is the valuational character of particular natural goods in all personal contexts, contexts in which individual considerations are paramount and where a question of duty does not arise in the determination of the object of the will. As Kant states it,

> ... and this is the case with all acts not motivated by the absolute law of reason (by duty), but by an end arbitrarily proposed by ourselves. For that end is part of the sum of all ends, whose attainment we call happiness; and one act can do more for my happiness, the other less, so that each can be better or worse than the other.
>
> But *preferring* one state of determining the will to another is simply a free act (*res merae facultatis,* as the lawyers say). It is an act in which no consideration is given to the question whether the determination of the will is good or evil in itself, and in which alternatives are therefore equivalent [*gleichgeltend*].[59]

Here personal preferences or privileges alone determine how one estimates the worth of particular natural goods since there is no moral issue involved. From the standpoint of the moral law natural goods are of equal value as long as they do not conflict with duty. The person may choose now one, now another; the law is indifferent.[60]

The society in which the individual lives provides a second context in which natural goods are subject to qualification. Societies tend to exhibit group preferences and value certain objects over others. There is a societal or cultural relativity of natural goods. But the valuational character of particular natural goods is not essentially different in this context from what it was in the personal context. Here too there can be a comparison of the value of natural goods; here,

---

58 TP, 282: TaP, 49. I have inserted Kant's terms parenthetically in the translation. I also translated *komparativ-böse* as "comparatively bad" rather than "evil." I have noted that Kant is not consistent in his usage. Cf. KpV, 25–26: CprR, 136–37.

59 TP, 282: TaP, 49–50. I have inserted Kant's term, *gleichgeltend*, into the translation.

60 Even in striving to help others attain their happiness, which is an end that is also a duty for us, "It is for them to decide what they count as belonging to their happiness" (MS, 388: MOM, 519). Note that: "It is an act of violence to force another to be happy in one's own way, though that is a pretext used, for example, by the upper classes in their dealings with their dependents" (VüE, 60: LoE, 51). Kant can take this position because the law is indifferent regarding many of our personal preferences.

as in the first context, valuation is based upon inclination with or without the support of understanding and prudence. If no moral issue is involved, the moral law is as indifferent to cultural preferences as it is to personal preferences.[61]

Natural goods can be viewed from a genuinely different perspective if we assume a constancy of desires in individuals and societies and consider the value of natural goods in the context of their relation to other natural goods. This we shall call the natural context. The value of natural goods is relative not merely to the preference of particular persons or particular cultures but also to the presence or absence of other natural goods. Consider the value of a baby stroller to a childless couple who desire children as compared with its value to new parents. The first couple may have an equally strong natural inclination as the second couple to have children and to own a stroller. Even assuming that the desires in the two cases are equal and constant, the value of the stroller will fluctuate with the presence or absence of the baby. Or consider the comparative value of a loaded rifle with that of an empty one in the presence or absence of a grizzly bear, or in a shooting gallery. As natural contexts vary, the value of the natural goods to individuals and to societies is subject to drastic fluctuation. The degree of fluctuation depends in part on the interest which a person (or a society) takes in the objects in the various contexts. This is why the natural goods will have comparative values. As long as there is no shift from a morally indifferent situation to one that is charged with moral implications, the law will be indifferent to assessment of natural value.

The natural context is a distinct one in which natural goods qualify and condition the value of each other even where desires are constant. The natural context in which natural goods are found may be as significant in conditioning values as the personal (or social) context. The personal appraisal of the natural good is made partly by reference to the natural context. The relativity of the natural context is reflected implicitly in the relativity of the personal context. But the converse is not true. We have noted examples in which personal desires are necessarily altered by the alteration of the natural context. But it is easy to cite cases in which the personal desires fluctuate without there being any change in the natural context.

For example, the owner of an automobile may prefer to get out of his or her car and walk for a while, not because the car or the natural context has been altered, but simply because he or she wants the exercise. The value of the automobile depreciates in this personal context because of conditions which are

61 For a discussion of the implications of this point in the application of the categorical imperative, see Chapter VII on moral schematism.

extraneous to the natural context. Some of the fluctuations in desire, in short, do not stem from alterations in the objects or the objective natural context but from alterations in the subject. The relativity of the natural context need not reflect the relativity of the personal context in a manner analogous to the way in which the relativity of the former is reflected in the relativity of the latter. The natural and personal contexts are therefore necessarily distinct.

In making this distinction, however, we must take care not to exaggerate its significance. Any overall personal assessment of particular natural goods must be made from the standpoint of the personal context which is included in the natural context. The natural context and the objects within it are seen and evaluated in terms of the individual's personal, sensible reaction.

Thus far we have been careful to discuss the value of natural goods in situations of moral indifference. We must now consider the moral context, in which the value of particular natural goods can be drastically qualified. Particular natural goods such as "moderation in affections and passions, self-control, and sober reflexion are not only good in many respects: they may even seem to constitute part of the *inner* worth of a person."[62] Yet, Kant insists,

> ... they are far from being properly described as good without qualification (however unconditionally they have been commended by the ancients). For without the principles of a good will they may become exceedingly bad; and the very coolness of a scoundrel makes him, not merely more dangerous, but also immediately more abominable in our eyes than we should have taken him to be without it.[63]

Particular natural goods have "no inner unconditioned worth, but rather presuppose a good will which *sets a limit to the esteem* in which they are rightly held."[64] Here Kant again asserts the capacity of the moral law to qualify the value of natural goods. He does not argue that the good will exhaustively determines the value of natural goods, but he does insist that the good will conditions and alters their value. It *sets a limit* to the value which we should place upon natural goods. If we find that particular natural goods are means to natural ills, we recognize at once that the worth of the natural goods has been qualified. If, for example, a scoundrel uses his or her intelligence to injure other people without detection, the natural goodness of that intelligence is qualified and perhaps completely offset when viewed in the context of the natural ill to which it is a means.

62 GMS, 394: GMM, 61.
63 Ibid., 394: ibid., 61–62.
64 Ibid., 393–94: ibid., 61. My italics.

This might seem to involve no determination of value by the moral law but simply a determination of natural values by means of personal comparison of objects in the total context of natural goods and an appraisal of them on the basis of desire. Such, however, is not the case; one cannot assume that persons will try to assess the value of the natural good from the total context, e.g. from the standpoint of the victim as well as from the standpoint of the scoundrel. Persons, as sensible creatures of desire, are under no constraint to do so. Even a society is privileged by desire to ignore the valuational perspective of its unfortunate members or of its neighboring societies. It is only the moral will under the imperative of the law which obligates individuals and societies to assess the natural good from all of these standpoints. Only will, under the direction of the law, demands that the esteem in which a particular natural good is held be qualified by the assessment of its consequences for other natural objects including other people.

This demand, in turn, reveals one of the essential ways in which the law determines the value of the natural good *as naturally good*. Reason does *not* establish a moral standard for judging between natural goods in this context. It merely requires us to consider the total natural context. Within this broader context, desire is the standard for evaluation. But only the moral law can demand that the objective appraisal of natural value, as natural value, be made not from a limited perspective of an interested party but rather in the light of the total context. Once this demand is made, the law keeps silent in the determination of the natural value of a particular object. Its value then can and must be assessed by reference to the influences and effects of the object in question on other natural objects. If in the totality of its influence it brings fulfillment and well-being to sensible-rational beings, then it *is* naturally good. If in the total context, however, it destroys the well-being of sensible-rational beings, then it is not naturally good. More precisely, we can say that it is both naturally good and naturally bad but that its natural badness outweighs its natural goodness.[65]

The natural goods are qualified in the moral context in additional ways. If we return our attention to the passages cited above,[66] we note that the moral good qualifies the natural good in still another way. Kant says that a scoundrel's coolness (which in other contexts is a naturally good quality) is not merely more dangerous (that is, naturally worse when viewed in the larger moral context, which includes the consequences of the cool scoundrel's acts); the naturally good quality of coolness makes the scoundrel more reprehensible than he or

65 TP, 282: TaP, 49.
66 See p. 137 of this chapter supra; also, Chapter II.

she would have been had he or she committed bad actions under emotional stress. An apparent ambiguity is avoided if we bear in mind that Kant is not here speaking of a qualification of the natural good at all. He is speaking, rather, of the moral character of the scoundrel, of the moral quality of the scoundrel's will. Kant is here concerned with a qualification of moral goodness by its being in a context which includes the natural good of cool-headedness. We noted earlier that the will is to be judged in terms of its exercise of its freedom, and that the responsibility of the will increases as the natural hindrances to its performance of duty decrease.[67] Cool-headedness, that is, the power to control one's passions and spontaneous inclinations, does in fact lessen the natural hindrances to the performance of duty. Kant is quite consistent, therefore, when he says that a vicious act performed with a cool head is morally more reprehensible than one done in passion. Such an act is a more serious transgression of the law. Unless we deny the unconditionality of freedom and the will, however, we cannot hold that this natural good of cool-headedness is a means to greater moral evil. In fact, Kant insists on the opposite. If cool-headedness were able in any way to prompt the will to action, it should prompt it to good action. Hence the evil of the cool-headed scoundrel is greater because despite possession of a natural good which should have made it easier for him or her to act in accord with the moral law, he or she acted contrary to it. The evil of the scoundrel, from this point of view, is moral evil, as the expression of his or her own misuse of freedom, and, as such, the scoundrel's moral evil is unqualifiedly and unconditionally evil. It is greater in this situation not because cool-headedness is extrinsically morally bad but because greater freedom is involved and the degree of imputation must be estimated by the degree of freedom.[68] The contributory influence of cool-headedness to moral evil, even if granted, is cancelled out by the fact that the moral worth of the scoundrel is assessed on a sliding scale which compensates for any such influence.

A particular natural good can, in addition, be qualified in a moral context by the norm of moral value as well as by the norm of natural value. We noted in the preceding paragraph that the moral good as the expression of freedom cannot be conditioned by the natural good. This is impossible because inclinations are subject to being affected by the will and by reason. If this were not the case, reason could not be practical.[69] The objects which the will as the faculty

67 See p. 123 of this chapter supra.

68 MS, 228, cf. 226–7: MOM, 382, cf. 380–1; VüE, 71, 212: LoE, 62, 197.

69 KpV, 48–50, 67–68, 75–76, 87–88, and especially 119: CprR, 158–59, 176, 183–84, 194–195, and especially 223. See Chapter VIII, "The Role of Judgment in Determining the Embodiment of the Highest Good," for a fuller consideration of this issue.

of desire poses for itself as natural goods can be altered by the dictates of reason. Thus a morally good person may cease to desire an object, such as the property of another, because of the strength of his or her reverence for the law. Moral goodness does not demand that the desire cease, only that it not be gratified. But in a person of well-developed moral character, the desire itself will cease because of its moral unworthiness. In this way, also, the moral good can determine the natural value of an object.

An implication of this fact adds further evidence for the view that the ambiguity referred to earlier is only apparent. Once we recognize that the will has an influence on the inclinations and their gratification, we see that the natural goods are potentially at the mercy of the will. Consider any natural good. Unlike the will, a natural good is not protected by the moat of freedom which prevents its being qualified and compromised except by its own agency. No particular natural good is capable of volition. But its value is dependent on both desire and volition of the free moral being. As we saw in the discussion of the personal context, a natural good is subject to the caprice of the faculty of desire – that is, to *Willkür* as natural volition. But now we see that in the moral context it is also affected by moral volition. Moral volition can affect the natural good *indirectly* by altering the desire – by thrusting the object into a new personal context of desire or aversion. Moral volition can also alter the natural goodness of an object by thrusting it into a new natural context. By so doing, the moral volition can transform the natural goodness of an object into an object of natural badness.[70]

For example, Iago could have been guilty of great moral evil without most of his natural talents, because the degree of moral evil is judged according to the degree of capacity, and hence greater capacity need not imply either greater moral virtue or moral vice. But Iago could not have produced such phenomenal natural evil, such destruction of natural goods, such destruction of personal well-being, had it not been for his natural virtues. Without the particular natural goods of intelligence, cool-headedness, wit, rhetoric, and knowledge of human beings, Iago would have been a puppet in the hands of the powerful Othello. Yet all these natural goods which Iago possessed became naturally bad because Iago's bad will used them in contexts in which they were means to great natural loss and moral evil. Thus, for all their goodness as means to the well-being of Iago and other persons, they became naturally bad as the necessary means to the destruction of the happiness and well-being of Othello and Desdemona. This example shows clearly the extent to which the natural value of particular

70 It can also enhance the natural value of an object.

natural goods is qualified and determined by the moral quality of the will. In the moral context particular natural goods are subject not only to objective appraisal in the light of the totality of their influence, but are also subject to qualification by the agency of the will. The will may qualify and condition them either by altering the personal (or social) context in which they exist or by altering the natural context and their relation to other natural goods. The will may also qualify the natural goodness of particular natural goods in both ways at once.

5 The Qualification of the Natural Good by the Moral Good

We have thus far limited our discussion of the relativity of natural goodness to that evidenced in particular natural goods, which have no intrinsic or inner goodness, but are good merely as means to happiness. The relativity of the natural good, as opposed to particular natural goods, must now be considered. Although Kant claims that the natural good, in the general sense of sensible well-being, has intrinsic worth, he also holds that its value is not immune from qualification. We must consider the way in which the natural good in this general sense can be qualified. As the ground of the natural value of all particular natural goods, the natural good as such cannot be qualified by them. If it is to be qualified at all, it must be by its relation to the moral good. Consequently, there is only one context, the moral context, in which to discuss the relativity of the natural good.

In trying to determine the relation of the natural good to the moral good, we face a formidable difficulty at the outset. As we noted earlier, particular natural goods are comparable. But they are comparable only among themselves and in relation to the natural good, being qualified by their relation to other natural goods and by their relation to desire. The natural good as happiness, however, is not subject to this sort of comparison and evaluation. Happiness, which is the fulfillment of the needs and wants of finite sensible beings, is the only intrinsic natural good. As we have already noted, it cannot be compared to or conditioned by any particular natural good, and there is no other natural good with which it can be compared. If, then, it is to be compared or qualified in any way it must be by reference to the moral good, that is, by reference to virtue. But Kant has suggested that virtue differs in kind from happiness, because it has a dignity and an incomparability about it.

On the other hand, although particular natural goods have a price, there is nothing that can be substituted for the natural good itself. Both the moral good, as virtue, and the natural good, as happiness, seem to be ultimate and *sui generis*, and therefore incommensurate. Virtue is the only moral good and happiness is the only intrinsic natural good, and we have not yet discerned what it is they have in common. If we are to follow Kant's point of view, however, we must insist that virtue and happiness are related and open to comparison.

Kant finds their common ground not in an additional good in which both virtue and happiness participate, but in the nature of humankind. This common ground is found in the relation of a person's sensible nature (the ground of the natural good) to his or her rational nature (the ground of the moral good). Theoretically, the natural good and the moral good are incomparable; practically, they are not. Despite the duality of human nature, each human being as a person is a living unity of both sensible and rational natures. In this unity happiness as the good of a person's sensible nature is related to virtue as the good of his or her rational nature.

Looking then to the relation of sensibility to rationality in humankind, we find that while the interests of sensibility and happiness are often (though not necessarily)[71] in conflict with the interests of rationality and virtue, the interests of the former pair are always subject to conditioning by the interests of the latter pair. A person's desire for happiness and that person's pursuit of sensible interests whereby that happiness is attained are qualified by his or her concern to be virtuous or worthy of happiness. As Kant states it,

> virtue (as the worthiness to be happy) is the supreme condition of whatever appears to us to be desirable and thus of all our pursuit of happiness .... Virtue is always the supreme good, being the condition having no condition superior to it, while happiness, though something always pleasant to him who possesses it, is not of itself absolutely good in every respect but always presupposes conduct in accordance with the moral law as its condition.[72]

Kant not only affirms the supremacy of rational, moral concern over the natural desire for happiness, but he also offers a measure by which to gauge this relationship. Since the law of morality "has no other motive than *worthiness of being happy*,"[73] and since morality is both "the worth of a person and his worthiness to be happy,"[74] the command of the law can be expressed as the obligation to "*Do that through which thou becomest worthy to be happy.*"[75]

---

71 KpV, 93: CprR, 199.
72 Ibid., 110: ibid., 215.
73 KrV, B834: CpR, 636.
74 KpV, 110: CprR, 215.
75 KrV, B836–7: CpR, 638.

If we try to compare the natural good to the moral good directly, we face the barrier of their heterogeneity. But we can compare them if we seek their relation to one another indirectly through their interconnection in the life of a person. The natural good is always naturally good. It is pleasant to the person who possesses it[76] because it represents a fulfillment of the sensible nature which is an essential part of human nature. But the delight a person takes in personal happiness and its pursuit is qualified by the assessment a person makes of his or her own worthiness. In assessing one's worth, one must consider only the exercise of one's freedom.

> Being worthy of happiness is a personal quality based on the subject's own will. Due to this quality, a generally legislative reason (one making laws for nature as well as for free will) would harmonize with all of a person's ends. Hence it is totally different from skill in the achievement of some kind of happiness. For a man is not worthy even of this skill, nor of the talent for it lent to him by nature, if his will does not conform to, and cannot be contained in, the only will fit for a universal legislation of reason (i.e. if it is a will that conflicts with morality).[77]

How much unqualified delight or pleasure could one derive from one's gifts of mind and body while knowing that one has misused his or her freedom and violated the law of morality? If guilty, the person must judge himself or herself to be worthless, no matter how happy that person may be. For what had he or she to do with the bounty of nature, with the possession of a fine intellect or a well-formed body, with health or a favorable turn of the market? The fine intellect and the excellent body, the health and wealth, in short, the happiness, are things which happened to him or her and over which he or she had little control. "Happiness," Kant says, "contains whatever (and no more than) nature can obtain for us."[78] But virtue, he adds, "contains what nobody but a person himself can give to or take from himself."[79] Only in the area of moral action can a person express himself or herself with full freedom, and hence only in this area are a person's actions subject to imputation. In this area one is responsible, totally responsible, for what one does. Consequently, by transgression of the moral law a person shows that he or she is worthless – "reprehensible and

76 KpV, 110–1: CprR, 215.
77 TP, 278n: TaP, 45n; cf. RGV, 44: Rel, 40.
78 TP, 283n: TaP, 50n. It must be noted that health, wealth and other elements contributing to happiness may be gained by sustained efforts freely undertaken in accord with the moral law and not the result of luck or gifts of nature.
79 Idem: idem.

punishable in his own eyes."[80] How then can all the honors, all the wealth, and all the skill in the world make something good out of that self? Lady MacBeth shared the title to a kingdom and, with resolution and cunning, might have secured it and reaped all the benefits in ceremony and happiness. But could all the perfumes of Arabia sweeten her hands? Could all these natural goods transform her worthlessness into worthiness? To her credit, she was rightly overcome with guilt with the thought of her bloody hands.

When we raise the question of personal worth, we are asking about the quality of the person himself or herself. The estimation of personal worth necessarily concerns only the exercise of the will. For this alone is the ground of "personality, i.e., the freedom and independence from the mechanism of nature regarded as the capacity of a being which is subject to special laws (pure practical laws given by its own reason)."[81] A judgment of worth is a judgment of reason. We are not asking: Is this person happy, or does this person have certain attributes and goods as a result of a fortuitous nature? Rather, we are asking: Whatever be of value in this world, what *right* does this person have to it? What is his or her worthiness to possess whatever is of value? We know that goods are often distributed in this world without any rational justification: the rain falls on the just and the unjust. We are not concerned therefore with whether or not a person has *possession* of these goods. We are asking what would constitute a rational distribution of goods, that is, what constitutes one's *worthiness* or one's *right* to possess these goods.

A person's justification for possessing goods must be based on what that particular person is or does. To say that one is *justified* in possession of wealth simply because one has it (without regard to how it was acquired) is to mistake completely what is involved in justifying something. This would make "justification" and "possession" synonymous. Justification in the possession of goods cannot be based on the fact of possession; rather, it must be grounded on the internal quality of the person, upon one's exercise of freedom. Moreover, since excellence in the exercise of one's freedom is "virtue," it is virtue which constitutes the worthiness of a person to the possession of whatever goods are of value to that person. And because all the goods other than virtue itself are summed in happiness, as the fulfillment of a human being's sensible nature, we can conclude with Kant that virtue is the worthiness to be happy.

A person may, of course, be happy despite a lack of virtue. Kant, unlike the Stoics and Plato, is a sufficiently keen observer of human experience to know

---

80 Ibid., 288: ibid., 55; cf. KpV, 37: CprR, 149.
81 KpV, 87: CprR, 193; cf. TP, 283: TaP, 50.

this. But he also recognizes that without virtue one can never consider oneself to be worthy of happiness. It is a demand of reason that one should be happy in proportion to one's virtue, that is, in proportion to one's worthiness to be happy.[82] Thus if a person with a sensible nature no less than a rational nature is worthy of happiness, he or she should be happy in that proportion, "for to be in need of happiness and also worthy of it and yet not to partake of it could not be in accordance with the complete volition of an omnipotent rational being."[83] In like manner, by transgressing the moral law a person forfeits his or her worthiness to be happy and acquires instead a worthiness to have happiness withdrawn from him or her. Thus Kant insists that:

> Punishment is physical harm which, even if not bound as a natural consequence to the morally bad, ought to be bound to it as a consequence according to principles of moral legislation .... [E]very crime, without regard to the physical consequences to him who commits it, is punishable, i.e., involves a forfeiture of happiness at least in part.[84]

Even a criminal, if aware of the rational dimension of his or her nature, accepts unhappiness as the natural badness of punishment and also as a means to later improvement which will probably benefit society more than himself or herself. The criminal accepts punishment with the recognition that it was justified "and that his reward perfectly fitted his behavior."[85]

Here we see how the value of the natural good is deflated in the presence of the moral good. The criminal is fully aware of the pain of his or her punishment. Obviously as a natural being the criminal neither desires it nor finds it agreeable. From the standpoint of natural good he or she does not admit that punishment is good. From the narrow standpoint of the natural good, punishment must appear to be nothing more than the following of one act which was

---

82 KpV, 110: CprR, 215.
83 Idem: idem.
84 Ibid., 37: ibid., 149. It is important to note in this connection that Kant's view of punishment rests upon the assumption of the inner worth of happiness and the fact of freedom which together constitute the heterogeneity of the good. For unless the heterogeneity of the good is assumed one faces the absurd conclusion (faced by Plato, the Epicureans and the Stoics) "that the crime consists just in the fact that one has brought punishment upon himself and thus has injured his own happiness (which, according to the principle of self-love, must be the correct concept of all crime). In this way, the punishment would be the reason for calling anything a crime, and justice would consist in withholding all punishment and even hindering natural punishment, for there would be no longer any evil in an action" (ibid., 37–8: ibid., 149).
85 Ibid., 37: Ibid., 149.

destructive of some natural good by still another destructive act. From this standpoint, punishment is merely that second wrong that never makes a right, but which may perhaps prevent a third wrong. Because the natural good is incapable of standing in judgment on itself, from its isolated standpoint there can therefore be no depreciation of its value. But in the moral context of the total person, a criminal can recognize the legitimacy of the depreciation of the value of the natural good. The person's rational nature rejects or deflates the claims of his or her sensible nature. While the value of the natural good may be constant with respect to the person's sensible nature, it is relative with respect to the person as a whole. By a suppression of the claims of the sensible nature, the person may reduce the importance and value of his or her personal desires and their fulfillment. Faced with personal worthlessness, a moral individual cannot justify the continuation of his or her happiness; to the contrary, can only justify its discontinuance.[86] The desires of one's sensible nature may urge a person to seek the natural good, but the maxims of happiness merely advise, while the maxims of the moral law command.[87] The law commands that one not passively accept the delights of happiness as gifts of nature, but rather that one justify possession of these delights. It further demands that if by transgression of the law one has forfeited all worthiness of the natural good, he or she then forfeits the actual delights that accompany its possession. In this situation "the person as belonging to the world of sense is subject to his own personality so far as he belongs to the intelligible world."[88] Our rational nature sets a limit to the esteem in which we can rightly regard our sensible nature. That is, the moral good, the will, sets a limit to the esteem in which all particular goods and even the natural good itself are rightly held.[89]

For a person to be happy without being virtuous is an affront to that person's rational nature. When this situation obtains, the moral good depreciates the value of the natural good in the context of the total person. In this way the moral good again determines at least to some extent even the value of the natural good itself by conditioning the value which the person can place upon his or her own sensible nature. When his sensible nature is in conflict with one's rational nature, one is required by reason to devaluate one's sensible nature, a requirement which he or she may not fulfill but which cannot be abrogated.

The unconditioned, absolute quality of the moral good obtrudes. For while the value of one's happiness is diminished by one's failure to deserve it, one's

---

86 GMS, 393: GMM, 61.

87 KrV, B834: CpR, 636; KpV, 110–1: CprR, 215.

88 KpV, 87, cf. 61: CprR, 193, cf. 170.

89 GMS, 393–4: GMM, 61.

worthiness to be happy is in no way diminished by one's failure to be happy. Kant asks:

> In the greatest misfortunes of his life which he could have avoided if he could have disregarded duty, does not a righteous man hold up his head thanks to the consciousness that he has honored and preserved humanity in his own person and in its dignity, so that he does not have to shame himself in his own eyes or have reason to fear the inner scrutiny of self-examination?[90]

Through fidelity to duty, such an individual proves the worth and value of his or her person even after the natural value of his or her circumstances has been diminished or lost. One's value as a person, far from being diminished by the absence of happiness proportionate to one's virtue, seems actually enhanced because "we convince ourselves, by contemplating it, that human nature is capable of such an elevation above everything that nature can present as an incentive in opposition to it."[91] Such an example reveals to us the power of the incentive of duty, in Juvenal's words, makes us "count it the greatest of all sins to prefer life to honor, and to lose, for the sake of living, all that makes life worth living."[92] A virtuous individual may lose everything pertaining to the natural good save this: he or she cannot lose his or her worthiness to its possession. Life can be lost, but an individual's rational claim upon life to give him or her of its natural bounty can never be lost. This right is grounded in the exercise of a person's freedom, in one's attainment of virtue; it is not diminished in the slightest by the failure of a stepmotherly nature to provide for someone. In fact, through reason an individual stands in judgment on nature and says that if reason rules, an adjustment will be made.[93] Such an individual may lose his or her life, but not its meaning. Were we to sacrifice our rational nature in order to fulfill our sensuous nature, we might gain life and happiness for a span of years, but would divest our life of all meaning, that is, of all that makes life worthwhile for a rational being.

Kant is not saying that a virtuous person is merely a rational being and that happiness is of no value to him or her. For such a person to be in need of happiness and to be worthy of it and yet not to have it is an affront to reason.[94] In saying this, Kant is stressing the primacy of a human being's rational nature over his or her sensible nature. Since freedom and personal fulfillment rest

---

90 Ibid., 88: ibid., 194.
91 Ibid., 158: ibid., 255.
92 Ibid., 159: ibid., 256; Juvenal, *Satire* 8, 83–84.
93 This is the basis of Kant's moral argument for the existence of God and immortality.
94 GMS, 110: GMM, 215; KrV, B840–1: CpR, 639–40.

upon rational nature, Kant feels justified in having made this subordination. Kant still insists, nevertheless, that "pure practical reason does not require that we should renounce the claims of happiness."[95] But Kant adds, "I must first be sure that I am not acting counter to my duty; not until then am I permitted to look for all the happiness compatible with my morally (not physically) good state."[96] The virtuous individual without happiness is far worse off than the virtuous individual who is happy, for both have a right to natural good, but only one enjoys it. Nor is it correct to say that the natural good ceases when it is in conflict with the moral good. Kant's point is merely that in the event of conflict, the value of the natural good is obscured and eclipsed by that of the moral good.

6 Summary

The common misinterpretation that Kant stresses duty and repudiates all concern for happiness is refuted by Kant's insistence that there are two basic goods – the natural good and the moral good – and that both have intrinsic worth. This point of view requires the reinterpretation of a few of Kant's own statements on the nature of the good. The text is not final and Kant himself admits that an author inadvertently can often speak at cross purposes to his own theory.[97] We have offered an interpretation of the good which not only finds support in most of the texts but also comports with his theory as a whole. Any attempt to provide a consistent account of Kant's theory must reject a few isolated passages, since some of Kant's statements, apart from interpretation, are contradictory. Because of this fact, any consistent view of Kant's theory will find occasional opposition in the text. My interpretation finds general support in the text and offers an account which cannot be challenged without denying the central doctrines of Kant's ethics.

Kant insists that the good will is neither the sole nor the complete good. This statement cannot be true, however, unless the natural good has genuine intrinsic worth. If the natural good were good only as a means, it would have to be extrinsically good as a means to the moral good – the only other good. But nothing external to the will as the moral good can be a means to its enactment without qualifying its freedom. If, however, its freedom were qualified, the

---

95 KpV, 93: CprR, 199.

96 TP, 283: TaP, 50.

97 KrV, B370: CpR, 310. Kant adds, "It is by no means unusual ... to find that we understand [an author] better than he has understood himself." (Idem: idem).

moral good itself would not be of unconditioned worth. Therefore the natural good cannot be good as a means to the moral good. But if the natural good cannot be good as a means, and if we deny it has intrinsic value, it can have no value at all. The moral good would then be the sole good. An interpretation which denies that the natural good has intrinsic worth thus leads to this *reductio ad absurdum*.

But suppose one were to suggest, as some of Kant's interpreters have, that Kant spoke at cross purposes to his own theory when he said that the moral good is not the sole and complete good. Suppose one tried to offer a consistent view of his ethics by holding that the moral good is the sole good. This interpretation of Kant's thought, aside from textual difficulties, involves the denial of almost every central doctrine of Kantian ethics! First, the heterogeneity of the good is denied and Kant's position is reduced to stoicism. Secondly, if the good is homogeneous, as it must be on this interpretation, there can be no experience of duty, and, hence, no awareness of the moral law and of freedom. Third, there can be no moral doctrine of punishment since there will be nothing of negative value which can punish vice or anything of positive value which can reward virtue. Fourth, there can be no doctrine of the highest good in which the strife between the natural good and the moral good is recognized and finally overcome. Fifth, apart from the intrinsic worth of the natural good and the doctrine of the highest good, which depends upon it, there can be no application of the moral law to the sensible world.

Any interpretation of Kant's views so thoroughly destructive of his theory as a whole could not be right even if it had extensive textual support. As a matter of fact, however, the interpretation which is rejected here has far less support than the interpretation I have proposed: Kant's views regarding the heterogeneity of the good, the experience of obligation, the nature of duty, punishment, the highest good, etc., are found in the text and in fact constitute the largest part of it.

I have proposed that the basic distinction between the moral good and the natural good is this: the moral good is an intrinsic good whose goodness is absolute and unconditioned, whereas the natural good is an intrinsic good whose goodness is relative and conditioned. The valuational properties of the good, both as moral and as natural, have been determined by reference to the being in relation to which they stand as norms. The moral good derives its property of absoluteness and unconditionedness from freedom, from the autonomy of a human being's rational nature. The intrinsic worth of the natural good is grounded in the inescapable needs and inclinations for happiness arising from humanity's sensible nature. But the natural good is relative to the presence or absence of the moral good, because the value that the person assigns to his or her own sensible nature and its demands is relative to the fulfillment of his or her rational nature. Although the intrinsic worth of the natural good is not qualified relative to a person's sensible nature, it is qualified relative to the person as a unitary whole, who judges himself or herself from the standpoint of the moral good. In this sense the moral good is found to qualify and condition the natural good.

On this interpretation, a distinction is made between the natural good *in general*, as happiness, the fulfillment of a human being's sensible needs and desires, and *particular* natural goods as momentary objects of the faculty of desire. Particular natural goods as objects of desire have no intrinsic worth at all but are good merely as means to the attainment of the natural good in general. Hence they have merely relative, extrinsic worth. This distinction enabled us to resolve most of the textual problems, since we may suppose that Kant had particular natural goods in mind when he said that non-moral goods have no intrinsic worth but are merely of conditional, relative worth. Furthermore, the value of particular natural goods was found to be relative and conditioned in many different ways. Their worth is relative not only to conditioning by the moral good; their value can also be qualified in different ways according as they are considered in personal, social, natural, or moral contexts. In the last context, the moral good qualifies the goodness of particular natural goods in terms of the standard of the natural good, either by altering the desires of persons, by considering the particular goods in their total context, or by thrusting them through the agency of the will into new contexts.

There is no way, however, in which the moral good can qualify the value of particular natural goods in terms of the standard of the moral good. This, strictly speaking, can never occur, although it seems to occur in the qualification of the natural good in general by the moral good. In this case, however, the value of the natural good in general is merely obscured because moral persons – by viewing their own persons from the ultimate standpoint of their free rational nature – devalue their entire sensible nature either because of the opposition of sensibility to duty or because in failing to fulfill the demands of their rational nature, they find themselves unworthy of the rewards of sensible fulfillment.

The heterogeneity of the good is central to Kant's ethics, and this analysis offers a clearer idea of the nature and source of that heterogeneity. In discussing the relation of the moral good to the natural good whereby the latter is qualified by the former as its condition, we have faced again Kant's insistence that the basic concepts of good and evil are determined by the law and cannot be presupposed as material objects of the will from which the law is to be derived. Likewise, we have seen the reinforcement of Kant's insistence that there must be an object of volition, that material must be added to the law. Suggestions as to the source and nature of that material and the means whereby it can be incorporated into the form of the law are gained from recognizing that for Kant the comparative worth of the moral good and the natural good can never be assumed on a merely theoretical basis, but only in the context of the living being who is within himself or herself, as a product of his or her own freedom in relation to natural endowments, a unity of those heterogeneous components of reason and sensibility.

Chapter V: The Highest Good As The Material Object Of Moral Volition

1 The Centrality of the Highest Good in Kant's Ethics

Kant's ethics in its completeness cannot be understood without considering the importance of his theory of the good. But strangely enough, no aspect of Kant's thought has received less attention or been more frequently misunderstood. Several excellent scholars, including Jeffrie Murphy, Lewis Beck, and to some extent, Stephen Engstrom, question the importance or centrality of the highest good in Kant's ethics.[1] But they are hard put to explain the emphasis Kant places on this concept. He not only organized the *Critique of Practical Reason* around the concept of the highest good, but in the *Critique of Pure Reason* he devotes chapter II of the transcendental doctrine of method to a discussion of the highest good as the canon of pure reason. How can one offer an accurate account of Kant's ethics without accounting for the important role that Kant assigns to this concept? Kant may be wrong, but his position needs to be considered in the most plausible and compelling light.

Kant's ethics is reduced to a caricature when it is presented merely as an ethics of duty as the paradigm of deontology. In Chapter II, we began our discussion of Kant's ethics with an examination of his theory of the good because from this standpoint, as from no other, Kant's ethical theory as a whole can be seen and compared with those of his predecessors and successors in the history of ethics.

Kant insisted that a careful delineation of the parts or details of a theory is only the first step in a responsible inquiry. "But still another thing must be attended to," he added, "which is of a more philosophical and architectonic character. It is to grasp correctly the idea of the whole, and then to see all those parts in their reciprocal interrelations, in the light of their derivation from the concept of the whole."[2] One can begin to understand Kant's ethics by an examination of the concept of duty. But one may understand this concept quite well without acquiring an idea of the whole of Kant's ethics. Moreover, one cannot adequately understand Kant's concept of duty without also understanding his concept of the good and all the other essential components of Kant's ethics in their interrelation.

---

1 See Murphy; Beck, *A Commentary*; Engstrom.
2 KpV, 10–11: CprR, 124.

It is, I believe, because the concept of the good pulls together so many strands of Kant's ethics that Kant organized the *Critique of Practical Reason* around it. Nevertheless, it is easy to overlook the centrality of the doctrine of the good in the second *Critique*. Like Schopenhauer, we may be so greatly influenced by the *Groundwork* with its focus directed almost exclusively on the purely formal aspects of ethics that the startling shift of emphasis and organization in the second *Critique* is easily overlooked.[3] Unquestionably, Kant's concept of duty has obscured Kant's extensive discussion of the good and has been accepted as the central doctrine of his ethics. And scholars may have to some extent been preoccupied with the formal schemes of organization, the section titles, and the rubrics of the second *Critique*. But if we look beyond these matters to examine the actual content of the second *Critique*, the centrality of the theory of the good becomes apparent.

In Part I, Book I, Chapter I of the second *Critique* Kant offers his proof that the experience of obligation cannot be accounted for nor the distinction between virtue and happiness maintained unless the concept of the good is derived from the moral law rather than the reverse.[4] The theorems of pure practical reason present Kant's conclusions on this basic issue.

In Part I, Book I, Chapter II, "The Concept of an Object of Pure Practical Reason," Kant develops the implications of his first chapter. Realizing that every act of will must have an object and denying that ethics can be grounded on any object defined prior to the law as an object of the will, Kant is compelled to determine an object for the will by means of the law itself. That is why he is concerned in this chapter with the nature of the good as the object of pure practical reason. Knowing also that the object of pure practical reason fails to meet the need of the will for a material object in the act of volition so long as it lacks sensible interpretation, Kant offers an interpretation of it in terms of the sensible world. In the section of Chapter II entitled "Of the Typic of Pure Practical Judgment," Kant attempts to show that the concepts of good and evil can determine definite sensible objects for the will – objects involving happiness in proportion to virtue. They can do this, however, only after they them-

---

3 Schopenhauer, for example, did not notice the fundamental shift of interest and focus in the second *Critique*. Between the *Groundwork* and the second *Critique* he found only an increase in garrulity and diffusion of thought. Thus he writes: "The *Critique of Practical Reason* contains essentially the same material as is contained in the above mentioned Foundations, only the latter gives it in a conciser and stricter form, whereas the former handles the matter with great prolixity of argument, interrupted by digressions and supported by a few moral declamations in order to enhance the impression." Schopenhauer, 51.

4 KpV, 19–57: CprR, 130–66.

selves have been determined by reason as the *a priori* objects of the will. Kant hopes in this way to have succeeded in providing a genuine material object (the good) for the act of volition without having defined it prior to the concept of law.

Chapter III of Part I, Book I concerns the incentives of the will and attempts to prove that the good, as the object of the will, does not determine the will to action by virtue of its material but by virtue of its form. The will, it is argued, is still self-determined, and it is obligated to seek any particular object in question only by reference to the law which legislates in terms of specific content provided by sensibility. Any pleasure that the will feels in regard to an object to which it is obligated is found, therefore, to follow as an effect of the law and not to precede the law as the cause of its influence. Chapter III thus exhibits the consistency and mutual support of the views presented in Chapters I and II.

In Book II of Part I, entitled "The Dialectic of Pure Practical Reason," Kant faces the problem of unifying the elements of virtue and happiness in the concept of the highest good. Having ruled out the good as the material object of the will defined prior to the law, Kant, nonetheless, must restore this object of volition subsequent to the establishment of the law. Since the will must have an object,[5] failure to re-establish the good in this fashion would leave the will without direction in the performance of its duty. The law by itself defines the moral good as virtue; sensibility, for its part, provides happiness as the natural good.[6] But the law, in need of the material of sensibility, cannot avail itself of the material of the natural good apart from the re-establishment of the unity of the good. In this unity the sensible material of happiness must be structured by the formality of the law without the sacrifice of the law's purity.

In order to offer a unitary, though material, object of pure practical reason, Kant introduces the concept of the highest good. In so doing, Kant is confronted by an apparent antinomy that threatens the possibility of the highest good. Since happiness and virtue are heterogeneous concepts they cannot be united analytically in the concept of the highest good. Hence, they must be united synthetically. Since the highest good is the practical object of the will – an object that the will must produce through its own actions – the unity of happiness and virtue in the highest good must be causally derived. Either happiness must be the cause of virtue or virtue the cause of happiness. Either alternative, however, seems impossible. The former is not possible because happiness

5 KpV, 34: CprR, 145.

6 See Chapter IV, 116ff., supra, for a discussion of Kant's distinction between moral and natural good.

cannot cause virtue, the latter because the effects of willing depend not only on the intention of the will but also on the support of the natural world. Kant resolves this apparent antinomy by showing that the latter alternative is not impossible but only improbable. Nevertheless, it is sometimes capable of partial, contingent fulfillment apart from supplementary mediation by God. The postulates of pure practical reason are offered to ensure the possibility of virtue promoting happiness and, thereby, the possibility of the concept of the highest good.[7]

In Part II of the second *Critique*, the methodology of pure practical reason is discussed. In this context the incentives of pure practical reason are once again examined. This time, however, they are discussed from the standpoint of their effective employment in moral edification, that is, in the production of good actions, rather than (as in Chapter III of Part I, Book I) from the standpoint of the theoretical difficulties involved in their very existence.

These discussions demonstrate the central importance of the good in the *Critique of Practical Reason*. The discussion of the good in its various aspects as the object of pure practical reason provides the unifying theme of the work as a whole. Comparatively speaking, concepts of duty and the categorical imperative assume minor roles in the discussion although they are fundamental components of the total theory of the good.

By presenting an extensive discussion of the good in the second *Critique*, Kant relates himself unequivocally to the classical tradition in ethics.[8] His theory of the good shows clearly both his conformity to, and his departure from, traditional points of view. The Copernican revolution in ethics reversed the traditional procedure by establishing first the moral law and then deriving the good from it. This led Kant to assert the heterogeneity of the good.[9]

---

7 Murphy questions how I can suppose that an individual can be virtuous even if he or she is not happy. (Murphy, 106). He believes I have introduced and used the concept in "just the way Kant has chosen." But he argues that "Kant's introduction of this notion was unnecessary and ill-advised." In one minor point, Murphy overlooks a subtle but important point in the relation of virtue to happiness. They are not equal because virtue establishes the worthiness to be happy and consequently Murphy errs in supposing that Kant has a problem in showing that one is obligated to be virtuous if happiness is denied. If one is virtuous, one should be happy in proportion to his or her virtue. But Kant recognizes that this relationship is not confirmed automatically in experience. If one is not happy, one should not cease to be virtuous, because the obligation to be virtuous is categorical and within one's power, while to be happy in proportion to one's virtue is not.

8 I am not alone in this observation. See Düsing; see also Kramling.

9 See Chapter II supra.

This duality of the good confronted Kant with the problem of providing for the unity of these components. In addition, there was the problem of determining the good as the material object of the will by reference to the demand of the moral law. He found his solution in the concept of the highest good as the synthesis of the dual aspects of the good. Kant thereby reaffirmed the importance of this traditional concept to ethical thought by making, albeit in a new and different manner, the concept of the highest good the object of the will.

But the mere existence of the concept of the highest good as the object of the will is of little value until it can be given sufficient content to guide moral volition. In the next three sections I shall systematically trace Kant's development of this concept toward this end.

2 Perfection (the Moral Good) as a Component of the Highest Good

In full accord with the ethical tradition, Kant repeatedly insisted that every volition must have an object.[10] He argued, further, that if the categorical imperative is to have meaning the will must be bound with necessity to an object that is defined by practical reason, that is, by reference to the moral law. If some object of sensibility (however refined) were accepted by the will as the good and made into the object of volition, the will would not stand under a categorical obligation. Its relation to any particular object would be conditioned in two ways: first, by the success or failure of the moral agent to achieve the object held to be good, and second, by the relation of the will to the object, which would be through desire and, hence, either contingent upon the continuation of the feeling binding the object to the will or determined by natural causation. Since in categorical obligation, however, there must be an unconditional relation of the free will to the object, the object to which the will is obligated must be of unconditioned worth. But the only unconditioned object that can be related necessarily to the will without conditioning the will and destroying its freedom is the good will itself.[11] The good will, therefore, is itself the object of the will, and in its act of volition it wills

10 KpV, 34: CprR, 145.

11 In being related with necessity to its object, the will is conditioned only by its own action in accordance with the moral law, that is, only by itself. The act of willing which accords with the law (and is thus fully autonomous), by virtue of its universality, transcends all conditions and can be determined by none.

nothing more or less than its own perfection (free willing) as an end which is also a duty.[12]

Kant believes that in this way material can be added to the law. The law not only insists that for every act of volition there must be an object, thereby stating a formal demand for a material component in ethics; the law now also projects a material object for itself in the form of the embodiment of the law in a good will. The will, at the behest of the moral law, projects for itself the good as an end which is also a duty. And this end toward which the will must strive is its own moral perfection. The will, that is, must seek to attain virtue.[13]

This conception of the material object of pure practical reason is, however, not yet an object for volition with actual material content. As noted above, the will must seek virtue as its own perfection. But what does this mean in terms of the specific intention of the will? The intention of the will can thus far be understood only in formal terms, as when one speaks of a person's having a good moral disposition, for here the object of volition is merely the intention to follow the law. This moral disposition is of pre-eminent importance in the assessment of a person's character. Nevertheless, in an act of volition one does not simply will a good disposition. Rather one expresses a good disposition by willing something more concrete. If, in consequence, the moral law is to be of any use to a person in supplying the good as the material object of volition, it must be more instructive than it has thus far been shown to be.

Kant himself is well aware of the need to say more. He is quite ruthless in his denunciation of the rationalistic ethics of Wolff and Baumgarten.[14] He thinks their first ethical principle, *"Fac Bonum et Omitte Malum,"* to be classic in its ineptitude. In regard to this principle Kant says,

> The meaning of the proposition is simply, "it is good that you should do what is good," which is tautological. It tells us nothing about what is good, but merely that we ought to do what we ought to do.[15]

---

12 MS, 385ff.: MOM, 516ff.

13 In *A Commentary*, Beck recognizes the importance of this aspect of the highest good, namely, the supreme good.

14 When Kant lectured on ethics, he used as his texts two works by A. G. Baumgarten, *Initia philosophiae practicae primae* and *Ethica philosophica*. The German universities were required by state law to use textbooks in all courses, which helps to explain why Kant would use works by Baumgarten while disagreeing with him so completely (Macmurray, xi; see also Paulsen, 59–60).

15 VüE, 31: LoE, 25.

Then raising his sights to include the field of ethics in general, he adds, "There is no branch of knowledge which so abounds in tautological propositions as ethics, offering as the answer what was in fact the question."[16] Kant felt the folly of this practice so strongly that he says of some of his colleagues:

> ... teachers are prone to believe that they have done everything required of them when their explanations and indications to their pupils are as if a medical man told a patient suffering from constipation that he ought to loosen his bowels and to perspire freely and digest his food well. This is just telling him to do what he wants to know how to do. Such propositions are tautological rules of decision.[17]

Kant is obviously unwilling, therefore, to leave the definition of the good as the object of volition in this indefinite and as yet merely formal state.

Can anything more definite be said about the object toward which the moral person must strive when seeking his or her moral perfection? Kant suggests: "This duty can therefore consist only in *cultivating* one's *faculties* (or natural predispositions), the highest of which is *understanding*, the faculty of concepts and so too of those concepts that have to do with duty. At the same time, this duty includes the cultivation of one's *will* [*Willen*] (moral cast of mind) so as to satisfy all the requirements of duty."[18] The last part of this explanation merely repeats that the object of the will is its own moral perfection. It is, therefore, of no help in adding material significance to the object of pure practical reason. The first part, however, seems more promising. Kant suggests that, in the cultivation of one's powers, one has a duty to educate and refine oneself to the fullest extent possible. Reason commands one to fulfill the potentialities of his or her rational nature so as to be worthy of the humanity that is within.[19] At this point genuine material content seems to be added to the object of volition. In the process of willing his or her own perfection, the person now wills to educate himself or herself, to develop reason and understanding, and thereby to become free from the rudenesses of the state of nature. Still we must remember that Kant says that one is to do all these things so that he or she shall be worthy of the humanity within. All these activities are carried out as a means to virtue.[20]

16 Idem: idem.

17 Idem: ibid., 25–26. Elsewhere Kant makes the observation: "A practical proposition is tautological when no performance can follow from it." (Ibid., 177: ibid., 141).

18 MS, 386–87: MOM, 518.

19 Idem: idem.

20 As Keith Ward notes, Kant objected to the rationalistic ethics of Wolff on the ground that, as Ward states, "One cannot *start* with an 'empty,' non-moral concept of metaphysical perfection and derive specific moral duties from it." Ward, 85–86.

The individual must develop his or her faculties to the point that he or she can live a moral life because this is the condition of the attainment of moral perfection. Kant writes,

> Moral goodness thus lies in the perfection, not of the faculties, but of the will. But the functional completeness of all our powers is required in order that the dictates of the will should be made operative. Perfection [of the faculties], therefore, appertains to morality indirectly.[21]

But if this natural perfection of our powers is of value merely as a means to the attainment of moral perfection by providing us with the conditions for living moral lives, then it cannot provide a material object of volition. One educates oneself and develops one's humanity so that the conditions for the exercise of one's will are met. Once these conditions are met, however, what then does a person will when he or she wills in a manner befitting a person with a good moral disposition? What does he or she will when seeking moral perfection? An object of moral volition with material content has not yet been provided.

Perhaps Kant does not regard the perfection of one's faculties of mind and body simply as a means to moral perfection. Perhaps he intends to argue, rather, that one is obligated to fulfill one's capacities because they are natural ends whose fulfillment is good in itself. We find Kant saying occasionally that the cultivation of the powers of mind, soul, and body is the end or goal of human existence.[22] If this is Kant's view, then he is clearly in possession of an object of volition with material content. Under this interpretation, one no longer wills the perfection of his or her natural faculties merely as a means for the exercise of moral volition. Having attained to the conditions of moral volition already, one fulfills one's duty and attains moral perfection in part by striving to fulfill one's natural capacities. It may thus be thought that Kant (following Aristotle, Wolff, Baumgarten, and others) attributes goodness to the perfection of capacities simply because the perfection of these ends is good in itself.

This interpretation, however, does not bear up under scrutiny; it overlooks the fact that, for Kant, the good is always related to desire. The natural good (the pleasant) is that which satisfies the desires of individuals. The moral good is that which satisfies everyone.[23] Kant insists that "what we call good [morally good] must be, in the judgment of every *reasonable* man, an object of the faculty of desire, and the evil must be, in everyone's eyes, an object of

---

21 VüE, 32: LoE, 26.
22 MS, 444ff.: MOM, 565ff.; cf. GMS, 423: GMM, 90.
23 VüE, 30: LoE, 24.

aversion."[24] In the third *Critique,* Kant again insists that goodness, whether natural or moral, involves a reference to the faculty of desire and a concern for the real existence of the object that is regarded as good.[25] If the object itself arouses the faculty of desire, then it is naturally good. If, however, the object of desire is defined by the moral law and presented to the faculty of desire as the object it ought necessarily to desire, then the object is morally good. But unless an object is related to the faculty of desire in one way or the other it cannot be good in either sense. Kant finds no third way by which an object can be related to the faculty of desire. The perfection of capabilities, therefore, cannot be regarded as good unless it is either naturally good, by being essential to the fulfillment of sensible needs and inclinations, or morally good by being demanded by the moral law. It cannot be regarded as a third kind of intrinsic goodness; for unless the moral law demands it, or sensible desire delights in it, the perfection of natural capacities does not stand in relation to the faculty of desire at all. And apart from some relation to the faculty of desire, an object cannot be good.

Nor can Kant be interpreted to say that if one has no desire, for example, to develop one's capacity to read and if reading is not essential to the moral life, then learning to read is not good. Though perhaps not immediately desirable, reading may be an essential means to the fulfillment of something else which is desired. Consequently, the cultivation of one's capacity to read may be naturally good in accordance with a maxim of prudence under the idea of happiness as the total well-being of the individual.[26] Kant's point is this: if the perfection of natural capacities is to be good in any sense, this perfection must be desired either indirectly or directly, or it must be a necessary object of the faculty of desire demanded by the moral law.[27]

Apart from moral perfection, which we have already discussed, perfection is related to human beings as a natural good and, hence, as the object of desire according to maxims of happiness. And most of the talents and skills of which a

---

24 KpV, 60–61: CprR, 169. My italics. For an instructive discussion of this point, see Beck, *A Commentary*, 138–39.
25 KU, 209: CoAJ, 48.
26 GMS, 415–16: GMM, 78–83.
27 For this reason I think it is more in keeping with Kant's thought to stress the two-fold division of the good into the moral good and the natural good than to stress the three-fold division into *bonitas problematica*, *bonitas pragmatica*, and *bonitas moralis*, distinctions found in Baumgarten. Although this division corresponds, as Beck shows, to the three kinds of imperative, both *bonitas problematica* and *bonitas pragmatica* belong to the class of natural goods. Beck, *A Commentary*, 131.

person is capable are good, if at all, only as natural goods. Kant's position on this subject is well summarized in his refutation of Baumgarten's view that the perfection of all the natural ends of humankind is to be included in the list of duties that we have toward ourselves. Kant says of Baumgarten's theory:

> He includes in his list all human perfections, even those which relate to our talents. He speaks of the perfection of all the powers of the soul. On this argument, logic and all the sciences which go to perfect the understanding and satisfy our thirst for knowledge would need to be included; but there is nothing moral in these. Morality does not tell us what we ought to do in order to become perfect in the skilled use of our powers; any such precepts are merely pragmatic, they are rules of prudence for amplifying our powers because this conduces to our welfare.[28]

Kant thus insists that unless our powers and their cultivation are essential to the fulfillment of the moral law, they are good only as they contribute to the happiness of humanity.

> Nor can such perfections acquire a distinct quality of goodness by being grounded on the command of God. Unless a command of God is itself derived from the moral law, it is not binding on the will except by means of threats and promises that concern the will's eternal happiness. Consequently, the perfection of talents which God might command would be demanded either upon moral grounds, and therefore be morally good, or upon grounds of sensible well-being, and hence be naturally good.[29] Again we see that perfection does not constitute a third kind of goodness.

Once it is noted, however, that perfection is good only as a natural or as a moral good, we see that it does not offer us a sufficiently determinate object for moral volition. As a moral good, perfection provides only preliminary objects of volition in terms of which the will attains to the conditions of significant moral existence. (For example, moral perfection directs the will to pay attention to the first signs of an emerging conscience, and to its nurture.) Once these conditions are met, however, moral perfection ceases to be an instructive object of volition. As a natural good, moreover, perfection is grounded only upon prudential maxims; consequently, it can never be presented as a necessary object of volition. Kant has rightly said that there is nothing moral in this notion of perfection. It seems, therefore, that *bonum supremum* (virtue) cannot function as a sufficiently determinate object of moral volition or provide material content for it.

---

28 VüE, 176: LoE, 141.
29 KpV, 41: CprR, 151–2.

Before leaving this question we must note, however, that Kant sometimes suggests that the perfection of natural capacities can provide a necessary and also concretely determinate object of volition. Unfortunately, Kant occasionally makes this claim at the expense of the consistency of his theory of the good. When he addresses the duties one has toward oneself in the *Metaphysics of Morals*, Kant says that the cultivation of the natural powers of mind, soul, and body – as means to all sorts of possible ends – is a duty of a human being to himself or herself. One must not permit one's talents to rust and atrophy through neglect, nor should one be content to leave natural capacities undeveloped beyond their condition at birth. Hence, according to Kant,

> the basis on which he should develop his capacities (for all sorts of ends) is not regard for the *advantages* that their cultivation can provide; for the advantage might (according to Rousseau's principles) turn out on the side of his crude natural needs. Instead, it is a command of morally practical reason and a *duty* of a human being to himself to cultivate his capacities (some among them more than others, insofar as people have different ends), and to be in a pragmatic respect a human being equal [*angemessener*] to the end of his existence.[30]

In this passage Kant does not find the individual committed by desire to the cultivation of these powers as a natural good. He admits with Rousseau that human beings might be better off in the rawness of the state of nature. On the other hand, we have noted that Kant does not argue that the perfection of all these powers of mind, soul, and body is essential to moral volition. These are powers that, when attained, are of use to human beings for a variety of purposes. While some of them may be of help in living a moral life, not many of these powers nor a very great refinement of them can be required for purposes of morality, because the moral life can be lived by common folk who lack such refinements. Kant seems to be arguing, therefore, that, apart from the service of these powers to a human's well-being and/or moral development, their development is nevertheless morally obligatory. As Kant puts it in this context, "as a rational being he [a person] necessarily wills that all his powers should be developed."[31]

Kant thus appears to be advocating the same view of perfection – that the perfection of one's natural aptitudes is a duty to oneself – that he refuted when it was advanced by Baumgarten. The theory of perfection was rejected again by Kant in the second *Critique* on the grounds that it was based on the determina-

---

30 MS, 444–45: MOM, 565.
31 GMS, 423: GMM, 90.

tion of a material object of volition prior to the moral law and consequently was incapable of relating itself to the will as duty.[32] Nevertheless, in the passages cited in the preceding paragraph, Kant not only introduced this material concept of perfection into his theory *ad hoc;* moreover, by insisting that the attainment of such perfection is a duty, he contradicted the central thesis of the Analytic of the second *Critique* in addition to many explicit statements on the subject.

Since I am not interested in making capital of such a contradiction but hope, rather, to suggest the systematic unity of Kant's doctrine of the good, I dismiss the few isolated passages in which Kant introduces perfection of capacities as a third sort of good (that is, as a material object defined *prior to* the law that is nonetheless binding upon the will) as unintentional lapses back into the rationalistic ethics of Wolff and Baumgarten. More consistent with Kant's theory taken as a whole is his claim that under the idea of moral perfection as an end which is also a duty, a person is obligated to perfect only those powers of mind and body that are essential to the exercise of moral volition.

There is no goodness other than moral or natural goodness on which Kant could ground an obligation to seek the perfection of one's capacities. If one were to adapt Kant's theory to include the cultivation of all powers of mind, soul, and body as good in a sense neither moral nor natural, one would have to do so by relating these ends to desire. This could be done most easily by developing the implications of reason itself as the faculty of desire. Reason does have ends. It is a practical faculty that seeks the embodiment of ideas and ideals. The ideas of the soul, the world, and good as well as the ideas of freedom, God, and immortality are among those ends that reason poses for itself as tasks. The realization of these ideas constitutes the desire of reason, and, hence, these ideas may be said to be good. Now, if one were to show that all the powers of mind, soul, and body were essential to these ends of reason, one could perhaps present a theory of the goodness of the perfection of these powers that was distinct either from moral goodness or natural goodness. The goodness of this perfection, however, would still be conditioned by the relative goodness of the ends of reason. At this point one might have to conclude that the goodness of any particular end of reason is subject to final evaluation in terms of the highest good as the canon of pure reason. From this standpoint, however, all the ideas and ideals of reason are to be evaluated in terms of their contribution to the highest good in which moral goodness and natural goodness are combined, the former providing the supreme condition of the

---

32 KpV, 40ff.: CprR, 151ff.

latter. Consequently, all the ends of reason, save the highest good itself (as reason's final goal), would be evaluated in terms of a concept of the good that simply unified the demands of both the natural good and the moral good. Thus the perfection of talents would be good either morally, as means to the attainment of the supreme condition of the highest good, or naturally, as a part of the completion of the highest good. We would still be at a loss, therefore, to point out a third sort of goodness constituted by the perfection of natural capacities.

3 Happiness (the Natural Good) as a Component of the Highest Good

At this point Kant has gone as far as he can from the side of the law alone in the determination of a material object of volition.[33] He now confronts an ethical paradox at least as serious as those which confronted the Stoics, the Epicureans and Socrates – namely, the paradox of willing the willing of nothing. Every action must have an object or end. That end prescribed by the moral law is the moral good, which is the good will itself. Thus the will is obligated to will willing itself (that is, moral perfection) as its end. But if the will is to be good, it must will *something* in the act of volition. While the moral law prescribes the conditions of willing and sets these conditions before the will as its object, these conditions cannot be fulfilled until the will itself *embodies* these conditions as the *form* of an *actual*, *concrete* volition whose material (while subject to the law) must be acquired through sensibility, that is, through the faculty of desire. If, therefore, the law is not extended to the condition of humankind, then the law cannot provide a material object of volition, and Kant is left with the paradox of willing the willing of nothing.

Kant avoids this problem by building his ethics on the foundation of the experience of obligation. This is the experience, not of a pure rational being, but of a person as a rational-sensible being. This is the experience of the heterogeneity of the good in which both the natural good as the fulfillment of a person's sensible nature and the moral good as the fulfillment of a person's rational nature are presupposed. Having recognized the fact of humankind's sensibility from the outset – not only as an essential part of human nature

33 One must not make the mistake of supposing that Kant was opposed to there being a material object of volition. He knew that there must be one for moral practice, but he insisted that the obligation to will a material object could never stem from the object itself. The obligation must stem from the law.

but also as a condition of the experience of obligation[34] – Kant, in keeping with the foundations of his theory, can extend reason beyond the consideration of humans merely as rational beings to their limits as both rational and sensible.

Kant does not stop, therefore, with perfection as the sole end which is also a duty. He insists rather that one is likewise obligated to seek the happiness of others as a second end which is also a duty.[35] Human beings have happiness as their natural good, and happiness is defined as that satisfaction taken in the fulfillment of needs and inclinations. Kant observes: "To be happy is necessarily the desire of every rational but finite being, and thus it is an unavoidable determinant of its faculty of desire."[36] As it is applied in a specific volition, the moral law can only prescribe the form of its own universality to which material, supplied by the faculty of desire, must be added. Since we are finite, rational-sensible beings, we all have happiness as the object of desire; hence, we can introduce our own happiness as material content of our volition if one condition is met – namely, if we have included within the content and structure of our volition the happiness of others. We are morally obligated to seek the happiness of others because we, in addition to being finite, sensible beings, who naturally and invariably seek our own happiness, are also rational beings, who are constrained to act according to the universal demand of the moral law. This constrains our will to pursue the happiness of others as the prior condition of the *moral right* to pursue our own. Kant reasons as follows:

> The law that we should further the happiness of others arises not from the presupposition that this law is an object of everyone's choice but from the fact that the form of universality, which reason requires as condition for giving to the maxim of self-love [personal happiness] the objectivity of law, is itself the determining ground of the will.[37]
>
> ... The reason why I ought to promote the happiness of others is not because the realization of their happiness is of consequence to myself (whether on account of immediate inclination or on account of some satisfaction gained indirectly through reason), but solely

---

34 KpV, 32, 91–92: CprR, 143, 197–98. Although I do not agree fully with Beck's discussion of the degrees of purity in Kant's ethical theory, I find his views singularly instructive. See Beck, *A Commentary*, 53–54.
35 MS, 387, 393ff.: MOM, 518, 524ff.
36 KpV, 25, cf. 60–1: CprR, 136, cf. 170. In the Groundwork Kant states: "... there is one purpose which they not only *can* have, but which we can assume with certainty that they all *do* have by a natural necessity – the purpose, namely, of *happiness... a purpose which we can presuppose* a priori*and with certainty to be present in every man because it belongs to his very being.*" (GMS, 415: GMM, 83; my italics from "a purpose" through "being").
37 KpV, 34: CprR, 146.

> because a maxim which excludes this cannot also be present in one and the same volition as a universal law.[38]

As finite, rational, yet sensible beings, we naturally and necessarily desire and seek our own happiness; yet this is never possible in accordance with law unless we also seek the happiness of others. We do not necessarily care for others. As far as our own desires are concerned, we may have indifference or contempt for the welfare of others. But we can never will an object according to a universal maxim unless, in the determination of that maxim, consideration is given to the fulfillment of the happiness of others.

Kant now has a material object of volition that can inform and direct the will in the act of volition. And yet, remarkably, this material stands under the determination of law because it is a demand of the *law* and not of *inclination* that one must seek the happiness of others. It is the law's demand of universality that finds one wrong to desire others to further one's interests (a desire shared by all human beings) unless one at the same time furthers their interests. Unless a person also wills the interests of others he or she has no *right,* no justification under the law, for having others will his or her own. But if one has no respect for the law and chooses to disregard its demand, one is certainly able and even inclined to have others seek one's interest while one totally disregards theirs. An individual may act in the manner of a politically astute person. He or she may find it prudent to hand out a favor here and a favor there in order to get what he or she wants. In this case, however, such a person is bargaining and gives only in order to receive something in return then or at some later time. But when one considers one's needs and wants as a sensible being under the jurisdiction of the law of one's rational nature, he or she must forego any desire to exploit others, or to trade on mutually advantageous terms, or to ignore their needs altogether. For one cannot rationally will the attainment of the natural good for oneself except under the condition of one's worthiness to do so – that is, under the condition that one also wills the attainment of the natural good universally according to the demand of the law. A person must seek the happiness of others as a condition of his or her *worthiness* to seek personal happiness which he or she in fact desires to seek. *Hence we see that it is not one's concern for happiness that leads one to consider the happiness of others. On the contrary, the concern for virtue, that is, for the*

38 GMS, 441: GMM, 109. It is very important to note that this doctrine, though not developed to any extent in the *Groundwork*, is nonetheless present there. Thus Kant does partially prepare – even in his formal treatise on ethics – for the material application of the moral law.

worthiness to be happy, motivates a person to do so. An individual pursues his or her own moral perfection by pursuing the happiness of others along with his or her own.

In admitting the content of sensibility into the maxim of the will, the law does not resign its claim to determine the object of volition. It continues to impose its form upon the material of the faculty of desire. As a consequence the material object of volition, in spite of its sensible content, is not defined prior to the law, but is defined by the law itself. Apart from the law, any material of the faculty of desire is merely a contingently desired end. Only after the imposition of the form of universality upon the content of desire does that content (now drastically altered) become the good as the material object of moral volition.

4 The Unity of Perfection and Happiness in the Highest Good

In presenting our own perfection and the happiness of others as distinct ends which are also duties, Kant has come closer to his goal: determining a material object of volition by reference to the law. The goal is not reached, however, until he can show the unity of these two ends in a single object that is also a duty. The relation of these ends to one another is not adequately answered by Kant's assertion that one gives expression to one's moral perfection by seeking the happiness of others. This is neither the only way nor even a completely satisfactory way of attaining virtue. For example, since a person recognizes that his or her own worthiness to be happy depends on seeking the happiness of others, he or she must wonder whether his or her duty to pursue the happiness of others is not to some extent conditioned by their worthiness to receive it. Thus, the will is left in great confusion in the absence of the definition of an object that can in some way unify these two morally necessary ends. But in reasserting this need for a unified end or object of volition, we must keep clearly in mind that we are not discussing a need of the law. The moral law does not have its foundation in some object, nor is it incomplete as the *law* of morality if it fails to determine an object. The concern for the determination of an object stems from a human need.[39] It is the need of the human will for an object in the act of volition that forces Kant to this consideration of ends and to

---

39 TP, 279–80n: TaP, 46–7n. The "concept of duty need not be based upon any particular end, but that, rather, it *introduced* another end for the human will." Ibid., 279: ibid., 46; cf. RGV, 4: Rel, 4.

the extension of the law beyond its own limits alone to the condition of humankind.

Once this extension is made, however, we see that these ends of one's own perfection and the happiness of others are not to be regarded as separate and distinct objects of volition. Rather they are united in the duty "to strive as best he can for the highest good that is possible in the world (universal happiness linked to and in accordance with the purest morality in the world as a whole)."[40] This obligation – to "make the highest good possible in the world your own final end"[41] – Kant notes,

> is a synthetic proposition *a priori*, which is introduced by the moral law. This extension is possible because of the moral law's being taken in relation to the natural characteristics of man, that for all his actions he must conceive an end over and above the law (a characteristic which makes man an object of experience).[42]

Because of humanity's sensible as well as rational nature, a person's obligation must be presented in terms of action in the *sensible world* and not merely in terms of the form of the action itself, as mere autonomy or virtue. The concept of the highest good enunciates a unity of the heterogeneous components of virtue and happiness by means of an extension of the law of humankind's rational nature to the needs and desires of its sensible nature. It enunciates, therefore, a unity of the moral good and the natural good.

The concept of the highest good, according to Kant, "is a *synthesis* of concepts,"[43] and it must never be confused with the "supreme good."[44] When the term "highest" *[höchste]* is used in the phrase "the highest good," it can mean either "supreme" *(supremum) [oberste]* or "complete" or "perfect" *(consummatum) [vollendete]*. The supreme good "is the unconditional condition, i.e. the condition which is subordinate to no other *(originarium),*"[45] while the complete or perfect good is "that whole which is no part of a yet larger whole of the same kind *(perfectissimum).*"[46] It is indeed true that "virtue (as the worthiness to be happy) is *the supreme condition* of whatever appears to us to be

40 TP, 279: TaP, 46.
41 RGV, 7n: Rel, 7n.
42 Idem: idem; cf. KpV, 110ff.: CprR, 214ff.; MS, 384–5: MOM, 516–7.
43 KpV, 113: CprR, 217.
44 Paton seems to have overlooked this point for he holds that Kant asserted that the good will is the highest good. See Paton, *Categorical Imperative*, 41–45.
45 KpV, 110: CprR, 214–15.
46 Idem: idem.

desirable and thus of all our pursuit of happiness and consequently that it is the *supreme* good *[das oberste Gut]*."[47] Nevertheless, Kant denies that virtue, as the supreme good,

> is the entire and perfect good *[das ganze und vollendete Gut]* as the object of the faculty of desire of rational finite beings. In order to be this, *happiness* is also required, and indeed not merely in the partial eyes of a person who makes himself his end but even in the judgment of an impartial reason, which in general regards persons in the world as ends-in-themselves.[48]

It is clear from this that the moral good, virtue, is by no means the highest good. It is rather the supreme condition of the highest good, and, therefore, Kant says "it is the supreme good [*das oberste Gut*]."[49] But happiness as the natural good must be added to virtue in order to realize the highest good. For, Kant insists:

> the highest good [*das höchste Gut*] means the whole [*das Ganze*], the perfect good [*das vollendete Gut*] wherein virtue is always the supreme good [*das oberste Gut*], being the condition having no condition superior to it.[50]

The highest good, is, therefore, the synthesis of the moral good and the natural good. And since the moral good is the supreme condition of this unity, we find that in the fulfillment of the highest good happiness must be present in exact proportion to morality "[i]nasmuch as virtue and happiness together constitute the possession of the highest good for one person."[51] As we saw in Section 2, "happiness in exact proportion to morality (as the worth of a person and his worthiness to be happy) constitutes that [the highest good] of a possible world."[52] An individual recognizes a defect in his or her moral goodness by his transgression of the law, and a defect in his or her natural goodness by unrequited needs and desires. But a person recognizes a defect in the highest good for himself or herself in two different ways – either by failure to attain virtue, which is the supreme condition of a person's highest good as the worthi-

---

47 Ibid., 110: ibid., 215. Kant's italics.
48 Ibid., 110–11: ibid., 215. Kant's italics. See KrV, B841ff.: CpR, 640ff.
49 KpV,110–11: CprR, 215.
50 Ibid.: ibid. It is important to note that Kemp Smith in his splendidly accurate translation appears on one occasion to have mistakenly translated "*das höchste Gut*" as "the supreme good." He thereby contributed to the confusion of the highest good with the supreme good. (KrV, B842: CpR, 641).
51 Idem: idem.
52 Idem: idem.

ness to be happy, or by the existence of a disproportion between one's virtue and happiness. The highest good of the individual – to the extent that the highest good can be attained by the individual – is never attained so long as the individual is deficient in virtue. Nevertheless, taking the degree of one's moral attainment for what it is, there is also a violation of one's highest good if one is not happy in exact proportion to the degree of his or her virtuous attainments.

Once the highest good is recognized by an individual as a personal obligation, he or she recognizes that an integral part of the attainment of virtue consists in striving to achieve the right proportion between personal happiness and virtue. Thus, if one recognizes that one is not worthy of the happiness one enjoys, one may find oneself morally obligated, in terms of the supreme good, to renounce this happiness. The criminal who turns himself or herself in can be seen to pursue both the moral good and the highest good by establishing that proportion between virtue and happiness that is demanded by the highest good and by the moral good, as its supreme condition. In the act of turning himself or herself in, the criminal increases his or her worthiness to be happy in the future, albeit perhaps insufficiently to permit a suspended sentence. Another individual, of course, may lack happiness commensurate with his or her virtue. Such a one, in striving to attain the highest good, has an indirect duty to increase his or her own happiness.[53]

It is not morally possible, of course, for this individual, in light of his or her duty to promote the highest good, to compromise his or her virtue in order to increase personal happiness or in order to make it commensurate with virtue. Because the attainment of virtue is the supreme condition of the highest good, to compromise one's virtue – regardless of the disparity of happiness to virtue – involves acting contrary to one's duty to promote the highest good. Were one to compromise one's virtue, that erstwhile virtuous person may not only fail to increase personal happiness, but will certainly find himself or herself less than worthy of whatever happiness he or she does possess. The virtuous but unhappy person must recognize that the moral law does not promise happiness but only the worthiness of it. Since one has acquired a *right* to happiness, however, any excess unhappiness in one's life is an affront to reason. As a rational being one must strive to remedy it. Failing this, the virtuous person may have a rational faith that this affront will be remedied by God. But as a virtuous person in

53 This discussion suggests the answer to Beck's question, What am I to do to promote the highest good? (Beck, *A Commentary*, 244). This is the issue that has given rise to the so-called Beck v. Silber discussion. Many critics have supposed Beck is right. Beck, however, leaves the issue unsettled, while Kant has an answer. On most issues regarding Kant's ethics Beck and I are in general agreement.

pursuit of the attainment of the highest good, he or she must be prepared to endure steadfastly in virtue without benefit of the happiness which he or she deserves.[54]

These observations pertain merely to the idea of the highest good for individual persons. When we generalize this basic conception of the relation of virtue to happiness to include the totality of finite rational beings, we attain to the idea of the highest good possible in the world, an idea in terms of which the happiness of all finite rational-sensible beings is sought under the sole limitation of their worthiness to be happy. Thus under the idea of the highest good, one is not merely concerned to achieve virtue and to seek happiness proportionate to virtue in one's own life; one is obligated in addition to strive for the realization of happiness in proportion to virtue in the lives of all human beings. Furthermore, one strives for this goal with the realization that it is likewise the obligatory goal of all human beings' efforts. Although this task is God-like in dimension, it does not totally transcend the powers of citizens, teachers, scientists, legislators and rulers who sometimes have the power to advance this task.[55]

Many questions concerning the nature of the highest good and its function in Kant's ethics remain. Nevertheless, a few conclusions of importance for the interpretation of Kant's second *Critique* and his system of ethics can be drawn. First, the central importance in Kant's ethics of the concept of the highest good must be recognized. The concept of the good – as a material, determinate object of volition – is necessary in order to give concrete direction to moral volition. Kant likewise recognized that the good must be determined by the moral law if it is to be categorically obligatory on the will. Therefore, he sought to provide, by means of the application of the moral law to the condition of humankind, material content for the good as this necessary object. Second, in attempting to provide material content for the good, Kant showed that moral perfection is an end which is also a duty. Moral perfection, however, does not provide a sufficiently determinate content for the good. Third, Kant demonstrated that the happiness of others is an end which is also a duty. Fourth, in recognition of the difficulty in determining the relation of these two ends as duties, Kant proposed

---

54 To this extent Kant's ethics is closely aligned with that of the Stoics. For my discussion of the highest good as a basis for an argument for the existence of God see Chapters VI and VII.
55 There is an important social and historical dimension to the pursuit of the highest good that other scholars have begun to address. See, for example, Gerald W. Barnes, "In Defense of Kant's Doctrine of the Highest Good"; Yirmiahu Yovel, "The Highest Good and History in Kant's Thought"; Sharon Anderson-Gold, "Kant's Ethical Commonwealth: The Highest Good as a Social Goal."

to unify perfection and happiness in one material object determined formally by the moral law as applied to the actual material of human desire. The unitary, necessary, material object of volition thus determined is the highest good. In light of these four conclusions the basic importance of the concept of the highest good, both for ethical practice and for the understanding of the second *Critique* and Kant's ethics, cannot be denied.

Chapter VI: The Highest Good As Immanent And As Transcendent

1 The Highest Good as the Canon of Pure Reason

The full significance of the highest good cannot be understood even as an ethical concept of practical reason until it is also understood as a metaphysical concept of pure reason. "Reason," Kant insists,

> is impelled by a tendency of its nature to go out beyond the field of its empirical employment, and to venture in a pure employment, by means of ideas alone, to the utmost limits of all knowledge, and not to find rest, save through the completion of its course in [the apprehension of] a self-subsistent systematic whole.[1]

Reason, whether in its moral, theoretical, or speculative employments, is a faculty of striving.

When Kant stresses the primacy of practical reason, he is not merely pointing out that a human being must view himself or herself first and foremost as a moral person and from this standpoint relate himself or herself in action to the world of nature. In addition, as we noted in Chapter I, Kant argues that because reason projects ends and seeks their realization in all its employments, it can function in its theoretical and speculative employments only because it also has a practical employment to undergird, guide, and direct them. In its practical striving, reason reveals a spontaneity that far outstrips that which it exhibits in its theoretical employment as understanding. Kant writes:

> Understanding – although it too is spontaneous activity and is not, like sense, confined to ideas which arise only when we are affected by things (and therefore are passive) – understanding cannot produce by its own activity any concepts other than those whose sole service is *to bring sensuous ideas under rules* and so to unite them in one consciousness: without this employment of sensibility it would think nothing at all. Reason, on the other hand – in what are called "Ideas" – shows a spontaneity so pure that it goes far beyond anything that sensibility can offer: it manifests its highest function in distinguishing the sensible and intelligible worlds from one another and so in marking out limits for understanding itself.[2]

---

1 KrV, B825: CpR, 630. I fail to see the need for Kemp Smith's insertion [the apprehension of] and I have altered his translation from "not to be satisfied" to "not to find rest." Kant's words are clear enough: "*Ruhe zu finden*." Kant definitely stresses the active, striving impulse of reason.
2 GMS, 452: GMM, 120.

Reason produces of its own spontaneity ideas which are its own necessary objects and to which no corresponding objects can be given in sense experience. But these ideas which transcend sense experience are not arbitrary inventions nor are they trivial. As the necessary objects which reason projects for itself, they are the ends of reason and guide reason in all its employments.

Having projected these ideas as its necessary ends, reason reveals additional spontaneity in striving toward their realization. A demand of reason, for example, drives the understanding toward the unification of its conceptions.[3] By insisting that the understanding make a regulative use of the principle of totality, reason expresses its demand that nature be apprehended in its unity. The principle of totality is a law of reason for the understanding, a law which is essential not only to the successful employment of the understanding but also to reason itself, since the end it proposes is an essential end of reason. Without this law, Kant insists,

> we should have no reason at all, and without reason no coherent employment of the understanding, and in the absence of this no sufficient criterion of empirical truth. In order, therefore, to secure an empirical criterion we have no option save to presuppose the systematic unity of nature as objectively valid and necessary.[4]

The movement of the understanding toward unity reveals, therefore, the spontaneity of reason in its two aspects: the projection of the idea of totality and the regulative employment of it by judgment.

In this latter role, moreover, reason functions simultaneously in more than one employment. Judgment in the operation of the faculty of understanding (to continue using this faculty as our example) not only follows the speculative principle of totality, it also functions under the direction of reason in its moral-practical employment. Both scientific inquiry and the use made of its findings, for example, are practical concerns of reason and involve its spontaneous employment as will. The will "either impels the understanding toward inquiry into a truth or holds it back therefrom."[5] Reason is therefore practical in two employments at once: as judgment in the technical-practical (theoretical) employment, and as will in the moral-practical employment under whose direction

3 "As a matter of fact," Kant says, "multiplicity of rules and unity of principles is a demand of reason for the purpose of bringing the understanding into thoroughgoing accordance with itself, just as the understanding brings the manifold of intuition under concepts and thereby connects the manifold." KrV, B362–3: CpR, 305.
4 KrV, B679: CpR, 538.
5 Log, 74: Logic, 577.

the theoretical activity is carried out. In addition, of course, reason is practical in both employments as the source of the ideas under which it itself operates as agent.

The realization, however, that reason is not only practical and active in projecting ideas and in striving for their realization, but is also active in several employments simultaneously, leads to the conclusion that reason must have some supreme or comprehensive end. There must be some general idea in terms of which reason itself can be directed so that all its ideas and interests are capable of realization in a way that satisfies its demands. Kant insists that the end of reason is to press beyond the limits of knowledge to a "self-subsistent systematic whole." And this goal, he says, has its source in the practical interest of reason. All other aims and ideas of reason are related as means to the end of morality which is the highest interest of humanity and of reason itself.[6]

Kant arrives at this conclusion not only on the basis of a prior concern for human beings and the interests of humanity, but also from a metaphysical concern: pure reason itself can reach its own goal of systematic unity only by a subordination of all its other interests to the practical.[7] Reason profits greatly from its theoretical employment for by means of it reason together with sensibility provides sense experience and partially satisfies its desire to know. But reason cannot find complete satisfaction in this employment for its results are limited and fragmentary. There is neither experience of living things (organisms) nor experience of the complete interconnectedness of all events in space and time. Hence, reason moves on to a speculative employment.

Employing the idea of totality – together with the teleological principle of finality, which is derived by judgment from the principle of totality – reason, in its speculative employment, extends the scope of knowledge and more closely approximates the unity of nature as a system. But the full demands of reason are not yet attained by this means, because the speculative employment of reason terminates in a return to experience, that is, in a return to the findings of its merely theoretical employment. "In so doing," says Kant, "the ideas fulfilled their purpose, but in a manner which, though useful, is not in accordance with our expectation."[8] The theoretical and speculative interests of reason, for all their importance, can never finally satisfy the demands of reason in respect to its final ends.

6 KrV, B825–26, cf. B828–9: CpR, 630–31, cf. 632–33.
7 As used here in contrast to *theoretical* and *speculative*, *practical* refers to that employment of reason which, strictly speaking, is morally practical.
8 KrV, B832: CpR, 635.

Kant insists, as we noted in Chapter I, that all the interests of reason, speculative as well as practical, combine in the three questions: What can I know? What ought I to do? and What may I hope? But the theoretical and speculative employments of reason succeed in answering only the first of these questions. Even the use of the ideas of God, the world, and the soul as regulative principles for speculation is fruitless. Their employment merely adds to our knowledge of the world, or as Kant states it, leads "us back to experience."[9] Their employment in speculation – even if we assume the success of this employment – provides nothing more than a partial answer to the first of the three questions. The interests of reason remain unsatisfied until an answer to all three questions is attained.

Reason has no alternative, therefore, but to turn to its practical employment and to seek there the ideas which will finally satisfy it. In this sphere, the ideas of the soul, the world, and God are encountered in such a way that they can indeed carry reason to its highest ends by providing answers to its remaining questions. In the practical sphere, reason finds the final idea in terms of which its activities in all employments can be unified both in comprehension and in practice.

In the practical sphere, the ideas of the soul, the world, and God are not encountered simply as speculative ideas. As such, they were of slight use to reason, as no determinate object could be found for them. In speculation they were limited to a merely regulative employment and were satisfactory only from a theoretical standpoint. Hence, Kant insists that for the purposes of metaphysics these ideas must be dropped, at least in their speculative form. If metaphysics is ever to satisfy the demands of reason, Kant holds, it must proceed through the practical employment of reason to the examination of the ideas of God, freedom, and immortality:

> Metaphysics has as the proper object of its inquiries three ideas only: *God*, *freedom*, and *immortality* .... It does not need the ideas for the purposes of natural science, but in order to pass beyond nature.[10]

Reason in metaphysics is not abandoning its concern for the ideas of the soul, the world, and God. But in speculation it is impossible to attain any understanding of them since no object was given for the idea of soul, and even if there were such an object, no movement could be made from it to the idea of world,

---

9 Idem: idem.
10 KrV, B395n: CpR, 325n.

nor any movement thence to the idea of God. Therefore Kant proposes that reason now turn in a more hopeful direction by seeking the ideas of the practical employment of reason, that is, by making freedom, God, and immortality the objects of its search.

Strangely, however, only three sentences after his statement that metaphysics has the moral ideas of freedom, God, and immortality as the sole proper objects of its inquiry, Kant states that metaphysics should begin with the theoretical idea of soul and move thence to the idea of the world and thence to God, advancing, that is, "from the doctrine of *soul*, to the doctrine of the *world*, and thence to the knowledge of *God*."[11] In this way Kant thinks that the morally-oriented inquiry of metaphysics will succeed, since it will be following the analytic method of considering first that which is given in experience.

That Kant should immediately substitute the theoretical ideas for the moral ideas clearly indicates that he considers these sets of ideas to be in some sense correlates of one another. The former set (soul, world, and God) is given by speculative reason, and the latter (freedom, God, and immortality) by morally practical reason. But the objects of these ideas must be either the same or closely related, such that (*a*) the metaphysical interest of reason is satisfied in the grasp of the moral ideas of reason and (*b*) the metaphysical grasp of the moral ideas of reason can be attained by means of an examination of the speculative ideas from a morally practical standpoint. That is to say, the metaphysical and the moral concerns of reason must be so intimately related, and reason must be so unified, that for the purposes of metaphysical inquiry an identity obtains between the speculative and the moral ideas of reason. This identity is such that reason can pursue the ends of metaphysics – which are the moral ideas of reason – by means of an examination of the speculative ideas of reason. Kant finds he must make only two changes in his substitution of the speculative ideas for the moral ones: the order of consideration of the speculative ideas must be altered to fit the character of what is given in moral experience, and their meaning and significance must stem from the moral perspective on which their apprehension and the striving after them is grounded.

Since Kant insists that metaphysics must begin with the idea of soul as that which is disclosed in experience, it is clear that he regards the idea of freedom as the correlate of the idea of soul. In the experience of duty, the moral law directly reveals to human beings the reality of freedom. Thus, Kant says,

---

11 Idem: idem.

> One idea of reason, strange to say, is to be found among the matters of fact – an idea which does not of itself admit to any presentation in intuition, or, consequently, of any theoretical proof of its possibility. The idea in question is that of freedom. Its reality is the reality of a particular kind of causality (the conception of which would be transcendent if considered theoretically), and as a causality of that kind it admits of verification by means of practical laws of pure reason and in the actual actions that take place in obedience to them, and, consequently, in experience. – It is the only one of all the ideas of pure reason whose object is a matter of fact and must be included among the *scibilia*.[12]

Freedom is revealed in moral experience as a fact. More than this, freedom has an object which is also a matter of fact, and that object is humanity. In the experience of obligation, wherein his or her freedom is revealed, a person becomes aware of the full dimensions of his or her being. In this experience one cannot regard oneself merely as a series of appearances. Rather,

> beyond this character of himself as a subject made up, as it is, of mere appearances he must suppose there to be something else which is its ground – namely, his Ego as this may be constituted in itself; and thus as regards mere perception and the capacity for receiving sensations he must count himself as belonging to the *sensible world*, but as regards whatever there may be in him of pure activity (whatever comes into consciousness, not through affectation of the senses, but immediately) he must count himself as belonging to the *intellectual world*, of which, however, he knows nothing further.[13]

A human being, in the awareness of his or her rational nature, recognizes the power of his or her will to act independently of determination by causes in the sensible world. In the free action of one's will, wherein one reveals oneself as the matter-of-fact object of the idea of freedom, one likewise reveals the reality of this idea of pure reason. The free will, as the supersensible ego and ground of personality, provides reason with a supersensible idea of personality. Meaning is thus given to the supersensible idea of soul. Whereas reason in its theoretical employment could regard the idea of soul merely as the idea of a thinking subject as an appearance to itself, reason, in the practical sphere, encounters the free will as the supersensible ego, as the ground of personality in which the *constitutive* reality of the idea of soul is revealed.

Having established the reality of the idea of freedom and the idea of soul, reason can now move on to the determination of its other objects. Yet reason can no longer proceed in terms of its moral ideas, because neither God nor

---

12 KU, 468: CoTJ, 142; cf. KpV, 6, 133: CprR, 120–21, 235.

13 GMS, 451: GMM, 119. See also KU, 181–82, 434–35, 473–74: CoAJ, 21, and CoTJ, 98–99, 147–49; KpV, 5–6: CprR, 120–21.

immortality can be derived directly from the idea of freedom. It now becomes clear why Kant suggested that metaphysics should investigate its objects – God, freedom, and immortality – by means of an examination in the moral sphere of the speculative ideas of the soul, the world, and God. Although reason cannot move from the idea of freedom to either of the other two moral ideas, it can move from the idea of soul (the correlate of the idea of freedom) to the idea of the world. And in this movement, the crucial metaphysical importance of the highest good and the factor which prompts Kant to refer to it as the canon of pure reason are revealed.[14]

The experience of obligation, in which freedom (and the soul as human will) is revealed, makes it possible to determine the highest good as the necessary object of the will.[15] But the idea of the highest good is precisely the idea of the moral world.[16] Under the idea of the highest good, which is projected by the moral law as another activity of practical reason, both reason and humankind find their final end and direction. Under this idea, "man conceives himself here in analogy to the deity which is destined to bring forth the highest good outside itself."[17] Accordingly, one considers "what sort of world he would create under the guidance of practical reason."[18] This would be a world "in which happiness is bound up with and proportioned to morality," a world in which all rational beings under the guidance of moral principles "would themselves be authors both of their own enduring well-being and of that of others."[19] The moral law applied to the condition of humankind suggests the reordering of the sensible world into a new world in which the moral law provides the form. The moral law, that is,

> ideally transfers us into a nature in which reason would bring forth the highest good were it accompanied by sufficient physical capacities; and it determines our will to impart to the sensuous world the form of a system of rational beings.[20]

---

14 See Heideman, I., *"Das Ideal des höchsten Guts."*

15 Reason finds, Kant says, that a human being "is the only natural creature whose peculiar objective characterization is nevertheless such as to enable us to recognize in him a supersensible faculty – his freedom – and to perceive both the law of the causality and the object of freedom which that faculty is able to set before itself as the highest end – the highest good in the world." (KU, 435: CoTJ, 99). Meredith mistakenly translates "*höchste Gut*" as "supreme good." I altered his translation to correct this error. See also KpV, 132ff.: CprR, 234ff.

16 KrV, B838–9: CpR, 639.

17 TP, 280: TaP, 47n.

18 RGV, 5: Rel, 5.

19 KrV, B837: CpR, 638.

20 KpV, 43: CprR, 154; cf. KrV, B836: CpR, 637–38; GMS, 436n: GMM, 104n.

In this idea of the highest good we find the practical correlate to the speculative idea of the world. We do not consider merely the systematic totality of the sensible world, but also the systematic reordering of the sensible world so that the moral-practical demands of reason can become a part of that systematic totality. In the idea of the highest good, reason envisages that systematic unity of ends in relation to one another whereby both the greatest moral and natural fulfillment takes place. And reason takes this idea as its final end and canon. The highest good, as the moral world determined by the moral law, is, according to Kant, "the conception of an object which reason alone is able to think, and which is meant to be realized in the world through our actions in conformity to that law." The idea of world, as revealed in the idea of the highest good, is "the idea of a final end in the employment of freedom in obedience to moral laws." As such, it "has, therefore, a reality that is subjectively *practical*."[21] Thus the reality of the idea of world, as well as the reality of the idea of soul, is ascertained in the practical sphere.[22]

Having ascertained the reality of both freedom (the soul) and the highest good (the world), reason can now attain to the ideas of God and immortality as the necessary postulates of the highest good.[23] At times Kant presents the argument for God and immortality in an entirely unsatisfactory manner. He sometimes argues, for example, that the denial of these postulates would result in the impossibility of the highest good and, hence, in the impossibility of the moral law which has commanded its attainment.[24] Usually, however, he presents the moral argument along sounder lines as an implication of the fact[25] that the moral law obligates human beings to promote (rather than to attain) the highest good.[26] When Kant speaks in consistency with the greatest part of his ethical writings, he argues that the highest good is a possible object of volition even though it is never fully realized, and he correctly insists that the proof of God and immortality

---

21 KU, 453: CoTJ, 122.

22 We must not forget, however, that the highest good is determined as the moral world which does not exist but which it is the duty of the will as practical reason to create. The practical drive of reason is by no means lessened in the apprehension of this idea; rather, it is increased by virtue of the direction which this idea provides for its efforts.

23 RGV, 5–7 and 6–8n: Rel, 5–7 and 5–7n; KpV, 122–3: CprR, 225–26.

24 KpV, 114: CprR, 218.

25 Ibid., 47: ibid., 157.

26 Ibid., 143, cf. 129–130, 142: ibid., 245, cf. 232, 244; RGV, 8n: Rel, 7n; TP, 279: TaP, 46; KU, 470–472: CoTJ, 144–146.

> does not imply that it is as necessary to assume the existence of God as it is to recognize the validity of the moral law, and that, consequently, one who is unable to convince himself of the former may deem himself absolved from the obligations of the latter. No! ... Every rational being would have to continue to recognize himself as firmly bound by the precept of morals, for their laws are formal and command unconditionally, paying no regard to ends (as the subject-matter of volition).[27]

The moral law and its object are valid apart from God's existence; one may deny the existence of God and immortality, therefore, without in any way circumventing the demand of the moral law.

Kant insists, nevertheless, that one cannot think consistently regarding matters of morality unless one does assume the existence of God and immortality.[28] Since it is a demand of reason (albeit one that humans need only promote) that the highest good be attained, reason cannot fail to be dissatisfied unless the conditions of its attainment can be secured. Reason cannot conclude from this, of course, that the conditions of the attainment of the highest good will in fact be secured, for the demands of reason may ultimately go unsatisfied. But in the context of the moral life, it is absurd to live according to the demands of reason – to strive to realize that ordering of the sensible world which most nearly accords with its demands – unless one supposes that reason itself does order the universe and that its demands will therefore be met. It is absurd, Kant argues, to deny the existence of God and immortality, which are the necessary conditions for the attainment of the demands of reason, and then to affirm, by risking one's life to do one's duty, the belief that the demands of reason are binding and certain of attainment. A person acts in a materially inconsistent manner when he or she stakes his or her very life on the validity of the demands of reason while believing that the world goes its way in total disregard of these demands.

---

27 KU, 450–51: CoTJ, 119.

28 See Wood, *Kant's Moral Religion*, 22–23. Wood suggests a kind of neutral agnosticism whereby as long as we do not explicitly deny the postulates of God's existence or the immortality of our souls, it does not follow from that that we have affirmed their existence. By the same token, Wood notes, "if we do not deny that the highest good is possible, we need not affirm positively that it is possible either." Support for this agnostic position can be found in Kant, who states that "the 'minimum' theology it is necessary to have is a belief that God is at least possible" (30). Wood recognizes the weakness of such an agnostic solution. He claims that an attitude of aloofness or skepticism is incompatible with the injunction to promote the highest good with all of our effort and will (31). As made clear in the quotation footnoted by number 29, it is volition, not belief, that is required. One may believe or be agnostic regarding God and immortality; either way he *must will* the existence of both. See Manfred Kühn's discussion of Kant's religious views in *Kant: A Biography.*

The moral agent recognizes that the attainment of the highest good – that happiness be distributed in proportion to virtue – is a part of the demand of reason. If the universe is rational, this proportion will therefore be realized. In order that this proportion be realized, the existence of God and the immortality of the soul are required. Consequently, if the universe is rational, there must be a God and the immortality of the soul. The moral person who wills the attainment of the highest good *wills*, therefore, the existence of God and immortality:

> Granted that the pure moral law inexorably binds every man as a command (not as a rule of prudence), the righteous man may say: *I will that there be a God*, that my existence in this world be also an existence in a pure world of the understanding outside the system of natural connections, and finally that my duration be endless.[29]

The moral argument is presented here as merely another aspect of consistent volition. At its strongest, the argument is this: no rational person can will consistently in accordance with the moral law of his or her rational nature unless he or she also *wills* the realization of the highest good and the existence of God and immortality as the necessary conditions thereto.

When this is done, the metaphysical interests of reason are satisfied. The speculative idea of world provides reason with the clue needed to complete the metaphysical inquiry. Unable to advance in ethics from the idea of freedom and the fact of humans as free beings, unable to advance in speculation from the idea of soul as merely regulative, reason is able, nevertheless, to advance in its morally-oriented metaphysical inquiry from the idea of soul (freedom) as grounded in moral experience to the idea of world. For, as the correlate in the moral domain of the idea of world, the idea of the highest good not only serves reason as the necessary object of moral volition, it also provides reason with its over-all end, comprehending within itself all of the concerns of reason in proper perspective. And from this idea of a world that is the goal of moral striving, reason can derive the ideas of God and immortality, ideas which were hopelessly beyond its grasp as long as reason remained within its speculative employment.

Admittedly, the metaphysical knowledge attained by means of the employment of the idea of the highest good in the context of moral experience is not theoretical knowledge. It is, nevertheless, genuine knowledge, inasmuch as it is grounded in the same experience on which the knowledge of morality is based. It cannot be dismissed, therefore, as transcendent illusion. It is clear from the

---

29 KpV, 143: CprR, 245. My italics beginning with "that there be a God."

first *Critique* that Kant supposes moral philosophy to be grounded in experience and to be concerned with principles that can be applied *in concreto* in possible experiences. Moral philosophy thus provides one of the modes of knowledge which reason, by means of its ideas, combines into a system.[30] The knowledge of God, the World, and Soul as derived from the employment of the idea of the highest good far outstrips the limits of the manifold of sensibility. This knowledge, though not theoretical, is not empty and unrestrained imagining, for it is grounded in and directed by the content and structure of moral experience.

That Kant should direct metaphysics to the objects of freedom, God, and immortality, only to carry out the inquiry into these objects in terms of the ideas of the soul, the world, and God, clearly shows that Kant presents the inquiry into the moral ideas of reason as a genuinely metaphysical and speculative inquiry as well as moral investigation.[31] (The discussion of the highest good, freedom, God, and immortality in the third *Critique* lends further support to this thesis, since the third *Critique* is not directly concerned with ethics at all.) This redirection of metaphysics and the fusion of moral and speculative ideas of reason which is achieved thereby reveal an aspect of the unity of Kant's thought that is easily overlooked. In all of the *Critiques*, the moral employment of reason is recognized as primary, for only in this employment does reason find the satisfaction of all its interests.

The highest good as the correlate of the idea of world is the crucial concept in the attainment of reason's interests. These interests – speculative, metaphysical, and moral – are largely fulfilled by answers to the questions: What ought I to do? and What may I hope? The idea of the highest good is indispensable for answering the first because it provides the necessary material object of moral volition; it answers the second by providing a proof of God and immortality. It now becomes clear why Kant regarded the concept of the highest good not merely as the object of pure practical reason but as the canon of pure reason. Without it both metaphysics and morals founder, and theoretical knowledge remains without direction.

---

30 KrV, B394, B452–3: CpR, 325, 396; cf. KpV, 47: CprR, 157.

31 That this inquiry into the practical employment of reason should be carried out in the first *Critique* indicates that the first *Critique* is perhaps better understood as a critique of all the employments of reason (as Kant originally intended it to be) rather than as a critique of theoretical reason alone. KrV, B375–6, cf. B832–3: CpR, 314, cf. 635; see also Kant's letter to Markus Herz, dated February 21, 1772, in BR (AA10), 126–7: Corr, 128–30.

2 The Immanence of the Highest Good

As we have seen, the role of the highest good in the whole of Kant's philosophy is found in its function as the canon of pure reason. In Kant's ethics, the concept of the highest good as the necessary material object of moral volition, whose analysis, deduction, and elaboration constitutes the central problem of the *Critique of Practical Reason,* gives concrete significance to moral obligation.[32] No longer obligated to strive for the abstraction of good-willing itself as its object, the will is now guided by means of the idea of the highest good to seek its own moral perfection and the happiness of others as its categorically obligated ends. The idea of the highest good thereby provides an initial answer to the second of Kant's three basic questions: "What ought I to do?"[33]

Since the will is obligated to strive for the embodiment of the highest good, the highest good must not be a utopian dream. The highest good is an idea, to be sure; but Kant insists that it is "at the same time a practical idea, which really can have, as it also ought to have, an influence upon the sensible world."[34] As practical, reason remains dissatisfied until that which ought to be done is done. Reason is dissatisfied until the idea of a moral world is embodied in the world of sense.

This development, however, poses a new problem for Kant's ethical theory. By an idea of reason, Kant understands "a necessary concept of reason to which no corresponding *[kongruierender]* object can be given in sense-experience."[35] If, however, the highest good is to be the object of volition, it must be possible to embody it in some way. On the other hand, if the idea of the highest good is like the other ideas of pure reason, it can never be introduced as an object in sense experience. Since Kant grants, however, that freedom is an exception to the rule that ideas of pure reason cannot be embodied or have objects as actual matters of fact, perhaps he regards the idea of the highest good as a similar exception. Unfortunately, this is not the case. Even if a virtuous person looks about, Kant observes,

---

32 There are scholars who agree that the highest good is of central importance to Kant's ethics but who differ in their interpretation of its role. Thus R.Z. Friedman argues that while the highest good is necessary for the *possibility* of the moral law, it is not necessary for giving the moral law a material content. See Friedman, "The Importance and Function of Kant's Highest Good."

33 KrV, B833: CpR, 635.

34 Ibid., B836: ibid., 637.

35 Ibid., B383: ibid., 318.

> he can never expect to find in nature a uniform agreement – a consistent agreement according to fixed rules, answering to what his maxims are and must be subjectively, with that end [the highest good] which yet he feels himself obliged and urged to realize. Deceit, violence, and envy will always be rife around him, although he himself is honest, peaceable, and benevolent; and other righteous men that he meets in the world, no matter how deserving they may be of happiness, will be subjected by nature, which takes no heed of such deserts, to all the evils of want, disease, and untimely death, just as are the other animals on the earth. And so it will continue to be until one wide grave engulfs them all – just and unjust, there is no distinction in the grave – and hurls them back into the abyss of the aimless chaos of matter from which they were taken.[36]

Kant does not confuse the world as it is with the world as it ought to be.[37] In the sensible world, happiness is not given in proportion to virtue, because virtue cannot guarantee happiness. Also, humans in their freedom are capable of rejecting the demands of the moral law. Humans are not merely powerless to attain in full the highest good; they are likewise frequently indifferent or positively opposed to the fulfillment of that part of the highest good that is within their power. In this regard, the highest good as the idea of a moral world is indeed no different from other ideas of reason.[38]

Because this idea seems incapable of sensible fulfillment, Kant must consider the charge that the moral law which commands the highest good is false. He states the problem as follows:

> If, therefore, the highest good is impossible according to practical rules, then the moral law which commands that it be furthered must be fantastic, directed to empty imaginary ends, and consequently inherently false.[39]

Kant proposes to overcome this difficulty with the moral argument for the existence of God and the immortality of the soul. By the introduction of God and immortality as postulates of pure practical reason, he hopes to account for the possibility of the highest good and show its suitability as an object of volition. To establish the postulate of God he argues:

> But if, now, the strictest obedience to moral laws is to be considered the cause of the ushering in of the highest good (as end), then, since human capacity does not suffice for bringing about happiness in the world proportionate to worthiness to be happy, an

36 KU, 542: CoTJ, 121.
37 KrV, B375: CpR, 313.
38 Ibid., B841: ibid., 640; KpV, 109–114: CprR, 214–28; RGV, 143: Rel, 134.
39 KpV, 114: CprR, 218.

> omnipotent moral Being must be postulated as the ruler of the world, under whose care this [balance] occurs.[40]

Since human beings by their finitude are incapable of rewarding virtue and vice with appropriate degrees of happiness, Kant argues that an omnipotent moral ruler is needed in order to sustain the concept of the highest good as the object of volition. Moreover, aware of humanity's moral limitations, he offers the following argument to establish the postulate of immortality:

> The achievement of the highest good in the world is the necessary object of a will determinable by the moral law. In such a will, however, the *complete fitness* of intentions to the moral law is the supreme condition of the highest good. This aptness, therefore, must be just as possible as its object, because it is contained in the command that requires us to promote the latter. But complete fitness of the will to the moral law is *holiness*, which is a perfection of which no rational being in the world of sense is at any time capable. But since it is required as practically necessary, it can be found only in an *endless progress* to that complete fitness .... This infinite progress is possible, however, only under the presupposition of an infinitely enduring existence and personality of the same rational being; this is called the immortality of the soul. Thus the highest good is practically possible only on the supposition of the immortality of the soul, and the latter, as inseparably bound to the moral law, is as a postulate of pure practical reason.[41]

The highest good is, of course, the necessary object of practical reason. But since no one is obligated to do the impossible, it follows that the possibility of the total realization of the highest good must be assured if it is to be the necessary object of practical reason. Kant concludes therefore that the immortality of the soul and the existence of God must be postulated in order to assure its possibility.[42]

The means by which the moral argument for God and immortality (discussed in the previous section) establishes the possibility of the full realization of the highest good are not clear. Nor is it clear why one must assume that it is possible to attain a full realization of the highest good. Here we find a genuine confusion in Kant's thought. Kant supposes that, because the highest good is an

---

40 RGV, 7–8n: Rel, 7n.

41 KpV, 122: CprR, 225–226. Kant's italics.

42 I am referring to and will now discuss Kant's moral argument as it is found in the passages just cited, in which Kant seems very confused. (For a clear example of Kant's confusion with regard to the moral argument, see KpV, 143–4n: CprR, 245n.) A sound argument can be made for the postulates of pure practical reason on grounds other than the ones Kant relies on in the passages cited; for the present, however, we shall confine our attention to this confused form of the moral argument which recurs several times in Kant's moral writings.

idea of reason and because reason seeks the full realization of this idea (as of all its ideas), human beings are therefore morally obligated to achieve the total realization of the highest good. This is Kant's first premise. Kant also supposes that persons cannot be obligated to attain the highest good unless it is a possible object of volition. His second premise, then, is: that to which a person is obligated must be possible. But Kant points out that as a matter of fact humankind's finitude and moral weakness make it impossible for individuals fully to attain the highest good. As his third premise, therefore, Kant concludes that the full attainment of the highest good by human beings is, in fact, impossible. On the basis of these three premises Kant develops the moral argument in the form which we are now examining.

We can recognize that all the premises must be true if Kant's argument is to succeed. If we deny the first premise (that humans are morally obligated to attain in full the highest good), then the introduction of God and immortality will not be required in order to insure the possibility of the highest good. If the full realization of the highest good is not demanded, humans might still be capable of realizing it to a sufficient degree. If we deny the second premise (that the object of a person's obligation must be possible), then the argument fails, for the highest good can be the object of one's moral volition even if it is impossible. Once again, neither God nor immortality is required. Finally, if we deny the third premise (that full realization of the highest good by humankind is impossible), then the attainment of the highest good becomes possible for humans; hence the attainment of the highest good can be the object of moral volition whether or not there is a God or immortality. Thus, unless all three premises are true, Kant needs no proof of the existence of God and immortality in order to establish the possibility of the highest good as the object of volition.

Granting, for the sake of the argument, that these premises are true, why does Kant think that their acceptance compels one to accept the postulates of God and immortality? The answer seems to be this: Kant recognizes that the affirmation of these three premises involves him in a contradiction which the moral argument alone can resolve. If the first and second premises are true, then the third is false. That is, if human beings are obligated to attain the highest good, and if they are not obligated to do the impossible, then it must be false that the attainment of the highest good is impossible. Furthermore, if the second and third premises are true, then the first is false; that is, if humans are not obligated to do the impossible, and if the attainment of the highest good is impossible, then it must be false that humans are obligated to attain the highest good. Finally, if the first and third premises are true, then the second is false; that is, if humans are obligated to attain the highest good and if the attainment of the highest good is impossible, then it must be false that humans are not obligated to do the impossible.

In light of the logical relationships between these premises, Kant recognizes that in affirming all three of them he is also at the same time denying them. To affirm the three together is thoroughly contradictory. Since Kant feels constrained to affirm all three premises, however, he seeks a means by which to resolve the contradiction. This he finds in the postulation of God and immortality. Since he affirms all three premises (and thereby involves himself in a contradiction which must be resolved) and since only the postulates of God and immortality will resolve this contradiction, he concludes that it is logically necessary to assume their existence. By means of this assumption, he believes that the three premises can be affirmed without contradiction, because the existence of God and immortality will assure the possibility of the attainment of the highest good.

The argument, however, is completely unsatisfactory. First of all, the argument purports to show that it is possible for humanity to attain the highest good. But God's existence and power do not establish this. If God is omnipotent, God can surely attain the highest good. The fact that God can attain the highest good does not prove, however, that a finite moral person can do so. Human potentiality is not increased by the introduction of God; the attainment of the highest good is as far beyond human capacity as it ever was even when the existence of God is assumed. If, by establishing the postulates of God and immortality, Kant were to prove that it is possible for humankind to attain the highest good, he would also prove that the third premise is false, for it asserts *as a matter of fact* that the attainment of the highest good is impossible for humankind. Now unless Kant intends to argue, in the manner of an extreme rationalist, that reason alone can determine matters of fact, he cannot reject the third premise on the ground that it is not consistent with the conclusion of his argument. Furthermore, if he were to throw out the third premise in order to regain consistency, he would destroy his argument, for the third premise is essential to it. This form of the moral argument is therefore totally unsatisfactory.

Since Kant's argument, which was advanced in order to resolve a contradiction in his premises, terminates in a contradiction of its own, we must reexamine the three premises.

One of the three original premises must be abandoned or revised, since they cannot all be true together. We cannot deny the third premise, for it is grounded on the fact of humanity's finitude and moral weakness. Hence either the first or second premise must be false in its present form. Either human beings are not morally obligated to attain the highest good or they can be obligated to do that which is impossible.

Since Kant wants to show that the highest good can be the object of moral volition, let us assume for the moment that the first premise is true. We begin our analysis, then, by denying the second premise; that is, we affirm that a person can be obligated to do that which exceeds his or her power. Many interpreters of Kant insist that this is in fact Kant's view; they argue that according to Kant "ought implies can."[43] It is argued that, according to Kant, whatever a person is obligated to do – even if it is theoretically impossible – that person must be able to do and is morally accountable if he or she fails to do it. But if we interpret the phrase "ought implies can" in this fashion (that is, if we deny the second premise), we present, as an interpretation of Kant, a view which is diametrically opposed to his. It is both ambiguous and highly misleading to say that Kant believes that "ought" implies "can." On the other hand, it is quite correct to say that Kant holds that "ought" presupposes "can." If one is *really* obligated to do something, one must be *able* to do it. But it is also true that, if a person cannot do something, he or she is not obligated to do it. "Cannot" implies no obligation.

Suppose we consider the implications for Kant's ethical theory of the claim that one has an obligation to do that which is actually impossible. First of all, Kant would have to abandon his fundamental doctrine that duty applies only to free beings – the doctrine that freedom is the *ratio essendi* of the moral law.[44] Autonomy could no longer be an essential component of Kant's ethical theory. But clearly it is central to his thought that duty presupposes freedom as its necessary condition. Reason does not command without regard to human capacity; rather, reason makes no demands upon a human being that exceed his or her capacity, "for reason," Kant argues, "will not order him to do the impossible."[45] If a person is not free to do something, he or she cannot be obligated to do it. Kant does not hold that the degree of freedom depends upon the degree of responsibility. To the contrary, he insists that "the degree of responsibility depends on the degree of freedom."[46] Accordingly, Kant says,

> Man *himself* must make or have made himself into whatever, in a moral sense, whether good or evil, he is or is to become. Either condition must be an effect of his free choice; for

43 For a typical account of this view see Doescher, "Kant's Postulate of Practical Freedom," 199ff. See also Stuart Brown, "Does Ought Imply Can?".

44 KpV, 4: CprR, 119.

45 Anth, 148: AN, 39. This is my translation.

46 VüE, 71: LoE, 62; cf. MS, 228: MOM, 382.

> otherwise he could not be held responsible for it and could therefore be *morally* neither good nor evil.[47]

To my knowledge, Kant never suggests, not even in a single passage, that moral responsibility can be grounded on anything other than human freedom.

In developing this fundamental principle, Kant *explicitly* argues from the impossibility of something to its unsuitability as a command of the moral law.[48] For example, Kant argues that no one has a duty to attain the virtue of others (which is incidentally a part of the highest good) because "it is self-contradictory to require that I do (make it my duty to do) something that only the other himself can do."[49] Since virtue is judged on the basis of one's own exercise of freedom, and since one can never be free for another person, one can never be obligated to attain another's moral perfection. There are numerous additional examples in which Kant argues along precisely the same lines. Among them, we note the argument that one can never be obligated to love God or one's neighbor if love be regarded as an emotionally grounded inclination. Kant reasons as follows:

> But love to God as inclination (pathological love) is impossible, for He is not an object of the senses. The latter [love as inclination] is indeed possible toward men, but it cannot be commanded, for it is not possible for man to love someone merely on command.[50]

Here again Kant argues that impossibility implies no obligability.

Thus Kant cannot abandon the second premise that a human being is never obligated to do the impossible; instead, he must abandon or alter the first premise that a human is duty-bound fully to attain the highest good. The highest good continues to be the object of volition, the necessary object of pure practical reason, and the canon of pure reason. But in regard to duty, Kant must be interpreted to hold that humans are obligated not to attain in full, but rather to approximate the highest good to the fullest extent possible. By means of this refinement, the contradiction between the first premise and the other two is

---

47 RGV, 44: Rel, 40.
48 We noted this very argument as a component in the moral argument which we examined. See KpV, 124: CprR, 218.
49 MS, 386: MOM, 518.
50 KpV, 83: CprR, 190. In his *Lectures on Ethics* Kant says, "Love is good-will from inclination. Now whatever depends upon my inclination and not upon my will cannot be laid upon me as a duty. I certainly cannot love at will, but only when I have an impulse to love" (VüE, 207: LoE, 192).

resolved. According to this interpretation – which is offered by Kant himself, though not always adhered to – we are not morally obligated to attain the highest good; rather, we are obligated to take this idea as an ideal, "as a model for the determination of our will."[51] As a demand of reason, as reason's ultimate end, the highest good continues to be an object of rational striving. But, because moral obligation cannot transcend the actual freedom and capacity of the moral agent, the idea of the highest good cannot define the extent of one's actual moral responsibility. It serves instead as the model to guide moral action. We are not duty-bound to attain in full the highest good, but to attain that part of "the highest good *possible through our collaboration*."[52] We have "a duty to realize the highest good *as far as it* lies within our power to do so."[53] As defined by the moral law our duty is not to *attain* but to *promote* with all our strength the highest good as the object and final end of pure practical reason.[54] Our strength is adequate to some of the demands contained within the idea of the highest good but insufficient to others. Each person is obligated to attain his own virtue, for this aspect of the highest good lies within his power.[55] One is not obligated, however, to attain the virtue of others nor the happiness (without qualification of degree) of oneself or others, for these aspects of the highest good are not possible of attainment. In regard to happiness, we are obligated only insofar as happiness "lies in our power ... [because the] fulfillment of duty consists in the form of the earnest will, not in the intervening causes that contribute to success."[56] We are obligated, thus, to attain only as much of the highest good as possible.

By restricting a human being's obligation to the actual limits of his or her capacity, that is, by defining the necessary object of moral volition as the duty to *promote* rather than to *attain* the highest good, Kant succeeds in making the idea of the highest good immanent in the life of humankind. The moral law, which poses the idea of the highest good as the material object of moral volition, is no longer threatened by the impossibility of the object which it demands. The good to which human beings are obligated now lies within their power to attain and is no longer utterly transcendent and irrelevant to them as beings of finite capacities.

51 KpV, 43: CprR, 154.
52 TP, 280n: TaP, 47n. The italics are mine. In the German this quotation reads: "als das höchste auch durch unsere Mitwirkung mögliche Gut."
53 KpV, 144n: CprR, 245n. The italics are mine.
54 Ibid., 142: ibid., 244; cf. RGV, 7–8n: Rel, 7n.
55 KU, 470, 472: CoTJ, 144–145.
56 Ibid., 451: ibid., 120.

3 The Transcendence of the Highest Good

By means of an immanent interpretation, Kant has solved the problem of assuring the possibility of the highest good as the object of volition. Kant now faces the problem of maintaining the normative character of the good. We are morally obligated to promote the highest good to the full limits of our power. But how do we determine the limits of our power? If one appears to violate the moral law, why may one not excuse one's action on the grounds of incapacity? Kant asks, "who knows what drove him to it? With his temperament, his wickedness may be no greater than a trifling fault of my own."[57] Thus a person may be judged guilty "though he is a victim of circumstances and temptation."[58] How, one may ask, can we ever know that we have an obligation, since we can never know whether or not we have the ability to fulfill it? Having argued that duty cannot exceed capacity, how can Kant defend his theory against attack by individuals who justify their lack of virtue and goodness on grounds of moral incapacity?

At this point the necessity and importance of the idea of the highest good as the transcendent object of pure practical reason becomes apparent. Although no one is obligated to do that which is impossible, neither can one define one's capacity in terms of actual performance. Both individually and generically, human beings cannot determine what they are capable of doing, and hence what they are accountable for doing, by observing what they have already done. Nor can one excuse oneself for having failed to do something merely on the grounds that one did not do it. If one were to argue that it is impossible for one to do anything which he or she has not already done, one would argue away most of one's real capacities. One may very well be free and able to attain a certain object or perform a certain task without being able to prove one's ability to do so in advance. The reason, as Kant notes, is simple: "as a rule we only first learn to know our powers by making trial of them."[59] This being so, the moral

---

57 VüE, 212: LoE, 197.

58 Ibid., 229: ibid., 213.

59 KU, 178n: CoAJ, 17n. Kant expresses this point with great clarity in the first "Introduction" to the third *Critique:* "In this, as in all else, nature seems to me to have made its arrangements wisely. For if we were not determined to apply our powers by the representation of an object until we had made sure of the adequacy of our capacity for producing it, then the latter would remain mostly unused. For we commonly learn to know our powers only by trying them out. Nature has therefore combined the determination of our power with the representation of the object even prior to knowledge of our capacity, which is often first brought forth precisely by this striving, which initially seemed to the mind itself to be an empty wish." (EEKU, 231n: CoPJ, 32n).

law – without exceeding the limitations either of human nature or of the particular human being in question – may indeed obligate a person to do that which he or she has never done before or never thought himself or herself capable of doing. One may be morally obligated, therefore, to attain a more complete embodiment of the highest good than one has ever achieved before. Thus Kant insists that: "Nothing is more reprehensible than to derive the laws prescribing what *ought to be done* from what *is done,* or to impose upon them the limits by which the latter is circumscribed."[60] Since the full limits of freedom and potentiality cannot be determined by an examination of actuality, the moral law, which can demand no more of a person than he or she is able to do, may demand far more than one *actually* does or even *shows* oneself capable of doing. Hence, although Kant makes the highest good immanent in the life of human beings by restricting their moral responsibility for its attainment to the actual limits of their freedom, he consistently argues that this idea of the highest good presents a moral obligation that is transcendent from the standpoint of human beings' actual performance.[61]

The inadequacy of a moral theory based on the observation of what actually takes place does not consist merely in the fact that the observation of actuality fails to reveal the full reaches of potentiality; it consists also in the fact that the observation of what happens can never reveal freedom at all. Positive knowledge both of the fact of our freedom and of its limits can be derived solely by reference to the moral law. Kant argues that

> the concept of the freedom of the will [*Willkür*] does not precede the consciousness of the moral law in us but is deduced from the determinability of our will by this law as an unconditional command. Of this we can soon be convinced by asking ourselves whether we are certainly and immediately conscious of power to overcome, by a firm resolve, every incentive, however great, to transgression .... Everyone will have to admit that he *does not know* whether, were such a situation to arise, he would not be shaken in his resolution. Still, duty commands him unconditionally: he *ought* to remain true to his resolve; and thence he rightly *concludes* that he must *be able* to do so, and that his will is therefore free.[62]

---

60 KrV, B375: CpR, 313. G. E. Moore should have borne in mind this statement and many others like it before charging Kant with having committed the naturalistic fallacy. In fact this quotation states the principle of the naturalistic fallacy in a much clearer manner than Moore was ever to express it.

61 Kant warns against ethical naturalism in the essay "Toward Eternal Peace." Here he writes, "[Politicians] make a great show of understanding *men* (which is certainly something to be expected of them, since they have to deal with so many) without understanding *man* and what can be made of him" (ZeF, 374: TEP, 334). Kant uses the word "Menschen" for both "men" and "man." The first is plural, the second is the generalizing singular.

62 RGV, 49n: Rel, 45n.

The moral law provides us with the only standard by which we can measure the extent of our powers and consequently our freedom. Thus the moral law is the *ratio cognoscendi* of our freedom.

We discover here an additional meaning of the phrase "ought implies can." We noted earlier that the phrase means that obligation presupposes freedom and that the denial of freedom implies the denial of obligability. We find now that the phrase has an additional significance of great epistemological importance for ethics. "Ought" implies "can" in the sense that the moral law provides us with the only, and therefore the best, positive indication of the extent of our freedom. "Ought" implies "can" in the sense that, apart from some direct proof of the impossibility of an action (in the face of which the moral law does not command), we must accept as valid the estimate of our powers which the moral law sets forth in the projection of the highest good. Apart from a direct proof of the impossibility of an action, we have no ground upon which to question the validity of an obligation; the only way we can prove that we are not obligated to attain in full the highest good as the object of the moral law is to prove by striving that we are incapable of it.

One may overestimate one's powers, of course, so that one may actually fulfill the demand of the moral law by exhausting one's capacities while failing to attain as complete a realization of the highest good as one thought oneself able and hence obligated to do. Kant does not hold that such a person is necessarily guilty simply by failing to attain as much of the highest good as he or she presumed himself or herself obligated to attain on the basis of a personal assessment of duty. Since one's obligation is fulfilled as soon as one actually exhausts one's powers in the partial attainment of the highest good, one may actually fulfill his or her duty while failing to attain in full the highest good.[63] It might seem therefore that Kant could dispense with the idea of the highest good altogether and argue merely

> that the rule, Do the most perfect thing that can be done by you is the primary formal principle of all obligation of commission, and the proposition Refrain from that whereby the greatest perfection possible through you is hindered is the primary formal principle with respect to the duty of omission.[64]

The substitution of these two complementary, formal principles of moral obligation for the idea of the highest good will not suffice, however, for as formal

63 VüE, 141: LoE, 128.
64 Untersuchung, 298: Inquiry, 283.

principles they are completely devoid of content. No one can gain any idea of the extent of his or her freedom or of the concrete nature of the goal toward which he or she must strive by reference to these principles alone. Without the highest good as the concrete object of volition no person could avoid underestimating his or her freedom and capacities.

Only the demand of the law to attain that which is totally beyond human capacity, at least as far as one can tell from experience, leads one to supreme effort and striving, and to a realization of the true limits of one's freedom. In terms of the idea of the highest good, a human being *estimates* the extent of his power and freedom.[65] And although this estimate is not necessarily correct, an error in estimation is not serious from a moral standpoint so long as one does not underestimate one's capacity. Overestimation is not serious because one's moral worth is determined by reference to one's *actual* freedom and not by reference to one's *estimate* of it. The moral agent, of course, may remain in ignorance of the full extent of his or her own virtue or vice. But a person need not know that he or she is good or evil in order to be so; hence, on this matter heaven can judge.[66]

If, however, the moral law did not confront human beings with the *total realization* of the highest good as the object of their practical reason in terms of which they are to estimate their capacity and the adequacy of their striving, humans would have to determine their obligation by reference to present and past performances, and the moral law would cease to function as an adequate normative principle. Each person could conclude with full justification that what he or she was doing was indeed the most perfect thing he or she could do. Since the upper limits of potentiality are never approached, much less attained, apart from desperate striving by an individual for that which he or she can never know himself or herself to be capable of in advance of its attainment, the full limits of one's capacities would never be engaged for the purposes of moral obligation unless that obligation were presented in terms of a transcendent idea of reason. By being forced to *estimate* one's powers and measure one's striving against a transcendent standard, the person who is faithful in the exercise of duty cannot fail to do all that is within his or her power to attain the highest good and thereby present himself or herself blameless before the moral law.[67] For this reason – and not because we are actually obligated to do the impossible – Kant insists that

65 A high jumper, for example, determines the extent of his or her ability by moving the bar higher and higher until he or she can no longer clear it. Then and only then he or she discovers his or her limits in this regard.

66 VüE, 229: LoE, 213.

67 This is not to suggest that there is such a person.

> moral laws must never take human weakness into account, but must be enunciated in their perfect holiness, purity and morality, without any regard to man's actual constitution .... The law in itself must be pure and holy, for the reason that it must be a model, a pattern, a standard, and as such must be exact and precise or it could not be a basis of judgment. It is, therefore, our highest duty to present the moral law in all its purity and holiness, as it is the height of transgression to detract a whit from its purity.[68]

The moral law and its object are taken in their purity because it is only in this way that they can serve as standards for moral judgment and bring human beings to the full awareness of themselves as autonomous.

At the same time, however (and I only repeat this point because it is so far removed from the traditional interpretation of Kant), a person's actual moral responsibility is not judged by reference to the highest good as the transcendent idea of pure reason. The idea of the highest good as transcendent – that is, the idea of the highest good as the object which a human being is obligated to *attain* in full – is the measure that one uses in assessing the limits of one's capacity. Such a standard assures against underestimation of one's capacities and hence of what may be one's duties. But the idea of the highest good as immanent – that is, the idea of the highest good as the object which human beings are obligated to *promote* to the full extent of their powers – is the measure which specifies a person's actual moral obligation.

The idea of the highest good, both as immanent and as transcendent, expresses in greater concreteness the objectives of the principles, "Do the most perfect thing that can be done by you," and "Refrain from that whereby the greatest perfection possible through you is hindered." As immanent, the highest good defines the limits of human beings' moral responsibility within the limits of their actual capacity. While Kant insists on presenting the highest good as transcendent in its employment as the ideal measure for human striving, he also insists on presenting it as immanent in its employment as the measure of moral accountability.

Therefore, Kant rejects any attempt to present the highest good either as immanent or as transcendent in both employments. If the attempt is made to naturalize the concept of the highest good and make it immanent even in the former employment (as the measure of human capacity), Kant argues, "Nothing is more reprehensible than to derive the laws prescribing what *ought to be done* from what *is* done."[69] Kant states further that the

---

68 VüE, 75: LoE, 66–67; cf. KrV, B369–77: CpR, 309–314; MS, 216–7: MOM, 371–2; VPR (AA28), 994: LdR, 342.
69 KrV, B375: CpR, 313.

> moral law is given, as an apodictically certain fact, as it were, of pure reason, a fact of which we are *a priori* conscious, even if it be granted that no example could be found in which it has been followed exactly.[70]

On the other hand, any theory which attempts to present the highest good as transcendent in the latter employment (as the measure of the actual moral accountability of human beings) is rejected by Kant as an ethics of illusion. Such an ethics, according to Kant, takes

> for actual what is in fact ideal .... It will therefore envisage a perfection, but a perfection to which we cannot attain, because it is not proportionate to human nature .... Such ethics is fanciful and visionary.[71]

Kant's understanding of the idea of the highest good – in terms of which it must be both immanent and transcendent, depending upon the use made of it – is reflected in his conception of the idea of holiness as an aspect of the highest good. Although Kant rejects the idea of holiness of the will as a component of the highest good in its immanent role (a person cannot be held responsible for its attainment since its attainment transcends his or her capacity), he nonetheless accepts this idea as a component of the highest good in its transcendent role; thus he asserts, "This holiness of the will is, however, a practical ideal which must necessarily serve as a model which all finite beings must strive after even though they cannot reach it."[72] Neither merely transcendent nor merely immanent, the idea of the highest good is both transcendent and immanent depending upon the use to be made of it.

4 The Constitutive Immanence and Regulative Transcendence of the Highest Good

Although complex and at times confusing, Kant's doctrine of the highest good is not just a highly subtle doctrine but is also remarkably well suited to the burden it must carry in his ethical theory. The idea of the highest good is not merely the object of moral volition; it is likewise an idea of pure reason, the canon of pure reason, the final idea toward which all rational striving is directed. As such, it is

---

70 KpV, 47: CprR, 157.
71 VüE, 90: LoE, 78.
72 KpV, 32: CprR, 144.

incapable of realization in the world of the senses. At the same time, however, Kant insists that it must be capable of realization lest the law that commands it be discredited as illusory and false. Recognizing these apparently contradictory aspects of the highest good – its obvious transcendence as an idea of reason and its necessary immanence as the obligatory object of moral volition – Kant presents the duty of human beings with regard to the highest good in two radically different ways. On the one hand, Kant often asserts that it is one's duty fully *to attain* the highest good. On the other hand, he often asserts that it is a human being's duty merely *to promote* the highest good to the full extent of his or her power. In passages of the former type he stresses the transcendence of the highest good as an idea of reason. In passages of the latter type he emphasizes its immanence as the object of volition.

But Kant never offers a systematic clarification of these divergent references to the highest good, nor does he explain how the highest good can be at once both incapable of realization and definitive of human obligation. Rather, he continues to express the duty of human beings in both ways – in terms of both immanence and transcendence – regardless of the confusion, and even contradiction, that ensues.

In order to bring some systematic unity into Kant's doctrine of the highest good while holding fast to his insistence on both the immanence and the transcendence of the good, I have sought to clarify Kant's position by analyzing the relation of the moral law to freedom, that is, the relation of "ought" to "can." Kant never says that the moral law is the essence of freedom or that freedom gives us knowledge of our obligations. Neither does he suggest that "ought" and "can" are equivalent terms. Rather, he says that experience of obligation leads us to knowledge of our freedom or capacity, whereas our freedom or capacity lies at the core of any obligation as the essential condition of its validity. Kant's words are these:

> To avoid having anyone imagine that there is an inconsistency when I say that freedom is the condition of the moral law and later assert that the moral law is the only condition under which freedom can be known, I will only remind the reader that, though freedom is certainly the *ratio essendi* of the moral law, the latter is the *ratio cognoscendi* of freedom. For had not the moral law already been distinctly thought in our reason, we would never have been justified in assuming anything like freedom, even though it is not self-contradictory. But if there were no freedom, the moral law would never have been encountered in us.[73]

73 KpV, 4n: CprR, 119n.

I have interpreted these words, with the support of many other passages and with the support of several basic doctrines of Kant's ethics, to mean that "ought" presupposes freedom, and hence that the general experience of moral obligation cannot be understood apart from the presupposition of freedom as its transcendental condition. But this is not to say that any particular expression of moral obligation in regard to concrete actions proves, apart from all evidence regarding the world of the senses, that the action which is demanded is possible. It seems to me, rather, that the experience of the command of the law provides us with a guide which is more accurate in the estimation of the limits of our freedom and potentiality than any other guide we have. At the same time, I have interpreted Kant to hold that in the absence of freedom there can be no moral obligation, and therefore, that any proof of the impossibility of an action constitutes clear proof of the absence of any duty to perform it. Thus I have argued that the general experience of obligation proves the reality of freedom; that impossibility unequivocally implies the absence of obligation; that a particular obligation provides the soundest, though not an infallible, guide in the estimation of our freedom; that direct proof of the impossibility of an act thought to be obligatory constitutes direct proof that it is not; and that in light of this analysis of the relation of "ought" to "can," the moral argument – regardless of its mode of presentation – provides no solution to the problem of explaining the immanence in moral volition of the transcendent idea of the highest good.

To solve the problem of explaining how the highest good as a transcendent idea of reason can at the same time be the immanent object of moral volition, two basic questions must be answered. First, how can the highest good be possible without losing its transcendence? And second, how can the highest good be immanent without losing its normative character? Inasmuch as the problem is one of relating an obligation which seems transcendent to a free moral agent whose freedom can never be transcendent, the solution should be found in a further examination of the relation of the moral law to freedom.

Whereas freedom, as the *ratio essendi* of the moral law, is a constitutive component of obligation, the moral law as the *ratio cognoscendi* of freedom can be either constitutive or regulative in regard to freedom, since knowledge can be either regulative or constitutive. Obligation can be presented as a constitutive requirement which the will must fulfill in its exercise of its freedom, or it can be presented as a regulative requirement that the will regard itself according to the idea of an obligation whether or not it has the capacity to fulfill that obligation. The distinction between regulative and constitutive obligation turns on the kind of knowledge that is afforded by the use of the obligation in moral decision. An obligation is constitutive if it provides the standard in terms of which one must assess one's actual, constitutive moral character. An obligation is regulative if it provides the standard in terms of which the will may estimate the extent of its freedom and capacity. No obligation which exceeds the power of the will can be a constitutive obligation, for the will can be held accountable only for the exercise of its freedom. A contradiction would follow were one to hold a person fully accountable for that which he or she was not free to do. An obligation may be regulative, however, even if it is in fact impossible. No contradiction follows from thinking oneself capable of doing something that in fact is impossible.

By employing this distinction between constitutive and regulative obligation, we can understand the obligatory character of the highest good even in its transcendence. Suppose our duty is presented as the command fully to attain the highest good. This command transcends a human being's finite capacity; it is impossible of fulfillment. Hence if this command is regarded as a constitutive employment of the moral law and if a person's actual moral worth is to be judged on the basis of his or her fulfillment of this command, it must be regarded as false. It is false because an assessment is made of the actual quality of the person's will in terms of an impossible standard. The actual impossibility of the idea implies the actual impossibility of its being related constitutively to the will as duty.

If, however, the total realization of the highest good is related to the will regulatively rather than constitutively, the highest good in its *transcendence* is not an impossible object of volition. It is quite possible for the will to use the idea of the full attainment of the highest good as a regulative principle in terms of which to estimate the extent of its freedom. The moral agent gains direction in the exercise of his or her will by acting as though the full attainment of the highest good were his or her duty, and therefore as though his or her freedom and power were adequate to its attainment. Thinking in terms of this regulative principle, one may then formulate one's obligation in the most strenuous terms and fully exhaust one's capacity in striving to attain this transcendent object.

If the will is to be categorically obligated to make the highest good the object of moral volition (as Kant insists), the highest good must be related to the will as a constitutive obligation in terms of which the moral worth of the will can be ascertained.[74] But if the will is constitutively obligated to the highest good, the fulfillment of this obligation must be within the power of the will. Just as no constitutive judgment of the will can be made if the norm for that

---

74 Only an omniscient being would be capable of assessing the *actual* moral worth of a person. But in making this assessment such a being would employ as its standard the highest good in its immanent role.

judgment exceeds the capacity of the will, likewise no constitutive obligation can obtain apart from the presence of freedom as its essence. For the purpose, therefore, of a constitutive employment of the idea of the highest good, a person's duty must be presented as the obligation to *promote* the attainment of the highest good to the fullest extent of his or her powers. When his duty is presented in this way, the object of one's volition is the idea of the highest good as immanent rather than transcendent, as possible rather than impossible. Since it lies within a person's power to promote the highest good to the full extent of his or her powers, success or failure in attaining as complete an embodiment of the highest good *as one is able to attain* can be imputed to a person constitutively. One may be regarded as a morally good or bad person on the basis of his or her performance. Without committing himself to the contradictory view that humans are morally obligated to do the impossible, Kant can present the highest good both as the necessary object of moral volition and as the standard in terms of which a constitutive judgment of moral worth can be made.

The complete statement of a person's duty is not expressed, however, in terms of the immanent idea of the highest good, which confronts human beings with the constitutive obligation to promote the highest good to the full extent of their powers. Without the transcendent idea of the highest good as the object of volition, human beings would have to judge themselves by reference to what they and others had actually done because they would have no other way of estimating the extent of their freedom and moral responsibility. But obligation does not express what persons have done; it states rather what they *ought to do*. Consequently, obligation may far exceed actuality; it is constrained only by the limits of possibility. And one cannot determine the limits of one's freedom and obligation by reference to actuality any better than one can determine his or her obligation by this means. Since the will cannot determine the limits of its own power in advance of striving, the will cannot have the slightest confidence of attaining even that part of the highest good that does lie within its powers unless it strives to do that which exceeds its known capacities. Unless, therefore, the highest good as transcendent is related to the will as the standard for estimating its freedom, the will must inevitably sell short its freedom and autonomy and acquire thereby constitutive moral guilt for its failure to fulfill even the highest good as immanent.

The demand of the moral law is not stated completely, therefore, as the constitutive demand to *promote* the highest good. The complete demand of the law also involves the duty to make a regulative employment of the transcendent idea of the highest good. The moral law must pose the *attainment* of the highest good as the necessary object of the will in order to carry out its function as the *ratio cognoscendi* of freedom. That is, the moral law must determine an object for the will in terms of which the full limits of human freedom can be exhausted. One is not obligated to suppose that one possesses the power to fulfill this transcendent demand; one is obligated, however, to estimate one's powers by reference to this idea so that one can never gain a false sense of security about one's moral worth until having exhausted in fact one's full power in the attempt to attain the highest good.

One cannot fulfill one's constitutive obligation to *promote* the highest good until one has estimated his or her power by reference to the regulative obligation to *attain* the highest good. This regulative obligation, by virtue of its transcendence, poses a task for the will that does in fact exceed its powers and thereby enables it to reach the limits of its constitutive obligation. Thus even the transcendent idea of the highest good is a necessary object of moral volition, though of course the will is obligated to make merely a regulative, rather than a constitutive, use of this transcendent object.

The wisdom implicit in Kant's admittedly confusing statements of human obligation with regard to the highest good is now explicit. The highest good *both as immanent and as transcendent* is the necessary and therefore possible object of moral volition. The possibility of the highest good as transcendent is assured by means of its regulative employment; its possibility as immanent is assured by the fact of its immanence. The necessity of the highest good as immanent is assured by means of its constitutive employment; its necessity as transcendent is assured because its employment as a regulative principle is a necessary condition of its fulfillment as an immanent constitutive principle. Thus the problem of relating the transcendent, impossible idea of the highest good to the will of humanity as its necessary, immanent, and possible object is resolved. Kant can account for both the transcendence and the immanence, the possibility and the necessity of this object.

As the moral agent seeks to reorder the sensible world in terms of the highest good as the idea of a morally-ordered world, the metaphysician seeks a unitary apprehension of the world as a systematic totality in terms of the interrelation and subordination of the various ideas and employments of pure reason by reference to the highest good as the canon of pure reason.

Chapter VII: The Moral Task: The Embodiment Of The Highest Good

1 The Moral Task as the Creation of Moral Schemata

Kant held that in all theories making reference to objects of intuition there must be a concern both for the theoretical formulation of the objects in question and for the practical application of that formulation. It cannot be said of such theories that they are true in theory but not in practice. Because they purport to offer a theoretical statement of practical occurrences, they cannot have theoretical validity unless they also have practical validity as well. Were an engineer or an artilleryman to suggest that the laws of mechanics hold true in theory but are of no use in building bridges or firing cannons, he or she would be regarded either as a comedian or a fool.[1]

The old saying "it may be true in theory but it doesn't work in practice" is nonsense when applied to science. If what ought to happen according to a scientific theory does not happen, the failure in practice indicates a failure in theory. But as regards ethical theory, if what ought to happen according to an ethical theory does not happen, the failure in practice may indicate merely the failure of a moral agent who has not done his or her duty. The old saying still makes sense. The validity of the moral law does not depend upon the actual fulfillment of all duties. The lapse of a single moral agent or even a large number of agents does not prove the ethical theory is invalid in practice, for it may correctly specify the guilt of the wayward agent. The ethical theory can therefore be sound without regard to the action that follows from it. But the old saying is still true in the ethical domain in the sense that what the ethics demands in theory must be what ought to be done in practice. In both science and ethics, practice must in ways appropriate to each domain be consonant with theory. Neither science nor ethics is theoretically sound unless it is also sound in practice.

The moral law demands that reason be practical, and reason as practical is always directed to the *existence* of something as a consequence of its agency.[2] The concept of duty is not an empty rational concept; rather, it has an essential relation to practice. It must therefore be possible to apply the concept of duty in experience. Kant argues,

---

1 TP, 276–277: TaP, 42–43.

2 KpV, 139: CprR, 241.

> For the pursuit of a certain *effect* of our will would be no duty if the effect were not also possible in *experience* [*Erfahrung*] (whether conceived as complete, or as constantly approaching completion).[3]

Kant's ethical theory is incomplete until he has shown that its application in experience is possible. That is, he must show both what duty requires in the daily life of the moral agent and that nothing other than the weakness or wickedness of the moral agent prevents the practical enactment of his or her duty.

Kant adumbrated the completeness of his ethics through its sound application by insisting that the moral law is not merely the supreme principle of obligation, but also the principle guiding the will in the determination of the good as the material object of volition.[4] The moral law requires that reason (or persons as rational beings) strive to bring something into existence as a result of its agency. It projects an object not for the purpose of apprehension or appreciation but for the purpose of enactment.

> Pure reason, then, contains, not indeed in its speculative employment, but in that practical employment which is also moral, principles of the *possibility of experience* [*Erfahrung*], namely, of such actions as, in accordance with moral precepts *might* be [*konnten*] met with in the *history* of mankind ... referring to the sensible world, viewed, however, as being an object of pure reason in its practical employment.[5]

The object of moral volition, if it is to be encountered in the sensible world, must be presented as the union of the formal and material which are elements in all experience and existence. Kant settled on the concept of the highest good as the *necessary material* object of volition because it synthesizes the formal and material components in the manner needed for determining an object of moral volition capable of realization in the sensible world.

As we noted in the preceding chapter, Kant presents moral obligation as the duty to create, after the analogy of the Deity, a world in which the moral law is fully obeyed. This would be a world in which finite rational beings live in full accord with the moral law and seek their mutual happiness. By so presenting duty, Kant brings the nature of the moral task into sharper focus. The moral task is neither to accept the world as it is nor to try to escape from it; it is, rather, to

---

3 TP, 276–277: TaP, 42–43. My italics.
4 See Chapter II.
5 KrV, B835–36: CpR, 637.

reorder the sensible world in terms of the highest good as the idea of a moral world.[6]

By presenting the moral task as one of creating a moral order in sensibility, Kant suggests that it is somewhat analogous to the theoretical task of pure reason. In both moral and theoretical employments, reason is concerned to order experience – that is, to attain a systematic unity of percepts in accordance with principles. Thus, in both employments there must be both form and material content and their schematism by the exercise of the judgment of the knower or the moral agent. Just as percepts without concepts are blind in the theoretical employment, inclinations and desires without conceptual direction and control are blind and slavish in the moral employment.[7] And just as concepts without percepts are empty in the former employment, the moral law without desires and inclinations is empty and barren in the latter.[8]

The analogy between the moral and the theoretical tasks breaks down, however, once we move from a consideration of the components of the moral and theoretical employments of reason to a consideration of the way in which these components are combined in their respective employments. In order to point out this difference, let us look first to the theoretical employment.

In its theoretical employment, reason begins with sensible intuition and moves from intuition to concepts and finally to principles. It begins, moreover, with an ordered sense manifold. Percepts are given in sensible intuition in spatial and temporal patterns or, in Kant's language, under the forms of intuition, space and time. Space and time are transcendental schemata providing the necessary link between concepts and percepts by being homogeneous with both. As empirically real, space and time are homogeneous with percepts; they are nothing more or less than the *de facto* order of sequence and arrangement in which percepts occur, the extensional and sequential patterns of the percepts. As transcendentally ideal, space and time are *a priori* matrices defining the

6 See Chapter V.

7 This conviction was one that Kant arrived at early in his career. In a letter to Markus Herz in 1773, Kant says, "A merely pure concept of reason, however, cannot specify the laws or percepts of what is wholly sensory, because as regards this the concept is entirely indeterminate." (Br (AA10), 145: Corr, 140). The quotation not only reaffirms Kant's fundamental insistence that concepts alone are empty; it also reaffirms the need for reason to be involved with sensible inclination if it is to be the guide for moral conduct. Reason must itself be practical; it must be actual as the moral will, which is both reason and the faculty of desire, so that the laws reason specifies are applicable to what is sensory.
See also the 1763 treatise, Untersuchung, 298–299: Inquiry, 283–284. For a later statement (1786) of the need for a material component in ethics, see Orientiren, 136–137: Orient, 296.

8 KpV, 118: CprR, 222.

properties of objective spatial and temporal orders. As conceptual definitions of spatio-temporal order, they are homogeneous with the categories of the understanding. Thus they permit the synthesis of the perceptual and conceptual elements of theoretical knowledge.

Schematization is a process by which a concept is rendered intelligible through the help of something sensible. For schematization to be possible, there must be a commensurability between the sensible and the conceptual – there must be something that is homogeneous to both components. That which is homogeneous to both components Kant calls a schema,[9] and its function is to fit concepts for an empirical use.[10]

Schematism in the theoretical employment of reason is effected by the synthesizing action of imagination. This is a productive act of reason as judgment.[11] Kant claims no understanding of this activity for as a free activity of the intellective faculty, it is inscrutable. It is an art, says Kant, "concealed in the depths of the human soul, whose real modes of activity nature is hardly likely ever to allow us to discover."[12]

Although the nature of this schematic activity, as free and spontaneous, cannot be understood in any employment of reason, Kant shows that its possibility depends both on the commensurability of the sensible and the conceptual and the nature of that commensurability. It consists largely in the fact that the order and structure to be found in the objective, phenomenal world made determinate by the categories of the understanding is already present in the given perceptual order of the sense manifold, even though it is not recognized or understood prior to the application of the categories. For example, in sensible intuition there are temporal sequences[13] which, according to the rule for the determination of objective succession of events in time (the category of causality), are objective. That is, certain pairs or groups of representations in the given time order of sensible intuition are related according to a pattern of irreversible succession. This pattern in time provides the basis for the schematization of the category of causality which, as schematized, provides the objective determination of time in which the objective succession of irreversibly related representations is recognized.[14] Similarly, there are pairs or groups of represen-

9 KrV, B177ff.: CpR, 180ff.

10 Orientiren, 133: Orient, 293; cf. RGV, 65n: Rel, 59n.

11 KrV, B176ff.: CpR, 180ff.

12 Ibid., B180: ibid., 183.

13 A comparable exposition can be given for space. For the purposes of this discussion, however, the examination of only one of the schemata is sufficient.

14 See the Second Analogy, KrV, B232–256: CpR, 218–33.

tations in the given time order of sensible intuition which are related by a pattern of reversible succession. The reversibility of the pattern of succession in empirically given time provides the schema for the category of reciprocity. The reversibility of the pattern of succession is the mark of its subjectivity. Hence, representations related by this pattern are given determinate location as contemporaries in the objective time order through the application of the category of reciprocity.[15]

These illustrations clearly show what Kant understood by the commensurability of the conceptual and the sensible in time (or space) as a schema. The commensurability does not consist in one-to-one correlations but in the establishment of test situations for judgment as it applies the categories of the understanding to the sense manifold. As defined in pure intuition, time is a set of *a priori* properties. But time as given in sensible intuition is a *de facto* pattern of concrete representations. In the former mode, time is objective but empty and abstract. In the latter it is subjective, but concrete and full. Now the problem of theoretical knowledge can be described as the problem of the determination of the objective space-time order. This is the task of the understanding. Understanding determines the objective temporal order by testing the compatibility of the *de facto* order of the sense manifold with the *a priori* properties of order in objective time. To illustrate, since one of the *a priori* characteristics of the temporal order is its one-directionality, reversible sequences have no place within an objective time order. Time in its sensible and *a priori* aspects functions as a kind of Rosetta Stone for judgment. Sequences whose patterns are compatible with the objective *a priori* characteristics of time are placed in the objective time order determined by the application of the categories of the understanding.[16] Those sequences whose patterns are incompatible with the objective *a priori* characteristics of time are not included in the objective time order except as subjective successions in the inner sense of individual knowers as given time coordinates in the objective system.

By the presence of time in sensible intuition, both as a given ordering of sensibility and as an *a priori* standard of objective temporal order, the com-

15 See the Third Analogy, ibid., B256–62: ibid., 233–37.

16 One cannot argue with certainty from the irreversibility of a sequence to its objectivity, for additional perception may reveal a reversal of sequence. This is the limitation that scientific verification stands under. While an absence of causal connectedness can be proved by reference to a single observation of reversibility, the verification of causal connectedness can never be more than indirect since it rests merely on the fact that thus far no reversibility in sequence has been observed.

mensurability of sensible intuition with the forms of the understanding is assured, and the process of schematism whereby form and content are united in determinate, phenomenal experience is made possible. In the theoretical employment, consequently, reason begins with a sensibility in which form is already present as a guide to the application of concepts. The task of reason in this employment is not to reorder sensibility but merely to make explicit the order already present in it. The objective sequence of time is implicitly given. But no subject-knower can tell immediately which of his or her perceptions of sequence are objective and which are subjective. The objective ordering of time cannot be *known* until the knower applies the categories of the understanding (in this case the categories of relation) to the data of intuition by means of the test of reversibility. Thus the task of the knower in the theoretical employment is to discern but not to create the order that is given in sensibility. The task of the knower in the theoretical employment is merely to gain knowledge of the phenomenal world.

In the theoretical employment of reason, the human being, as knower, is primarily a spectator and an investigator, one whose problem is that of *discovering* the order implicit in the sensuous component of knowledge. This component is given to a person in a form that is already commensurate with the forms of understanding and, hence, in a form suitable for knowledge.

But in the moral employment of reason, the situation is very different. In order to succeed in its moral employment, in order to give expression in existence to the idea of the highest good, reason cannot accept the sensible order as given. As given it is devoid of moral form and, hence, is incommensurate with moral concepts. Reason as practical must strive, therefore, to create a new sensible order structured by the moral law.

Whereas in the theoretical employment, a rational being begins with intuition and seeks to apply concepts and principles to it, in the moral employment he or she follows a reverse procedure. In the attempt to fulfill the moral task, the moral agent begins with the principle of the moral law and by its application (still on the theoretical level) to the nature of humanity derives the concept of the highest good. But sensibility, structured by the highest good and in which the latter is embodied, is precisely what is lacking and what it is the task of the moral agent to produce.

The moral agent is not devoid of sensibility. His or her will is not merely a faculty of practical reason; it is also a sensuous faculty of desire. As a faculty of desire, the will contains the material for volition in the form of desires and inclinations. But if percepts in the context of theoretical knowledge are blind, we need a vocabulary to express the limitation of inclinations in the context of moral volition. Kant insists that "inclination, be it good-natured or otherwise, is blind and slavish."[17] The blindness of inclinations does not consist, however, in their being unintelligible or chaotic. There is well-ordered, inner experience of desires and inclinations, and there is considerable phenomenal experience of inclinations ordered by understanding. The blindness of inclinations consists in the fact that inclinations reveal nothing in themselves about their amenability or opposition to moral expression. Their slavishness consists in the fact that at every moment they constitute a threat to rational behavior by determining the self causally (slavishly) through sensation. Thus although the will has access to sensibility and is given sensible material prior to moral volition, this material as given is not morally ordered.

It is the responsibility of the moral agent so to order and redirect the content of the faculty of desire that he or she can achieve a material volition in which the form of the moral law is ingredient. That is, one has the duty to reorder the content of the faculty of desire in such a way that one's particular concrete volition will become an embodiment in intuition of the highest good. Desires and inclinations, the sensible content of the faculty of desire, blind and slavish though they may be, are necessary to the expression of the will and, hence, to the fulfillment of the moral task. The will must have access to sensible content if it is to present the moral law in intuition. And since the only access of the will to material content is through the faculty of desire, the content of the faculty of desire must provide the raw material for moral volition. The will must make use of this content in moral volitions even though it is not morally ordered as given.

This is a formidable demand. The difficulty of giving schematic expression to an idea of reason would appear insurmountable and thus would appear to preclude the structuring of sensible intuition in terms of the highest good.

A schema is precisely what is lacking in the moral situation. In the sensuous given of moral experience, which includes not only all the content of the moral agent's faculty of desire but also all of the agent's theoretical knowledge and inner experience, there is no ordering of representations or objects in terms of time as a schema of the highest good. Time is not a schema for the ideas of reason. While time as empirically real characterizes all areas of inner experience, it is not present in sensibility as the homogeneous third thing relating sensibility to the ideas of reason. Neither inclinations, nor inner sense in any of its aspects, has a *given* order in accordance with the idea of the highest good. There is no *given* sequence of time in which representations or objects are related to one another in such a way as to constitute a sensible embodiment of the highest good. There is no given moral ordering in intuition which can guide

17 KpV, 118: CprR, 222.

the moral agent. From the standpoint of the moral ideal of reason, sensibility is completely devoid of form, either conceptual or intuitional.

This should neither surprise nor alarm us. In the moral employment we are concerned with the will as agency, with reason as efficient cause, and with the causality of freedom as an agency which is not determined by sensibility. But if sensibility were adequate to the moral idea of reason, if there were a schema of the highest good, we would find ourselves in the morally absurd position of advocating that a person ought to do that which he or she is already constrained to do. If the highest good were already embodied in the sequence of temporal events, there would be no moral task at all. We would be talking of freedom and obligation in terms of a framework which ruled out both.[18] The moral task arises precisely from the fact that there is no morally ordered sensibility.

In order to be free, the moral agent must not be determined in his or her moral volition by an existing order of sensibility. It is the obligation of the moral agent to reorder the content of desire and of phenomenal experience in such a way that it becomes a morally ordered sensibility in which the moral law is embodied as a result of his or her volition. Thus Kant says, "Here, however, we are concerned not with the schema of a case occurring according to laws but with the schema (if this word is suitable here) of a law itself."[19] In the moral employment we cannot make determinate and plain to public gaze the instance of a concept by reference to a schema of it in experience; rather our task in morality is to produce the schema through an act of willing which others may indeed make explicit if they review a moral example by means of the moral law employed as a category. Our task in moral action is to *order* time as a schema for practical reason just as it is already given as a schema for the understanding. By our agency as moral subjects we must produce in inner experience that ordering of representations and objects that will be for ourselves and for all rational finite sensuous beings a rationally (morally) ordered sensibility – a world in which time is a schema for the moral law, a world in which the ordering of representations and objects is such that their relationship can be understood in terms of the categories of freedom,[20] a world which is not merely a natural world but which, as the embodiment of the highest good, is also a moral world.

---

18 KpV, 69ff.: CprR, 177ff.

19 Ibid., 69: ibid., 177.

20 Ibid., 67: ibid., 175. I have limited the discussion to a consideration of time as a moral schema for sake of brevity only. Space must also be ordered as a schema for the moral law.

2 The Symbolic Schematism of the Highest Good

In the preceding section we noted that the incommensurability of sensibility to the moral law, which consists in the absence of time as a moral schema, is not an insurmountable obstacle to the embodiment of the highest good. But we have not removed all the difficulties standing in the way of the embodiment of the highest good. The incommensurability of form and content in the moral employment consists not merely in the absence of time as a moral schema; it is far greater than this. Kant denies not only the reality of a moral schema as given (on the grounds that a given moral schema is a contradiction in terms); he also denies the possibility of offering a direct schema of any idea of reason.

> To call for a verification of the objective reality of rational concepts, i.e. of ideas ... is to demand an impossibility, because absolutely no intuition adequate to them can be given.[21]

The ideas of reason, including the moral idea of the highest good, are infinite ideas taking in the whole of reality, ideas which make an unconditional, absolute demand. I have suggested that the principle of totality is applied regulatively by reason for the benefit of the understanding, and that to this goal understanding can strive but not succeed. But the attainment of this goal of the systematic unity of nature is a demand of reason and not of the understanding. The schematism of the concepts of the understanding is possible and indeed actual in determining finite objects. That the infinite demand to relate all finite objects and all finite systems of experience into an infinite, homogeneous order of experience cannot be achieved does not detract from the limited objectification and finite ordering that is actually attained by means of the employment of the concepts of the understanding. Science attains knowledge; understanding stands secure in its theoretical inquiry on this less-than-final footing. From the standpoint of the understanding, the attainment of the infinite demand of reason is a luxury rather than a necessity.

In the moral employment of reason, however, we cannot restrict ourselves to limited concepts analogous to the categories of the understanding. The idea of the highest good as a transcendent idea of reason is the idea of a moral world. The embodiment of this idea requires the production of a world, a totality of experience each component of which occupies a position required by reason.

---

21 KU, 351: CoAJ, 221. See also KrV, B692, 693, 697, 707, 711: CpR, 546–7, 549, 555, 557–8; and KpV, 136, *passim*: CprR, 238, *passim*.

The highest good as a moral world cannot be embodied by means of isolated uncoordinated moral acts, but its embodiment is nevertheless the moral task. Its embodiment here is by no means the luxury that the idea of totality was in scientific inquiry. The moral demand of reason is not satisfied until the highest good is embodied. It is a demand upon existence and not merely upon knowledge.

The moral agent cannot be indifferent to his or her moral deficiency and that of other humans; nor can he or she be indifferent to the moral caprice of nature which frequently sets reason and sensibility at odds by rewarding the least rational and most corrupt of beings and by striking down and sensibly injuring the most reasonable, morally good persons. Kant suggests we consider a person who, taking the moral law seriously,

> allows the thought to occur to him (he can scarcely avoid doing so) of what sort of world he would create, under the guidance of practical reason, were such a thing in his power, a world into which, moreover, he would place himself as a member. He would not merely make the very choice which is determined by that moral idea of the highest good, were he vouchsafed solely the right to choose; *he would also will that [such] a world should by all means come into existence* (because the moral law demands that the highest good possible through our agency should be realized).[22]

The moral individual has, as his or her moral concern, the universe *in toto*. Omniscience and omnipotence are requisite powers for the attainment of the order demanded by the moral law that the universe be ordered by reason. The ideas of reason, and particularly the moral idea of the highest good, make an infinite demand and are not satisfied by finite attainments and embodiments.

A finite moral agent has trouble enough in controlling himself or herself, has little control over others and has practically no control over nature. In the face of these limitations he or she can never hope to provide a direct schema for the moral idea of reason. The schema cannot be attained in any single finite, narrowly restricted act (even if performed by God). And a human being is incapable, by virtue of human finitude, of any act more extensive than this. We see, therefore, that the moral agent lacks both wisdom and the power to transform time into a direct moral schema even if he or she had the good will to do so.[23]

---

22 RGV, 5: Rel, 5. My italics.

23 See the cited articles by Sharon Anderson-Gold, Jonathan Barnes, Yirmiyahu Yovel, and others who consider the task of realizing the highest good from a standpoint of all of humanity over historical time.

The schematization of the moral idea of reason can only be envisaged in the concept of a “Kingdom of God” in which the ordering of nature is attuned to the moral demand by an all powerful being, and in which all rational beings within the boundaries of this morally-structured nature, by their autonomous willing, act in full yet free accord with the moral demand. This kingdom as a whole, this totality of finite natural events and finite moral actions, could present a sensible given in which time would be a moral as well as a theoretical schema. But nothing short of this totality would be adequate to the demand of this moral idea.

Since we lack both the power to *determine* other persons to rational action through their own agency (a contradictory idea) and the power to order nature in accordance with the moral law, what then is our task as moral individuals? As we noted earlier in this chapter, the moral task must be in some sense capable of fulfillment, yet the task of producing by our wills a direct schema of the moral law is impossible. Kant is quite explicit about the limits of sensible, intuitive embodiment of concepts and ideas. He summarizes his position on this point as follows:

> Intuitions are always required to verify the reality of our concepts. If the concepts are empirical the intuitions are called *examples*: if they are pure concepts of the understanding the intuitions go by the name of *schemata*. But to call for a verification of the objective reality of rational concepts, i.e., of ideas, and, what is more, on behalf of the theoretical cognition of such a reality, is to demand an impossibility, because absolutely no intuition adequate to them can be given.[24]

This then is our problem: *The moral idea of reason demands the empirical embodiment of the idea itself; yet there is no sensible, empirical intuition adequate to such an embodiment.* If the moral idea is left in this predicament, moral experience is reduced to illusion. If the best efforts of the best individuals are utterly inadequate as vehicles of the idea of reason, then it would seem that the best person’s life is not better than that of the worst.[25] Kant is keenly aware of this problem and makes a deliberate effort to solve it.

Although Kant never wavers in his insistence that the moral law be given a sensible manifestation, he does redefine the requirements of such a manifesta-

---

24 KU, 351: CoAJ, 221.

25 I have not forgotten that the morality of an act consists in the maxim of the will and not in the attainment of the end toward which the will was striving. On the other hand, we must not forget Kant’s insistence that there must be an object for every volition, his insistence that the object of volition which is demanded by the moral law must be capable of realization in experience, and his repudiation of all forms of ethical utopianism.

tion. As noted in the last chapter,[26] although Kant presents the rational demand of reason in terms of the complete sensible realization of the highest good, he does not suggest that the moral agent has a constitutive obligation to attain this realization. Kant holds, rather, that the moral agent is obligated merely to *promote* the attainment of the highest good to the full extent of his or her powers. To this end the moral agent is constitutively obligated to use the transcendent idea of the full attainment of the highest good merely as a regulative principle in the estimation of his or her power. Thus Kant suggests that one should judge oneself in terms of the absolute, transcendent idea of the highest good in its full purity, while at the same time he insists that the moral worth of a person is to be determined by the degree to which he or she exhausts himself or herself in achieving in existence what is merely an approximation of the complete embodiment of the highest good. We can describe the moral task of reason with accuracy as the task of determining time as a direct schema of the moral law. But because the total embodiment of the highest good would be a world in which the moral law were a constitutive category, we cannot describe the moral task of human beings in these terms. For reasons discussed in Chapter VI, we must try to describe the moral task by reference to a human being's immanent, constitutive duty to *promote* the highest good. We must try to describe the moral task in terms of an approximate embodiment by human beings of the highest good to the extent that it lies within their power.

Such an embodiment of the moral law cannot be called a schema, strictly speaking; it can nevertheless be called a symbol, an analogon of a schema. All meaningful concepts or ideas must have some sensible notion appended to them. Otherwise concepts would be devoid of empirical use. Since Kant defines the moral demand in such a way as to require an empirical employment, he must offer some sensible notion to give meaning to this moral idea. This cannot be done directly since the sensibility is not commensurate to the moral demand; hence, it must be done analogically.

Because the emphasis in the first *Critique* is placed on schematism as the act whereby judgment applies the concepts of the understanding to sensible intuitions in the determination of objects, one may very easily overlook the broader application of this process beyond the categories of the understanding. Under a broader interpretation, Kant refers to schematism as the process whereby a concept is rendered intelligible "by help of an *analogy* to something sensible."[27] It is according to this broader interpretation of schematism that

26 See Chapter VI.
27 RGV, 65n: Rel, 59n. Italics are mine.

Kant calls for the employment of the idea of totality as a principle for the guidance of science. Although Kant is unable to offer a direct schematism of an idea of reason, and although no fulfillment of this idea is possible in experience, there is an analogy to the schematism of this idea in the "idea of the maximum in the division and unification of the knowledge of the understanding under one principle."[28] Kant insists,

> The idea of reason is an analogon of a schema of sensibility; but with this difference, that the application of the concepts of the understanding to the schema of reason does not yield knowledge of the object itself (as is the case in the application of categories to their sensible schemata), but only a rule or principle for the systematic unity of all employment of the understanding.[29]

The idea of reason (totality) achieves considerable embodiment not directly through empirical schemata but through an analogously schematic relation to the understanding itself, in which relation the understanding itself is given the direction requisite to its successful employment.[30] The knowledge and experience attained by the understanding, as it is guided by means of the principle of the unity of nature and assisted by teleological judgment with the concept of finality, offers something analogous to the schematization of the idea of reason itself.

The seeds for a broad conception of the schematism are thus found in the first *Critique*, although it is not until later, until the third *Critique* and the *Anthropology*, that Kant gives a systematic presentation of this conception. In the second *Critique*, Kant reintroduces the understanding, with its form and content as the typic of pure practical judgment, as analogous to a schema of the moral idea of reason. Since this treatment is a parallel to the theoretical analogy we have just considered, we need not go into it at this point. In the *Critique of Judgment*, Kant finally offers an extended discussion in which he introduces a new generic term – hypotyposis[31] – to cover all activities of designation whereby sensibility is brought to bear upon concepts or ideas to afford them an empirical use. Of this activity Kant says,

> All hypotyposis (presentation, *subjectio sub adspectum*) as a rendering in terms of sense, is two-fold. Either it is *schematic*, as where the intuition corresponding to a concept

---

28 KrV, B693: CpR, 546.
29 Ibid., B693: ibid., 546–47.
30 Ibid., B671–2: ibid., 533.
31 In the *Anthropologie*, Kant refers to it as the faculty of designation (*facultas signatrix*). See Anth, 191: AN, 84.

> comprehended by the understanding is given *a priori*, or else it is *symbolic*, as where the concept is one which only reason can think, and to which no sensible intuition can be adequate.[32]

The source of similarity, the justification of analogy between the symbolic and schematic modes of hypotyposis, stems from the presence in both of the procedure of judgment. In the case of a symbolic hypotypose,

> the concept is supplied with an intuition such that the procedure of judgment in dealing with it is merely analogous to that which it observes in schematism. In other words, what agrees with the concept is merely the rule of this procedure, and not the intuition itself. Hence the agreement is merely in the form of reflection, and not in the content.[33]

But we are not to conclude that the symbolic mode of representation is opposed to the intuitive (schematic) mode. Judgment is able to proceed in a similar fashion in both cases only because "the intuitive mode of representation is, in fact, divisible into the *schematic* and the *symbolic*."[34] But both are hypotyposes (*Hypotyposen*) (*exhibitiones*) and not "symbols" in the modern logical sense of the term. Their sense is better designated perhaps by "signs" (*Zeichen*) rather than by "symbols." Signs designate concepts by means of sensible marks (*Anzeichen*); but the marks so used have no necessary or internal connection with the intuition of the object in question. The sole function of signs "is to afford a means of reinvoking the concepts according to the imagination's law of association – a purely subjective role."[35] Signs then are to be distinguished from true symbols with respect to the conventionality of their employment. Words and logical, mathematical, or musical signs are expressions for concepts without in any way providing an intuition of what is symbolic of the concept – that is, without ever providing an object that *represents* the concept even imperfectly and by analogy.

Under this broad conception of schematism, *a priori* concepts are given sensible, existential employment in intuitions which are either direct presentations of the concepts, that is, schemata, or indirect, that is, symbols. Kant's explanation of the schematization in denotations or marks stresses the importance of the creative employment of judgment as imagination. In his discussion of the attainment of the symbolic presentation of concepts by analogy, Kant

32 KU, 351: CoAJ, 221.
33 Ibid., 351: ibid., 221–22.
34 Ibid., 351: ibid., 222.
35 Ibid., 352: ibid., 222.

emphasizes again the important dual role of judgment. First, judgment must attain a schematic presentation of a concept by applying one or more concepts of the understanding to the manifold of sensible intuition in the determination of a sensible object. Second, judgment must then use this object as a symbol for (or sign of) the concept which is incapable of direct presentation. In this second task, judgment applies its rule of reflection on the object of intuition to a concept different from the one that was employed in making the object of intuition determinate so that by means of a process of judgment, the object of intuition becomes a symbolic presentation of the new concept. The symbolic hypotypose in this way provides an expression for concepts,

> without employing a direct intuition for the purpose, but only drawing upon an analogy with one, i.e., transferring the reflection upon an object of intuition to quite a new concept, and one with which perhaps no intuition could ever directly correspond.[36]

Kant is thus able to make some headway in meeting the demands of the ideas of reason by making them pertinent to sensible employment. Although the moral agent is utterly lacking in the capacity directly to embody the moral idea of reason, perhaps he or she is able to provide symbolic presentations of this idea. In the best of moral acts of the best of moral persons we can perhaps see the symbolic presentation of the moral idea of reason. The universal concern for the poor revealed in every act of Mother Teresa, for example, suggests a world ordered by unstinting compassion. We must not confuse this symbolic representation with a schematic one; on the other hand, we must not deprecate this symbolic representation for it does provide us with an intuitive, sensible dimension to moral experience that is essential to the reality of moral experience. In knowing one another as rational beings, we must appeal to the sensible manifestations of ourselves as symbols of what is more than phenomenal; yet we must not forget that these symbolic presentations are by no means directly revelatory of our noumenal natures. In symbolic hypotypose we find ourselves in a dialectical position between reason and sensibility, drawn toward both, but lost if we accede to either attraction.

We must not shrink from the use of symbols, for they are essential to the fulfillment of the moral life; without them, that life is either reduced to an inadequately normative naturalism or to an impossible and therefore vain utopianism. The transcendence of the moral demand, and the basic incommensurability of the ideas of reason and sensibility, force us to the symbolic mode

36 Ibid., 352–53: ibid., 223.

of presentation in order to make the transcendent moral demand immanent. We must use symbols if we are to make the highest good capable of significant embodiment. But the symbol must never be regarded as a direct manifestation of the idea of reason. To do so would involve the abandonment of the idea of reason altogether and the loss of an optimally normative ethics. That would leave us with only concepts of the understanding at best, and at worst, with nothing at all to restrain us from fantasy and fanaticism. We must, however, regard symbols as symbols, and recognize that the demand of this idea of reason remains transcendent, that is, unembodied in even the most adequate hypotypose.

This examination requires us to refine our earlier statement of the nature of the moral task. We can no longer suppose it to be the creation of space and time as moral schemata; rather, it is one which demands the presentation of space/ time as a symbolic structure for moral experience. We may continue to refer to time and space as moral schemata, but in so doing we must bear in mind that this is a use of "schema" in the indirect symbolic sense.

A concrete illustration of this task may be found in Kant's view of perfection. The charge of the Gospel is "Be ye perfect as your father in heaven is perfect." With understanding and interpretation, this is an acceptable statement of the moral demand of reason. Yet if perfection is conceived of in an unqualified way, we have seen that it can never be attained. There can be no hope of a direct schematic presentation of perfection. However, our sensible phenomenal acts can and ought to present a symbolic hypotypose of perfection. With this in mind, perfection, or holiness, can be understood as the immanent demand of the moral law, and the task for the moral will. Regarded symbolically, as the moral task confronting the individual, perfection (or holiness) is "the highest, most perfect moral good which we can derive from ourselves, from our understanding."[37] According to the symbolic interpretation of the moral task, the rule

> *Do the most perfect thing that can be done by you* is the primary formal principle of all obligation of commissions, and the proposition *Refrain from that whereby the greatest perfection possible through you is hindered* is the primary formal principle with respect to the duty of omission.[38]

That the moral task can be considered in its transcendent purity and still, as pure, be regarded as in some sense attainable in terms of the finite capacities of

37 VüE, 87: LoE, 75.
38 Untersuchung, 299: Inquiry, 283.

human beings is a view Kant held most of his philosophical life. The passage just quoted was published in 1763, and Kant reiterated this same point of view in the first and second *Critiques*, and in his lectures on ethics. But it was not until the third *Critique* that Kant finally introduced explicitly the symbolic conception of schematism in terms of which we can understand how the infinite and transcendent demand to embody the highest good can be maintained while at the same time the sensible realization of this idea is reduced to a point commensurate with the moral agent's capacity. In terms of the concept of the symbolic hypotypose, the phenomenal less-than-complete embodiment of the highest good by the less-than-perfect moral agent can be regarded as a genuine symbol of the complete and perfect attainment of the highest good. A person can now be understood to have attained a kind of moral perfection when his or her actions are *symbolic* of the complete attainment of the highest good. One's actions are to be regarded as symbolic of this demand when one wills specific concrete volitions determined by the faithful exercise of judgment in following the procedure used in applying the concepts of the understanding to sensibility. When judgment faithfully performs its theoretical schematic procedure in terms of the concept of the highest good in regard to the objects of sensibility and the content of the faculty of desire, judgment brings an order to the content of sensibility in which the concept of the highest good is symbolically present. This is also an order in which time and space are structured as schemata of the moral law.

This symbolic embodiment of the highest good is all that can be produced by a human being in experience, in sensible intuition; it is, therefore, all that can be constitutively demanded of him or her by the moral law. Although the transcendent demand of reason remains unattainable by human beings, it can be approximated by them as they fulfill the immanent demand of reason in the attainment of symbolic manifestations of this idea.

Through symbolic schematism Kant provides a means for practical as well as theoretical mediation between the infinite and the finite, the formal and the material. The finite ordering of sensibility that is symbolic of the infinite idea of reason may be regarded as a schema in the sense that by analogy it is homogeneous with both sensibility and with the idea of reason. It is homogeneous with both in that it has not been ordered merely in terms of the categories of the understanding but has been ordered by judgment which, though it has followed its usual procedure of schematism, has been guided not only by the categories of the understanding, but also by reference to the idea of the highest good. The symbolic embodiment is homogeneous, therefore, in the sense that the phenomenal order is structured by an activity of judgment that is directed by an idea of reason and not merely by the forms of sensible intuition and the categories of the understanding. Its homogeneity consists in its bringing into existence an ordering in space and time that transforms space and time to the limits of its extension and duration into moral schemata. Time itself is ordered by the symbolic form determined by judgment and produced in existence by moral volition. In the duration of the symbolic embodiment time is symbolically homogeneous with both sensibility and the idea of reason.

In order to make clearer the nature of the symbolically sensible embodiment as an analogical, homogeneous unity of both sensible immanence and conceptual transcendence, perhaps we should refer to this "schema" as an "incarnation." To use this term is to admit that it is to a degree inscrutable. But to call it this is to emphasize the difficulty that a moral theorist faces in trying to relate a truly normative standard of conduct to the life of the moral person. To refer to this schema as an incarnation is, moreover, to stress the creative and spontaneous volition that is required of the person who seeks to fulfill the moral demand. *Im Anfang war die Tat, nicht nur das Wort*. This is the idea we convey by referring to the symbolic embodiment as an incarnation. Here we are talking about the product of a free act which, as free, stands beyond full conceptualization. In the discussion of the embodiment of the highest good in experience, we can only point to ideas that are in a way analogous to that which we are trying to comprehend. In this light, the task confronting the moral agent is to live a life that oneself and others can regard as an "incarnation" of the moral idea of reason. The life of the moral person will never be infinite. But in its finitude it can give the *most complete* symbolic expression of the infinite that is within its finite power. The capacity of the sensibility to receive the infinite can be exhausted. In sensibility, the infinite is nevertheless made symbolically incarnate through the life of the moral agent.[39]

Let us now consider the agent whose creativity is responsible for this achievement. In terms of Kant's formulation of the moral task as the problem of producing a symbolic schematization of the highest good, we see at once that the moral agent cannot be an imitator. The moral agent cannot be directed from without, either indirectly by moral examples or directly by commands of

---

39 The symbolic expression of the highest good will be achieved, as we will note in Chapters VIII and IX, by the aid of both judgment and understanding. The understanding will provide the moral agent with a typic for the symbolic expression of the moral idea in the concept of natural law. Judgment will use this typic in carrying out the procedure of symbolic schematism. Furthermore, judgment in the idea of beauty and sublimity will offer a guide to the appreciation of moral demand by its symbolic exemplification (reflectively) in art and nature. (KpV, 68–69: CprR, 176–77); KU, 351ff.: CoAJ, 221ff.).

custom, religion, law or ethics.[40] The moral agent must be rational not historical; he or she must be autonomous and not heteronomous. On the basis of one's own free employment of one's reason and judgment one must determine for oneself the action which will be a symbolic representation of the highest good.

Just as we found the Kantian knower to be a revolutionary, creative Copernican, we now find the moral person to be a revolutionary, creative Rousseau. Rousseau's ethical discoveries were so important in Kant's judgment that he accords Rousseau the distinction of having done for morality what Newton did for science. Kant notes that

> Newton was the first to discern order and regularity in combination with great simplicity, where before him men had encountered disorder and unrelated diversity. Since Newton, the comets follow geometric orbits.
>
> Rousseau was the first who discovered underneath the manifoldness of the forms assumed by man his deeply hidden nature and the concealed law.[41]

Rousseau cut away the conventions of society to ground morality in the individual moral agent. He pointed to the way in which society and conventionality had robbed human beings of their essence, of their purity in direct and original action according to the dictates of their own reason. Kant saw this as the plea for autonomy and as the source of human dignity. This was Kant's interpretation of Rousseau's return to nature. According to Kant, it was not a simple-minded panegyric of forest-life; Kant saw in Rousseau's ideal of the noble savage in the

---

40 Allen Wood argues that Kant's assertion that humans could not have as a duty the promotion of the moral perfection of others is inconsistent with his moral theory because the moral good of others is an important component in Kant's conception of the highest good. Wood states, "The mutual improvement of men's moral characters through education and religious community play such an important role in Kant's overall view of the moral destiny of man that it is impossible to take as Kant's best thinking the passage cited in which he denies that one can promote the moral good of others." Rather, Wood argues, it is more logical to hold that "the moral good of *all* finite rational beings is the unqualified and unconditioned end of the finite rational moral agent." Wood, *Kant's Moral Religion*, 78. I do not think Wood's position is tenable because it is not consistent with Kant's ethical theory. Human beings cannot in any essential way assist others to moral perfection because no person can legislate for the will of another without in the process undermining the autonomy, freedom and responsibility of the other. Humans can only provide conditions that may reduce the temptation and hindrances others face in attempting to do their duty or offer incentives to virtuous action. But in either case the imputation of responsibility is reduced by this assistance which thus offers no real help in adding to another's moral perfection.
41 Hartenstein, 630: my translation. Cassirer, 18.

state of nature a poetic symbol standing in judgment on conventionality and *all* varieties of heteronomy.[42] It was this insight of Rousseau's which led Kant to his famous statement that there was a time when he despised the ignorant, common herd.

> Rousseau has set me right. This deluding advantage disappears; I learn to honor men, and would find myself much less useful than the common laborer if I did not believe that this contemplation is able to give worth to all others, to establish the rights of mankind.[43]

By tearing away the excesses and distracting accretions from the moral life, Rousseau revealed that life in a new and clearer light – in a light which revealed a unitary law beneath the hodge-podge of custom morality, a law which placed on each individual the demand of autonomous living and thereby endowed each with a dignity, a fundamental irrevocable worth.[44]

Rousseau, like Copernicus and Newton, forced a revolution in Kant's thinking. Rousseau's revolution found its way into Kantian philosophy in the concept of autonomy – in the awareness of the awful power and responsibility that falls upon each human being as a moral agent. The good, the right, the object of moral fervor, all these are products of individual human action. They are not external impositions of society or God.

Thus Rousseau led Kant to focus his attention on the full dimensions of human nature. He evidently reminded Kant of the presence in every person of practical reason – the ability to act independently of the demands of the

---

42 Anth, 325–27: AN, 231–2. Cassirer notes that Kant was one of the few of Rousseau's contemporaries who saw this profound significance in the plea for a return to nature and who did not interpret Rousseau in a direct, prosaic fashion, which would deprive Rousseau of serious attention from anyone who recognizes that one cannot develop as a full human being in utter isolation from one's fellows. For a detailed discussion of Rousseau's influence on Kant, see Cassirer, 1–18. We must note that Kant never accepted Rousseau's wholesale rejection of social convention and law.

43 Hartenstein, 624. My translation.

44 Schilpp insists that it is foolish to suppose that Kant took over these ideas from Rousseau, since they were a part of Kant's pietistic background. (Schilpp does agree that Rousseau was a great source of inspiration to Kant.) Schilpp's contention does not explain, however, why Kant praised Rousseau so lavishly and credited him as the source of these ideas. No doubt Kant's reflection on the beauty of his own home life, on the love and respect which pervaded his home in the midst of trade disputes among the harness-makers, prompts Schilpp to this suggestion. But over against this, we must recall Kant's abhorrence of the religious slavery he suffered under in the Collegium which may have blinded him to all the truth of pietism until Rousseau awakened him from his moral slumbers. See Schilpp, 49; Paulsen, 38–39; and Greene, xxviii. See also Kühn, 53–54.

sensible world and, instead, to act according to the demands of one's own rational, sensible nature. A human being so conceived is recognized by Kant as the agent of the symbolic schematism of the highest good. In order for an idea of reason to find expression in the sensible world – even a symbolic expression – there must be some direct contact, some commensurability, between reason and sensibility. The human being is the direct union of the sensible and the rational, existing in both the sensible world and the world of reason. As the object in the empirical world of the idea of freedom,[45] a human feels internally the pulls and strains of both reason and sensibility. The experience of obligation is the experience of the conflicting demands of humanity's dual nature. It is in this experience, in fact, that an individual becomes aware of this duality.

> When a human being is conscious of a duty to himself, he views himself, as the subject of duty, under two attributes: first as a *sensible being*, that is, as a human being (a member of one of the animal species), and secondly as an *intelligible being* (not merely as a being that has reason, since reason as a theoretical faculty could well be an attribute of a living corporeal being). The senses cannot attain this latter aspect of a human being; it can be cognized only in morally practical relations, where the incomprehensible property of *freedom* is revealed by the influence of reason on the inner law-giving will.
>
> Now the human being as a *natural being* that has reason (*homo phaenomenon*) can be determined by his reason, as a *cause*, to actions in the sensible world, and so far the concept of obligation does not come into consideration. But the same human being thought in terms of his *personality*, that is, as a being endowed with *inner freedom* (*homo noumenon*), is regarded as a being that can be put under obligation.[46]

Only human beings can be the agents of moral schematism because they alone are beings cognizant both of the moral law and of the content of the sensible faculty of desire. They alone are aware of an active and a passive employment whereby they can find themselves motivated by external forces to seek an object that is merely of natural value or, on the other hand, find themselves motivated by their own faculty of reason to attain the moral good through the embodiment of an order in sensibility in which virtue and happiness are combined in the symbolic embodiment of the highest good. Since one's faculties of volition and judgment are informed both by the idea of reason and by sensible intuition and desire, one's judgment can function schematically in terms of the idea of the highest good in relation to the content of sensibility and desire. Once judgment has attained an ordering of sensibility *in imagination* by means of this schematic

45 KU, 468: CoTJ, 141–42; KpV, 6, 132–133: CprR, 120–21, 234–35.
46 MS, 418: MOM, 543–4; cf. ibid., 429–436: ibid., 552–8.

procedure, one can commit all one's volitional power to the attainment of that ordering *in experience*.

Since the qualifications which fit a human being for the task of symbolic schematism are revealed in the experience of obligation, one's fitness to fulfill the moral task is as certain as the experience of obligation, which Kant called the absolutely certain fact of pure reason. Thus Kant's ethical theory offers an account of both the moral task and the moral agent that permits the realization of the former by the latter. By means of symbolic schematism the moral person can strive in practice, no less than in theory, to embody the highest good.

Chapter VIII: The Role Of Judgment In Kant's Procedural Formalism

1 The Procedure of Judgment in All Employments

In the preceding chapter, we discussed the general structure of the moral task after having described it as the duty to achieve the symbolic schematization of the highest good. We saw that the source of the homogeneity between sensibility and the idea of the highest good consists in the procedure that judgment – or the will in volition – goes through in determining an order in sensibility that is symbolic of this idea. The employment of judgment is therefore necessary for the application of the moral law and the sensible embodiment of the highest good.

Moral theory is by no means unique in its dependence upon judgment for its application. Judgment is a creative faculty of the human mind or will that stands as the active link between any theory and its application, whether it be a theory of science, morality, or aesthetics:

> However complete the theory may be, it is obvious that between theory and practice there must be a link, a connection and transition from one to the other. To the intellectual concept that contains the rule, an act of judgment must be added whereby the practitioner distinguishes whether or not something is an instance of the rule. And since we cannot always lay down rules for our judgment to observe in subsumption (as this would go on ad infinitum), there may be theoreticians who, for the lack of judgment, can never be practical: physicians or jurists, for example, who have been well schooled but do not know what to do when they are summoned to a consultation.[1]

The embodiment of the highest good as the union of virtue and happiness as the moral task requires, in addition, an act of judgment to determine that concrete state of affairs which constitutes the most adequate embodiment of the highest good in each particular act of volition. The moral law and the highest good, as the material object of volition determined by the moral law, are not complete and sufficient for practice as they stand:

> [They] require in addition a power of judgment sharpened by experience, partly *in order to distinguish the cases to which they apply,* partly to procure for them admittance to the will of man and influence over practice.[2]

---

1 TP, 275: TaP, 41.

2 GMS, 389: GMM, 57. Italics are mine.

Kant thus lays heavy stress on the role of judgment in the application of moral theory to practice. Judgment has responsibility both to determine the nature of one's specific duty and also to see to its enactment. Kant must explain how judgment is able to fulfill both functions in order to demonstrate the validity of his moral theory in practice. Since these functions are distinct, our examination of them will be clearer if we discuss one at a time. In this chapter we will consider judgment's role in the determination of one's duty, reserving to Chapter IX the examination of judgment's role in effecting, i.e. motivating, the will to moral action.

Turning to the role of judgment in determining the specific obligations of the moral agent, we must be clear about what sort of explanation we seek. We know at the outset that we are not trying to explain the nature of free acts of judgment. Kant's insistence on the inscrutable origins of this power is well known. Furthermore, and this point is more likely to be overlooked, we are not looking for rules to tell us how to apply the moral law. No instruction of this sort can ever be given:

> If there were to be doctrines for the power of judgment, then there would have to be general rules according to which one could decide whether something was an instance of the rule or not, which would generate a further inquiry on into infinity. Thus the power of judgment is, as we say, the understanding that comes only with years; it is based on one's long experience.[3]

If this is the sort of explanation we are seeking in order to understand how judgment can determine one's specific duty, we had as well abandon the search. This sort of explanation is impossible in principle. If we introduce a rule to guide judgment in deciding which cases fall under rules, we contribute nothing to the understanding of judgment's activities. Unless judgment already knows how to determine which cases fall under rules, it will not be able to make use of the new rule. If we feel constrained to offer judgment a new rule to guide it in the application of other rules, then we should likewise feel constrained to offer judgment an additional rule to guide it in the application of the new rule which is to guide it in the application of the earlier rules, *ad infinitum.*

If there is any merit in an ethical theory, it must entail the ability to guide moral judgment in acts of volition. If the theory offers no instruction to judgment, then it is indeed invalid in practice: while it claims to provide the principles of obligation and the good as the normative object of volition, it

3 Anth, 199: AN, 93.

cannot give meaning either to good or bad, or right or wrong in the context of moral decisions.

The guidance provided by moral theory consists in its specification of the procedure that judgment must follow if it is to function soundly. The moral theory does not pretend to offer a rule for applying the moral law, but the moral law is itself to be understood as a principle which specifies the procedure of judgment in the act of moral schematism. On this interpretation, the correct application of the moral law would consist in the fulfillment by judgment of a *procedure* whereby a particular object or action is designated in imagination as the fulfillment of duty, that is, as the embodiment of the highest good in a particular act of moral volition. Following the determination of the act that most adequately fulfills one's duty, judgment assists the will in the enactment of that act.

The norm or guide to successful achievement in the various employments of the faculty of cognition is never given in terms of some substantive goal to be achieved. Rather the guide or norm consists in a statement of the procedure for judgment which, if followed, can be expected to lead to the attainment of the substantive goal of the employment in question. We might all agree, for example, that the goal of science is the attainment of a systematic account of the relationship of phenomena such that the future as well as the present and past ordering of phenomena can be known. But although this may be regarded as the goal of science, it is not the method of science. One cannot look to this goal in order to learn how to be a scientist. In order to think and act as a scientist one must observe the norms of scientific method, that is, one must follow the procedures of judgment prescribed for scientists. To be sure, a scientist is obligated to observe the procedures of scientific method only because this is the only way he or she can attain the goal of scientific endeavor. Nevertheless, the goal and the method of science are quite distinct and it is not the goal but rather the method which guides the activities of the scientist.

Kant holds a similar point of view regarding ethics. The goal of the moral person is to attain the highest good. But the highest good as a transcendent idea of reason does not reveal what state of affairs constitutes the most adequate sensible embodiment of it. In fact we do not begin in ethics with the concept of the highest good at all. The highest good must be determined as the material object of volition by the moral agent in an act of judgment by reference to the moral law.[4] In order to determine the highest good the

4 See Chapter II.

moral agent must exercise his or her judgment according to sound procedures prescribed by the moral law. Kant can thus introduce guides for judgment without being involved in an infinite regress because he does not offer a rule for applying the moral law; rather, the moral law is itself a principle specifying the procedures judgment must follow in order to determine and then to attain the highest good. The moral law merely specifies the procedure of judgment in the act of moral schematism, that is, in the act of determining that action which best accords with duty and embodies the highest good.

Before we turn to a direct examination of the moral law as it defines the procedures of judgment in ethics, we must consider at greater length the procedure of judgment in all the employments of the faculty of cognition. In the act of symbolic schematism, judgment does not perform a radically different sort of act than it performs in the direct schematism of the understanding. Although judgment in the former operates in terms of an idea of reason whereas in the latter it operates in terms of the concepts of the understanding, the procedure in both cases is essentially the same. Since there is only one reason underlying a variety of rational employments, there is likewise only one rational or judgmental process in all its employments.[5] Consequently, we should be better able to understand the nature of reasoning in ethics and the procedure of judgment there if we examine first the nature of reasoning and the procedure of judgment in a variety of rational employments.

If we wish to understand what it means to be rational in logic, science, ethics, law, and in matters of taste, we can ignore all consideration of the beliefs held in any or all of these employments. A person's rationality in any of these fields cannot be assessed on the basis of the opinions he or she holds. In each of these fields one may acquire one's opinions in a passive, imitative fashion without the exercise of reason. On the basis of opinion alone a horse can be a mathematician since it can easily be trained to nod its head four times whenever it is shown a card calling for the addition of two plus two. But this horse is no more rational than the child who has memorized a flash card giving the sum of two plus two. Both the horse and the child can give a correct *response* to a given *stimulus* but neither is reasoning.[6] Reasoning and behavior that expresses rationality must not be simplistically identified. This mistake of behaviorism leads to serious confusion.

---

5 GMS, 391: GMM, 59.
6 See KrV, B864: CpR, 656; cf. Log, 22: Logic, 535–6.

The procedure that is followed in these employments, however, reveals the rationality in these fields. One shows oneself to be rational in logic, science, ethics, and in matters of taste by the way one proceeds in the employment of reason in judgment, that is, by the actual process of one's thought and action.

We find, moreover, that there is a striking similarity between the procedures of judgment in all its employments. In his *Logik*, for example, Kant states the general rules for the avoidance of error in thinking as follows: "1) to think for oneself; 2) to think oneself in the position of someone else; and 3) always to think in agreement with oneself."[7] In the *Anthropologie* Kant reintroduces these same procedures in slightly variant forms as "maxims for the class of thinkers" and as the rules for the attainment of wisdom, which for Kant was the idea of a perfect, practical use of reason, conformable to law. Here are the descriptions:

1) To think *for oneself.*
2) In communication with men to imagine (*sich denken*) oneself in the place of every other person.
3) Always to think in *agreement with oneself.*

> The first principle is negative (*nullius addictus jurare in verba Magistri*)[8] that of *freedom from coercion*; the second is positive, that of liberals who accommodate themselves to the concepts of other thinkers; the third is the consistent (logical) mode of thinking.[9]

And in the *Critique of Aesthetic Judgment* Kant says,

> While the following maxims of common human understanding do not properly come in here as constituent parts of the Critique of Taste, they still may serve to elucidate its fundamental propositions. They are these: (1) to think for oneself; (2) to think from the standpoint of everyone else; (3) always to think consistently.[10]

In the third *Critique* Kant elaborates the implications of these maxims in more detail than is found in his other works. It is significant to note that Kant concludes the paragraph following his elucidation of these maxims with the statement:

> We might even define taste as the faculty of estimating what makes our feeling in a given representation *universally communicable* without the mediation of a concept.[11]

7 Log, 57: Logic, 563.
8 See Horace, *Epistle 1.1* line 14, 252.
9 Anth, 228–29, cf. 200: AN, 124, cf. 95. The text cited is my translation.
10 KU, 294: CoAJ, 152.
11 Ibid., 295: ibid., 153.

The ability of the faculty of taste to form an "*a priori* estimate of the communicability of the feelings that, without the mediation of a concept, are connected in a given representation"[12] stems from the mediation of judgment as it follows the procedures outlined in the maxims. Taste is able to judge universal communicability of the feeling that it has as a result of the stirrings of the understanding by the imagination in its freedom only because in the act of aesthetic judgment the person of taste has, in a special sense, "felt" or "thought" for himself or herself, in the place and point of view of others, and "consistently."

That judgments of taste are universally communicable indicates they must contain some universal element in them. This universal element cannot be a concept, for then aesthetic judgment would be cognitive in the same sense as the understanding is cognitive. Rather that which is the source of the universal communicability of aesthetic judgments is the presence in all persons of taste of the same faculties and the practice of the same procedure of judgment. But the fact that judgment in matters of taste does indeed follow the procedure specified by the three maxims for its use in all of the employments of the faculty of cognition does point to the presence in aesthetic judgments of cognitive significance, for it is the act of judgment which is the source of analogy in the attainment of symbolic hypotyposis of ideas of reason and aesthetic ideas. And it is the conception of hypotyposis, broad enough to include the symbolic as well as the direct schematism of concepts, that provides the foundation for cognitive significance apart from direct subsumption of particulars under concepts.

In all of the employments of the faculties of mind, Kant presents the test for the sound use of reason, for reasonableness, not in terms of static goals, opinions, or facts, but rather as maxims for the guidance of the reasoning process. He has prescribed procedures for judgment to follow where a reasoned outcome is desired. The rationality of a process of thought consists in the faithfulness with which mind, or will, or taste, has carried out these procedures. Only if rules of thought, norms of morality, and rules of aesthetic judgment are regarded as procedural statements can there be genuinely rational knowledge in science, autonomous action in moral experience, and free play of sensibility and understanding in aesthetic experience. Although judgment employs concepts in many of these employments, it is not given explicit guidance in the application of these concepts. Here it must express itself in subsumptive or inductive acts of freedom unaided (or unencumbered) by rules for the application of rules. The act of judgment is guided instead by reference to procedural

---

12 Ibid., 296: ibid., 154.

norms in terms of which it functions in relating concepts and ideas to sensibility.

2 The Procedures of Judgment in Ethics

The procedural interpretation of rationality, that is, the attempt to account for the rationality of thought and action in terms of the process or activity of judgment, receives its greatest emphasis and amplification in Kant's ethics. This interpretation is emphasized particularly in the *Groundwork*. In his exposition of the categorical imperative Kant presents the several formulae of the imperative as various ways of looking at the procedures judgment must follow in the determination of one's specific duties. Kant does not suggest that there are several categorical imperatives. He insists rather that there is "only a single categorical imperative and it is this: *'Act only on that maxim through which you can at the same time will that it should become a universal law.'*"[13] This is the one categorical imperative. Having stated the imperative in this form, Kant offers four examples in terms of which he tries to illustrate the function of the categorical imperative in concrete moral situations.[14] In these examples, Kant speaks continually of the process of thought through which the moral person goes, and how he or she tests the actual procedure of his or her thought against the procedure demanded by the law. Kant derives conclusions in regard to the concrete duties of persons in each of the examples. But then Kant does not make the mistake many of his interpreters have made: he does not say, "Here then are a few of the many actual duties which we must always fulfill if we are to be morally good." Kant says instead "These are some of the many actual duties – *or at least of what we take to be such* – whose derivation from the single principle cited above leaps to the eye."[15] Kant does not say that these are actual duties or categorical imperatives. They are offered merely as apparent examples, hurriedly determined, of what willing in accordance with the categorical imperative involves. Kant insists that the one categorical imperative is a procedure of judgment. If we follow it, "We must *be able to will* that a maxim of our action should become a universal law."[16] And this, Kant states further, "is the general *canon* for all moral judgment of action."[17] The meaning of this principle can be

13 GMS, 421: GMM, 88.
14 Ibid., 421ff.: ibid., 89ff.
15 Ibid., 423–4: ibid., 91. Italics are mine.
16 Idem: idem.
17 Idem: idem. Italics are mine.

found only by attending to the process of moral judgment itself. If we attend to the way in which we have thought about an action in which we fail in our duty, Kant observes that:

> we find that we in fact do not will that our maxim should become a universal law – since this is impossible for us – but rather that its opposite should remain a law universally: we only take the liberty of making an *exception* to it for ourselves (or even just for this once) to the advantage of our inclination. Consequently if we weighed it all up from one and the same point of view – that of reason – we should find a contradiction in our own will .... This *procedure*, though in our own impartial judgment it cannot be justified, proves none the less that we in fact recognize the validity of the categorical imperative and (with all respect for it) merely permit ourselves a few exceptions which are, as we pretend, inconsiderable and apparently forced upon us.[18]

Thus while referring to the categorical imperative as the *canon* for all moral judgment, Kant offers, in addition, an example of the procedure of moral judgment both in obeying and in transgressing this principle. In the case of transgressions, the procedure is demonstrably flawed.

Bearing in mind Kant's statement that the categorical imperative is the canon for moral judgment, and that there is only one categorical imperative, what are we to make of all the formulations of the imperative which Kant presents? Traditionally it has been supposed that there are three formulae of the categorical imperative. They are given as follows:

I. *"Act only on that maxim through which you can at the same time will that it should become a universal law."*[19]
II. *"Act in such a way that you always treat humanity, whether in your own person or in the person of any other, never simply as a means, but always at the same time as an end."*[20]
III. "*Every rational being must so act as if he were through his maxims always a law-making member in the universal kingdom of ends.*"[21]

The first formula is often referred to as the Formula of Universal Law, the second as the Formula of the End in Itself, and the third as the Formula of the Kingdom of Ends.

These formulations of the categorical imperative cannot be regarded as final. Paton points out that there are in fact five formulations of the categorical

18 Ibid., 424: ibid., 91–2. The final italics are mine.
19 Ibid., 421: ibid., 88.
20 Ibid., 429: ibid., 96.
21 Ibid., 438: ibid., 106. Italics are mine.

imperative.[22] In addition to the three given above, he finds that there is the Formula of the Universal Law of Nature: *"Act as if the maxim of your action were to become through your will a* Universal Law of Nature."[23] He also singles out the Formula of Autonomy: So act *"that the will can regard itself as at the same time making universal law by means of its maxim."*[24]

Actually one may find not five but seven or eight formulae of the categorical imperative. The number is indeterminate because Kant begins with the moral law as a single formal principle and attempts to make its meaning increasingly clear or intuitive by a variety of formulations. Kant notes the curious feature of ethics as opposed to epistemology: while in epistemology we begin with sensible intuition (the aesthetic) and move to the conceptual, in moral philosophy we begin with the concept of the moral law and move toward intuition and sensibility. Once we recognize that the characteristic movement in ethics is from the abstract to the concrete, we see that there is no basis for asking how many formulations of the categorical imperative there are, for the number of formulations is as unlimited as sensibility is diverse.

After Kant lists and discusses the formulations of the categorical imperative, he summarizes his discussion by saying that the "three ways of representing the principle of morality are at bottom merely so many formulations of precisely the same law."[25] The difference between them is not objective but subjective. That is, the first formulation of the categorical imperative is stated in purely formal terms, whereas the subsequent formulations, while following from the first, are designed to "bring an Idea of reason nearer to intuition (in accordance with a certain analogy) and so nearer to feeling."[26]

Kant's movement of thought in the *Groundwork* directly parallels his movement of thought in the second *Critique.* We see the moral law, the formal principle, and seek to exhibit it in intuition. But the difference is this: in the second *Critique* Kant is concerned to determine the object of pure practical reason, namely the good; in the *Groundwork* he is concerned to make intuitive the demand of the moral law in terms of the maxims of moral judgment. Kant focuses his attention in the second *Critique* on the findings of reason, on the

---

22 Paton, *The Categorical Imperative*, 129ff.
23 Ibid., 421: ibid., 89.
24 Ibid., 434: ibid., 101. See Singer, *Generalization in Ethics*, 9ff. Although Singer was not interested in an historical presentation of Kant's ethics, he offers important insights into Kant's treatment of the categorical imperative.
25 Ibid., 436: ibid., 103.
26 Idem: idem.

ends reason projects as it acts in accordance with the moral law; but in the *Groundwork* he limits himself to the specification of the procedure of judgment in fulfilling the demands of the moral law.

Accordingly Kant summarizes his discussion of all the formulations of the categorical imperative by saying:

> All maxims have in short,
>
> 1. a *form*, which consists in their universality; and in this respect the formula of the moral imperative is expressed thus: "Maxims must be chosen as if they had to hold as universal laws of nature";
> 2. a *matter* – that is, an end; and in this respect the formula says: "A rational being, as by his very nature an end and consequently an end in himself, must serve for every maxim as a condition limiting all merely relative and arbitrary ends";
> 3. a *complete determination* of all maxims by the following formula, namely: "All maxims as proceeding from our own making of law ought to harmonize with a possible kingdom of ends as a kingdom of nature." This progression may be said to take place through the categories of the *unity* of the form of will (its universality); of the *multiplicity* of its matter (its objects – that is, its ends); and of the *totality* or completeness of its system of ends. It is, however, better if in moral *judgment* we proceed always in accordance with the strict method and take as our basis the universal formula of the categorical imperative: "*Act on the maxim which can at the same time be made a universal law.*" If, however, we wish also to secure acceptance for the moral law, it is very useful to bring one and the same action under the above-mentioned three concepts and so, as far as we can, to bring the universal formula nearer to intuition.[27]

In this passage Kant stresses the importance of the categorical imperative in its various formulations as a guide to moral judgment. By insisting that this one principle is sufficient for moral practice, Kant presupposes the human context in which reason and sensibility are present in every act of volition. Unless the categorical imperative is a principle for the guidance of the human will, the will of a rational yet sensible being, it cannot possibly be sufficient in itself. All maxims of volition have both form and content in unity. But unless we assume that Formula I is the law for humans, or some other rational and sensible being, Formula I alone, together with the judgment it informs, could not give expression to maxims containing both form and matter. Furthermore, Formula I would not be an obligation at all unless it constituted the form of moral judgment for a being who is tempted to reject reason in favor of desire in the determination of a moral action. The moral law would be a descriptive law of a holy will, that is, a pure rational will, not tempted by sensibility. It becomes a categorical imperative only for those rational beings who are also subject to the enticements of

27 Ibid., 436–7: ibid., 103–4.

sensible inclinations. The categorical imperative cannot be presented, therefore, as a concept unrelated to the will; it is revealed in the life experience of a being who is both rational and sensible and who strives through his or her power of judgment to express the rational aspect of his or her nature in action. Kant does not have the problem of relating the categorical imperative to the moral context for it emerges from it. Kant's problem is rather to make clear what the demand of the categorical imperative actually involves.

The union of sensibility and the idea of reason in the moral schematism rests upon the activity of judgment. This activity of judgment consists in the production of maxims the form of which is stated in the categorical imperative, and the matter of which is given in the ends posed by actual finite rational and sensible beings. But the unity of form and content which it is the moral task to produce is not given. The achievement of this unity in the specification of each maxim is the moral task. And its attainment depends upon the way in which judgment proceeds.

From the standpoint of form, nothing more than Formula I is needed. No one can claim that the maxim of his or her act is morally good unless it is based on a maxim which is objective as well as subjective. A maxim is objective if the grounds for the determination of the will in a given action are not based merely on subjective conditions of the particular individual but are valid for all other rational beings. In determining the maxim of a moral act, judgment must incorporate the form of universality. Only by acting on the basis of a universal maxim is a person able to maintain the independence of his or her will in a specific moral act. By acting on the basis of a universal maxim, one takes account of all conditions and points of interest, not merely one's own. By so acting, one transcends the subjectivity of personal inclination and acts in terms of the *idea* of law rather than in terms of personal desires. By virtue of the universality of one's act, one asserts one's freedom and autonomy, and preserves one's rationality. To be rational means

> nothing more than to ask one's self, with regard to everything that is to be assumed, whether he finds it practicable to make the ground of the assumption or the rule which follows from the assumption a universal principle of the use of his reason.[28]

In order to assure one's self of one's rationality, Kant urges him or her to try the procedure of universalizing his or her assumption and the rules of argument. Kant thus holds that the test for rationality and for moral integrity is the

---

28 Orientiren, 146–7n: Orient, 305n.

same. Kant calls this procedure "the maxim of self-preservation of reason." If the principles of a person's thought are sound when applied universally, then such a person is thinking rationally. For example, in practice one may convert the proposition "All bachelors are unmarried men" without limitation and say "All unmarried men are bachelors." The simple conversion of this universal affirmative proposition can be carried out without leading to a false conclusion. But one would not be thinking on the basis of a sound rule of reason unless one tried to universalize this rule of conversion. If one makes this method of conversion a universal rule of reason one will soon come to grief. By reasoning, for example, that since all human beings are mortal, all mortals are human beings, one will discover the deficiency in his or her reasoning. Kant insists that the attempt to universalize all assumptions and rules of reason will assure one of preserving one's own rationality. This procedure of testing leads one to transcend subjective thought by appeal to the universality of law.

A person's moral autonomy is assured when he or she completes a similar procedure: one is morally alive and rational and fully free if in willing he or she engages in a process of universalization that will ensure the rationality of his or her thought and volition. When one acts on the basis of a maxim that can at the same time be a universal law, one cannot be said to act on the basis of the influence of some specific natural cause. Rather that person must be recognized as a responsible being thinking and acting for himself or herself. Such a person shows himself or herself to be unconditioned, and, hence, of unconditioned worth; such individuals reveal themselves as ends in themselves. Thus we see that by acting in accordance with the Formula of Universal Law we also act in accord with the Formula of Autonomy, and we meet the conditions of the Formula of the End in Itself. We show ourselves to be thinking and willing for ourselves.

In elaborating the maxims of common understanding in the third *Critique*, Kant said that thinking for oneself is the maxim of a never-passive reason. "To be given to such passivity, consequently to the heteronomy of reason, is called *prejudice*."[29] This passivity or heteronomy of reason is avoided by adopting the procedure which is specified by the maxim of the self-preservation of reason. Following this procedure one cannot fail to engage in rational thought and to restore or raise oneself to the status of a rational autonomous thinker. Adopting the procedure outlined in Formula I and articulating the maxims of one's volition on the basis of this procedure of judgment, one cannot fail to will in a

29 KU, 294: CoAJ, 152.

morally autonomous manner. One wills as a law giver so that one's maxims of volition are specifications of the laws of a moral nature.

Formula I of the categorical imperative leads us to alternative formulations which, though more intuitive, are nonetheless a statement of the same procedure of judgment in determining the form of moral maxims. In order to determine the form of our maxims Kant says, "Maxims must be chosen as if they had to hold as universal laws of nature." This statement of the categorical imperative expresses exactly the same demand as was expressed in the formula "Act as if the maxim of your act were to become through your will a universal law of nature." This formulation – let us call it Formula Ia – is in my judgment the most important formulation of the categorical imperative for the purpose of making clear the practical relevance of Kant's theory and the way that the will fulfills the moral schematism in practice. The moral schematism is projected in imagination as one imagines the consequences of one's maxim if it were to become a causally necessary law of nature.

The importance of this formulation is evident in Kant's writings since it is this formulation which Kant develops in the second *Critique* in the discussion of the understanding as the typic of pure practical judgment. And this formulation makes it abundantly clear that Kant thought of the embodiment of the highest good in terms of symbolic schematism.

In moral experience, judgment must decide on an action which in the world of sense will be recognized as an instance of a law that is not constitutive of that world of sense but is a law of freedom that may or may not be present in it but that from a moral point of view should be present in it. Unlike the category of causality that is always applicable because it is schematized in the temporal ordering of sensibility, the moral law must be applied through the agency of the moral person. The moral agent must so arrange events in the spatio-temporal order that time and space become schemata for the moral law no less than for the category of causality. The moral agent attempts to structure the spatio-temporal order so that the moral law is descriptive of sequences that occur there.

Confronted with this problem, Kant reasons as follows:

> A schema is a universal procedure [*Verfahren*] of the imagination in presenting *a priori* to the senses a pure concept of the understanding which is determined by the law; and a schema must correspond to natural laws as laws to which objects of sensuous intuition as such are subject. But to the law of freedom (which is a causality not sensuously conditioned), and consequently to the concept of the absolutely good, no intuition and hence no schema can be supplied for the purpose of applying it *in concreto*. Thus the moral law has no other cognitive faculty to mediate its application to objects of nature than the understanding (not the imagination); and the understanding can supply to an idea of

> reason not a schema of sensibility but a law. This law, as one which can be exhibited *in concreto* in objects of the senses, is a natural law. But this natural law can be used only in its formal aspect, for the purpose of judgment, and it may, therefore, be called the type [*typus*] of the moral law.[30]

Judgment can borrow from the understanding the concept of natural law itself, and by use of this, as a typic of pure practical reason, better succeed in the application of the moral law itself. Devoid of a schema in sensibility for testing its employment, judgment can set up its own test apart from such a schema with the concept of a natural law projected in imagination. The rule of judgment under the typic of pure practical judgment (the gift of understanding) is:

> Ask yourself whether, if the action you propose should take place by a law of nature of which you yourself were a part, you could regard it as possible through your will. Everyone does, in fact, decide by this rule whether actions are morally good or bad .... If the maxim of action is not so constituted as to stand the test of being made the form of natural law in general, it is morally impossible.[31]

In order to determine that maxim which can be willed universally in a concrete situation, judgment follows the procedure of assuming that whatever is willed by the moral agent will become a universal law of nature. Kant thus proposes a thought experiment for the moral agent. Judgment assumes that all human beings will begin to perform by natural causation the action that is willed in the particular instant. If the action willed expresses a maxim of universal validity, then the will should not object to finding itself in a world of nature in which all humans in comparable situations observed the same principle. If one is not willing in contradiction to oneself, that is, if one is not willing that all human beings should observe a certain moral precept while he or she alone acts in opposition to it, then one should be prepared to will that the maxim of one's act become a constitutive law of the phenomenal world binding on him or her and everyone else. If one does not want the maxim of one's act to become a universal law of nature, then one is not willing in a universal manner but on the basis of one's subjective interests.

By means of this formulation, judgment follows a procedure which definitely involves Kant in a consideration of consequences. It has been objected by Mill, Dewey, Schopenhauer, and many others that Kant involved himself in an

30 KpV, 69: CprR, 177.
31 Ibid., 69–70: ibid., 178.

inconsistency by appealing to consequences. It has been argued that since Kant insisted that the moral agent must perform his or her duty for its own sake, the agent is not privileged to consider the consequences of his or her actions in trying to determine this duty. But this criticism of Kant is misguided. Kant says that our motive must not derive from a consideration of the consequences; on the other hand, in determining what our duty is and what we are and ought to be trying to do, we must consider the consequences of our action in light of our intention. We would have no intention at all if it was not to produce some specific consequence, and our moral obligation is to ensure that our intention can be universalized. Our calculation of duty is not to rest on *empirical prognostication* of the consequences of our action. Rather it is our duty to consider all of the consequences willed by our action. We determine the willed consequences of our action by projecting in imagination the sort of world that would come into existence were the maxim of our act to become a universal law of nature.

Thus Kant successfully avoids several of the criticisms raised against his theory: when one follows the procedure called for in Formula Ia one never confronts the question, "what happens if other people act as I do?" Empirical observation may show that they don't. But that empirical observation is beside the point. Kant asks instead, "what would happen if the maxim of my act became a law of nature, that is, if as a consequence of my act everyone in my position would subsequently, out of inexorable causal laws, act precisely as I have?" Kant suggests that one develop in imagination the details of this thought experiment, that is, that one see in the mind's eye the kind of world that would come into existence if a new natural law were introduced by the adoption of one's specific maxim. By means of this thought experiment the moral agent gains a clearer intuitive sense of the demand of consistency and universality in volition.

If Kant made reference to consequences after the fashion of utilitarians, he would appeal to an empirically observed prediction of the consequences of one's action. Such an appeal would offer no guidance concerning the conformity of one's maxim to the moral law. Suppose, for example, in World War II an Englishman wished to evade military service. If he asked himself, what would actually happen as a consequence of his avoiding military service, he could assure himself that patriotism and respect for the law of typical Englishmen would ensure that most men served. The actual consequences of his action would not leave England defenseless but merely save him from the risks of battle. In this case, however, he does not appeal to consequences in the manner prescribed by Formula Ia. He should have asked, what would happen if the decision I make to avoid military service were by my will to become a law of nature according to which all Englishmen would evade military service? The contradiction in his volition would be instantly apparent. The Englishman does not will that his country be destroyed but rather that other men will fight while he exempts himself from this obligation. Kant requires the moral agent to determine not empirically but a priori the consequences that would follow from his or her volition. These consequences are determined by reference to the formula of the law of nature. One must ask, what are the inevitable consequences of my action if the maxim of my act becomes a law of nature?

Thus the moral agent, on Kant's theory, does not consider what other persons will *actually* do as a result of his or her having acted in a certain fashion. Rather the moral agent considers what other persons *would necessarily do* if his or her maxim were a universal law. The moral agent is not trying to predict the future, but is simply applying a procedure of judgment in terms of which the future he or she intends is determined in imagination. The examination of this willed future reveals whether or not the moral agent is willing in a universal manner.

Thus we see that Kant can make a direct appeal to consequences without resting his determination of duty on empirically grounded probabilities that are extremely difficult if not impossible to ascertain. The consequences to which he refers are a rationally determined set of consequences which follow from the subjection of one's maxim to a procedure of judgment called for by Formula Ia. In terms of this procedure the *a priori* determined consequences of the universalization of one's maxim provide an intuitive check on the universality of one's volition. Kant can never hope to prove that all human beings will actually do the same thing he does. But Kant recognizes that all humans have an equal right to do whatever he does. Hence in order to determine the rationality and universality of his or her maxim the moral agent must consider whether or not he or she wills a world in which all individuals actually do that which they have as much right as he or she to do. In this way the demands of the moral law are revealed in specific moral decisions.

In concluding our discussion of Formula Ia, we must bear in mind that this is not a material principle, nor a guide for determining the material content of moral maxims. Rather, Formula Ia makes intuitively clear the meaning of universality in the form of a maxim by commanding judgment to follow the procedure it specifies.

The matter of moral maxims is determined by reference to an end. As Kant observes, "the formula says, 'A rational being, as by his very nature an end and consequently an end in himself, must serve for every maxim as a condition limiting all merely relative and arbitrary ends.'"[32] By the exercise of judgment

32 GMS, 436: GMM, 104.

in accord with Formula I or Formula Ia the moral agent reveals his or her freedom, the ability to act in terms of his or her own idea of law (whether he or she does so or not) rather than in terms of natural causation whose power lies in a source external to the will. The moral agent thus shows himself or herself to be a being whose worth lies within and worth cannot be conditioned or qualified by anything external to himself or herself.[33] As such a rational being exists as an end in himself or herself. In this regard, such a being must recognize a limit to the formulation of his or her maxims. The categorical imperative states the form of moral judgment in the determination of one's specific duty. As such, it does not spin out any specific content. But the moral maxim cannot be devoid of content. It is Kant's explicit insistence that every act of volition must have an object and hence that every maxim must have a content.[34] The act of moral judgment is an act of relating form to sensibility, and although the form does not, *qua* form, specify the content, it does, nevertheless, so direct the process of moral judgment that certain restrictions and ordering are imposed on the content of volition. The most important of these restrictions consists in the demand that judgment recognize the integrity of every rational being as an end in itself, as a condition *limiting* all ends of sensibility which are less final and less unconditioned than it.

The law itself determines the unconditioned worth of rational beings. It is the presence of the law within each rational being that is the condition of its having the power to be free. And it is likewise the presence of the universality of the law as a condition for the fulfillment of freedom that compels the rational being to acknowledge all other rational beings as ends in themselves.

Reason likewise determines the primacy of the rational being as an unconditioned end in himself or herself over all other ends, which are, in relation to the rational being, of conditioned even if not arbitrary worth. The freedom of human beings is the source of their worth as persons and hence their right to happiness. Happiness is therefore qualified within the life of the rational being and subject to the limiting condition of his or her moral worth.

Moral judgment, following Formula II of the categorical imperative, to treat others as ends in themselves and never as means merely, will accept content as it is introduced by the faculty of desire. Moral judgment will accept the content of sensibility without question until it encounters rational beings among the contents for moral volition. At this point judgment must reorder the content of sensibility so that the natural good (happiness as relative though intrinsic good-

---

33 See Chapter III, Sections 2 and 3.
34 GMS, 435–6: GMM, 102–4.

ness) is never willed at the expense of a rational being (an unconditioned end). Of course, the situation is rarely as simple as this. Rational beings who are also human have sensible interests and relative ends to which they are fondly attached. Hence judgment must take care in the formulation of a maxim of volition not to violate the rights of a rational being as an unconditioned end by disregarding that rational being's relative ends of happiness as he or she rather than the moral agent defines them.

But Formula II is still very abstract. It is regrettable that Kant did not think to express Formula II of the categorical imperative in terms of his second maxim of common human understanding: instead of writing about treating humankind as an end in itself, Kant should have suggested putting oneself in thought in the place and point of view of others. Kant amplifies the intent of Formula II effectively when he says:

> However small the range and degree to which a man's natural endowments extend, [it] still indicates a man of *enlarged mind* [provided] he detaches himself from the subjective personal conditions of his judgment, which cramp the minds of so many others, and reflects upon his own judgment from a *universal standpoint* (which he can only determine by shifting his ground to the standpoint of others.)[35]

This statement makes intuitively clear the procedure of judgment in determining the content of moral maxims: it gives specific meaning to the imperative of treating others as ends in themselves. In order to respect the humanity of all rational, sensible beings, the moral agent must in imagination put himself or herself in the place and point of view of all those, including the moral agent, who are affected by his or her actions. In this way the moral agent will understand the values and needs of other beings and by moving beyond self will limit his or her tendency to focus on the fulfillment of his or her own needs and desires to the neglect of the needs and legitimate desires of others.

It is obvious that to put oneself in the place and point of view of others in determining one's action expresses the categorical imperative to treat others as ends in themselves and never as means merely. Objections have been raised, however, to Formula II. It has been argued that because human beings are free and unconditioned as rational beings, they cannot be treated as a means merely even if one tries. Since one's freedom cannot be qualified, it may be argued, one is therefore impervious to whatever others may do to him or her. But here again is a serious confusion. In the first place, this objection does not prove that we cannot *will* to treat others as means merely. It suggests only that it is impossible

---

35 KU, 295: CoAJ, 153.

for us to reduce human beings to that status no matter how abusively we may treat them. It is impossible to reduce a human being to a means merely so long as he or she continues to have any vestige of freedom. But it is clearly possible through drugs and torture to destroy a rational being by stages or to kill him or her outright. In the second place, a human being is not merely a rational being, but is also a natural, sensible being whose happiness is of legitimate concern to him or her for it is an intrinsic good. Since we can destroy the happiness of others, we can therefore treat them as means merely by ignoring their needs as ends. In the third place, arguments such as this ignore the procedural character of the categorical imperative. In reaching moral decisions we often fail to move beyond ourselves to consider the interests and needs of others from their own points of view. It is the failure to engage in this procedure of judgment that Kant is warning against. The procedural character of Formula II is not so apparent in its formulation as in Kant's remark that this formula sets "a limit on all arbitrary treatment of them [rational beings]."[36]

The Formula of the End in Itself does not require that we never use others as means. It is simply a limiting concept on all arbitrary treatment of them. There is no way to specify the exact limits to which other persons can be used as means. These limits depend upon the determination of the rational versus the arbitrary uses of others. In some situations one might be using a person arbitrarily by smoking in a closed room in which a non-smoker was present. On the other hand, one might not be arbitrary in another situation in demanding that a person give up his life, as when a soldier is given a combat order that may save the lives of the men in his platoon although he will very likely forfeit his own. Whether or not the treatment of a person is arbitrary depends on whether the treatment of that person is grounded on rational willing. If in the decision regarding the treatment of others, one has placed himself in thought in the place and point of view of others,[37] and also followed the other procedures of judgment, we must presume that the treatment of others would not be arbitrary since the affected parties would if rational presumably concur. In this case, however, a given action might, even if willed in good faith, be mistaken if all parties incorrectly assessed the situation. Given the finitude of knowledge and the constant influence of self-interest, that possibility is always present.

36 GMS, 428: GMM, 96.

37 We must acknowledge, however, that it is difficult truly to put oneself in the place and point of view of others, for self-love can easily cloud one's judgment. Reinhold Niebuhr emphasized the ever-present tendency of human beings to fail in this regard through self-deception.

Thus far we have discussed the formulae for the determination of the form and matter of maxims. But all of this discussion was in the nature of analysis. In the actual moral decision these are but moments in the unified operation of judgment as it establishes the link between the idea of reason and sensibility. In all moral volition there must be "a *complete determination* of all maxims by the following formula, namely: 'All maxims as proceeding from our making of law ought to harmonize with a possible kingdom of ends as a kingdom of nature.'"[38] In terms of this formulation the procedure of judgment is once again stated in its unity. The concern for universality and its test in terms of the projection of a law of nature, along with the concern for material with the recognition of a hierarchical arrangement of ends such that some may be subject to arbitrary volition while others may not, are combined in this maxim. According to this maxim, judgment seeks to reassert its own autonomy contained in the principle of universality after having enlarged its perspective by taking the place of others as ends in themselves. The progression of judgment from the form of the maxim to the matter of the maxim and finally to that of complete delineation takes place "through the categories of the *unity* of the form of will (its universality); of the *multiplicity* of its matter (its objects – that is, its ends); and of the *totality* or completeness of its system of ends."[39]

The unity of the self depends upon the exercise of freedom, which in turn depends on the will's acting in terms of the universality of the law apart from the grounds of action which have their origin outside the unity of the person. Hence in the act of willing as a unity, moral judgment in order to preserve the unity and autonomy of the person is forced to go beyond itself, to project itself into the contexts of other rational beings. In the multiplicity of other contexts it finds the needed material and the necessary perspective for an escape from the subjectivity and heteronomy of willing, that is, from the isolated perspective conditioned by private inclinations of the moral agent. But in the movement beyond itself to the multiplicity of ends, judgment runs the danger of losing its autonomy and unity by absorption in the multiplicity of standpoints. Hence, in terms of the category of totality it must forge a new autonomous unity, or totality, beyond the power of its individual unity now informed by the multiplicity of perspectives.

By examining the procedures of judgment we see how Kant's third maxim of common human understanding – always to think consistently – applies in an ethical context. This maxim of consistent thought, he insists,

38 Ibid., 436: ibid., 104.

39 Idem: idem.

> is the hardest of attainment, and is only attainable by the union of both the former [to think for oneself, and to think from the standpoint of everyone else] and after constant attention to them has made one at home in their observance.[40]

This is the maxim which Kant expressed in the *Anthropologie*: "Always to think in agreement with one's self."[41] This formulation of the final procedure of judgment, like the other two, stresses the overall unity of form and matter, in terms of the power of judgment as a unified faculty of each rational will to arrive at a concrete course of action in which the moral law is expressed. This course of action must be subject to the unity of the individual's autonomy, enlarged by reference to his or her self projection in acquiring the material content of volition. It also stresses the additional procedure of judgment in willing this harmonious unity of a kingdom of ends as a system of nature.

But what is the harmonious unity of a kingdom of ends as a system of nature if not the symbolic embodiment of the highest good as the systematic unity of a moral world? As judgment proceeds to assert its freedom through the universality of the form of maxims, the will moves toward the attainment of its moral perfection. But its freedom and universality cannot be attained unless it commits itself to the content of sensibility and to relationship with other ends. Thus its moral perfection depends on its material involvement with other ends and its ability to reassert its individuality and autonomy through the universality of its form in terms of its material response to other ends and its avoidance of arbitrary treatment of them.

When judgment has followed these procedures, the concrete determination of the moral task is achieved. And the moral task itself is completed as soon as the will commits itself to action in accordance with the maxim designated by judgment as the outcome of its procedures. The complete delineation of the maxim of moral volition is the outcome of a process of judgment defined by the moral law as the categorical imperative for a finite rational sensible being. This complete delineation is the symbolic embodiment of the highest good. The process whereby it is determined is the act of moral schematism and the realization of the categorical imperative. When this process has been completed and the will has acted on the basis of judgment's determination of the maxim of moral volition, Kant has no additional problem of applying the moral law or showing the validity of his ethical theory in practice. Once judgment completes

---

40 KU, 295: CoAJ, 153. I have added the words in brackets.
41 Anth, 228: AN, 124. My translation.

the procedure for the determination of the moral maxim and the will acts on the basis of it, the categorical imperative has been applied.

3 The Procedural Formalism of Kant's Ethics

i. The Non-Substantive Character of Kant's Formalism

In light of Kant's exposition of the moral task in terms of the symbolic embodiment of the highest good, of his insistence that there is but one categorical imperative, and of his explication of that imperative in terms of a variety of procedures designed to guide moral judgment, and finally in light of Kant's continual insistence on the need for autonomy and rationality, it becomes obvious that the Kantian theory of ethics cannot support any legalistic interpretation. Furthermore, Kant's rejection of a substantive interpretation of duty can be seen in many isolated passages as well as in the major emphases of his theory as a whole.

It is highly important to note Kant's distinction between the duty of ethics and the duties of virtue. There is only one duty of ethics. It is the duty, stated formally again, of fulfilling the categorical imperative. The duties of virtue, however, are the specific determinant duties that only arise in the process of applying the categorical imperative. One wonders, however, if a conflict of duties might arise when specific actions are interpreted as genuinely substantive duties, valid in many contexts apart from fresh determination by the moral agent.

Kant denies that there can ever be a conflict of duties, and since there is only one categorical imperative, we have no reason to suppose that Kant should have difficulty in sustaining this view. In regard to the possibility of a conflict of duties Kant says:

> *A conflict of duties* (*collisio officiorum s. obligationum*) would be a relation between them in which one of them would cancel the other (wholly or in part). – But since duty and obligation are concepts that express the objective practical *necessity* of certain actions and two rules opposed to each other cannot be necessary at the same time, if it is a duty to act in accordance with one rule, to act in accordance with the opposite rule is not a duty but even contrary to duty; so a *collision of duties* and obligations is inconceivable (*obligationes non colliduntur*) .... When two such grounds conflict with each other, practical philosophy says, not that the stronger obligation takes precedence (*fortior obligatio vincit*) but that the stronger *ground of obligation* prevails (*fortior obligandi ratio vincit*).[42]

42 MS, 224: MOM, 378–9.

Kant's views on the impossibility of a conflict in duties accord perfectly with the central doctrines of his ethics: his insistence on autonomy and on a single categorical imperative.

But it is an inevitable consequence of Kant's theory of ethics that the ethical life is difficult. "Virtue", he says,

> is not to be defined and valued merely as an *aptitude* and ... a long-standing *habit* of morally good actions acquired by practice. For unless this aptitude results from considered, firm, and continually purified principles, then, like any other mechanism of technically practical reason, *it is neither armed for all situations nor adequately secured against the chances that new temptations could bring about.*[43]

Kant's ethics is an ethics of rationality, of autonomy. One's duty is not defined by some set of legalistic actions, some codification of substantive duties. One's duty as a human being is simply the demand of reason that in all circumstances one express oneself in terms of the freedom of one's rational nature. Kant's ethics leaves no place for imitators:

> The *imitator* (in moral matters) is without character; for character consists precisely in originality in the way of thinking. He who has character derives his conduct from a source that he has opened by himself. However, the rational human being must not be an *eccentric*; indeed, he never will be, since he relies on principles that are valid for everyone.[44]

The moral individual can be neither irresponsible nor passive. Each must creatively attempt to determine his or her duty afresh for every moral situation. Of course, as one's judgment becomes sharpened by experience, one may be able to determine his or her duty swiftly and with considerable assurance. But one can never take one's virtue for granted. Since an individual is easily deceived about his or her own goodness, Kant says it is never wise to encourage a state of confidence in this regard. Rather, he suggests – quoting from Philippians – it is much wiser and more "advantageous (to morality) to 'work out our own salvation *with fear and trembling.*'"[45] Kant does not urge men and women to despair over their moral life. But he does think that serious concern is in order and that the moral agent must be ever on the alert to preserve in all acts of volition the freedom of his or her rational nature.

---

43 MS, 383–84: MOM, 515–6. Italics in the last clause are mine.

44 Anth, 293: AN, 158; cf. HN (AA19), No. 6954, 212–13. See also RGV, 64: Rel, 58.

45 RGV, 68: Rel, 62.

Given Kant's articulation and emphasis of these points, it is curious that many critics should have accused him of holding a legalistic position. The essential criticism of many philosophers is exemplified by Paul Weiss when he states that Kant "thought it absolutely, unqualifiedly wrong for a starving man afloat on a raft to eat a rotting can of beans to which he had no commercial claim."[46]

This popular caricature of Kant's position ignores, first, Kant's many explicit statements that there is only one categorical imperative. Second, even if we suppose that Kant would always regard stealing to be wrong, we must recognize that each person is morally obligated to treat himself or herself as an end in himself or herself. In terms of the Formula of the End in Itself, the man on the raft would have to place himself as an unconditioned end before a can of beans as a relative end. On the assumption that it is wrong to steal, nothing more serious than a conflict in duty will arise. But Kant insists that conflicts in duty are only apparent, and that the only duty in such a situation is the duty for which a stronger ground of obligation in the law can be given. It is inconceivable that Kant would regard the claim of the absentee owner of a can of rotten beans as superior to the claim of a rational being to life. Third, in his *Theory of Law* Kant recognizes and accepts the right of necessity as to some extent *qualifying* (though not abrogating) one's right even to take another's life when in peril of ones own.[47] And, finally, Kant accepts the right of *usucapio*, in terms of which one may acquire title to the property of another because of the failure of the owner to maintain control over his or her property.[48] The starving man thus could claim the rotting beans on the basis of *usucapio*.[49]

Let us suppose, however, that Kant made a statement that was clearly legalistic. What should we conclude from it with regard to Kant's ethical theory? We should only conclude that the statement in question is inconsistent with the remainder of his theory. Faced with such an inconsistency we would then have to determine which position, the legalistic one or the procedural one, is in closer

46 Weiss, *Man's Freedom*, 56.

47 MS, 235: MOM, 391–2.

48 Ibid., 291–2: ibid., 439–40.

49 Professor Blanshard offers a criticism of Kant's theory very similar to Weiss's. He pictures starving men in a life boat with foodstuffs belonging to someone else. Now they have a duty to refrain from stealing and to refrain from taking life. But if they don't steal they will have to starve, which means they would be taking their own lives. On the other hand if they obey the duty to preserve life, then they must steal. I think all the objections raised against Weiss's example apply equally well here. See Blanshard, *Preface to Philosophy*, 149.

accord with the main tenets of Kant's ethics. There could be no doubt about the answer.

We find ourselves forced to choose between contradictory statements on this very issue raised in Kant's article on the "Supposed Right to Lie." Here Kant does argue in a highly legalistic manner. But are we supposed to throw out the doctrine of the *Groundwork*, the second *Critique*, the third *Critique*, and the *Metaphysics of Morals* so that we can interpret Kant's ethics on the basis of this single article? Paton meets this issue squarely and judiciously by dismissing Kant's article on the "Supposed Right to Lie" on grounds that it is internally inconsistent, that it flagrantly contradicts his major ethical writings, and that it was written when Kant was in a rage and well advanced in years.[50]

The attribution to Kant of a substantive formalism and the criticism of his position on this basis derives primarily from Hegel, who is considered by many to be the most effective of Kant's critics. Although Hegel does not mention Kant by name in his *Phenomenology of Mind*, he assesses in his discussion of "the ethical view of life" a position thought to be Kantian. Hegel opens his criticism of what has been taken to be Kant's position by noting in the chapter on "Reason as Lawgiver" that on the ethical view, substantive laws of the ethical life are directly accepted. There is no argument to justify them or to reveal their origin, because the *other*, which could give such warrant, could only be self-consciousness, which is for Hegel nothing else than this reality of the ethical life. Therefore,

> Since self-consciousness knows itself to be a moment of this substance, the moment of self-existence (of independence and self-determination), it expresses the existence of the law within itself in the form: "the healthy natural reason knows immediately what is right and good."[51]

---

50 Paton, "An Alleged Right to Lie." As a matter of fact I think a better justification can be made for the article and for Kant's rejection of the right to lie than Paton seems to think possible. Lying is a very serious offense for anyone who prizes communication between persons. Also, Kant thought that reason was dependent upon such intercommunication. Thus he seems to feel that to lie is to abandon one's very nature as a rational being. (See also Singer, "The Categorical Imperative.")
Important statements on the controversy surrounding this article, including the relevant Kantian texts, have been assembled by Georg Geismann and Hariolf Oberer, eds. *Kant und das Recht der Lüge*.
51 Hegel, 302: Baillie, 441.

This argument may be directed against Kant, but only if we mean by the knowledge of right and good nothing more than the general *form*, that is, the concept of duty. But Hegel continues:

> As healthy reason knows the law immediately so the law is valid for it also immediately, and it says directly: "this is right and good." The emphasis is on "*this*": there are *determinate specific laws*; there is the "fact itself" with concrete filling and content.[52]

Hegel attributes to Kant the notion that reason alone can with immediacy determine specific duties and tell the agent what is right and good.[53]

Hegel tests the soundness of this position by considering two of Kant's examples. Taking the maxim, "Everyone ought to speak the truth," Hegel immediately notes that we must add the condition, "if he knows the truth." The healthy reason explains that this is what it meant all the time. But then we note that the healthy reason has not spoken the truth, since it spoke in a fashion other than it had intended to speak. To avoid this embarrassment, Hegel suggests the new form, "Each must speak the truth according to his knowledge and conviction about it on each occasion."[54] But now we no longer have the universal assurance that truth will be uttered, which was promised by the ethical maxim. Now the content is contingent: "Each must speak the truth" now asserts no more than "Each is sincere." And Hegel warns that we can no longer improve on this maxim; if we were to remove this difficulty

> by saying that the contingency of the knowledge and the conviction as to the truth should be dropped, and that the *truth* too, "*ought*" to be known, then this would be a command which contradicts straightway what we started from.[55]

We started with the assurance that the healthy reason could immediately express the truth, and now we are saying that it does not possess this power but is, instead, obligated to look for it. Reason, pretending to dictate substantive law, produced instead a content that was purely contingent. More important, Hegel adds,

---

52 Idem: idem. Italics are mine. This italicized phrase states clearly the position of substantive formalism.

53 We have noted already that Kant does not hold the view that Hegel may be attributing to him.

54 Ibid., 303: ibid., 442.

55 Idem: ibid., 442–3.

> When we try to get the required universality and necessity by making the law refer to the knowledge [instead of to the content], then the content really disappears altogether.[56]

Hegel develops a similar dialectic in connection with the command, "Love thy neighbor as thyself." He points out that love must be active (practical in Kant's terminology) since inactive love is non-existent, and, consequently, that this command enjoins us to do someone good and/or remove evil from our neighbor. But this presupposes that we treat our neighbor intelligently, with knowledge of good and evil in general, and with knowledge in particular of the constitution of his or her well-being. Since the state carries out this concern on a vast scale far beyond the capacity of any single individual to add or detract, all that is left for the individual to do is to offer particular assistance which, says Hegel, "is as contingent as it is momentary."[57] The action which is commanded may thus exist or not exist, may result in good or not. The confusion of contingent factors deprives an imperative to such action of any substantive, universal content. "In other words," Hegel says, "such laws never get further than the '*ought to be*,' they have no actual reality; they are not laws, but merely commands."[58]

Hegel concludes that we should not be surprised at this result because it is the nature of concrete, substantive situations to be determinate and particular; consequently, any determinate, substantial command will by its nature be inadequate to the universality demanded by reason. And conversely, any and every command of reason in order to be universal must forego content of an absolute sort and restrict itself to formal universality, which is universality devoid of content. Stripped of all particularity,

> there is thus nothing left with which to make a law but the bare form of universality, in fact, the mere tautology of consciousness, a tautology which stands over against the content, and consists in the knowledge, not of the content actually existing, the content proper, but of its ultimate essence only, a knowledge of its self-identity.[59]

The inner ethical essence is, therefore, not to be considered as content; rather, it offers a criterion for the determination of the suitability of content to be law – the criterion being that such content must not contradict itself. Reason as

56 Ibid., 303: ibid., 443.
57 Ibid., 304: ibid., 444.
58 Idem: idem. Hegel assumes that since reason does not give a substantive law (as Kant himself holds) it can give no law. Apparently Hegel does not even consider the concept of procedural laws.
59 Ibid., 305: ibid., 445.

lawgiver is thus reduced to reason as tester of what is, from some other source, laid down as law.

Before considering Hegel's criticism of reason in his chapter on "Reason as Tester of the Law," we must assess his criticism of reason as the giver of law. He presents the "ethical view" as one in which the healthy reason knows the law immediately and by reference to the law knows immediately specific determinate laws which are right and good. Reason presents the right or the good in terms of concrete, specific actions. If this were Kant's position, I think we could agree that Hegel had refuted it. But, as we have seen, Kant does not hold this substantive position. Kant comes closer to speaking of a "healthy reason" in the second *Critique* than anywhere else. In one passage he even says, "It is always in everyone's power to satisfy the commands of the categorical command of morality."[60] But this hardly supports Hegel's interpretation of Kant, because Kant immediately goes on to say that the reason why it is always in everyone's power to fulfill the command of morality is that "it is only a question of the maxim which must be genuine and pure."[61] While it is true that the maxim of moral volition has content as well as form according to Kant, it is also true for Kant that the determination of the maxim is not given immediately but is the product of a rather complex procedure of judgment. Hence even here Kant is not speaking of a healthy reason which mechanically or immediately delivers substantive law.

Hegel and Kant are essentially in agreement that reason does not of itself give substantive law. And Kant should agree with Hegel on the inadequacies of the examples Hegel discussed.[62]

Hegel's third criticism is, however, much more important. The essence of this criticism is that there can never be any content to the law, for if the law has a determinate content it will lack the universality of reason, and if it has the universality of law it will fail to have determinate content. This is a formidable problem which faces any non-naturalistic theory of ethics. But this problem, as it seems to me, is one which Kant's ethics has solved. Kant's attempt to relate the infinite to the finite, the universal form to particular sensibility, is made possible in two ways. First, Kant establishes a procedure that while rejecting any claimants to universality that are already determinant, ensures the ultimate

60 KpV, 36: CprR, 148.
61 Ibid., 37: ibid., 148.
62 Hegel does not specifically claim that these examples are Kant's; they are introduced out of any context so that it is difficult to know. But granting that they are Kant's, and granting that Hegel has shown that these examples are in error, no substantial criticism of Kant's ethics follows. Kant himself has apologized for the shortcomings of some of his own examples.

achievement of determinateness that is universalizable. Thus, the law, though it does not immediately provide content, provides a procedure whereby determinate content can be added; the determinate content will indeed be particular but not merely particular; it will be made particular through a procedure ensuring universalizability. It can never be said that the particular is universal, but rather that the particular is capable of universalization.

We must admit that Kant's solution to this problem is not systematically stated and emphasized in any of his writings. So perhaps there is some plausibility in Hegel's criticism of Kant's writings on this particular issue. On the other hand, I have tried to systematize Kant's solution to this problem, and we have seen, in fact, that Kant himself was occasionally fully explicit on these points.

To conclude our discussion of the non-substantive formalism of Kant's ethics: in light of the definition of the moral task, the singularity of the categorical imperative, the indeterminacy of duties of virtue, the importance of autonomy, and the insistence that each moral agent must live his or her own ethical life in fear and trembling, we can only conclude that Kant does not regard the moral law and the categorical formulations of it as substantive principles.

ii. The Non-Logical Character of Kant's Formalism

Once Hegel shows that reason cannot present a substantive law, he proceeds to argue that reason as tester of the law is simply a formal, logical principle and incapable of directing the moral agent in the act of volition. Having shown that the inner ethical essence is devoid of content, Hegel shows that it offers instead a criterion of self-consistency for the determination of the suitability of content to be law.

Hegel has no difficulty in showing that this criterion of consistency is inadequate and, thus, that reason is ineffectual both as lawgiver and as tester of laws. He can justly insist, following the analysis we have recapitulated, that "just because the standard is a tautology and indifferent to the content, it accepts one content just as readily as the opposite."[63] And he is able to exemplify this by pointing to examples of the internal consistency and inconsistency of both property and no property. Having interpreted the "moral law" or "categorical imperative" as the principle of contradiction, Hegel argues that it would be strange,

---

63 Hegel, 307: Baillie, 447.

> if tautology, the principle of contradiction, which is allowed to be merely a formal criterion for knowledge of theoretical truth, i.e. something which is quite indifferent to truth and untruth alike, were to be more than this for knowledge of practical truth.[64]

The law is therefore found to be devoid of content and indeterminate. And this necessarily implies that when the law is made determinate it will have an accidental content. It will be a law made by a particular individual, conscious of a particular, accidental content. If the law, then, is enacted with immediacy on the basis of this accidental content in the experience of the particular agent, caprice, as Hegel says, is made into law.[65] It will be of no avail to say that something is not consistent, for any given action can be made consistent. I can universalize stealing the property of another simply by insisting that the property I have taken is no longer the property of another. By changing points of view all this can be accomplished, and no contradiction is involved in changing points of view.[66]

By attributing to Kant the view that reason alone can determine specific duties with immediacy, Hegel deprives Kant of an appeal to sensibility. According to Hegel's interpretation of Kant, the content of the faculty of desire is not given any consideration in the determination of concrete, specific duties. On this interpretation the content of sensibility and desire is superfluous, since Hegel attributes to Kant the view that reason alone can produce the content as well as the form of duties. Once Hegel presents Kant's position in this fashion, he has no trouble in showing that reason is incapable of producing determinate concrete duties.

Presented in this fashion, Hegel's objections to Kant's position cannot be met by considering the various formulations of the categorical imperative. Admittedly, Hegel did not consider whether there was anything more than the principle of contradiction contained in the idea of being able to *will* one's maxim as a law of nature. But there is no way to establish the relevance of the procedures of the categorical imperative once the sensibility has been removed. When access to sensibility is removed, so is the phenomenal world, the knowledge of others, the knowledge of the self, metaphysics, science, and art. As Hegel rightly saw, only logic remains.

The radical separation of the sensibility and reason and their necessary conflict are crucial points in Hegel's mistaken exposition of Kant's view of the

64 Ibid., 308: ibid., 449.
65 An insightful and comprehensive discussion of Hegel's critique of Kant's ethical theory is the article by David Couzens Hoy, "Hegel's Critique of Kantian Morality."
66 Hegel, 309–11: Baillie, 450–53.

moral moment.[67] Kant is alleged to hold: that reason alone is self-sufficient in ethics; that reason is in conflict with sensibility; that reason postulates the harmony of duty and nature and falls thereby into inconsistency and dissemblance. If reason has no recourse to sensibility, a rational command (duty) must require the realization of pure universality. But pure universality cannot be actualized. Duty, which is universal, is actualized only as particular; hence duty is impossible and is necessarily illusory.[68] To avoid this consequence Kant's only recourse is to ignore content, to deny in effect all meaning to moral action since any act can then be both moral and immoral at once.[69] And since Hegel insists that Kant accepts the postulate of the harmony of duty and the world (after asserting their opposition), the individual's moral self is lost in contradiction and dissemblance.

We find a similar situation if we examine this issue from the standpoint of moral conscience. Kant is alleged to hold that pure duty is the essence of the moral act.[70] (By essence, Hegel means more than mere form.) Thus, according to Hegel, duty is opposed to the self, which is a concrete being. Duty for Kant then becomes a law for the sake of which the self exists.[71] In conscience one beholds this pure empty duty, the emptiness of which reflects the absence of any and all conviction in the Kantian conscience.[72] But since action requires determination, we must find content for this negative conscience, this immediate certainty of the self. Since we cannot rely on sensibility (it being in conflict with duty and conscience), we must rely on caprice for particularity, and conscience is indifferent to capricious particularity. Any content, therefore, will do.[73]

Hegel's criticism of reason as the tester of the law is, again, a perfectly sound criticism. However, it is not directed against Kant's ethics. If interpreted as a critic of Kant, Hegel is basically in error by insisting on the radical separation and opposition of sensibility and reason in the moral situation. In Chapter II, Section 2, we examined the heterogeneity of the good at considerable length and acknowledged the sharp difference between the natural good as happiness and the moral good as virtue. We have seen that whereas reason provides the norm for the latter, sensibility and reason as prudence provide the

---

67 Ibid., 427: ibid., 618.
68 Ibid., 448, 452: ibid., 648, 654.
69 Ibid., 430–432, 437: ibid., 621–623, 632.
70 Ibid., 448: ibid., 648.
71 Ibid., 449: ibid., 649.
72 Ibid., 452–3: ibid., 653–4.
73 Idem: idem.

norm for the former. But we have also seen that although the moral (formal) good and the natural (material, sensible) good "strongly limit and check each other," they do so "in the same subject."[74] Clearly Kant thought that reason and sensibility were closely related to one another, indeed that both are present in moral experience and Kant's theory takes this into account.

Furthermore, Kant gives a very different account of the opposition between reason and sensibility in ethics than the one Hegel attributed to him. Kant says:

> But this *distinction* of the principle of happiness from that of morality is not for this reason an *opposition* between them, and pure practical reason does not require that we should renounce the claims to happiness; it requires *only that we take no account* of them whenever duty is in question.[75]

Kant does not say that there is an inevitable opposition between form and content in ethics. He says merely that there is a conflict between reason and sensibility in regard to the *determination* of the will. But when reason attempts to determine the will, it must recognize the legitimate claims of sensibility. One of the ends of reason which is also its duty is to seek the happiness of others. We noted at great length in Section 1 of this chapter Kant's insistence that every maxim must have both form and content and the complete delineation of the two in a unity of totality. We must not forget, moreover, that the material object of moral volition and the canon of pure reason is the highest good as a union of form and content. If Hegel's target is Kant's ethics, Hegel's mistake is increasingly obvious once we consider the broader reaches of Kantian philosophy: theoretical and aesthetic experience clearly depend upon the unity of form and matter through the agency of the knower.

The only possible source of irreconcilability of form and content in Kant's ethics would be the incommensurability of sensibility to an idea of reason. But we have already considered this issue and have suggested that Kant's theory solves the problem of the union of such incommensurables.[76] We must conclude, therefore, that Hegel was mistaken in his criticism of Kant on this issue of the relation of reason to sensibility or that the philosophical tradition has erred in supposing that Hegel was discussing Kant's ethics.

Consider the famous Hegelian insistence that reason as tester of the law cannot function in terms of the criterion of consistency. His argument that this

---

74 KpV, 113: CprR, 217.
75 Ibid., 93: Ibid., 199. Italics are Kant's.
76 See Chapters VI and VII.

standard, as a tautology, and therefore as indifferent to content, can accept one content as readily as any other seems sound enough. But here again the difficulty with Hegel's criticism is that it does not apply to Kant. Kant does insist that if there is a logical inconsistency contained in the mere idea of the maxim of our act, then it is clearly incapable of universalization and moral willing. But this test of logical consistency is not the primary test of the law. The law also requires *volitional* consistency, not merely formal consistency. The categorical imperative prescribes what moral judgment must do to *will* in a universal manner. It does not prescribe mere consistent thought; rather, it demands that willing be done, not merely on the basis of mutually consistent maxims but on the basis of universally valid maxims. We are not obligated merely to think about various possibilities that could be consistent, but to *will* a state of nature in which certain maxims would become laws of nature. This transports us into a realm of action in which content becomes determinate.

The superficiality of Hegel's criticism is most easily seen if we consider his example about stealing. He points out that the rule of consistency can justify stealing just as easily as not. One simply says that the property of another belongs to one as soon as he or she takes it. Therefore one never takes what does not belong to him or her, and hence never has in his or her possession the belongings of others. But this bit of casuistry does not satisfy the demand of the moral law in Kant's ethics. The moral demand is stated in terms of the formulations of the categorical imperative which specify not what is logically possible but what is volitionally possible. Reason that is the tester of the law is not mere logical reason but practical reason. Suppose we try to justify stealing while striving to will in a manner that is universally valid. In order to will in this manner I must put myself in thought in the place and point of view of the person from whom I plan to steal. From that person's standpoint I cannot regard the property in question as my possession. Rather, by taking the other's standpoint I see the situation from a universal point of view in which the concept of property cannot be manipulated by a mere act of illegal possession. I cannot shift the title of the property without rejecting that enlarged perspective and thereby exposing my failure to observe the morally imperative procedures of moral judgment. Some cases of stealing may indeed be justifiable. Since Kant is not a legalist, it is quite possible that one could will universally the theft of another's property in certain restricted situations – as, for example, where human life hangs in the balance. But it will not be possible to do so simply by defining the meaning of ownership as mere possession or to suit oneself. Kant's theory is not refuted by the Hegelian attack, for Hegel's mistake lay in confusing Kant's formalism with logical formalism.

iii. The Procedural Character of Kant's Formalism

Hegel's criticism of reason as the giver of the law was based upon a substantive interpretation of Kant's formalism which cannot be sustained. His criticism of reason as tester of the law was based upon a logical interpretation of Kant's formalism, which is likewise indefensible. Kant's formalism cannot be understood either as a substantive or as a logical formalism; rather it is a procedural formalism. The categorical imperative sets forth the procedure which moral judgment must follow in order to will rationally.[77] As in thought, rationality in volition depends upon the process of thinking and willing and not upon substantive belief. When the procedures that reason specifies for moral judgment have been carried out, the will has acted rationally and in a universal manner.

Since moral action is the task of each individual knower, there can be no moral examples. Kant is not being cynical; he does not deny that some individuals have lived exemplary lives. Jesus and Socrates are among those in whom Kant finds great apparent worth. But even these men are not moral examples in the sense that we should model our lives after theirs in any literal fashion. We determine, in fact, which individuals seem to be particularly good by recourse to our own autonomous understanding of the demand of the moral law. Kant asks how we can know the holy ones of the Scriptures except by applying the moral test to all the characters in the Bible. Each person must judge in such matters for himself or herself.

Kant also insists that

> No one can obligate anyone else except by a necessary agreement of the will of others with his own according to universal rules of freedom. He can, therefore, never obligate another except by means of that other's own will.[78]

No human being can delegate his or her moral responsibility; each must be moral for himself or herself and also accept responsibility for his or her immorality.

It is for this reason that the problem of the application of Kant's ethics to practice assumes such importance. If one could only delegate some of one's

---

77 Schilpp, 126, *passim*. Professor Schilpp was the first, to my knowledge, to interpret Kant's moral law in a thorough-going procedural manner. But by restricting himself to Kant's precritical writings he never made as much of his point as the point itself warrants. I found his fragmentary suggestions on this point extremely helpful.

78 HN (AA19), no. 6954, 212–13: Schilpp, 126.

moral responsibility, then the problem of the application of ethics could be left to experts. In fact, however, creativity and independent judgment are required in the application of any theory to practice – whether in architecture, science, military tactics, medicine or other fields. In fields such as these we can delegate responsibility to architects, scientists, generals and doctors. They must, in turn, follow procedures of judgment appropriate to their professions. But the gap between theory and practice in ethics must burden each of us because there is no way of delegating it. The problem of relating ethical theory to practice is one that confronts each rational being; therefore each person must be concerned with the application of ethical theory to moral practice.

For Kant, applying the categorical imperative, while demanding, does not present a problem. The problem is to embody the highest good to the fullest extent possible through symbolic representation. The categorical imperative is simply a statement of the actual procedure of moral judging. The agent seeks to will in a universal manner so that his or her actions fulfill his or her freedom. But the only way the will determines what does in fact constitute universal acts of moral volition is by going through a variety of procedures designed to carry the agent beyond the merely subjective conditions of volition.

The extent to which the will is guided by these procedures depends upon the faithfulness with which the moral agent carries out these procedures in his or her consciousness. Rational autonomous willing must be judged on the basis of the character of the thought process the moral agent engages in, rather than in terms of the substantive opinions he or she holds. In consequence, the virtue of the will must consist not in the attainment of some external goal but in the faithfulness with which the moral agent fulfills the procedures of moral volition. No rational being can be certain that he or she holds only true opinions or that he or she has always determined correctly the indeterminate duties of virtue. But one can be certain that one has fulfilled the rational procedures of moral judgment. That much lies wholly within one's power. Kant, therefore, concludes:

> For while I can indeed be mistaken at times in my objective judgment as to whether something is a duty or not, I cannot be mistaken in my subjective judgment as to whether I have submitted it to my practical reason (here in its role as judge) for such a judgment; for if I could be mistaken in that, I would have made no practical judgment at all, and in that case there would be neither truth nor error. *Unconscientiousness* is not lack of conscience but rather the propensity to pay no heed to its judgment. But if someone is aware that he has acted in accordance with his conscience, then as far as guilt or innocence is concerned nothing more can be required of him. It is incumbent upon him only to enlighten his *understanding* in the matter of what is or is not duty.[79]

---

79 MS, 401: MOM, 529–530.

Because of his repudiation of substantive formalism, Kant consistently argues that moral guilt or innocence is to be judged not in terms of the agent's fulfillment of particular actions or attainment of certain goals, but rather in terms of his or her conscientiousness, the faithfulness with which he or she carries out the maxims of moral judgment in ethical practice. And if a moral agent does not carry out the moral procedure of judgment to the best of his or her ability, then he or she fails to fulfill the immanent duty to promote the embodiment of the highest good. The moral agent tries to will the universal form of the moral law in terms of the content of sensible desire while accepting a condition limiting all relative ends to the consideration of all rational beings as ends in themselves. This procedure constitutes the source of unity between the highest good as an idea of reason and the sensible world. The reordering of the sensible world by the moral agent in accordance with the determinations of his or her moral judgment constitutes a symbolic representation of the highest good.

The first task of judgment, establishing the practical validity of Kant's ethical theory, is made reasonably plausible. We must now consider the role of judgment in motivating the moral agent to complete his or her acts of judgment in terms of the procedure designated by the formulae of the categorical imperative. The validity of Kant's ethics turns also on this consideration.

Chapter IX: The Role Of Judgment In The Embodiment Of The Highest Good

1 Moral Feeling

Judgment's role in the fulfillment of the moral task is only half done when judgment arrives at the "regulative" determination of actions which, if acted upon by will, would be symbolic realizations of the highest good. Judgment's task is not complete until the will has been aroused to *will* such symbolic enactments through moral action.

In order to understand how judgment wins acceptance for the moral law in the human will, we must determine the conditions necessary to motivate the will to action. It is not sufficient for a person to know what he or she should do. The will may be informed by judgment of that action which the moral law demands of him or her without effecting that action in concrete volition. If one had a holy will, if one were a pure rational being, one would act in this fashion. But a person is not such a being and, consequently, judgment's task in applying the moral law in action is not complete when judgment merely determines the particular action that is a proper symbol of the highest good and an adequate expression of one's duty. The action commanded by reason must become the object of volition; it must not only be *known*, it must be *willed*.

There is a distinction between knowing and willing for all rational beings. For human beings possessed of sensibility, there is a struggle between sensible desires and reason for control of the will. In the presence of sensible desires, the will is under a constant temptation to reject the command of reason (the moral good) in favor of the delights of inclination (the natural good). For humans, therefore, the moral law becomes a categorical imperative. Furthermore, if the action demanded by the categorical imperative is to be realized, the will must be motivated to action by the aid of a certain feeling of pleasure which the law itself effects in the will. This pleasure must be a delight the will takes in the fulfillment of duty.

> If we are to will actions for which reason by itself prescribes an "ought" to a rational, yet sensuously affected, being, it is admittedly necessary that reason should have a power of *infusing a feeling of pleasure* or satisfaction in the fulfillment of duty ... by which it can determine sensibility in accordance with rational principles.[1]

1 GMS, 460: GMM, 128.

Reason must be able not only to legislate the law for the human will, it must be able to produce in this will a sensible incentive to fulfill the law.

It is here that judgment enters as the power of mind to provide *a priori* principles for the feeling of pleasure and pain. Judgment is that power of reason to produce a feeling of pleasure in sensibility associated with the fulfillment of duty.[2] Hence, in trying to understand how it is that judgment can win acceptance of the moral law in the will of human beings we are concerned with the question, How can reason be practical? Another way of putting this question is to ask, How can reason be an efficient cause in the determination of an effect (feeling) in sensibility?[3]

If this is our question, however, we must not suppose that it can be answered directly. Kant always insisted that when one acts morally one must not act from inclination as the principle of one's action. Although in every act of volition one must have a material object, one must not be determined in willing by the attractiveness of that object to the faculty of desire. Whenever one acts from sensible inclination, one acts heteronomously; one acts as though one were an animal. One's sensible faculty of desire leads one to action just as though there were a causal connection between the object of one's desire and his or her act of willing. In such an act – assuming it has moral dimensions and is not merely a morally indifferent act, such as drinking water when thirsty and water is abundant – the person is morally deficient, and his or her freedom is not fully realized. If a person acts out of fear or hope for some object, then this act is morally worthless.[4] If one would will in a morally commendable manner, one must act both according to the moral law and for its sake. In every act one takes an interest in an object, a delight (satisfaction) in its existence. This is necessary in order to will a particular action.[5] But this delight and interest must not derive from the object, which is sensible, but from reason as the moral law which can never be sensible. This is the difficulty we face in attempting a direct answer to the above question. Kant states:

> It is, however, wholly impossible to comprehend – that is, to make intelligible a *priori* – how a mere thought containing nothing sensible in itself can bring about a sensation of pleasure or displeasure; for there is here a special kind of causality, and – as with all

2 EEKU, 245: CoPJ, 45; GMS, 389: GMM, 57.
3 See KpV, 76–82: CprR, 184–9.
4 KpV, 22–23: CprR, 133–4. Note, however, such a person is still free though not autonomous. The person is therefore responsible for his or her bad action. Heteronomy is, as I have shown, a deficient mode of freedom.
5 KU, 209: CoAJ, 48.

> causality – we are totally unable to determine its character *a priori*: on this we must consult experience alone.[6]

Experience, however, can only determine relations of cause and effect between objects of experience, because,

> here pure reason by means of mere Ideas (which furnish absolutely no objects for experience) has to be the cause of an effect admittedly found in experience. Hence for us men [*Menschen*] it is wholly impossible to explain how and why the *universality of a maxim as a law* – and therefore morality – should interest us.[7]

It is therefore impossible to *explain* in theoretical terms how reason can be practical, for this would require "explaining *how freedom is possible*."[8]

A theoretical explanation of freedom would involve the denial of freedom, since theoretical explanations involve determining objects by the laws of nature. It is precisely the nature of freedom that it cannot be so determined, since it is of the essence of freedom that an *idea* should itself become an efficient cause.[9] The will is not free if it is determined either by sense stimuli, by conceptions which necessarily constitute the content of one's thought, or if it is explicable in terms of principles. Free action depends upon independence from necessitating conditions of a past time. In order *to explain* something, however, one must make it determinate by reference to the conditions which necessitate it.[10] If, then, we are to hold that reason is practical and that the will is free, we must resign ourselves to the predicament in which our understanding rests. Our concern with the question "How can reason be practical?" and its derivative question, "How can reason provide an incentive for the will?" cannot be understood as a concern to explain this possibility. Freedom of the will, which is the reality of reason as practical, is presupposed in the experience of obligation from which Kant begins.[11]

It is also clear from this that the employment of judgment as practical reason in producing the feeling of pleasure in the human will, as the unitary faculty of both reason and the faculty of desire, is reason effecting a sensible

---

6 GMS, 460: GMM, 128.

7 Idem: idem. We must bear in mind that interest is one kind of pleasure. (KU, 205–7, 209–11: CoAJ, 44–5, 48–50).

8 GMS, 458–459: GMM, 127. See also KpV, 75: CprR, 180.

9 GMS, 412–413: GMM, 80.

10 KpV, 96: CprR, 202; GMS, 461–62: GMM, 129–30.

11 GMS, 455: GMM, 123.

occasion. It follows that we cannot explain how judgment is able to arouse this feeling in the will, since this employment of judgment as reason in practice is free and, consequently, beyond explanation.

What then is our concern in asking how judgment can produce a feeling of pleasure in the fulfillment of duty, such that the will is thereby provided with a necessary incentive to moral action? In asking this question we wish to know what kind of feeling is produced in the will by judgment whereby the will takes a sensible interest in the fulfillment of the moral law. We want to know what the moral law, through judgment, "effects (or better, must effect) in the mind, so far as it is an incentive."[12] We wish, therefore, to learn two things: first, what this sensible feeling is like, and second, how it differs from other feelings of pleasure and pain, which can also affect the will.[13]

As regards the first question, since none of the desires and inclinations entertained by the agent's will through the faculty of desire can be allowed to determine the will by means of natural inclination, nothing is left to determine the will objectively speaking except the moral law. And subjectively speaking, the only remaining feeling that can determine a person's will is the feeling of reverence aroused by the law itself.[14] The moral law demands that the will dismiss all sensuous inclinations, not from its consideration, but from its determination to moral action.[15] But to the extent that determination of the will by the moral law restricts and spurns our sensuous feelings and desires, to that extent the moral law "must produce a feeling which can be called pain."[16] This feeling of pain which follows from the determination of the will by reason[17]

---

12 KpV, 72: CprR, 180.

13 The second question is particularly important, since we shall leave Kant open to the charge of resting morality on empirical grounds unless we can distinguish in principle this feeling from others which serve as motives to action.

14 GMS, 400: GMM, 68–9.

15 Schopenhauer and Hegel have argued that Kant wished to dismiss from moral deliberation all reference to the sensibility, but this is clearly a mistake as we have progressively seen. Kant does not find it necessary to disregard the sensibility in determining moral action; he merely insists that in moral action the moral law "blocks the inclinations and the propensity to make them the supreme practical condition (i.e., self-love) from all participation in supreme legislation." (KpV, 74: CprR, 182). To say that the inclinations must not determine the will is one thing. To say that the inclinations cannot even provide content for which reason determines the form is quite another. Kant affirms the former and denies the latter. (TP, 280–81: TaP, 47–48; RGV, 6–7n: Rel, 6–7n).

16 KpV, 73: CprR, 181.

17 Since our sensible desires strive to determine our will and since pleasure results from the attainment of dominance over the will by these desires (the pleasure of anticipating the fruition of these wants by the action the will directs to their attainment), it follows that

does not seem likely, at first glance, to provide an incentive to moral action. Rather, it would appear to offer a strong deterrent to moral action. And indeed, the immediate direct effect of the moral law on feeling is precisely this. But we must not overlook the indirect effect on feeling which is also produced. In striking down a person's inclinations the moral law strikes down the pretensions of a person's sensible nature to control that person. This law thereby reveals to a human being his or her full nature as a personality, his or her possession of freedom and volition. In this a person recognizes himself or herself as worthy of respect, for the law teaches one that the determination of one's actions lies within oneself and not in pre-existing sensuously given inclinations.

As revealed by the law, one is unconditioned; one's worth cannot be conditioned. As a free law-giver one sees oneself not as a pawn of fated inclinations, but as one's own master. As servant of the same law, one is humbled, and recognizes that the condition of one's unconditionedness, one's dignity, lies not in the senses nor in self-conceit, but in the law which alone frees one from the control of external stimuli. In the pain of humiliation that follows this revelation, one finally arrives at the positive feeling of respect for freedom and for the law that reveals it. This positive feeling of respect is moral feeling[18] which becomes an incentive to action in accordance with the law, since, Kant writes,

> it has an influence on the sensibility of the subject and effects a feeling which promotes the influence of the law on the will .... Thus respect for the law ... is morality itself, regarded subjectively as an incentive, inasmuch as pure practical reason, by rejecting all rival claims of self-love, gives authority and absolute sovereignty to the law.[19]

Thus practical reason, as an efficient cause with power to act freely apart from determination by external causes, strikes down claims of inclination to dominion over the will. Kant is convinced that until one has understood this, one has not understood the phenomena of moral experience. Kant insisted throughout his life (both before and after the completion of the *Critiques*) that

> the supreme ground of morality must not only permit a conclusion in the direction of delight, but must itself afford delight in the highest degree; for it is no merely speculative

---

determination of the will by reason which reduces to naught the pretension of the sensible desires produces pain. (Idem: idem).

18 Ibid., 71–77, 94–101: ibid., 180–185, 200–206.

19 Ibid., 75–76: ibid., 183–4.

> concept, but must have driving power and, although it is intellectual, it yet must have a direct bearing upon the primary incentives of the will.[20]

Since it is the nature of the moral law, the supreme ground of morality, to be dynamic and to produce moral feeling, moral beings must have this feeling. Kant insists that

> No human being is entirely without moral feeling, for were he completely lacking in receptivity to it he would be morally dead; and if (to speak in medical terms) the moral vital force could no longer excite this feeling, then humanity would dissolve (by chemical laws, as it were) into mere animality.[21]

This provides us with an answer to the derivative question regarding the practicality of reason. While we cannot directly answer the question, "How can reason be practical?"[22] we can say something about how reason provides an incentive to the will. The nature of this incentive is ambivalent. As the feeling of respect, it is both painful and pleasurable. But even when the moral law confronts our wills in a painful manner, it also makes us aware of the supreme unconditioned worth of our nature as a moral being. It reminds us that our virtue is the condition of our worthiness to be happy. The moral law creates in our wills – as the faculty of desire and practical reason – a desire to fulfill the demands of the categorical imperative. As long as we are humans, as long as our reason is in the least degree practical, the law arouses in us a feeling of respect for our own free natures. "We have, rather, a *susceptibility* on the part of free choice [*Willkür*] to be moved by pure practical reason [*Wille*] (and its law), and this is what we call moral feeling."[23]

A second question must now be considered. If Kant says that there is a sensible incentive, a feeling which aids the will in the fulfillment of duty, how can Kant preserve the categorical quality of the moral imperative? How can he escape the pitfalls of empirical morality which he so carefully described and warned against? How can he avoid the conclusion that one is obligated only so long as he or she has the sensible feeling of respect? Though often misunderstood, Kant's answer to this problem is direct and unequivocal. Since it is true that feelings of pleasure and pain provide the conditions for moral feeling, no such feeling would be possible were humans not sensuous as well

---

20 Kant to Herz, (Fall) 1773, Br (AA 10) 145: Corr, 140, as translated by Schilpp, 120.
21 MS, 400: MOM, 529.
22 GMS, 459: GMM, 119.
23 MS, 400: MOM, 529.

as rational.[24] Reason as practical is the sole cause of the moral feeling. In moral action the will takes delight in the existence of something,[25] but that object is not determined by sensibility but rather by practical reason itself.[26] It is true, of course, that

> the will must have *motives*; but these are not specific objects presumed as ends and relating to *physical feelings*. They are nothing but the unconditioned *law* itself, and the will's receptivity in subjecting itself to that law as an unconditional constraint is called *moral feelings. This is not the cause but the effect of the will's determination* [my italics], of which we would not have the slightest inner perception if that inner constraint were not already present within us. This is why the old litany–that this feeling (and thus a pleasure which we make our end) constitutes the will's first determining cause, and that happiness (of which that pleasure is an element) therefore constitutes the ground of all objective necessity to act, hence of all obligation.[27]

It is nonsense, Kant argues, to claim that because one knows it will make one unhappy to violate the moral law, therefore, one obeys the moral law from the motive of happiness and self-love. It is all right, if one wishes to be careless with language, to regard moral satisfaction as a form of happiness and moral dissatisfaction as a form of unhappiness. Kant thinks this is a clumsy use of language, but he won't quibble. He doesn't need to. The point is that even if one relates happiness and moral satisfaction in the manner just considered, one must face the fact that

> none but the virtuous, or he who is about to become virtuous, is capable of this pure moral discontent (not with the disadvantages resulting from his act, but with its sheer illegality). The discontent is thus not the *cause* but rather the *effect* of his being virtuous, and the ground that motivated him to be virtuous could not come from that unhappiness (if the pain following a misdeed be so called).[28]

As we saw in our earlier discussion of Socrates with regard to the nature of the good, one would not be made unhappy by the consciousness of the immorality

---

24 Kant says, "It should be noticed that, as respect is an effect on feeling and thus on the sensibility of a rational being, it presupposes the sensuousness and hence the finitude of such beings on whom respect for the moral law is imposed; thus respect for the law cannot be attributed to a supreme being or even to one free from all sensibility, since to such a being there could be no obstacle to practical reason." KpV, 76: CprR, 184.

25 KU, 209: CoAJ, 48.

26 See Chapter IV, Section 3.

27 TP, 283–84: TaP, 50–51. See Chapter II, Section 2.

28 TP, 283n: TaP, 50n. My italics.

of his or her actions if the good as a natural object of volition were the only standard of judgment. A person's action in opposition to the moral law cannot be the source of "unhappiness" unless that person has recognized the moral law and his or her obligation to it as a condition of worthiness to be happy. Hence, although the moral feeling produced in sensibility by the moral law is a sensible incentive to moral behavior,[29] it is nevertheless a rational incentive. Moral feeling is the *effect* rather than the *cause* of the influence of the moral law upon the will. Respect, therefore

> in contrast to the enjoyment or gratification of happiness, is something for which there can be no feeling basic and prior to reason, for such a feeling would always be sensuous and pathological. Respect as the consciousness of the direct constraint of the will through law is hardly analogous to the feeling of pleasure, although in relation to the faculty of desire it produces exactly the same effect, but from different sources.[30]

Having seen again that in spite of the sensible condition of this feeling, its source lies in reason as practical, let us consider in more detail the moral feeling itself and how this feeling compares with other types of sensation. The moral feeling, along with other feelings, is to be found in the faculty of pleasure and pain. This faculty of mind is the ground of the faculty of judgment; judgment, on the other hand, is the faculty which provides the principles for the determination of pleasure and pain. As judgment functions in this employment to determine the feelings of pleasure and pain, "judgment is related solely to the subject and does not produce any concepts of objects for itself alone."[31] While the understanding and sensibility, along with reason and the faculty of desire, contain within themselves as faculties "an objective relation to representations," the faculty of pleasure and pain contains nothing more than "the receptivity of a determination of the subject."[32] Hence,

---

29 We must note that it is only an incentive to, and not the motive of, moral behavior. It is the sensible counterpart of the motive force of practical reason itself. As a sensible incentive it only assists the will to act morally; it does not compel or determine the will to do so.

30 KpV, 117: CprR, 221. Although Kant says that respect is hardly analogous to pleasure, he does not intend to say that it is not a pleasure for it clearly does excite and attract the will as the faculty of desire. But he does intend to say that it is hardly analogous to pleasure if by "pleasure" one means a feeling which is aroused in the faculty of desire by a material object whose existence gratifies this faculty. We must note carefully Kant's insistence here that the feeling of pleasure and the feeling of respect do not differ in their effects on the faculty of desire. They differ merely in their sources. The former affects the will whereas the latter is effected by the will itself as practical reason.

31 EEKU, 208: CoPJ, 12.

32 Idem: idem.

> if the power of judgment is to determine anything for itself alone, it could not be anything other than the feeling of pleasure, and, conversely, if the latter is to have an *a priori* principle at all, it will be found only in the power of judgment.[33]

To the extent that we find a principle in the feeling of pleasure and pain, to that extent we will find judgment present providing that principle, since judgment, alone among the faculties of cognition, relates itself to the subject without concepts as, in fact, do feelings of pleasure and pain.

We are not concerned here, however, to examine in detail this faculty of pleasure and pain, and the relationship of judgment to it. Our concern here is to determine the kind of pleasure or pain in moral feeling and to compare it with other types of pleasure and pain. Feelings of pleasure or displeasure are not attributable to an object. Rather it is the feeling that the subject has simply by being confronted with representations of one sort or another. If we consider the mere feeling of pleasure and pain as such, that is, if we concern ourselves with the *reaction of the subject* to the representation only, without being concerned to relate the representation to an object, then we encounter pure feelings of pleasure or pain. Judgments we make from this perspective will be, therefore, either judgments of mere agreeableness or aesthetic judgments of the beautiful. But suppose we are not content to revel either in our subjective response to an agreeable representation or in the harmonious free play of our faculties in the presence of a beautiful object. Suppose, instead, that we are concerned with the real existence of an object which understanding connects with this representation and that we take pleasure, or delight, in the real existence of this object. When these conditions are met, we have attained an *interest* in addition to a *feeling*. An interest, Kant says, is that particular type of pleasure "we connect with the representation of the real existence of an object."[34] This is not a pure feeling of pleasure, since we are involved already with the faculty of desire which is either the determining ground of this pleasure (as in the case of pleasure stemming from the realization of sensuous desires) or is "necessarily implicated with its determining ground,"[35] as in the case of a moral delight stemming from the realization of a moral object which is placed before the faculty of desire by practical reason. Here, then, we have three types of pleasure that Kant distinguishes: first, a pure, disinterested pleasure; second, a pleasure *following from* the interest taken in the existence of an object; and third, a

---

33 Idem: ibid, 12–13. Judgment has a determinate role in all the faculties of mind, but only in this employment does it determine something merely in terms of itself.

34 KU, 204: CoAJ, 42.

35 Idem: idem.

pleasure taken in the existence of an object *which produces* an interest. Kant calls these three types of pleasure (or delight) free delight in the beautiful, in the good, and in the agreeable.

Delight in the agreeable stems from the gratification or pleasure of the subject by the attainment of an object, the desire for which was aroused through sensation. When the faculty of desire is stimulated by the sensation of an object to desire that object, the delight expressed does not refer merely to the subject, but also refers back to the object. The judgment made of the object is that it is agreeable, and that consequently it both pleases and gratifies.[36]

Delight in the good likewise involves an interest in the object and permits a judgment in regard to the object. But in this case the delight in the object is not the result of the sensation of that object. Rather, the delight results from the activity of reason whereby the object is demanded and is therefore made attractive by reference to its concept. Hence, delight in the good is not a delight in being gratified by the realization of something. It is rather delight in the prospect of bringing something into existence which follows from reason's disclosure of the worthiness of the object. That object whose nature is such that reason commends it to the faculty of desire is called good; consequently, the object so regarded not only pleases, but is also esteemed and respected.[37]

Free delight is merely a subjective sensation, referring only to the subject and never to an object. A given representation, for example, a sensible object, can provide such delight; but in the free delight, there is no representation of an object in relation to this feeling "through which the object [which is indeed the stimulus of the sensation] is regarded as an Object of delight."[38] No cognition of the object as an object of delight is involved. No interest whatever is taken in the existence of the object. Instead, the interest is merely in the experience of delight itself. Delight in the beautiful refers neither to the object nor to some concept which specifies the form of the object. Delight in the beautiful arises from reflection on an object both apart from determination by sensation to possess the object (to be gratified by it), and from determination by reason of the worthiness of the object (to esteem it). In the judgment of this experience, the object is said non-cognitively to be beautiful, that is, the judgment asserts that the subject is pleased by it.[39]

---

36 Ibid., 205–7, 209–11: ibid., 44–5, 48–50.

37 KU, 209–11: CoAJ, 48–50.

38 Ibid., 206: ibid., 45.

39 If one might argue not only that the subject is pleased, but that the subject must be pleased (as Kant would say) by every judgment of the beautiful, then it would appear that a cognitive judgment of the *experience* of the object has been made, even though no such judgment of the object itself has been made.

Of these three different experiences of delight, the last one is quite different from the first two since in this experience no interest is directly taken in the object. Here judgment functions in the free play of all powers of the faculty of cognition in generating feelings of pleasure and pain in regard to that which merely pleases, i.e. that which is beautiful. The first two types of feeling of pleasure and pain take an interest in the existence of the object. In both cases an appraisal of the object is made from which the feeling of pleasure or pain follows. Judgment, after completing the cognitive appraisal of the object (both from theoretical and moral standpoints), is involved in bringing about a feeling of pleasure or pain in the representation of the existence of the object or objects. (Kant would perhaps hold that this activity of judgment is unnecessary in regard to an object judged merely to be agreeable or disagreeable. He might prefer to say here that the feeling of pleasure or pain follows physiologically (causally) from the sensation of the object as mere stimulus.)

In regard to the good object, we have already seen that judgment is active in producing the feeling of pleasure; we have also seen that it is active in producing the feeling of aversion in regard to an evil object. We have further noted that in the exercise of this power, which as an activity of freedom cannot be explained, judgment reveals itself in the role of practical reason. By examining the role of judgment in the feeling of pleasure and pain, we see that Kant has not fallen into an ethical empiricism by introducing moral feeling. The feeling of pleasure and pain can be aroused in three significantly different ways as judgment follows three different procedures. Judgment operates differently in the determination of the object related to these three modes of feeling. Judgment also operates differently in arousing the feeling of pleasure or pain after the designation of the object has been completed in these three modes of feeling. The admittance, by Kant, of the feeling of pleasure and pain in moral experience does not reduce his ethics to an empirical one for the feeling of pleasure and pain is aroused, not merely by sensation in the judgment of something as agreeable, but rather by concepts in the judgment of something as good. Hence, Kant, in his treatment of the feeling of pleasure and pain, consistently clarifies the context in which the feeling of respect is aroused. At the same time he neither succeeds in showing nor attempts to show how judgment is capable of arousing feelings of pleasure and pain from the mere representation of an object as good. This capacity of judgment is presupposed by the fact of practical reason.

2 The Cultivation of Moral Feeling

Although we can never hope to explain how the power of judgment gains admittance for the moral law into the will of human beings, we can note the devices that judgment employs, not to create but to cultivate this moral feeling.[40]

Moral feeling is a delight that is not the product of sensation but rather the interest judgment takes in the representation of an object whose existence is a worthy expression of freedom. It follows that in any cognitive or non-cognitive employment of judgment, in which pleasure as distinct from mere sensation is aroused, the subject's moral sense will thereby be sensitized and strengthened. The delight taken by a mathematician (or a logician) in an elegant demonstration or proof is an example of the way judgment cultivates our moral feeling. In such a demonstration,

> understanding, as the faculty of conceptions, and imagination, as the faculty of presenting them *a priori*, get a feeling of invigoration (which, with the addition of the precision introduced by reason, is called the elegance of the demonstration).[41]

The delight in this case, although founded on concepts, is nonetheless subjective and belongs to feeling rather than cognition. As sensitivity to such delights increases, Kant expects, as did Plato before him, that moral feeling will be refined.

The development of taste in aesthetic experience also increases moral sensitivity. Kant does not go to the extreme of saying that a person who takes delight in the beautiful is therefore a good moral person. But he does insist that to be capable of such a disinterested delight is "at least indicative of a temper of mind favorable to moral feeling."[42] Kant therefore cautions his readers against an indifferent or destructive attitude toward the beauty of the natural world. In writing of the duties that one owes to oneself Kant says:

---

40 In the *Metaphysics of Morals*, Kant states: "Since any consciousness of obligation depends upon moral feeling [as its foundation] to make us aware of the constraint present in the thought of duty, there can be no duty to have moral feeling or to acquire it; instead, every human being (as a moral being) has it in him or her originally. Obligation with regard to moral feeling can be only to *cultivate* it and to strengthen it through wonder at its inscrutable source." (MS, 399–400: MOM, 528–9).

41 KU, 366: CoTJ, 12.

42 KU, 299: CoAJ, 157. See also ibid., 296–8, 354–6: ibid., 154–6, 225–7.

> A propensity to wanton destruction of what is *beautiful* in inanimate nature (*spiritus destructionis*) is opposed to a human being's duty to himself; for it weakens or uproots that feeling in him which, though not of itself moral, is still a disposition of sensibility that greatly promotes morality or at least prepares the way for it: the disposition, namely, to love something (e.g., beautiful crystal formations, the indescribable beauty of plants) even apart from any intention to use it.[43]

The person who can wantonly destroy a beautiful rock formation or wantonly kill an animal reveals his or her insensitivity to the value of something for its own sake apart from its capacity to gratify him or her. A person who is sensitive to the beauties of nature, who takes intense emotional delight in things apart from their utility, is thereby prepared to have moral feeling aroused in him or her by the confrontation of the moral law. Judgment, in seeking to gain admittance of the moral law to the will of a human being, finds a means to that end through cultivation of the human's aesthetic nature.[44]

Developing one's taste also enhances moral feeling since, as the subject in aesthetic experience, in the process of making a judgment of taste, one reveals oneself to oneself as a free being. One can never acquire taste by imitation, "for taste must be an original faculty."[45] "Hence," says Kant,

> it follows that the highest model, the archetype of taste, is a mere idea, which each person must beget in his own consciousness, and according to which he must form his estimate of everything that is an Object of taste, or that is an example of critical taste.[46]

In the process of judging aesthetically, one becomes aware of the free play of one's faculties from which one's aesthetic judgments emerge. Thus the individual becomes aware from a non-moral perspective of the autonomy and dignity of his or her person as a free being.

The awareness of one's autonomy and full dignity is even more dramatically revealed in the aesthetic experience of the sublime. In the experience of the sublime, there is no presentation of an object in sensibility which, by virtue of

---

43 MS, 443: MOM, 564. See also Anth, 239–244: AN, 106–112. Kant would not be surprised to note the frequent tendency of graffiti artists who wantonly destroy or deface objects to be guilty of more serious offenses, including drive-by killings. Moral feeling is clearly diminished by the destructive spirit.

44 We must not forget, however, that a decision of the will as practical reason is required to marshal the forces of judgment to this and any other cultivation of moral feeling. Thus the activity of judgment is really the activity of reason as practical.

45 KU, 232: CoAJ, 75.

46 Idem: ibid, 75–6.

its form prior to organization in terms of concepts, commends itself as pre-adapted to the ends of judgment, and thereby arouses a feeling of delight. Granted, pleasure in the merely beautiful is also of this nature, resulting from the adequacy of the representation in the free play of imagination and the understanding apart from the intervention of concepts. But the experience of the sublime stems rather from the inadequacy of sensibility. Pleasure arises indirectly when the mind, after recoiling from the inadequacy of sensibility, surges to a realization of its supersensible nature.

The feeling of the sublime may be of two sorts – mathematical or dynamic. The mathematically sublime is that which is of transcending grandeur – an experience in which the mind is driven from sensibility to the idea of totality in reason, and, in this way, to an awareness of the supersensible dimension of the rational being. In trying to grasp in sensibility something very great, the imagination strives (*ad infinitum*) to find something greater than the representation in question in terms of which to gauge its greatness. But no matter how far the imagination goes, it sinks to insignificance before the idea of reason which is satisfied with nothing less than totality. In attempting to comprehend totality in intuition the imagination reveals its limits and its proper function in serving the ideas of reason. The experience of the mathematically sublime is, consequently,

> at once a feeling of displeasure, arising from the inadequacy of imagination in the aesthetic estimation of magnitude to attain to its estimation by reason, and a simultaneously awakened pleasure, arising from this very judgment of the inadequacy of the greatest faculty of sense being in accord with ideas of reason, so far as the effort to attain to these is for us a law. It is, in other words, for us a law (of reason), which goes to make us what we are, that we should esteem as small in comparison with ideas of reason everything which for us is great in nature as an object of sense; and that which makes us alive to the feeling of this supersensible side of our being harmonizes with that law.[47]

The superiority of our cognitive faculties over the greatest faculty of sensibility arouses in us the feeling of sublimity "for the idea of humanity in our own self – the Subject," which by subreption only (never constitutively) "we attribute to an Object of nature."[48]

In the experience of the dynamically sublime the mind moves from imagination to the faculty of desire. As in the experience of the mathematically sublime, we again find the double movement of repulsion and delight united in the one experience. The dynamically sublime is experienced in the dual reaction

---

47 Ibid., 257: ibid., 106.
48 Idem: idem.

of the subject to the confrontation of nature in all its might and fury. In this confrontation, the subject recognizes his or her pitiful frailty as a sensible being before the might of nature while at the same time recognizing himself or herself as a super-sensible being who has dominion over the might of nature and need not bow to its threats. Thus this experience "saves humanity in our person from humiliation, even though as mortal men we have to submit to external violence."[49] Aesthetic judgment regards nature as sublime not because it excites fear in us, but

> rather because it challenges our power (one not of nature) to regard as small those things of which we are wont to be solicitous (worldly goods, health, and life), and hence to regard its might (to which in these matters we are no doubt subject) as exercising over us and our personality no such rude dominion that we should bow down before it, once the question becomes one of our highest principles and of our asserting or forsaking them. Therefore nature is here called sublime merely because it raises the imagination to a presentation of those cases in which the mind can make itself sensible of the appropriate sublimity of the sphere of its own being, even above nature.[50]

The delight in this experience of the sublime is a delight, Kant says, in "the sublimity of our faculty of soul."[51]

The similarity of the feeling of the sublime to that of moral feeling itself is quite striking, since in both there is an awareness by the individual of his or her freedom, of the reality of practical reason. The distinction between the feeling of the sublime and moral feeling lies in the fact that the feeling of the sublime, as an aesthetic judgment, has no determinate object and takes no interest in the existence of something. Its delight is not dependent on bringing something into existence as is the case with moral feeling. The delight in the aesthetic judgment of the sublime is merely aesthetic delight in the reflection of judgment on the freedom of the will, on the independence of a human being from control by the sensible world. In merely reflecting on the triumph of spirit over flesh, the feeling of sublimity is aroused. The moral feeling is encountered in its purity, on the other hand, in one's recognition *in a moment of decision* of the dominion of the spirit and the capacity of the self *to act* counter to the demands of sensibility.

It is clear, nevertheless, that moral feeling is cultivated by judgment in the experience of the sublime, for in these experiences the person comes to moral

---

49 Ibid., 261–2: ibid., 111.
50 Ibid., 262: ibid., 111–12.
51 Idem: ibid., 112.

consciousness. Kant's treatment of war is a case in point. He discusses the phenomenon of war as an example of the sublime. War, which Kant detests from the standpoint of moral judgment as the most flagrant and costly denial of reason, is, nonetheless, regarded as sublime from the aesthetic point of view.[52] The sublimity of war stems from the fact that it can only occur when humans are cognizant both of the might of nature and of their ability to exhibit dominance in the face of that might. By contrast, consider the forces of nature. Atoms do not war when they collide, nor do animals war when they struggle to lead the herd or take a mate. In these conflicts, there is no awareness of death, and hence no awareness of the might of the forces of nature and their capacity to destroy the sensible being. Furthermore, there is no decision to do battle, for the conflict is merely the inevitable product of the forces of might. When the forces of might collide, they simply collide; when they are in harmony, they harmonize.

But war is waged between humans who, as sensible beings, know the might of nature in war and its capacity to destroy them. No threat of violence or destruction can force a person to make war, for the threat of violence reaches its extreme limit in threatening the destruction of persons as sensible beings, and to engage in war places one under the shadow of this self-same destruction. Human beings bring force against force only when they recognize the dominion of personality, of their humanity, over the might of war. Human beings war instead of accepting the boot of an oppressor, not because they think they will survive the struggle, but because they know that to submit to the dominion of an enemy over oneself destroys oneself as a person – as a supersensible being – even though it may gain for oneself survival as a sensible being. One also knows that by refusing to accept domination by another one elevates oneself above the enemy as a supersensible being and leaves only one's sensible nature at the enemy's mercy. One knows that in spite of the suffering one may endure as a physical being, the refusal to bow to the might of one's enemy wins dominion over that enemy even if it be in death. As the poet Dylan Thomas observed, "death shall have no dominion."[53] Even in death, by the fact that one's death

52 Ibid., 262–63: ibid., 112–13. The flexibility and honesty of Kant's thought is seen in this example. Here, Kant shows an amazing capacity to appreciate aesthetic experience on its own terms, and to refrain from moralizing in this context. Kant's view concerning the sublimity of war is echoed in the comments of leading generals. General Robert E. Lee said, regarding the Battle of Fredericksburg, "It is well that war is so terrible–otherwise we would grow too fond of it." And General George S. Patton said, "Magnificent! Compared to war all other forms of human endeavor shrink to insignificance. God help me, I do love it so!"

53 "And Death Shall Have No Dominion," in *The Poems of Dylan Thomas*.

occurs in a war in which one freely engages, one reveals that one's principles, that one's personality, cannot be ruled by might. The warrior reveals the frailty of his or her body, but the dominion of his or her spirit, which stands beyond the circle of the sword. An enemy can destroy a person, but cannot make that person either fight or submit. War is entered upon by a decision to accept if necessary the might of another, but to reject the pretensions of another to have dominion over oneself. In this decision, one reveals one's dominion over the enemy by the total disregard taken of the enemy's power to injure or destroy him or her. Thus, a person reveals contempt for that power, by virtue of the resources of his or her free self that far transcend it.

The ability to appreciate the sublimity of war presupposes that one has arrived at moral consciousness and has experienced moral feeling. But it is equally true that the experience of the feeling of the sublimity of war cultivates moral feeling in return. In this experience a person is again reminded of his or her autonomy, of his or her power as a free being, of the presence in oneself of practical reason. Judgment can further its task of cultivating moral feeling, therefore, by developing the aesthetic appreciation of both the sublime and the beautiful.

We are brought by the experience of the sublime, moreover, to the most direct method at judgment's disposal for developing moral feeling – that of confronting the person with moral examples. By pointing out the purity of the maxims of such actions, judgment relies on practical reason itself to produce a desire in a person to emulate the one whose acts are held up for examination.

It may be wondered how Kant could ever have recourse to moral examples, since we have noted at some length the impossibility of the direct embodiment of the moral law and the inability to judge completely the adequacy of any person's action to that law. Although we may realize our own failing as individuals to live up to the moral law just as we may doubt the adequacy of another's behavior to that law, we can never have the assurance that we have encountered a perfect moral example. Kant does not forget this. While he notes that the good in human beings is always defective and distorted he also notes that

> the law made visible in an example always humbles my pride, since the man whom I see before me provides me with a standard, by clearly appearing to me in a more favorable light regardless of his imperfections, which, though perhaps always with him, are not so well known to me as my own.[54]

54 KpV, 77: CprR, 184–5.

In observing the action of another, we can determine that, to the best of our judgment, his or her action is legal in the moral sense and hence probably conforms to the moral law. And because we find such a person's inclinations and desires are violated by what he or she does, and because, therefore, we can find nothing in that person's example to suggest an ulterior motive of selfishness, we can and do suppose that his or her action is also moral. We suppose, that is, that it is done both in accordance with the law and for the sake of the law.

By regarding the moral example in this fashion, Kant is not contradicting his earlier position, namely that sensibility is incommensurate with the moral idea of reason. He does not say that moral examples can show us what particular acts are our duty to perform. (If he did, this use of examples would not only run counter to the incommensurability of the sensible and the conceptual, it would also run counter to the principle of autonomy according to which each person must determine the commands of the moral law for himself or herself and also judge whether a given person or action provides a moral example.) Kant uses moral examples only in order to further the cultivation of moral feeling by showing the agent his or her own potential nature as a free moral being as it is reflected in another – by showing the agent that what one feels obligated to do one can do because others have done it. Only in the confrontation with moral examples is the feeling of respect – the pure moral feeling – aroused. The feeling of admiration, or of sublimity, is indeed aroused by:

> volcanoes, lofty mountains, the magnitude, number and distance of the heavenly bodies, the strength and swiftness of animals, etc. All of this, however, is not respect. A man can also be an object of love, fear or admiration even to astonishment, and yet not be an object of respect. His jocular humor, his courage and strength, and his power resulting from his rank among others may inspire me with such feelings, though inner respect for him is still lacking. Fontanelle says "I bow to a great man, but my mind does not bow." I can add: to an humble plain man, in whom I perceive righteousness in a higher degree than I am conscious of in myself, *my mind bows* whether I choose or not, and however high I carry my head that he may not forget my superior position. Why? His example holds a law before me which strikes down my self-conceit when I compare my own conduct with it; that it is a law which can be obeyed, and consequently is one that can actually be put to practice, is proved before my eyes by the act.[55]

Since pure moral feeling is cultivated by putative examples of moral action, judgment's influence on the will of human beings on behalf of the moral law is

---

55 Ibid., 76–7: ibid., 184.

increased by careful attention to such examples. As a consequence, Kant suggests that the education of the young in matters of morality should proceed along two main lines: first, a moral catechism should be instituted in which the judgment is sharpened for moral assessment by casuistry. This allows the student to arrive at the principles of morality by debating the various sides of particular questions of duty. Second, the young should be offered a series of biographical examples which they are to test in terms of the principles which they have learned. In selecting examples, the teacher should avoid examples of noble deeds since they lead children to ignore the humble duties of daily life and lose themselves in romantic illusion. Furthermore such examples may lead the young to take pride in themselves as persons who exceed their duty in acts of supererogation, rather than to stand with humility before the law whose demand cannot be exceeded and, rather, is not likely to be fulfilled. But if this restriction is observed, the judgment of children in the presence of examples of human behavior sharpens quickly. They discern at once the difference between prudence and moral action, and their moral feeling is aroused in direct relation to the exemplified action's freedom from all selfish motives. Kant suggests that we watch the reaction of a youngster to the example of a person who is asked to make false accusations against one who is innocent. Suppose a man is offered a reward for giving false witness but rejects it. The child will only applaud this. But if instead the man is threatened with loss of estates, friends, family, and finally life itself, and still remains true to his duty, the child will be led, Kant believes,

> step by step from mere approval, to admiration, and from admiration to amazement, and finally to the greatest veneration and a lively wish that he himself could be such a man (though certainly not in his circumstances).[56]

By stripping away the possibilities that action done in accordance with the moral law might be done for the sake of anything other than the law itself, the moral example is made purer. And it is noteworthy that morality has "more power over the human heart the more purely it is represented."[57] As the purity of the moral person's actions is progressively revealed, as happens when all considerations of individual welfare vanish, the moral feeling, the desire to be such a person, is strengthened in the observer. The faculty of feeling is intensely

---

56 KpV, 156: CprR, 253. Kant would doubtless recommend the example of Thomas More as presented in "A Man For All Seasons."
57 Idem: idem.

aroused by this, for in the thought that one can be like the person disclosed in the example, one is taught to feel one's own worth, to become aware of one's own power

> to pull himself loose from all sensuous attachments… and in the independence of his intelligible nature and in the greatness of soul to which he sees himself called, to find himself richly compensated for the sacrifices he makes.[58]

Thus, in all these many ways – by directing the attention of the will to the elegance of rational thought, to the beauties of nature, to the beauty of art, to the sublime, and to examples in the lives of good men and women – judgment gains admittance for the moral law to the will of human beings, whereby the power of reason to be practical is both exercised and strengthened.

How is practical reason possible? This we cannot know directly. But Kant insists that we do know that its possibility is factually grounded on the ability of practical reason to have an effect on sensible inclination in the production of a moral feeling. We know how this feeling differs in kind from feelings of pleasure in the agreeable and in the beautiful. And we know some of the devices that judgment can use to bring each person to an awareness of his or her freedom and to an expression of that freedom in the embodiment of the highest good. Admittedly, this is merely a behavioral account of reason in practice. But this is the only account that Kant can give, for the true explanation lies hidden within the inscrutable depths of freedom.

58 Ibid., 152: ibid., 250.

Chapter X: Summary And Assessment

We began this study by reviewing the place of Kant's ethics in the context of the rest of his philosophy. In the Introduction we noted that Kant wrote his first *Critique* and established the limits of knowledge "in order to make room for faith."[1] We also noted in the introduction that Diderot, though convinced that there is nothing in the world better than a good man or woman, was troubled by his inability to find a sufficient reason or motive for virtuous conduct but incapable of accepting the moral indifference that appeared to follow from Newtonianism. Kant hoped to complete that "sublime work" that Diderot found beyond his ability – that is, "to seek out and establish *the supreme principle of morality*"[2] along with the principles and doctrines of religion on the basis of reason to ensure that the laws of practical reason have "access to the human mind and an influence on its maxims."[3]

1 Kant's Attempt to Reconcile the Christian and Scientific Worldviews

Kant recognized, perhaps more clearly than Diderot, that after the challenges to faith presented by modern science there was no going back. No one, least of all Kant, could minimize the appeal of the new scientific *Weltanschauung*. As a contributor to the Newtonian philosophy, he recognized, like King Canute, that he could not hold back the tide, even though he was as concerned as Diderot to save morality and the essential tenets of the Christian religion rightly interpreted.

Christianity proclaimed a good news that could be understood by the most ordinary person. As Becker said,

> No interpretation of the life of mankind ever more exactly reflected the experience or more effectively responded to the hopes of average men .... The importance of the Christian story was that it announced with authority (whether truly or not matters little) that the life of man has significance, a universal significance transcending and including the temporal experience of the individual. This was the secret of its enduring strength, that it irradiated pessimism with hope: it liberated the mind of man from the cycles in which classical

1 KrV, Bxxx: CpR, 29.
2 GMS, 392: GMM, 60.
3 KpV, 151: CprR, 249.

> philosophy had enclosed it as in prison, and by transferring the golden age from the past to the future substituted an optimistic for a disillusioned view of human destiny.[4]

That Kant was concerned to preserve this good news for the average human being through a rational interpretation of the Christian message is obvious, even from the most casual reading of Part One, Book Two, and Part Two of the *Critique of Practical Reason.* And though less obvious, this concern is still evident in his *Religion Within the Limits of Reason Alone.* Where the Christian religion reassured each individual, no matter how common, of his or her infinite worth as a child of God – the hairs of whose head were numbered and whose life counted more than those of sparrows, no one of which fell without God's knowledge – Kant enunciated the secular good news of the infinite moral worth of the individual personality that was beyond all price and that to will in accordance with and for the sake of the moral law entailed as a matter of consistency willing the existence of God and personal immortality. This was Kant's rationally grounded good news.

Kant offered this secular account of Christianity's good news when he began the *Groundwork of the Metaphysic of Morals* with these words: "It is impossible to conceive of anything at all in the world, or even out of it, which can be taken as good without qualification, except a *good will.*" "A good will," he continued, "seems to constitute the indispensable condition of our very worthiness to be happy."[5] Thus Kant assured each person of good will of his or her infinite worth and, by his or her consistent volition, of the existence of God and of personal immortality.

2 The Heterogeneity of the Good

These conclusions entailed many original contributions to ethics that fundamentally reshaped the subject thereafter. First, he clarified the experience of obligation by demonstrating the heterogeneity of the good. If the good were a homogeneous quality, desire or inclination would naturally attract us to it and, hence, if we knew the good we would do it. But Kant observed two fundamental difficulties with this conclusion. First of all, it denies the experience of obligation on which our moral experience is grounded, in which the will is torn between duty and desire. In the experience of obligation the moral agent is

4 Becker, 126, 128.
5 GMS, 393: GMM, 61.

acutely aware of two different and conflicting goods: the moral good required by obedience to the moral law and the subordination of the natural good as a material object of desire. Kant offers as an example a commonplace experience. A man cheats at cards and wins handsomely. He then passes not one but two judgments on himself. He is pleased by his cunning and skill that enabled him to win and to prosper from that winning, but at the same time he condemns and despises himself because he cheated in order to win.[6] In moral choice, Kant showed, we are torn between the demands of the moral law that determines the moral good and the objects of our personal desires which constitute the natural good. In reaching these conclusions Kant relies on the common moral experience of ordinary individuals.

3 The Clarification of the Concept of Freedom

Kant's second major contribution was his classification of the will as the faculty of freedom. Kant defined the will as the capacity to act in accordance with its own idea of law. If our will were determined by the good as the natural object of desire, the will would not be free. It is the law as revealed in the maxim of the will that determines the moral object of volition, rather than the desireability of the object itself. Hence, whether acting autonomously in accordance with the moral law or heteronomously in accordance with desire as the law or principle of one's actions, the will is free.

Kant's second major contribution was discussed in Chapter III. It consists in his elucidating the dynamic tripartite nature of the will. He showed that in order to qualify as a person who is responsible and accountable for his or her acts and to whom the personal pronoun can properly be assigned, the human will must be transcendentally free from determination by alien and antecedent influences (free, that is, according to Kant's negative definition of freedom). Transcendental freedom guarantees the possibility of both freedom in the positive sense of possessing the potentiality for freedom in its fulfilled mode as autonomy and also in its deficient mode as heteronomy. Because of its unconditioned and self-determining nature, the will possesses whatever moral qualities it has (whether good or evil) without qualification. The moral law defines the conditions of personal fulfillment and those conditions are recognized as part of the given nature of any and every person. A being lacking either transcendental freedom or the potentiality of autonomy or heteronomy lacks the conditions

6 KpV, 39: CprR, 149.

essential to being a person. But one who has these characteristics is a self-determining cause and totally responsible for whatever one makes of oneself in the process of exercising one's freedom. Autonomy is achieved by acting in accordance with the moral law and for its sake, that is, by acting in accordance with the principle of universality that by virtue of its universality ensures the individual's transcendence of all particular motives for action. The individual by his or her volition establishes a moral worth that becomes the basis for his or her right to happiness:

> Man *himself* must make or have made himself into whatever, in a moral sense, whether good or evil, he is or is to become. Either condition must be an effect of his free choice; for otherwise he could not be held responsible for it and could therefore be *morally* neither good nor evil.[7]

I am baffled by those students of Kant who fail to recognize that heteronomy is a mode (albeit a deficient mode) of freedom. If it were not a mode of freedom, the individual would not be responsible for morally deficient acts. The will would either be freely good or cease to be a will at all. The person would be either good morally or cease to be a person. The experience of obligation in which one confronts the demand of autonomy in the context of one's ability to reject it would be illusory. That is, if we deny heteronomy as a mode of freedom, the human will would in effect disappear. The human will would either cease to exist or the will in question, capable only of autonomous action, would be a holy will.

Observing society and history without distortion, Kant recognized that there was nothing to guarantee distribution of happiness in this world on the basis of moral deserts. And consequently, Kant argued that consistent volition requires that the free moral individual should *will* that there be a God and personal immortality.[8] Thus, having established the supreme principle of morality, Kant used that principle in its full development to establish religion on the basis of reason alone.[9] Under this interpretation freedom of the moral agent is not undermined by the introduction of God and immortality. There are no independent theoretical proofs for their existence; there is only a moral proof that

---

7 RGV, 44: Rel, 40. The responsibility for the origin of evil is thus transferred from God to humanity. It is a possibility that is introduced by freedom and, though not logically or causally necessary, appears to be an ineluctable consequence of human volition.

8 KpV, 143: CprR, 245.

9 For a fuller explication of these views, see Chapter V, The Highest Good as the Material Object of Moral Volition.

follows as a condition of consistent volition from the recognition of one's duty.[10]

Since every person is possessed of freedom, the achievement of a good will is within the potentiality of each person. To this extent, there is secular good news for every person. But there is no guarantee of happiness. If one is a person of good will who has made a consistent effort to universalize the maxims of one's acts, to put oneself in the place and point of view of others, to treat humanity, whether in oneself or in another, always as an end in itself and never as a means merely, one has established a worthiness to be happy.

> In a word a person who has made honesty and integrity [*Wahrhaftigkeit*] his supreme maxim in the core of his confessing to himself as well as in his behavior toward everyone else, is the only proof within a human being's consciousness that he has character.[11]

This is both the most and the least that can be demanded of a person. To do less than this is to fail morally; to do more is impossible.

In this context failure is not defined by the occurrence of specifically immoral acts but only by the loss of a genuinely moral disposition or that *Wahrhaftigkeit* in relation to one's self and in actions towards others as one's supreme rule of life. A person who has achieved an essentially good will by making reason practical in his or her life and by subordinating sensible interests to the achievement of rational action has clearly demonstrated commitment to a universe that is also rational. That is, such a person is committed by his or her acts and consistent volition – at perhaps the cost of happiness or even of life – to a universe in which there is God and immortality. Having willed the ends, the morally good person likewise wills the means.

This does not prove theoretically the existence of God or the immortality of the soul, but it establishes God and immortality as part of a context of coherence and meaning in the life of the individual that becomes in itself, Kant

10 KpV, 30: CprR, 232.

11 Anth, 295: AN, 195. The English translation is my own, though here I cite Louden's translation. The words "truthfulness," "honesty," "sincerity" or "integrity," singly and alone, inadequately translate "*Wahrhaftigkeit.*" In this context the meaning encompasses not only "truthfulness" but also "sincerity" (*Aufrichtigkeit*) and conscientiousness (*Gewissenhaftigkeit*). "Integrity" (an English word for which there is no single German equivalent other than the Latinate *Integrität*) presupposes a consistent and dependable moral character through time in contrast with sincerity and honesty, virtues that can be achieved in an instant. Integrity, therefore, most adequately conveys the full meaning of *Wahrhaftigkeit* as used here by Kant.

believed, a powerful motive for moral conduct. If our dignity and self-respect as free moral persons is well established, says Kant,

> so that a man fears nothing more than to find himself on self-examination to be worthless and contemptible in his own eyes, every good moral disposition [*Gesinnung*] can be grafted on to this self-respect, for the consciousness of freedom is the best, indeed the only, guard that can keep ignoble and corrupting influences from bursting in upon the mind.[12]

Within this general framework Kant believed that he had brought about the synthesis of the Christian and the Newtonian worldviews and concluded the *Critique of Practical Reason* with these famous lines:

> Two things fill the mind with ever new and increasing admiration and awe, the oftener and more steadily they are reflected on: the starry heavens above me and the moral law within me .... The former begins from the place I occupy in the external world of sense, and it broadens the connection in which I stand into an unbounded magnitude of worlds beyond worlds ... and into the limitless times of their periodic motion, their beginning and continuance. The latter begins from my invisible self, my personality, and exhibits me in a world which has true infinity but which is comprehensible only to the understanding – a world with which I recognize myself as existing in a universal and necessary ... connection, and thereby also in connection with all those visible worlds. The former view of a countless multitude of worlds annihilates, as it were, my importance as an animal creature .... The latter, on the contrary, infinitely raises my worth as that of an intelligence by my personality, in which the moral law reveals a life independent of all animality and even of the whole world of sense – at least so far as it may be inferred from the purposive destination assigned to my existence by this law, a destination which is not restricted to the conditions and limits of this life but reaches into the infinite.[13]

Diderot asked for a sufficient reason for just conduct. He said it was necessary to demonstrate that philosophy makes more good men and women than sufficient or efficacious grace. Kant's reply may be summarized as follows: If we reflect rationally on the presuppositions of our natures as persons, of our ability to function as responsible, accountable individuals, we become aware of our freedom and the law of its fulfillment. We recognize that through the fulfillment of our freedom in autonomy we establish our infinite worth, our ultimate significance, on the basis of which we can expect whatever significance and fulfillment the universe has to offer will in fact be ours.

---

12 KpV, 161: CprR, 258.
13 Ibid., 161–162: ibid., 258–259.

4 Kant's Response to Diderot's Demand for Moral Guidance

In responding to Diderot's concern to offer adequate guidance in the determination of one's duty, Kant did not make the mistake of offering a new principle of morality. Rather he offered, as he put it, "only a *new formula*."[14] That formula, as we have shown, is a procedure of thought, imagination and judgment, by which one can assure oneself that the maxim of one's act is not defined by a particular inclination but in accordance with the demand of universality, that is, in accordance with the moral law.[15]

In presenting the one categorical imperative as a procedure of judgment in testing the universality of one's maxims, Kant offered useful instruction in what is required if we are to act in accordance with the moral law. There is no rigid legalism in Kant's formulation, for there is only one categorical imperative which must be applied by the will in an unlimited number of different situations. Each situation of choice must be responded to thoughtfully by going through a procedure of testing. Of the various formulations of the one categorical imperative, "to treat all persons as ends in themselves and never as means merely" and "to will in accordance with the maxim that by one's will can become a universal law of nature" are perhaps the most helpful. These procedures require thought experiments carried out by judgment and imagination as guides to the will in formulating a maxim of choice that has the universality required by the moral law, a universality that clearly transcends the particularity of any desire or inclination. The requirement of treating ourselves and others always as ends and never merely as means is clarified by the requirement to place ourselves in imagination in the place and point of view of others. When we subordinate our thought to this imaginative requirement we must look at our decision in an entirely different way. We don't ask merely what's in it for us, but rather how what we propose to do will affect all of those influenced by our action.

If those affected by our action are morally responsible, they should recognize the maxim of our action as one that they themselves would act upon. If what we propose to do would not be recognized by others as something fair to them, again assuming them to be morally responsible, then we would know that our maxim lacks the universality required by the moral law. If I propose a maxim that cheats other persons, I clearly violate their interest and well-being, and so fail to treat them as ends in themselves. If, on the other hand, I spank a child (too young and inexperienced to understand the risk it has taken) who has

14 KpV, 8n: CprR, 123n.
15 See Chapter VII.

endangered its life by rushing into a heavily trafficked street without looking, the child and its parents, if rational, would know that the punishment, however unpleasant, is in accordance with the child's best interests.

The procedure of willing one's maxim as a universal *law of nature* also stretches the mind and the imagination. The agent must consider his or her responsibility to act so that he or she wills a morally phenomenal world in which the order of events is structured not only by the laws of causality but also by the moral law. That is, the moral law through one's will becomes constitutive in the spatio/temporal order so that one can recognize the objectivity and correctness of one's moral act by the sequence of events in that morally structured phenomenal order. It also assists moral agents in avoiding the temptation to excuse themselves from doing their duty because they know that others will not act as they have. Under this formulation one *wills* a world in which everyone would necessarily act in accordance with one's maxim. From that standpoint one can better judge whether his or her maxim meets the criterion of universality.[16]

Kant's procedural formalism repudiates any legalistic interpretation, for every act must be assessed not on the basis of some rigorous formulation to be applied literally in all contexts but rather by criteria confirmed or considered in the procedural process. One's duty is never determined until a creative interpretation is developed to determine its demands.

But neither is Kant's formalism a logical formalism. By taking into account the interests of all those affected by our actions and the nature of a sensible order if our actions were to become by our will constitutive of that order, Kant clearly rejects an empty logical formalism.

Before considering the adequacy of Kant's moral incentives, we must ask: Has Kant with his procedural formalism and his various formulations of the categorical imperative along with many examples offered sufficient moral guidance? In Prelude 4 of *Fear and Trembling,* Kierkegaard was later to observe, "When the child must be weaned, the mother has stronger food in readiness, lest the child should perish."[17] Was Kant's procedural formalism and his explanation of moral feeling the stronger food, the guidance, that Diderot had insisted on if the Christian worldview was to be salvaged? Could one say of Kant's moral philosophy not only that it was true in theory but that it also worked in practice?

By rejecting a merely formal interpretation of the categorical imperative in favor of a procedural interpretation according to which the will is guided by

16 Singer, *Generalization in Ethics*, 9ff.
17 Kierkegaard, *Fear and Trembling*, 29.

the extensive exercise of judgment and imagination in determining a universal maxim, Kant made, I believe, a third major contribution to ethics. When the moral agent uses judgment and imagination to enlarge his or her awareness by seeking maxims that by his or her will can structure a moral world, then the moral agent puts particular concerns aside. One also does so when one puts oneself in thought in the place and point of view of others in order never to treat them merely as means. It is relatively easy to show in many examples, perhaps in most examples that one confronts in life, that this procedure demonstrates that one is not acting according to universal maxims but rather according to maxims that ignore the interests of others while being of advantage to oneself.

Here, however, Reinhold Niebuhr might ask: how, in the absence of a standard independent of the moral agent, can one be sure that one has faithfully followed the demands of the moral law? Does one, can one, really understand and feel the needs and desires of others as if they were one's own? Is one capable of that degree of empathy? Can one actually know how to structure the morally ordered world it is one's duty to bring into being as a law of nature? We have the example of Martin Luther, who by his relentless efforts to assess the moral quality of each of his intentions and deeds, discovered that he could never be sure of his moral purity or his good faith. Can any of us do better following Kant's procedures?

Kant himself observed that we can never know for sure our own moral worth, for "the dear self" always intrudes. Often after our choice has been made and our action taken we realize our failure to assess truly the interests of another, that we have failed despite our intention to treat others never as means but as ends in themselves.

On this issue Kant gave, I believe, the right answer. We can never be sure, nor have we any need for such assurance, for it would only lead to a moral arrogance that can be blinding. The only proof, as noted earlier,[18] Kant insists, "lies in the consciousness of a man that he has character" – that is, that he or she is a person who has achieved "honesty and integrity (*Wahrhaftigkeit*) in the innermost depths of the self, both in relation to oneself and in actions toward others as the supreme maxim of one's life." In an exercise of reasonableness, Kant rejects Luther's moral fanaticism. Nevertheless, Kant must admit that there is no absolute proof of one's virtue. Kant insists that this test is both the most and the least that can be demanded by law. Here I agree with Kant, though I doubt seriously that we can successfully put ourselves in the place and point of

---

18 See Section 3, page 285 supra of this chapter.

view of others to a degree sufficient to guarantee that we always treat them as ends in themselves. The procedural interpretation of one's duty is, I have concluded, very helpful even though it cannot guarantee that the right choices will always be made. This procedure is quite effective nevertheless in exposing obvious violations of universality and duty in our moral decisions.

The individual's inability to find certainty with regard to his or her moral actions and moral worth is a straightforward consequence of Kant's decision to assign freedom to the noumenal realm and to the noumenal person as a *Ding an sich*. The moral individual may know that he or she is also a free noumenal being but can know nothing further. All one can know is oneself as an appearance to oneself with all of the uncertainty that that entails.

5 Kant's Absolute Concept of Freedom

A question remains, however, concerning Kant's claim that obedience to the categorical imperative is enforced by the diminution of freedom and personality and final extinction of both through the violation of the moral law. We have noted Kant's acceptance of the fact that humans knowingly do evil and his argument that freedom is essentially rational and his expansion of the concept of the rational to include the irrational. Since the rejection of reason is a mode of the rational, freedom encompasses the irrational mode of heteronomy no less than the rational mode of autonomy. We observe that, in terms of his conception of freedom and rationality, the will is free to reject the rational moral law but must ultimately pay the price of self-annihilation in the forfeit of freedom and thus personality. And we saw in Chapter III, Section 3, that Kant offered experiential support for his concept of freedom by showing in the *Religion* the concomitant decline of virtue and personality. This demonstration reached its critical point in the discussion of wickedness and devilishness. Wickedness was shown to be a weakness, because freedom is a power, and the rejection of its rational nature is therefore an impotence.

Devilishness was shown to be an illusion, because no one can deliberately and on principle subordinate the law to inclinations since the power of the person (its freedom) is derived from the law. Kant thus seemed to offer in the *Religion* a final clarification and experiential support for his conception of freedom.[19]

19 This view does not compromise the freedom of the will in the heteronomy of action through impurity or weakness. In these cases the person has not rejected the law but merely failed to act in accordance with its demands.

But in dismissing the devilish rejection of the law as an illusion, Kant called attention to the possible limitations of his conception of freedom rather than to the limits of human freedom itself. In denying the power of individuals deliberately to reject the law, Kant, I believe, may have repeated the methodological mistake of Plato when he denied that humans can knowingly do evil. Kant, like Plato before him, explicitly considered the data which seemed to contradict his theory and, like Plato, used his theory to dismiss the contravening evidence as illusory.[20] He gave his theory momentary support, but he exposed a possible weakness.

Kant's insistence to the contrary, a person's free power to reject the law in defiance seems to be an ineradicable fact of human experience. St. Paul consolidated the opposition to Plato's moral optimism by asserting the power of humans knowingly to do evil; Kierkegaard consolidated the opposition to Kant's moral optimism in asserting the power of humans to fulfill their personalities in the despair of defiance.[21] Nietzsche joined Kierkegaard in affirming that human freedom can be diabolically, no less than heteronomously, expressed. Novelists and historians have supplemented their arguments with many observations and facts. Melville created Ahab, who, having thrown both prudence and morality to the winds, stalks the deck of the Pequod in deliberate search of destruction – Moby Dick's and if necessary his own and even that of his ship and crew. Far from languishing in the impotency of personality demanded by Kant's conception of freedom, Ahab infuses the excess of his personal strength into the spirits of his men, into the rigging of his ship, and even into the artificial limb on which he stamps out his defiance of the law. History in turn records the deeds of Napoleon, Stalin and Hitler. No weak personality loses an entire army in Egypt only to recruit and lose yet another in Russia and finally a third at Waterloo. No weak personality leads a civilized nation as Hitler did to moral disaster and a continent to ruin.

Kant was right, perhaps, to insist with Plato that the *realization* of freedom depends on rationality. He was certainly right in going beyond Plato to distinguish the volitional and theoretical uses of reason and to argue that the former provides the foundation and direction of the latter (the primacy of practical reason). But Kant may have erred in failing to note that the power of volitional rationality can be fully asserted either in rational or irrational acts. Because the

---

20 The use of one's theory to establish the factual value of data is nonetheless unavoidable. The frequent occurrence of this practice in science is considered by Michael Polanyi, in *Personal Knowledge*. See also Chapter I of *Reality*, by Paul Weiss, for a general statement of the interdependence of fact and theory.

21 See Kierkegaard, *Sickness unto Death*.

power of theoretical reason depends upon its observance of the laws of thought and is reduced to incoherence when these laws are violated, Kant assumed that volitional rationality[22] loses its power in the rejection of the moral law. Although theoretical irrationality is an impotence, since it is separated from its source of power in experience, understanding and logic, volitional irrationality is separated from its power in the moral law but can derive its power elsewhere. One source of its free power is doubtlessly the theoretical employment of reason itself. The industrial and financial tyrants of the 19th Century may have been ruthless, but they were never stupid and rarely imprudent in the rational determination and fulfillment of their perceived interests. Both Hitler and Stalin harnessed the power of science and technology to support their programs. Ahab abandoned the prudential use of reason, but he took prodigious care in charting the habits of Moby Dick and in judging the temper of his crew. Volitional irrationality, whether the subordination of the law to non moral interests, or the willful rejection of the law itself, finds power of realization in a parasitic use of theoretical reason. One may argue, moreover, that there are other non-rational sources for the power of freedom and personality, such as Nietzsche's will to power, which ascribed power to volition with or without reason.

But even if we agree with Kant that reason supplies the power of freedom, we must still conclude that his conception of freedom is inadequate. On Kant's own premises we must admit that personal fulfillment is possible for the irrational will as long as it uses the theoretical and prudential capacities of rationality to its perverse ends.

The implications of this conclusion for Kant's answer to the question, How is the categorical imperative possible? are plain: it would require that the concept of freedom does not relate the will to an action required by the moral law with necessary obligation as a condition of being a person. The will appears to be free to fulfill itself in some ways without the law, for it has a source of free power apart from its observance of the law.

Some interpreters might hold that Kant never conceived of the force of the categorical imperative in anything other than logical terms. This interpretation is over-intellectual. Of course it is illogical to reject the moral law when the law is a condition of one's being. But Kant did not intend to say that a wicked person is guilty merely of an intellectual faux pas. Such a person has lost the worthiness to be happy, though he or she may continue to be happy; a wicked person has lost all that makes life worthwhile, though he or she may continue to

22 I am using rationality in a generic sense which includes both the rationally sound and the irrational rejection of rationality.

live; the wicked person has bankrupted himself or herself as a person and is worthless as a human being even though others may defer to his or her power. In all these ways, Kant speaks of the here-and-now enforcement of the demand of the moral law. If one rejects the moral law, one forfeits personal fulfillment, fulfillment as a free being, in favor of fulfillment as an animal. In his discussion of the impotence of immorality in the *Metaphysic of Morals* Kant speaks of immorality as the disability of the will much in the way that Plato speaks of injustice as the disease of the soul.[23] The force of Kant's answer to the question, How is the categorical imperative possible? consists in his showing that freedom is of such a nature that to disobey the moral law involves the loss of one's freedom. And since freedom is the basis of individuality, the individual who loses freedom loses his or her own self.

If Kant's demonstration of the categorical imperative fails, it is not because it never aimed to succeed. Even its success, on the logical interpretation, would be a gross failure, for in the heights of personal fulfillment a wicked person could ask, "Why be logical?" And such a person could not be told that anything essential to his or her personal fulfillment was lacking. Kant had more to say than this. He was convinced that the universe was sufficiently rational to assure the payment of a penalty for irrational behavior even without appeal to a God to restore the balance of happiness and virtue.

Suppose we grant for the sake of argument, however, that Kant's analysis of wickedness and devilishness is sound. We still encounter a difficulty with his view of freedom: it would appear to shatter on the problem of forgiveness. Kant holds in the *Religion*, as elsewhere, that human freedom involves absolute spontaneity. Kant insists that "in the search for the rational origin of evil action, every such action must be regarded as though the individual had fallen into it directly from a state of innocence. For whatever his previous deportment may have been, whatever natural causes may have been influencing him, and whether these causes were to be found within him or outside him, his action is yet free and determined by none of these causes; hence, it can and must always be judged as an *original* use of his will [*Willkür*]."[24] The moral individual alone makes himself or herself into whatever he or she is from a moral standpoint. One acquires one's own virtues and vices through one's own free actions. Others may force us to act contrary to the moral law, but no one can make us violate it. Violation of the moral law can result only from a free decision and never from force. An individual himself or herself must fall into sin from a state of inno-

23 MS, 227: MOM, 381. See also MS, 384: MOM, 516.
24 RGV, 41: Rel, 36.

cence. If an individual's acts can be imputed to him or her, they must follow from the exercise of the individual's own freedom. This leaves us with an absolute concept of freedom.

It follows from this conception of freedom that no human being can be good for another. Kant rejected the doctrine of vicarious atonement because it runs counter to the nature of freedom. No matter how good another person is, his or her excess of goodness (were such an excess possible) would in no way remove another person's lack of goodness nor redeem that other person's evil. Any notion of forgiveness or absolution, moreover, would seem impossible in terms of this conception of freedom. A good person has the right to find satisfaction in his or her virtue. But even God cannot help the guilty individual without violating the moral law. If one is guilty, it is one's own fault and he or she must bear the full and non-transferable burden.

Kant sought a means of sustaining the human hope of forgiveness and absolution from guilt without compromising the absolute purity of the moral law.[25] By means of an imaginative interpretation of the mystery of atonement, Kant offered a plausible solution to the problem of forgiveness as it relates to guilt deriving from an evil disposition. He considered the change of disposition from ill to good to be so radical that it could accurately be called a new birth. And he thought that the difference between an evil and a good disposition is so great that the new *Willkür*, structured by a good disposition, is justified in denying identity with its preceding evil disposition. Since the disposition is itself the only basis for moral self-identity, this conclusion has an initial credibility.

Kant could see clearly the incompatibility of forgiveness and absolute freedom. And this incompatibility troubled him because he realized that an inescapable guilt could lead the moral individual to despair and far greater guilt. But how is one to gain absolution from the guilt that follows from the impurity and weakness of one's will? Such a person's disposition is already good when, through weakness or impurity, he or she violates the demands of the law. Kant was sorely troubled on this point. The problem is insoluble in terms of absolute

---

25 RGV, 76: Rel, 70. For Kant, forgiveness is impossible to accept without compromising the absolute nature of freedom. In the search for the rational origin of evil actions, every action must be regarded as though the individual had fallen into it directly from a state of innocence. See ibid, 41: ibid., 36. Kant faces a dilemma similar to that posed by Ivan in *The Brothers Karamazov* when he asserts forgiveness is impossible. Kant may be inconsistent in this view, for in discussing *Wahrhaftigkeit* as the key to moral assessment, Kant seems to admit that a person of good will can meet minimal moral standards though lacking in the moral perfection required by the law. See Section 3, supra.

freedom, for under this interpretation of freedom there is no context. The past experiences, friendships, suffering and pleasures that constitute the matrix of one's actions are all irrelevant.

Kant argues, nevertheless, that a person may, through effort, acquire grace; that is, a person may become worthy of receiving aid or absolution should the one who judges that person be disposed to offer it.[26] But why should God or any righteous judge decide to compromise the requirements of the moral law or fail to hold the absolutely free being responsible for his or her exercise of freedom? Kant himself knew, I think, that he was in trouble. On the same page in which he speaks of the possibility and necessity of grace in order to give hope to guilty moral beings so that they will not slacken their efforts, he also says, "The accuser within us would be more likely to propose a judgment of condemnation."[27]

When Kant confronted the Antinomies, he presented thesis and antithesis and then offered a resolution. On the issue of devilishness and forgiveness he merely vacillates. There is neither antinomy nor resolution. On the one hand his view of freedom as fundamentally rational, deriving its power from the moral law, makes the rejection of the law in devilishness impossible. On the other hand, his absolute conception of freedom precludes the need for grace, since every guilty person freely wills to become guilty from a state of innocence, and the purity of the moral law precludes the granting of grace, for grace violates the uncompromising nature of the law. But despite these theoretical implications of Kant's conceptions of absolute freedom and its foundation in the law, which are clear and precise on the issue, Kant denied the possibility of the evil rejection of law and continued to insist on the possibility of grace. On the latter issue, he insisted that the individual of good disposition who strives hard to live up to the moral law has the right to hope that his or her shortcomings will be excused or that the demands of the law will be reduced to his or her measure. Kant tries to reassure himself by saying that this of course implies that the individual has done all that he or she can. But if the individual has done all that he or she can, that individual does not need grace. And if the individual has not, even Kant agrees he or she should not get it.

If Kant had recognized these problems as genuine antinomies and devilishness as a mode of freedom he would, I believe, have been on sounder ground. In order to make sense of the idea of personal responsibility, Kant argued that freedom is absolute. Yet by holding that human responsibility is absolute, he

26 Ibid., 67–71, 75–6: ibid., 60–65, 70.
27 Ibid., 76: ibid., 70.

condemns humans to an insufferable burden of guilt. Although guilt is not predetermined or logically necessary, all human beings, nevertheless, fall short of perfection and find themselves guilty. The realization of oneself depends upon the recognition of absolute freedom; yet absolute freedom precludes the realization of oneself by destroying the individual through an overburdening guilt. These are moral antinomies worthy of Kant.

It is a tribute to Kant's reasonableness and humanity that he contradicted his theory by admitting the possibility of grace. But the contradiction involved is a serious one whose resolution demands either the redefinition of freedom or obligation or the introduction of the miracle of forgiveness.

If Kant had consistently held to his theory of unqualified freedom, he would have followed the line of argument taken by Ivan Karamazov.[28] In discussing the evil in this world, Ivan insisted that he would accept no Euclidian (i.e. scientific) nonsense about there being no freedom. And he saw quite clearly that if there is freedom (the absolute freedom of which Kant speaks), there can be no forgiveness. Consider the man who orders ravenous hunting dogs to tear a naked little boy to shreds because he accidentally hit a dog in the foot. Shall this man be forgiven, Ivan asked? Suppose the mother forgives? Suppose the boy forgives? How dare they forgive! Forgiveness, as Ivan observed following Kantian principles, is a moral outrage; it is itself a violation of the moral law.[29]

What then is the penalty of guilt? Ivan proposes three alternatives: sensuality, suicide, or insanity. Alyosha, his brother, proposes a fourth: the acceptance of a divine and miraculous forgiveness. Ivan rejects this fourth alternative. His rejection did not follow from the fact that a miracle is involved (although this in itself would have posed a serious obstacle for Kant). He refused to accept forgiveness on moral principle. In so doing he remained faithful to the implications of Kant's view of the purity of the law and the absolute nature of freedom.[30]

---

28 See the "Pro and Contra" from *The Brothers Karamazov*, by F. Dostoevsky.

29 Kierkegaard's discussion of the offense of Christianity is illuminating on this point. Cf. *Sickness Unto Death*, Appendix II, 2.

30 Allen Wood (in *Kant's Moral Religion*) disagrees with my view that "since for Kant human freedom is absolute, man is responsible for all evil he does … if man truly did everything in his power to avoid evil, … he would not need grace. But if he has not done all in his power, even Kant agrees that he ought not to receive God's aid or forgiveness." Wood quotes my statement "following Kant's principles, forgiveness is a moral outrage." Wood would agree that "for Kant, all of man's guilt follows from the exercise of freedom, and that man is responsible for every use he makes of this freedom" (242). But Wood still insists that human guilt may be forgiven. He believes I "confuse the forgiveness of a deed with giving and accepting an excuse for it, even with declining responsibility for it." He argues that these concepts are very different, and that it is only reasonable for someone to forgive something for which one is responsible and

With regard to Kant's denial of the possibility of devilishness – that is, of the deliberate subordination of the moral law to inclinations – the jury, for me, is still out. I can make the case that Ahab clearly rejected the law, but like Milton's Satan, he is a fictional invention. Kant will not be influenced by evidence based not on fact but only on imagination.

But what do we do with Hitler and the evils of the Third Reich? All this lies within the realm not of fancy but of fact. Can we actually discern, however, what Hitler really intended? Did he not will the good of Germany? Doesn't he appear to be more like Plato's tyrant who, through ignorance of the good, does evil and ultimately destroys himself in the process? In the exercise of his devilish purpose was he not powerful?

Not so, Kant would argue. When did Hitler test the maxims of his acts following the procedure of putting oneself in thought in the place and point of view of others? If he had considered his acts from the standpoint of his victims – Jews, gypsies, homosexuals, Poles, Czechs, Slovaks – the impossibility of universalizing his actions would have been apparent. The procedure of willing his maxim as a universal law of nature might have pleased Hitler. Wouldn't he have been delighted if Britain, France, and the United States had shared his desire to rid the world of undesirables and allow all persons of Germanic heritage to become citizens of an enlarged Germany? The mistake from a Kantian point of view is obvious: that world includes all the so-called undesirables and all the victims of his pursuit of *Lebensraum.* Casuistry is a dangerous game and can easily mislead one.

On the other hand, I am impressed by Sebastian Haffner's examination of Hitler in *Anmerkungen zu Hitler.*[31] He notes Hitler's continuing success was undiminished until the Battle of Stalingrad, and his shift of policy. The extermi-

---

blameworthy. When asking for forgiveness, he writes, "I admit my responsibility and my guilt for the deed in question, but I ask that this guilt be lifted from me, that the evil I have done not be held against me. Forgiveness does not exclude evil, it justifies the agent in spite of his evil." If a person is responsible and guilty for the deed in question, on what basis does one expunge the evil and justify the agent? That requires a miracle of atonement or something comparable contradicting all Kant holds with regard to freedom and responsibility. Perhaps it is useful to recall that Kant asserted that if a man had been condemned to death and was in prison and the community in which the prison stands are about to depart, they should hang him before they left. Wood supposes that in forgiveness we absolve the wrongdoer of evil; that is, we justify the agent in spite of his or her evil. But I find nothing in Kant on which to justify the agent in face of his or her evil. Indeed, Kant does introduce the doctrine of grace, but it seems to me he contradicts his essential point of view when he does so. This inconsistency does Kant credit, but it also calls for a modification in his concept of freedom.

31 Haffner, Sebastian, *Anmerkungen zu Hitler.*

nation of the Jews was equally successful. But finally Hitler was unsuccessful in his ability to implement his order to apply the scorched earth policy to Germany itself after he had become convinced of his error in assuming German superiority. At that point his power terminated in his psychological collapse and suicide. But how can we deny the power of his personality in the implementation of his policies up until that last order that he could not persuade Albert Speer to implement?[32]

We cannot ignore the problem of forgiveness nor the problem of freedom in devilishness. These difficulties call for a reconsideration of Kant's assumptions regarding the nature of freedom as absolute and freedom's essential dependence on rationality, even if Kant were to accept the concept of rationality expanded to admit the full potential of the irrational as a mode of its expression. When freedom is considered in terms of rationality, it is inevitably narrowed to the limits of conscious intention and perhaps therefore made far too intellectual. And when it is considered as absolute, it ignores the fated, the given elements in the nature and experience of the individual. As such Kant's concept of freedom is highly abstract and thus far removed from our experience.

6 Moral Incentive in Kant's Ethics

Although Kant made a place for religion in order to offer a sufficient motivation for moral conduct, it is not at all clear that his religion has effective motivational force. For Kant's religion is devoid of mythic roots: all its doctrines are subjected to rational, essentially secular interpretations. The synthesis of Christian and Newtonian thought was genuine enough for Kant, and the motivational force that derived from Kant's religious upbringing continued to exert its influence on Kant long after he had completed his process of demythologizing Christianity. Kant continued, throughout his life, to speak at times with religious fervor, as in the passage, quoted above "on the starry heavens above and the moral law within," or as in his moving apostrophes to Duty and Sincerity.[33]

---

32 For a fuller examination of this issue please consider the appendix, "Kant at Auschwitz."

33 "O *sincerity*! Thou Astraea, that hast fled from earth to heaven, how mayest thou (the basis of conscience and hence of all inner religion) be drawn down thence to us again?" (RGV, 190n: Rel, 178n; see also Ovid, Book I, verses 149–150, p. 2); and "Duty! Thou sublime and mighty name that dost embrace nothing charming or insinuating but requirest submission and yet seekest not to move the will by threatening aught that would arouse natural aversion or terror but only holdest forth a law which of itself finds entrance into the mind and yet gains reluctant reverence (though not always obedience) – a law before which all inclinations are dumb even

But Kant's religious fervor did not derive from his demythologized religion within the limits of reason alone. It came rather from the emotionally and mythically rich pietism of his parental home. Kant could hear the voice of duty as if it were the voice of God because as a child he had heard the voice of God issue the categorical imperative: "Be ye perfect, as your Father in heaven is perfect." The refined stem of Kant's rational ethics had been grafted onto the hardy emotional root of Christianity. What effect would the demythologized religion of reason alone, itself derivative from a rational theory of ethics, exert on individuals devoid of childhood nurture in the mythic religious tradition?

No one can question the success of Kant's philosophical horticulture. His grafting of a secular interpretation onto mythic Christianity was brilliant. Those reared in a mythic religious tradition have, generation after generation, developed from childhood to adulthood along essentially Kantian lines. As children they have spoken as children, articulating their moral obligation in essentially religious terms as commands of God, but on maturing, they have put away the myths of childhood and continued to do their duty as the requirement of practical reason and to reinterpret the religion of their childhood in a secular, demythologized form.

The theological movements of the nineteenth and twentieth centuries from Schweitzer to Bultmann and Tillich illustrate the feasibility of Kant's program. But we must also note the inability of demythologized branches of Christianity to reproduce themselves. The Unitarian Church and the Congregational Church in the United States, for example, have not been able to recruit sufficient numbers of ministers from their own congregations but have had to draw for their ministry on the mythically richer traditions of the Baptist, Methodist, and other evangelical traditions. In recent years, following the Second Vatican Council and steps toward the demythologizing of Catholicism, it has become increasingly difficult for the Catholic Church to recruit individuals for its religious orders. Whitehead, in *The Adventures of Ideas*, pointed out that the platonic idea of psyche had lacked widespread influence until it was given motivational force through the Christian idea of soul. Had not Kant perhaps reduced the Christian idea of soul to an equally abstract and motivationally inert concept of personality?

---

though they secretly work against it: what origin is there worthy of thee, and where is to be found the root of thy noble descent which proudly rejects all kinship with the inclinations and from which to be descended is the indispensable condition of the only worth which men can give themselves?" (KpV, 86: CprR, 193).

This is the position taken by Reinhold Niebuhr. In *An Interpretation of Christian Ethics*, he wrote,

> no rational moral idealism can create moral conduct. It can provide principles of criticism and reasons; but such norms do not contain a dynamic for their realization .... Rationalism not only suppresses the emotional supports of moral action unduly, but it has failed dismally in encouraging men toward the realization of the ideals which it has projected.[34]

Niebuhr would grant, I think, that Kant answered a part of Diderot's concern in that he offered a reason for just conduct. But Niebuhr denied that Kant offered a sufficient reason – a "philosophy [that] makes more good men than sufficient or efficacious grace."

Although Niebuhr may be correct in his conclusion, it is clear that Kant, no less than his critics, is aware of the insufficiency of the moral law and the categorical imperative as formulae. For the purpose of moral life, Kant insists, they "require in addition a power of judgment sharpened by experience, partly in order to distinguish the cases to which they apply, partly to procure for them admittance to the will of man and influence over practice."[35] Judgment, Kant insists, must provide the incentive that moves the will to do that which it knows it ought to do. Kant's recognition of the need to provide moral incentives is seen in his distinction between the moral law and the categorical imperative.

Kant observed that if human beings had holy wills, that is, if they were pure rational beings, they would act in accordance with the moral law without overcoming temptation. They would have neither obligations nor the need of incentives to follow the moral law because it would be the descriptive law of their behavior. Humans are not pure, rational beings, however, and the human will consists not merely of practical reason (*Wille*) but also of the faculty of desire (*Begehrungsvermögen*) and *Willkür*. *Willkür*, free and self-determining, confronts both the demands of reason and the desires of sensibility; it is tempted to act in accordance with the appeals of the latter, while it is obligated to act in accordance with the principle of the former. The moral law for pure, rational beings thus becomes the categorical imperative for humans who, being both rational and sensible beings, require some sensible incentive for fulfilling the demands of reason.

---

34 Niebuhr, 206.
35 GMS, 389: GMM, 57. See Chapter VIII, in which I have dealt with the role of judgment in the application of the moral law at greater length.

In order to determine action in accordance with the categorical imperative, practical reason must gain control over the desires and inclinations that compete with it for determination of the will. And since reason cannot control non-rational desires and pleasures by means of argument, it must control them by means of pleasures and desires which the moral law itself can effect in the will. In order to fulfill the demands of the categorical imperative, the human will as a dynamic, unitary faculty must be able to find sufficient pleasure or delight in the fulfillment of duty. Thus, Kant argues

> if we are to will actions for which reason by itself prescribes an 'ought' to a rational, yet sensuously affected, being, it is admittedly necessary that reason should have a power of *infusing a feeling of pleasure* or satisfaction in the fulfillment of duty, and consequently that it should possess a kind of causality by which it can determine sensibility in accordance with rational principles.[36]

Kant insisted that reason must be able not merely to legislate the law for the human will; it must also be able to produce in the will a sensible incentive to fulfill the law.

It is here, as we have seen in Chapter IX, that judgment enters as the power of the mind to provide *a priori* principles for the feeling of pleasure and pain. It is that power or ability of reason to produce a feeling of pleasure in sensibility associated with the fulfillment of duty.[37] In providing for a moral incentive, Kant must show how judgment can win acceptance for the moral law in the human will. He must answer the question, how can judgment – as reason in its dynamic employment – be an efficient cause in the determination of an effect (a feeling) in sensibility? That is, he must answer the question, how can reason be practical?[38]

Before considering Kant's answer to this question, we must be sure the question is correctly interpreted. In the first place, it must not be understood as a question of whether or not reason can be practical. Freedom of the will – which involves the actual capacity of reason to be practical through the production of incentives – is presupposed in the experience of obligation from which Kantian ethics begins.[39] That reason is practical, that man does take an interest in enacting the demands of the moral law, is a fact of human experience for which no additional proof is required.[40]

---

36 Ibid., 460: ibid., 128.

37 KU, 209: CoAJ, 48.

38 GMS, 459–461: GMM, 127–129.

39 KpV, 32: CprR, 143.

40 GMS, 460–1: GMM, 128–9.

In the second place, granting that reason is practical, we must not suppose that a direct theoretical explanation of how it is practical is possible. The question, How is reason practical? is identical to the question, How is freedom possible? to which no direct answer can be given. These questions are identical because to explain how reason can be practical requires one to show "how a law in itself can be the direct determining ground of the will"[41] while the capacity of the will to act in terms of the idea of law is precisely what is meant by freedom. As Kant puts it, "a free will and the will under moral laws are one and the same."[42] Hence, any explanation of the way in which the moral law can determine the will necessarily involves an explanation of freedom. Once we grant that these are identical questions requiring an explanation of freedom, we must agree with Kant that no explanation for either is possible.[43]

Thus, in asking how reason or judgment can provide an incentive for the will, Kant appears to assume his conclusion by noting that we are not questioning that judgment can provide an incentive, and he denies that we are seeking a direct theoretical explanation of the conditions by which it does so. Rather we seek to know A) What kind of feeling is produced in the will by judgment whereby the will takes a sensible interest in the fulfillment of the moral law? B) How can Kant introduce feeling into his ethical theory as an incentive of the will without destroying the categorical imperative and inheriting the difficulties of ethical empiricism? And C) Presuming that Kant can satisfy the previous issues, what practical means can judgment employ in providing moral incentives?

On the first question, we explained in the previous chapter that the feeling in question is different in kind from other feelings in that it is not aroused by material objects. In the *Critique of Judgment*, Kant enumerates three varieties of delight: delight in the agreeable, delight in the beautiful, and delight in the good. Delight in the good results from the activity of reason whereby the object (the morally good) is demanded and made attractive by reference to the moral law. Feeling can be aroused not only by sensation in the judgment of something as agreeable, or by the play of imagination and understanding in the judgment of something as beautiful; it can also be aroused by the moral law in the judgment of something as good. The moral law (as an expression of *Wille*) produces an incentive in *Willkür* that is moral feeling, the delight or sensible interest taken in an object that is morally good.

---

41 KpV, 72: CprR, 180. See also GMS, 458–9: GMM, 127.

42 GMS, 447: GMM, 114.

43 Ibid., 461–463: ibid., 129–131.

As to the second question, the introduction of this incentive does not undermine the categorical imperative. Moral feeling, the sensible incentive that moves the will (*Willkür*) to the fulfillment of duty, does not reduce Kant's theory to one of ethical empiricism because moral feeling is rationally, not empirically, determined. Moral feeling is the *effect* of the moral law on the will, not its *cause*. One's desire to be happy or to avoid unhappiness cannot be the incentive that leads one to obey the law. Whatever satisfaction one derives from fulfilling one's moral obligation, and whatever suffering one experiences from a guilty conscience for having failed to do so, are the effects of one's virtue, not its causes.[44]

Our central concern here is to understand Kant's answer to the third question: what practical means or devices can judgment employ in providing adequate moral incentives? We recognized in Chapter IX that Kant offers techniques for the cultivation rather than the creation of moral feeling, for moral feeling is presupposed in every moral person. "Since any consciousness of obligation depends upon moral feeling," Kant argues, "to make us aware of the constraint present in the thought of duty, there can be no duty to have moral feeling or to acquire it; instead every human being (as a moral being) has it in him originally. Obligation with regard to moral feeling can be only to *cultivate* it and to strengthen it through wonder at its inscrutable source."[45]

Recognizing its proper task as the cultivation rather than the creation of moral feeling, judgment may enlarge the moral incentive of each individual by any of the following techniques: by directing the will's attention to the elegance of rational thought;[46] to the beauties of nature;[47] to the beauties of art;[48] to the sublime;[49] to the examination of the lives of good persons;[50] and to practices in moral casuistry.[51]

These various means for the cultivation of moral feeling and the encouragement of moral conduct are ingenious and imaginative but not convincing. There is on Kant's theory an inescapable dilemma inherent in moral education. If incentives and inducements are introduced to determine the will, they destroy in the process its freedom and thereby the will itself. On the other hand, if the moral incentives are merely inducements, guiding threads to encourage moral

44 TP, 283–284: TaP, 50–51; cf. KpV, 76: CprR, 184.
45 MS, 399–400: MOM, 528–9.
46 KU, 366: CoTJ, 12.
47 MS, 443: MOM, 564.
48 KU, 232–3, 298–9: CoAJ, 75–76, 157–8; see Sections 41, 59 and 60.
49 KU, 257–263: CoAJ, 105–114.
50 KpV, 76–77: CprR, 184–185.
51 Ibid., 152–156: ibid., 250–253; cf. MS, 428–441: MOM, 551–562.

volition, they are insufficient. That is, if one wishes a moral incentive that provides an incentive sufficiently strong to ensure moral action, one can only adopt an incentive so strong that it will either buy off or scare off the moral agent, and thus destroy his or her freedom. Morality is ineluctably contingent upon the exercise of freedom and cannot be guaranteed by force or sufficient incentive. Moral incentive is necessarily limited by the independence of the free will.

It was for this reason that Kant stressed the importance for morality of the fact that there is no theoretical proof of God and immortality. For if there were, the freedom of humankind would be destroyed and moral action would be determined simply by fear of Hell or hope of Heaven.[52] Consistent with his ethical theory, Kant recognized in *Über die Pädagogik* that "if one wants to ground morality, we must not punish. Morality is something so holy and sublime that one must not degrade it and place it on the same level as discipline."[53]

After making this sound observation, Kant proceeded to contradict himself by introducing and approving moral punishment. Apparently Kant failed to recognize that moral punishment, for example, the denial by the parent of love or respect for the child, is from the child's point of view more terrifying and severe than any reasonable form of physical punishment and can be just as heteronomous as a beating.[54] This irregularity aside, Kant is basically consistent in holding that no program of education which accords with his ethical theory could develop moral persons by means of social and psychological influences that would undermine the freedom of the students and destroy them as moral beings. Whatever a human being is in a moral sense, whether good or evil, must be a condition of his or her free choice. From this it follows, as we have already noted, that

> whatever his previous deportment may have been, whatever the natural causes may have been influencing him and whether these causes were to be found within him or outside him, his action is yet free and determined by none of these causes; hence it can and must always be judged as an *original* use of his will [*Willkür*].[55]

---

52 Päd, 494–495: Ed, 480–1. Kant would agree with Kierkegaard that faith presupposes an objective uncertainty.

53 Ibid., 481: ibid., 468–9.

54 Ibid., 482–484: ibid., 470–1.

55 RGV, 41: Rel, 36; cf. RGV, 44: Rel, 40. This, Kant adds, is the basis of original sin: it originates in the individual. Niebuhr, incidentally, offers an identical interpretation, Niebuhr, 89–90.

The inscrutable and irreducible nature of freedom which we comprehend only to the extent that we recognize its incomprehensibility precludes Kant's development of sufficient moral incentives or a genuine theory of education that is determinative of personal character.

He proposes in lieu of a theory of education a two-stage educational process that first encourages legality of action by insisting that the student act in accordance with the moral law and train his or her judgment in assessing his actions and those of others in terms of conformity to law. A second stage follows in which moral feeling is developed, in which the moral individual's growing sense of his or her own worth as a free moral person becomes itself the dominant incentive to action.[56]

In this two-stage process, Kant suggests, the metamorphosis of freedom will occur and the natural person, having become accustomed to acting in accordance with the moral law and to judging others in terms of that standard, will discover in himself or herself a growing sense of personal dignity as a moral individual and eventually desire above all else to become worthy in his or her own eyes. That is, Kant recognizes Aristotle's emphasis on the importance of developing habits of moral behavior.

Though Kant cannot, while preserving freedom, offer a genuine educational theory, he does offer educational counsel to assist in practice. On this view Kant merely offers observations on training, cultivation, and education. Kant's educational program is better understood in Aristotelian terms as a natural process of entelechy in which the individual, after being subjected to a series of educational influences, is not *made* moral but simply *becomes* a moral person. Just as in puberty the child suddenly and dramatically becomes sexually mature, so the moral person, attending the voice of conscience, naturally but inexplicably ceases to be led by the inclinations that dominated infancy and answers to the voice of his or her own practical reason. Kant would hold that reason and freedom are immanent in the human being from birth and that the unfolding of moral capacity is no more remarkable, and no more comprehensible, than the capacity for rationality in any of its other employments.

On Kant's theory, the moral individual cannot be "programmed" by sociological or educational techniques. To brainwash is to destroy freedom, not to build it. To educate, by contrast, is to develop the capacity for freedom which may yet express itself in ways that are either good or evil. Since the student's actions are his or her own and the responsibility for them radically his or her own, the teacher can never be blamed for the wrong actions of the student nor

---

56 KpV, 152, 159–160: CprR, 250, 256–7.

credited for the student's achievements. Recognizing the inscrutable depths of freedom, Kant cannot claim to know the conditions under which freedom is developed and its autonomous expression assured. Thus, Kant can offer only nostrums for moral instruction, including even his suggestion, ridiculed by Beck, that the life of Anne Boleyn might exemplify for children innocence punished.[57]

How, then, does one provide sufficient reason for moral conduct? Kant faces a dilemma: either the moral incentive is adequate and freedom is compromised, or it is only influential, that is, less than sufficient. Kant has no way to make humans morally good and worthy of happiness. Strictly speaking, they make themselves morally good and worthy by their own acts. The teacher in a moral community provides, to use a metaphor, oxygen for the tiny spark of reason until it bursts spontaneously into flame. Freedom is potential from the start, and education is no more than guardian and encourager of the flame. Programs are developed, exercises are completed, and free moral persons emerge by a process of moral entelechy. But they are never coerced.

In his concern to provide an adequate foundation for moral conduct, Kant was occasionally swept away by the extravagance and utopianism of the 18th century. At the close of his *Lectures on Ethics* he proposed an educational program to bring about the systematic betterment of humankind on a worldwide scale. Holding that the ultimate destiny of humankind is humanity's moral perfection, Kant asks: "How then is moral perfection to be sought? Wherein lies our hope?" And he answers:

> In education and in nothing else. Education must be adapted to all the ends of nature both civil and domestic .... Let education be conceived on right lines, let natural gifts be developed as they should, let character be formed on moral principles, and in time the effects of this will reach even the seat of government, when princes themselves are educated by teachers fitted for the task .... But the ruler cannot do it alone; men of all ranks in the state would have to be similarly trained; then would the state be built on a firm foundation .... Justice and equity, the authority, not of governments, but of conscience within us, will then rule the world. This is the destined final end, the highest moral perfection to which the human race can attain.[58]

57 Beck, *Essays on Hume and Kant*, 202; KpV, 155: CprR, 253. As a matter of historical record Kant seems to have been right in his assessment of Anne's virtue. If Beck had reviewed the nature of the evidence used to condemn Anne he probably would have concluded with Kant that she was indeed an innocent person convicted by fraud and perjured testimony arranged by a wicked king. I must thank John Howes, president of Learningguild, for this correction of Beck.

58 VüE, 270: LoE, 252–253.

Despite these pronouncements, for the most part Kant held his enthusiasm in check. His more characteristic and certainly more consistent view of the limits of education was clearly stated in the *Anthropologie* and serves as a correction to the panegyric on sincerity quoted above:

> The human being must therefore be *educated* to the good; but he who is to educate him is on the other hand a human being who still lies in the crudity of nature and who is now supposed to bring about what he himself needs .... Since, however, *good* human beings, who must themselves have been educated for this purpose, are necessary for moral education, and since there is probably not one among them who has no (innate or acquired) corruption in himself, the problem of moral education for our *species* remains unsolved even in the quality of the principle, not merely in degree.[59]

Kant discovered that his theory of morality contained the implication that it is impossible to make humans morally good. Hence, while he was successful in meeting Diderot's concern to establish morality on a rational basis and assist in determining their duty in situations of moral choice, he was unable to deal adequately with the other aspect of Diderot's concern: that philosophy make "more good men than sufficient or efficacious grace."

This concern, Kant would argue, is mistaken. It is a consequence of Diderot's confusion. First, is there any proof of the efficacy of divine grace in ensuring morality? Human history offers a doubtful record. Second, do we wish to encourage moral conduct, i.e. true morality? If so, virtue must be the free expression of the moral person. Or do we wish rather to encourage conformity to the moral law, i.e. mere legality? The latter can be motivated through laws and social pressure; the former can only be nurtured.

Similarly, Kant can answer a part of Niebuhr's concern. The moral law does in fact contain a mechanism for its realization: it produces moral feeling and thereby provides some emotional support for moral action. On the other hand, that support is so attenuated that Niebuhr may reasonably conclude that it "has failed dismally in encouraging men toward the realization of the ideals which it has projected."

7 Ethical Orthodoxy in Religious Education

But why did Kant reject a middle course? Why should we not rear the young child in a mythic tradition – as Kant himself had been reared – and after the

---

59 Anth, 325, 327: AN, 230, 232.

mythic religion with its motivational power had been established only then begin the process of rational pruning and grafting? Kant did not reject the mythic religion of his childhood either from personal whim or from prejudice against religion as such. Instead, his rejection is a logical consequence of his view that morality be introduced without the threat of punishment or the inducement of reward. Thus, ethics and moral education must precede rather than follow religion and religious education. As Kant says, “A religion which is founded merely on theology can never contain anything moral. In such a religion one will have only fear on the one hand, and intentions and dispositions in general toward reward on the other, resulting merely in a superstitious cult.”[60]

On ethical grounds, consistent with the implications of his moral theory, Kant would restrict the child’s experience of God and the child’s participation in religious practices. When God was explained to children in eighteenth-century religion, God was presented on the same footing as any other fact and was characterized as a being who knows the human heart and who directly rewards and punishes it according to its intent. Presented thus, the presence of God in the consciousness of the child destroys its freedom. Consequently, Kant would recommend that children be reared in their earliest years in the absence of religious rites and without hearing the name of God. Instead, they should be given instruction about the ends and aims of humankind, about the order and beauty of nature; their judgment should be exercised, and they should be provided with a wider knowledge of the universe and its laws, “and only then to reveal to them the concept of a supreme being – a lawgiver.”[61]

Having established religion on the foundation of ethics, Kant is consistent in holding that education should progress from ethics to religion: “Morality must therefore come first, theology then follow; and this is what is called religion.”[62] “Religion is the law in us, in so far as it receives emphasis from a law-giver and a judge above us; it is morals applied to the knowledge of God.”[63] “Religion without moral conscientiousness is a superstitious worship.”[64] Thus, Kant rules out the very process by which his acute moral awareness was developed in the pietism of his childhood.

In practice, nevertheless, Kant reluctantly recommends the introduction of religious education into early childhood education. This, however, is only be-

60 Päd, 494–495: Ed, 481.
61 Ibid., 493: ibid., 480.
62 Ibid., 495: ibid., 481.
63 Ibid., 494: idem.
64 Ibid., 495: idem.

cause it is absolutely necessary in order to prevent the miseducation that children would receive in their daily lives through contact with morally corrupting religious ideas. The religious education Kant would offer to counteract this problem is not, of course, an education in Christianity or in any mythic religion. It would be education – even for the youngest child – in the demythologized religion of reason alone. Rejecting the advice of St. Paul that a child be taught as a child and allowed to grow to adulthood before putting off childish things, a succinct description of Kant's own development, Kant proposes to teach the ethical religion of reason to the little child as if it were a little man or woman.[65]

With an eighteenth-century confidence that nature does nothing without purpose and is organized to ensure the maximum efficiency of means, Kant concluded that humans have not been created for happiness but for a moral pilgrimage that could establish their dignity, and their worthiness to be happy.

Kant could find no way to use historical Christianity or any other religion as a foundation for ethics. Christianity was presented to the public in many varieties of religious orthodoxy, each of which contained elements inimical to Kant's moral orthodoxy. But Kant had no way of imposing his moral orthodoxy on any branch of Christianity. Unable to make over the culture of his day, Kant was forced to accept it as a limiting condition for his theory of moral education. He concluded that a sound moral education would have to proceed with the simultaneous introduction of a moral interpretation of Christianity that would be understood as a derivative rather than as a foundation of morality.

As if these obstacles were not enough, there was an additional problem. The Christian worldview was being gradually eclipsed by the scientific. Even if Kant had proposed to ground moral education on historical Christianity, he would have found that project swept away by subsequent cultural changes. The project could not have succeeded in the climate of opinion of the nineteenth, twentieth and twenty-first centuries, in which the scientific worldview was enormously strengthened by the work of Darwin, Freud, Einstein, and their many brilliant collaborators and followers. Concomitantly, and without any direct encouragement from Kant, Christianity was rationalized and demythologized. As it gained in sophistication, Christianity lost much of its appeal to the average person. The scientific worldview was indifferent to the ultimate questions concerning the meaning of life, and left these to the realm of uncertainty. The civilization based on the Christian worldview was dissolving into smaller and competing social elements. Each of these could claim to be validated by the scientific worldview,

---

65 By this move, Kant disregards Rousseau's view of the child as a unique being to be understood on its own terms, a view Kant had praised so highly.

whose presumption of value neutrality and ethical relativism to some extent encouraged an intellectual climate of political and moral anarchy.

The pervasive influence of the scientific worldview in the twentieth and twenty-first centuries as the implications of value neutrality and ethical relativism were applied with extraordinary crassness to justify the opinions and beliefs of any and everyone has contributed to the disintegration of the social and legal order. The individual's respect for law and the discipline that the moral person imposes on himself or herself in the fulfillment of his or her freedom have been extensively undermined by social relativism and indifferentism.

Although Kant did not have the option of proposing the imposition of a religion that could provide the motivational force of a mythic religion, he was aware, of course, of this possibility from his reading of Plato.

Plato had proposed in the fourth century B.C. a scheme of general education whereby a society might be transformed and an ideal state of ideal citizens brought into existence. In order to achieve this social objective, Plato proposed a new myth whose tenets were consistent with the aims of the state. He proposed a great fable in which all citizens of his republic would be nurtured. They would be taught to believe that God had made humans of three basic substances: gold, silver, and iron or bronze. They would come to believe on faith, as if it were a mundane truth, that their natures were thus differentiated at birth. Those of gold would become rulers; those of silver, auxiliaries; and those of bronze or iron, farmers or craftsmen.[66]

Plato recognized that the first, and possibly even the second, generation of persons nurtured in this new religion would not likely believe it. In order to ensure the workability of the ideal state, Plato recommended finally that all citizens over ten years of age be sent out into the countryside so that their children, removed from the ways of their parents, might be brought up in accordance with the institutions of the new state and so believe its newly developed religious myth.[67]

By getting rid of everyone who was bound by older traditions, and by introducing a new orthodoxy fully congruent with the aims of the state, Plato proposed nothing less than a pervasive totalitarianism. He offered in support of his moral theory an educational system that appeared more capable than "sufficient or efficacious grace" in the production of good persons.

66 Plato, *The Republic*, 1050ff (415a, 546c-547b).
67 Ibid., 1155 (540c-541a).

Plato's proposal to invent mythic roots as incentives to moral conduct involved not merely the propagation of falsehoods and a mistaken concept of the good as homogeneous, but its success required also a totalitarian state that destroyed freedom and hence the possibility of morality. In providing moral incentives, Kant was not concerned to encourage mere legality; rather, he was concerned to encourage true morality. Plato's proposal to force men and women by thought control and regimentation to act in accordance with law could at best produce persons who conformed to law and who were brainwashed to believe that they were therefore happy. But Plato's citizen could not possibly be morally good or worthy of happiness by virtue of this heteronomously determined choice. To force moral goodness, Kant insisted, is as impossible as to force love: each must be the expression of the free individual, or it is nothing.[68] Once the mistaken notion of a homogeneous good is corrected, Plato's theory of motivation is destroyed.[69] Quite often, moreover, he finds that the moral good can be attained only at the sacrifice of the natural good. Thus, Plato fails to offer any genuinely moral incentive. He appears to encourage moral action but in fact encourages only legality of action by means of coercion.

Although Kant exposed a fundamental confusion in Plato's concept of the good and demolished Plato's theory of motivation, which derived its plausibility from that confused notion, Kant did not and could not refute the efficacy of Plato's educational proposal. He understood that it was entirely possible to change human behavior by a totalitarian educational program.

Unfortunately, subsequent history has amply shown that Plato's theory of totalitarian education works effectively in practice. In the twentieth century we witnessed many examples of societies that have produced remarkable changes in the social and moral order through the techniques of totalitarianism. Once the government assumes the role of a Dostoyevskian Grand Inquisitor who "saves" humankind from freedom in order to ensure the well-being and happiness of all, the technological advances of modern science are available to make easier and swifter the fulfillment of the totalitarian project.

---

68 In noting the totalitarian implications of the Platonic program, I wish to distance myself from the analysis by Professor Popper, who, in *The Open Society and Its Enemies*, tried to credit Plato with ideas that lay behind Hitler's National Socialism. It was Plato's position that the state should serve the individual and guarantee his or her greatest personal fulfillment. It is highly anachronistic for a scholar to attribute to Plato an abuse of democratic freedoms and a support of totalitarian schemes of which he had no knowledge and about which he had no intentions.

69 See Chapter II.

Marx, Lenin, Stalin, Mao and Hitler all proposed and all, save Marx, established educational programs with the scope and thoroughness of Plato's scheme, programs that put down the mythic roots of their secular religions. They projected new visions of society and of the new human being within that society. That vision is indoctrinated into the child as a mythic religion, and the child comes to consciousness in an ethos in which the state is watching and judging and will reward and punish him or her. The diabolical religion of National Socialism was inculcated in this way – by terror and totalitarianism. It incorporated Norse sagas into a new state religion whose end remained Ragnarok.

However benign or malignant their objectives, these totalitarian states have inculcated contrived mythic religions that promise to "free humankind." But the freedom that is promised is not the freedom more precious than life itself, the freedom that makes possible "all that makes life worth living,"[70] the freedom on which human dignity and one's worthiness to be happy are grounded. Rather, it is only an ersatz freedom of mere conformity to party objectives, a legality devoid of autonomy.

It would appear that Kant stood between two worlds – one dying and the other powerless to be born. The civilization based on mythic Christianity was dissolving in the solvent of the scientific worldview and the neo-religions of socialism were as yet scarcely emerging. Kant could not subvert the ethical by introducing the coercive motivations of mythic religion. But he was by no means indifferent to the need for moral incentive. He thus presented a theory of ethics of maximal rational purity, grounded in human freedom and the law of its expression that revealed the human person as a being worthy beyond price. Those who understand and accept Kant's conception of humankind are immunized against the temptations of the secular heterodoxies and all the totalitarian schemes for human betterment that destroy freedom.

Although Kant's ethics had its mythic roots in Christian pietism rather than in reason, his fully developed ethical theory proscribes the use of any mythic religion that is not subject to the test of ethical orthodoxy. By eschewing mythic roots, Kant's theory only lost what it could never really have had. Having reached the limits of reason in providing moral incentive, Kant stopped. And perhaps in regard to this issue he did enough: his ethical theory clearly provides the principles of criticism and procedural guidance for personal and political conduct. Although the force of moral feeling produced by reason may be weak, it continually gives rise to the conviction that freedom is the natural end of

70 KpV, 159: CprR, 256. See also ibid., 158: ibid., 255.

humankind and that each of us should subordinate life itself to those principles that make life worthwhile.

The limited incentive of moral feeling is perhaps best understood as a moral sea anchor that, although incapable of providing the motive power to move a ship to harbor, may yet prevent its foundering on the rocks.

The problem of forgiveness, the possibility of wickedness and devilishness, and the question posed by Kant's theory of two standpoints are lines of inquiry suggesting the inadequacy of Kant's conception of freedom. But this does not substantially distract us from Kant's monumental achievement in ethics. We do not question but rather confirm Kant's greatness by pursuing these lines of inquiry from the point at which his efforts terminated.

Like Plato, Aristotle, Hegel, Spinoza and all the greatest philosophers, Kant deepened our understanding of ourselves and bequeathed to his successors questions that remain to puzzle us, for Kant never minimized the extraordinary nature of the human species – its depth, complexity and inscrutability.

Kant made, as I believe to have shown, great advances in our understanding of ethics. And yet he has left us with sufficient puzzles to ensure that continuing attention will be paid to his philosophy for many generations to come.

Appendix: Kant at Auschwitz

1 The Holocaust

In assessing the enduring value of Kant's ethics I propose to put it to a test to which Kant subscribed: a sound theory must be effective in practice. Let us consider, then, how adequately Kant's ethics might have dealt with the great moral tragedy of genocide. How would one guided by Kant's ethics have dealt with Auschwitz?[1]

It would require a Chinese ideograph of the greatest complexity and inclusiveness to call forth the full range of conceptual, perceptual and emotional elements evoked by the word "Auschwitz." Auschwitz calls to mind what has been described as "the greatest crime in history," "the crime without a name," or, in what now appears to be its authoritative and enduring denomination, the Holocaust.

Commentators have not failed to notice the irony of the word "holocaust," whose root meaning is "fully burnt offering" and whose extended meaning, prior to the Third Reich, was "a great conflagration in which many human lives are lost." The extended meaning aptly characterizes what transpired in the fires that were ignited and maintained by the functionaries of the Nazi *Vernichtungslager* in the territories controlled by the Third Reich. But the root meaning – burnt offering – calls forth the question: offering to whom? Surely not God.

With the exception of those killed in isolated uprisings, such as the Warsaw Ghetto and Sobibór, the Holocaust's victims had no opportunity for the self-elected martyrdom of those who freely sacrifice themselves for some noble cause. They were not, like the martyrs of the fifteenth and sixteenth centuries, burned as contumacious heretics following trial and condemnation by an ecclesiastical court. They were worked, beaten, and starved; they were shot, gassed or killed with lethal injections; some were buried or burned alive. They were neither scapegoats nor suffering servants; they were not killed to appease any deity or to reconcile humans to other humans. They were wasted – utterly, systematically, without sentiment, or with visceral loathing – much as one would exterminate vermin, which indeed is how the Nazi leadership described its genocidal policy.

---

1 I want to express my indebtedness to the late Professor Klaus Hartmann of Tübingen and Professor Thomas Seebohm of Mainz for their helpful criticisms of an earlier draft of this study.

Nonetheless, in the context of the pervasive evil of the Third Reich, the victims were martyrs: confessors of the human spirit – burnt offerings, not to the worship or glory of God, but to God's absence from human affairs, and to humankind's capacity for great evil when possessed by a satanic ideology. In their intense suffering they bore witness to that humanity said to be created in God's image.

It is not my purpose, however, to evaluate the appositeness of the term Holocaust. It is now in common usage. Through the work of Elie Wiesel and others, the word now calls to mind and feeling the full horror of the historical reality to which it refers.[2]

This reality had indeed eclipsed all other meanings. The word has now become our "ideograph" for a crime of such magnitude that it extended over most of Europe, of such complexity that it strained the industrial and military resources of Germany as well as other European nations, of such purposelessness apart from a commitment to evil and of such monumental, deliberate, and sadistic cruelty that it has given a new dimension to the word "ruthless." It would appear to offer a factual example of the devilish use of freedom and reason which Kant held to be impossible. It is impossible to find any positive motive for this program other than the realization of great evil, the possibility of which is as inscrutable as freedom itself, and no more likely to be comprehended.

When Hitler willed the Final Solution to the Jewish Question, he also willed with full consistency the means to this end. But as an individual, he did not have those means and ordered others to provide them. His orders challenged the technical abilities of his key aides and associates and the organizations under their control: Reinhard Heydrich and his successor, Ernst Kaltenbrunner in the *Reichssicherheitshauptamt*; Heinrich Himmler, head of the SS; and especially Albert Speer, the most important Reich Minister, with responsibility for all systems of production and transportation. Eventually, even the *Wehrmacht* became involved, as did key officials and subjects of governments allied by choice or force to the Nazi cause.

It is important to note that a crime of this magnitude, though it required extraordinary skill and determination in the marshaling of the vast resources of the Third Reich and its allies in time of war with shortages of manpower and materials, poses no insuperable scientific or organizational challenges for any industrial society with sufficient police and military power. Though Hitler's

---

2 See, for example, Wiesel, *Nuit*; also Rosenfeld and Greenberg, *Confronting the Holocaust: The Impact of Elie Wiesel*.

policy of genocide was historically unique in Western civilization, a genocidal Holocaust could happen again. Indeed, it can happen in any society – industrial or non-industrial – when there is sufficient will on the part of a ruthless leadership.[3]

Although in its historical particularity the Holocaust will always be unique, we must be concerned to understand its universal significance. It is the paradigm of the crime against humanity or, as the French prosecutor at Nuremberg, François de Menthon, said, "a crime against the human status."[4] Persons operating with the sanction or at the behest of their regime who take human lives for no reason or purpose other than that their victims live – that their mere existence is an offense to those in power – commit a crime against the human status as such. The victims'"offense" is found in their existence; they are killed not for what they do but for what they are and cannot avoid being. We only understand the full malevolence of the agents of genocide if we recognize that the crime is not committed under a claim of necessity for which any objective evidence could conceivably be adduced, but solely for the purpose of satisfying the criminals' preference for the victims' nonexistence.

This universal aspect of the crime we call the Holocaust in no way diminishes the significance of the fact that Jews bore the brunt of the Nazi fury and were killed as Jews, or that Gypsies were killed as Gypsies. Though it is true that many Germans were also murdered at Auschwitz, they were not killed as Germans. They were executed as Jews, as communists, as "useless eaters," or as deviants from the Nazi program. Members of other groups believed to be racially inferior – Russians and Poles, in particular – were also treated harshly even

3 State-sponsored mass extermination had occurred earlier as, for example, in the Turkish massacre of Armenians. Although the Turkish government's policy was genocidal, it is distinguishable from the Nazi policy because the Nazi regime sought to annihilate on a global basis an entire people. The Turkish government's atrocities were as brutal as those of the Nazis. See Walker, *Armenia, Survival of a Nation*, 202–9. But they were not motivated by the same intention to exterminate all Armenians worldwide. They were rather designed to remove a minority that interfered with their national ambitions. Stalin annihilated millions of Ukrainians during the 1930s through starvation as well as direct killing. In this case, however, the objective was collectivization of agriculture, not the extermination of a race or nationality. Whether programs essentially like the Holocaust have occurred in other times and places has been the subject of intense discussion by German historians and philosophers. Ernst Nolte, Michael Stürmer, Jürgen Habermas, Thomas Nipperdey, Hans Mommsen, Steven T. Katz, and others have examined the issue of the uniqueness of the Holocaust in the public press and in scholarly books and articles. Many of the principal articles are collected in *Historiker-Streit*, Ernst Piper, ed.

4 Quoted in Arendt, *Eichmann in Jerusalem*, 257.

though they were not marked for total annihilation. In all such cases, the executioners brutalized and killed because these groups were deemed either unworthy of life altogether or inferior to the German *Volk*.

2 Eichmann's Claim to be a Kantian

The Holocaust confronts us as an ineradicable fact of human experience that begs for comprehension. It is time for philosophers to come to terms with the objective historical reality of the crimes of the Holocaust. It is time that Kant, in particular, come to Auschwitz.

Kant, the most important writer on ethics since Aristotle, set forth doctrines that were not just theoretical in nature but were intended to guide everyday human conduct – to provide a firm moral anchoring for individuals seeking to exercise their free will in accordance with the moral law.[5] Kant is relevant to the discussion not only because he examined the problem of freedom and evil in more depth than any philosopher before him, but because his philosophy, and particularly his moral philosophy, was widely and deeply influential in all those nations that participated in the Enlightenment – that movement in western thought that represented the triumph of reason over tradition and of science over superstition. Of special relevance for us, Adolph Eichmann used Kant's teachings in defending his participation in the Nazi machinery of mass murder.[6]

It seems obvious from all we know about Immanuel Kant that he would have been appalled by National Socialism and Hitler's extreme cruelty, especially his treatment of the Jews. It seems therefore outrageous, as Hannah Arendt noted, for Eichmann to appeal to Kant in justification of himself.

When we think of Kant's veneration of the moral examples of his parents and the centrality of one's obligation to act in accordance with law and for its sake, as the supreme principle of morality, we know he would have been outraged by Nazi extremes and in particular by Hitler's hatred and abuse of Jews

---

5 See Chapter X.

6 Kant's doctrines have generally been considered antithetical to the National Socialist ideology, which represented a calamitous setback to the Enlightenment in Germany. See Viereck, 9. On the other hand, efforts were made by a few, most notably the *völkisch* propagandist Houston Stewart Chamberlain, to find in Kant legitimation for a racialist authoritarian polity. Chamberlain observed, but without convincing argument, that Kantian idealism provided philosophical justification for German "cultural" idealism – the inner struggle against material self-interest and comfort in favor of self-sacrifice. Stackelberg, 132–44.

and his intention to use all the powers of the state to exterminate them. How would Kant, who insisted that we must put ourselves in the place and point of view of others in order to act morally, have countenanced the Nazi treatment of Jews and Gypsies and their extermination in the Final Solution?

But Kant's personal views are irrelevant to the issues raised by Eichmann. He was not a Kant scholar, but he had almost certainly read the *Groundwork of the Metaphysics of Morals* and possibly the *Critique of Practical Reason*. As an exercise of thought experiment, let us consider the merits of Eichmann's claim that he was a Kantian and living in accordance with the categorical imperative in light of all we know not of Kant personally but of what he has said in his writings.

What then would Kant have had to say about Auschwitz? Considering the primacy of practical reason in his philosophy and his emphatic insistence that sound theory must work in practice, it is reasonable to ask how his ethical and political teachings apply to the Holocaust. Is Kant's theory of moral responsibility adequate to the phenomena of the Holocaust? More specifically, by what criteria would Kant determine the individuals responsible and the degree of their responsibility?[7]

Just as the Holocaust is the paradigm of the crime against the human status, the Eichmann case offers itself as a paradigm for an understanding of moral responsibility under conditions of mass bureaucratized murder. Eichmann stood at considerable remove from both those who actually carried out the killings at the lowest level of the regime and the leaders of the Third Reich who conceived of the Final Solution and set it in motion.

When, at his trial at Jerusalem in 1961, Eichmann tried to absolve himself from responsibility, he told the court: "With the killing of the Jews I had nothing to do. I never killed a Jew, or a non-Jew, for that matter – I never killed any human being. I never gave an order to kill either a Jew or a non-Jew; I just did not do it."[8]

---

7 I am keenly aware of the impossibility and the folly of asking what would Kant or Jesus or any other historical figure have done confronted by Auschwitz and the Third Reich – a political system and its defining program of which they had no experience. This is rather an exercise of imagination in which we apply our knowledge of Kant's ethical and political writing to this historic phenomenon. We know that Kant personally – with his consistent defense of freedom to speak and to write, and with his concern never to treat others as means merely – would have been appalled by Hitler's program. But what could or would any of us including Kant have done in this situation guided only by his teachings? Had Kant lived during the Hitler years, I suspect he would have revised his views on the right of revolution and the justification for executing a head of state.

8 Arendt, 22.

Eichmann's first sentence, "With the killing of the Jews I had nothing to do," is distinct from his claim that he never killed any one or ordered anyone killed. The distinction is not unimportant from the standpoint of Kantian philosophy or our own legal tradition which holds, generally speaking, that for any criminal act there must be a *mens rea* and an *actus reus*.

But even if we grant the truth of Eichmann's claim that he did not personally kill anyone or directly order others to carry out executions, this does not warrant the conclusion that he had therefore nothing to do with the killing of the Jews. For his was not the ordinary trial for murder involving a simple suspect or a small group of suspects but an extraordinary criminal proceeding involving a bureaucracy of murder operating under the sanction of state authority. Eichmann's responsibility, the District Court in Jerusalem held, did not require proof that he knowingly and intentionally killed, or ordered others to kill, because, as the court expressed it, "the legal and moral responsibility of him who delivers the victim to his death is, in our opinion, no smaller and may even be greater than the liability of him who does the victim to death."[9]

What was the scope and nature of Eichmann's role and responsibility? The prosecution made extravagant claims about Eichmann's importance and suggested that he had considerable influence on Hitler and Himmler. As Hannah Arendt observed, Eichmann insisted that "he was guilty only of 'aiding and abetting' in the commission of the crimes with which he was charged." The Court did not dispute Eichmann's position in this regard. "To one's great relief," Arendt wrote, "[the court] in a way recognized that the prosecution had not succeeded in proving him wrong on this point."[10] Instead, the court found that Eichmann's activities "were mainly those of a person soliciting by giving counsel or advice to others and of one who enabled or aided others in [the criminal] act."[11] Eichmann was clearly not a central figure in the Third Reich's policy of genocide. Reinhard Heydrich – not Eichmann – has been described as the "real engineer of the Final Solution."[12] But even though Eichmann lacked the position and the ability to be a master engineer of the Final Solution, he was a successful negotiator who was capable of organizational innovations to expedite the Nazi program of mass murder.[13]

---

9 Arendt, 211.

10 Arendt, 246.

11 Arendt, 246.

12 Arendt, 36.

13 Arendt, 63. Eichmann declared himself free of anti-Semitic passions and claimed even to have saved hundreds of thousands of Jewish lives. That he exaggerated the number of Jews he had saved was demonstrable; nevertheless, he could establish that he had saved some.

Eichmann was also fully informed of what the Final Solution of the Jewish question meant – the physical annihilation of all of the Jews. Testimony at the trial revealed that Eichmann attended the Wannsee Conference. Having learned that the Final Solution was the Führer's decision, Eichmann at all times thereafter did "his best to make the Final Solution final."[14] Eichmann never denied but proudly admitted his fidelity to Hitler's orders. He shipped Jews to death camps and transferred Jews from one camp to another. Although he readily acknowledged his involvement as an accomplice in the crimes of which he was accused, Eichmann excused himself on the grounds that he acted under orders.

After his capture and just prior to his trial, Eichmann acknowledged to Avner Less, the Israeli police interrogator, that he lived by duty according to the categorical imperative, "the demand by Kant which I long assumed as my guiding principle. I fashioned my life according to this demand."[15] In the course of the trial, Judge Raveh asked Eichmann what he understood by his statement that he had tried all his life to live according to Kant's categorical imperative. Eichmann replied, "That the basis of my will and the pattern of my life should be such that at all times I should be a universal example of lawfulness. This is what I more or less understood by it."[16] Hannah Arendt rightly observed that that was a perfectly adequate unprofessional description of Kant's view.[17]

Judge Raveh then asked, "Would you say, then, that your activities within the framework of the deportation of Jews was consistent with Kant?" To which Eichmann replied: "No, certainly not. For I did not mean as I was living then, under the pressure of a third party. When I talked of the categorical imperative, I was referring to the time when I was my own master, with a will and aspirations of my own, and not when I was under the domination of a supreme force."[18] Eichmann, perhaps knowing or intuiting more of Kant than Hannah Arendt was inclined to believe, added: "Then I could not live in accordance with this principle [categorical imperative]. But I could include in this principle the concept of *obedience to authority*. This I must do, for this authority was then

---

Interestingly, Robert J. Lifton notes how some Nazi SS doctors managed both to participate fully in the death camp selection process while also behaving humanely towards individual concentration camp inmates. In this way, Lifton notes, they were able to sustain the sense of themselves as healers even while serving as active functionaries in the bureaucracy of mass murder. See Lifton, 430–65.

14 Arendt, 146.

15 Pearlman, 222.

16 Pearlman, 532.

17 Arendt, 136. Many of us have given our philosophy students academic credit for less accurate interpretations.

18 Pearlman, 532–3.

responsible for what happened."[19] While recognizing the apparent conflict between the demands of the categorical imperative and Hitler's order of the Final Solution, Eichmann claimed that the categorical imperative ("this principle") included the duty of obedience to authority.

It may seem outrageous to find Kant's ethical doctrine, grounded as it is in the dignity of the moral person as an end-in-himself, used to exculpate a confessed accomplice to mass murder. But it should come as no surprise to Kant scholars, for Kant's published views on the citizen's obligation to the sovereign strongly supported Eichmann's position.

In "Theory and Practice," Kant argues uncompromisingly that it is a citizen's duty to obey established law. Using an extreme case to make the point, he writes:

> If a law is so framed that all the people *could not possibly* give it their consent – as, for example, a law granting the hereditary *privilege* of *master status* to a certain class of *subjects* – the law is unjust; but if it is *at all possible* that a people might agree on it, then the people's duty is to look upon the law as just.[20]

Kant holds that, as citizens of a state, individuals should not assume the soundness of their own judgment. If, on the basis of individual judgment, each citizen were morally justified in determining the requirements of the law for himself or herself, a society under law would be impossible. "If a people were to judge," Kant writes,

> that a certain actual legislation will with the utmost probability deprive them of their happiness – what can such a people do? Should they not resist? The answer can be only: *They can do nothing but obey.* For the question is not what happiness the subject may expect from the establishment of a community or from its administration. Rather the issue is first of all the legal order which is thereby to be secured for all.[21]

---

19 Pearlman, 533. My italics. Germany has often been described as an *Obrigkeitsstaat* (authoritarian state). In his study of the contemporary German national character, John Ardagh notes how submission to law and to superiors has been seen as the citizen's most essential duty and also how Kantian teaching legitimated this attitude. Kant, he notes, stated emphatically that the characteristics of the child "must include, above all, obedience." Such obedience "prepares the child for adherence to the laws he will have to obey as a future citizen, whether he likes them or not." Ardagh, 408.

20 TP, 297: TaP, 65.

21 Ibid., 298: ibid., 66. My italics.

Kant recognizes that the lawmaker may err. Nevertheless, the existence of civil society under the rule of law is so important that:

> any resistance to the supreme lawmaking power, any incitement of dissatisfied subjects to action, any uprising that bursts into rebellion – that all this is the worst, most punishable crime in a community's foundations. And this ban is absolute, so unconditional that *even though that supreme power or its agent, the head of state, may have broken the original contract, even though in the subject's eyes he may have forfeited the right to legislate by empowering the government to rule tyrannically by sheer violence, even then the subject is allowed no resistance, no violent counteraction.* The reason is that once a civil constitution exists, a people no longer have the right to judge how that constitution ought to be administered.[22]

These passages, had Eichmann known of them and introduced them in court, would have given *prima facie* support to his claim that he followed Kant for it was his duty to obey Hitler. The point of view expressed in these passages is one that Kant elaborated with great consistency in many different works.[23] Kant explicitly comments, for example, on Gottfried Achenwall's defense on the right

---

22 Ibid., 299–300: ibid., 67–68. My italics. Allen Wood claims that "Kant does not hold, of course, that all italicized forms of rebellion are impossible. If morality has been presented to a man through the arbitrary and despotic will of a real or imagined sovereign, it might not at all be unlikely in Kant's view that this man, feeling his dignity as a person affronted and abused by such a despotism, would develop a strong natural inclination to disobey the commands of this sovereign and to rebel against them." (*Kant's Moral Religion*, 212n). Unfortunately no supporting evidence for Wood's view can be found in Kant's own writing, and it clearly contradicts Kant's position as noted above. I can't find Kant making any exception to the view that all forms of rebellion are morally outrageous and especially in cases where an assault is made on the person of the sovereign.
Wood's suggestion is, nevertheless, appealing because one can only wish that Kant had specifically allowed for this exception, and because most of us believe that had Kant been alive during the rise of the Nazi dictatorship, he would have advocated rebellion against Adolf Hitler. Unfortunately, however, this view is not endorsed by Kant, but is only our wish, and our belief, that had Kant been transferred in time from the 18th to the 20th century, he would have opposed Hitler's regime.

23 Thomas Seebohm has also noted the uncompromising nature of Kant's position. There is absolutely no right of resistance, no matter how odious the regime. On the other hand, Kant's ambivalence towards revolutions is clear, as Seebohm also notes. Kant allowed that some revolutions could further the progress of the human race and, indeed, could occur as a "natural event" – a reasonably predictable occurrence in regimes ruled by unjust sovereigns. This does not, however, provide any moral or legal justification for revolutions as "natural events." See Seebohm, "Kant's Theory of Revolution." Kant was, for example, somewhat approving of the American Revolution. But he was utterly appalled by the brutality and chaos of the French Revolution and the Reign of Terror that followed.

of revolution. Achenwall had argued that when the danger of injustice by a head of state poses more danger to the community than the threat of armed revolt, the people have the right to abrogate their contract of submission to the sovereign, to depose him or her as a tyrant, and to return to the state of nature.[24] Rejecting this argument, Kant doubts even that Achenwall and his supporters would ever have given their counsel or consent to such dangerous undertakings. The outcome of history, Kant notes:

> usually colors our judgment of the legal grounds [of any revolution] though it was uncertain while the latter are certain. As far as these legal grounds are concerned – granting even that such a rebellion might do no wrong to a prince (who may have violated, say, a *joyeuse entrée*, or an actual underlying contract with his people) – it is clear that the people by pursuing their rights in this manner have done the greatest wrong. For this manner, if adopted as a maxim, would render every legal constitution insecure and introduce a state of utter lawlessness (*status naturalis*) in which all rights would lose at least their effectiveness.[25]

This doctrine espoused by Kant, on behalf of both the head of state and the head of government, would appear to reduce or eliminate altogether the responsibility of those functionaries of the Third Reich, Eichmann among them, who were ordered by him to implement the Final Solution. Are we then driven to the conclusion that Kant's ethical doctrines are inconsistent: that an individual is morally obligated to act in accordance with the orders of his or her superior in violation of his or her conscience as guided by the categorical imperative? Does Kant, by resolving the apparent conflict of duties in favor of obedience, actually lend moral support to Eichmann and his associates?

3 Absolute Obedience in Kant's Ethics

To answer these questions we must first examine Kant's views on the nature of civil society and the basis for its legitimation. Civil society, according to Kant, is neither an imposition on humankind nor the consequence of an historical contract. The social contract by which civil society is established is an idea of reason and obligatory on the rational being as an aspect of consistent volition. Clearly influenced by Hobbes, Kant argues that the individual who wills to pursue his or her own freedom cannot do so consistently without respecting the

---

24 *Jus Naturae*, Editio 5ta, Pars Posterior, Sections 203–6. Cited in TP, 301n: TaP, 69n.
25 TP, 301: TaP, 69.

right of other individuals to exercise their own. The individual recognizes that he or she cannot protect himself or herself from neighbors' unrestrained exercise of their freedom except by engaging in continual war with neighbors, or by entering into civil society. The former alternative is the unendurable Hobbesian state of nature, the "war of all against all." Without the structure of civil society, each individual's enjoyment of the right to real property, for example, would require constant vigilance and the ability to defend that property from others. But since individuals desire a form of legal possession that guarantees their right to real property without having constantly to defend it, they must recognize the necessity of civil society.[26]

Kant's argument is not only strongly influenced by Luther and Hobbes but tracks closely the position developed by Socrates in Plato's *Republic* and *Crito*. Socrates observes that no individual is self-sufficient but is compelled by his or her insufficiency to enter into society as a condition of both survival and fulfillment. Therefore, the individual outside of the state lacks the conditions of his or her own existence and fulfillment.

Kant also recognizes, along with Plato, that in any civil society there must be a determination of who shall rule since it is not possible for each and every person to rule. Although Kant presents an argument for the superiority of the republican form of government, he recognizes that other forms can serve the purpose, including monarchies and aristocracies. But in any civil constitution there must be a single sovereign, whether a legislature acting under majority rule, a body of aristocrats or a monarch. Whatever the form, there must be an ultimate source of order, a sovereign beyond whom there is no appeal, in short, a commander-in-chief (*Oberbefehlshaber*).

But what if the sovereign abuses his or her subjects by imposing laws that treat them unfairly? Acutely aware of historic examples of despotism in which individuals had been mistreated and even killed by their rulers, Kant nevertheless states clearly and without compromise that:

---

26 MS, 256–7, 307–8: MoM, 409–410, 451–52. Kant summarizes his position as follows: "However well disposed and law-abiding human beings might be, it still lies *a priori* in the rational idea of such a condition (one that is not rightful) that before a public lawful condition is established, individual human beings, peoples and states can never be secure against violence from one another, since each has its own right to do what seems right and good to it and not to be dependent upon another's opinion about this. So, unless it wants to renounce any concepts of right, the first thing it has to resolve upon is the principle that it must leave the state of nature, in which each follows its own judgment, unite itself with all others (with whom it cannot avoid interacting), subject itself to a public lawful external coercion .... That is, it ought above all else to enter a civil condition." MS, 312: MoM, 456.

> there is, therefore, no right to *sedition* (*seditio*), still less to *rebellion* (*rebellio*), and least of all is there a right against the head of a state as an individual person (the monarch), *to attack his person* or even his life (*monarcho-machismus sub specie tyrannicidii*) on the pretext that he has abused his authority (*tyrannis*). – Any attempt whatsoever at this is *high treason* (*proditio eminens*), and whoever commits such treason must be punished by nothing less than death for attempting *to destroy his fatherland* (*parricida*). – The reason a people has a duty to put up with even what is held to be an unbearable abuse of supreme authority is that its resistance to the highest legislation can never be regarded as other than contrary to law, and indeed as abolishing the entire legal constitution. For a people to be authorized to resist, there would have to be a public law permitting it to resist .... This is self-contradictory, and the contradiction is evident.[27]

Kant would argue that there is no contradiction between his ethical and his political theories because the individual, in order to avoid the state of nature, is required by the categorical imperative to subordinate his or her own determination of law to the law as determined by the sovereign. After considering the command of the sovereign in terms of the procedures required by the categorical imperative, the individual may find it abhorrent. Nevertheless, he or she cannot universalize the maxim of acting in opposition to the sovereign's command, for it entails the rejection of all law and civil society. Kant avoids a conflict of duties by subordinating the individual's determination of law to the law of the state. Surely Kant must have found this subordination deeply troubling, but not so troubling as the chaos that would follow from the elevation of individual conscience above the will of the sovereign.

With full consistency Kant can admit that a revolution might, in fact, contribute to human progress while also insisting that there can be no *right* of revolution – an idea he held to be inherently contradictory. Since lesser acts of disobedience share logically with revolution the rejection of civil society, Kant rejects not only the right of revolution but the right of any kind of disobedience.

Was Eichmann so far off the mark, then, in appealing to Kant to justify his acceptance of the *Führerprinzip*?

Kant's moral idealism and the rectitude and decency of his personal life lead me and most Kant scholars to believe that Kant's philosophy could never be used in support of Hitler and the Third Reich. In his introduction to Kant's *Metaphysical Elements of Justice*, John Ladd tries to defend Kant from any such

---

27 Ibid., 320: ibid., 463. Kant clearly intended for this to apply not only to *active* efforts at resistance, whether nonviolent protest or violent revolution undertaken to *change* a policy or an entire regime, but even to an individual's refusing to carry out an order from the sovereign. See *infra*.

interpretation. Because coercion is only legitimate when it is used to preserve the rule of law, Ladd argues:

> a state founded on violence, like the Nazi one, definitely exceeds those limits, and I do not see how Kant could, consistently with his stated principles, condemn those who opposed the activities of that kind of regime, although he repeatedly asserts that we must obey the powers that be.[28]

Ladd attempts in this way to bypass Kant's repeated argument that individuals by entering into civil society forfeit their right to determine what the rule of law requires.

Ladd tries to avoid the inevitable implications of Kant's statement by claiming that the Nazi regime was "founded on violence." Unfortunately, his interpretation of the origins of the Hitler regime is more convenient than accurate. The Third Reich was violent, but while the Nazi party had earlier used violence to intimidate opponents, it came to power through lawful, democratic procedures. Hitler was also made Chancellor in a constitutionally proper manner. As President, Hindenburg had the constitutional authority to suspend the constitution, and Hitler had the right, as Chancellor, to ask that he do so. Had the Third Reich been introduced by force, all Germans would in fact have been obligated to oppose Hitler for he would have come to power through an act of unlawful rebellion against President Hindenburg and the Weimar Republic.

The reason individuals cannot interpret the law in accordance with their individual consciences is, according to Kant, that they lack the standing from which independently to determine a society's legal requirements. If any individual other than the sovereign were granted such standing, chaos would follow in the proclamation of conflicting laws. Kant is willing to grant people who suffer what they consider to be injustice and violence the right to complain and the right to put their complaints in writing,[29] but he denies at every opportunity the right to resist, to engage in sedition or to revolt. Rulers, like citizens, should obey the law. But once *lawfully* established in power, the sovereign has and must have the last word regarding what is and is not in accordance with the law.[30]

---

28 *The Metaphysical Elements of Justice* xxi.

29 The sovereign, of course, might suspend that right and impose censorship. TP, 304–5: TaP, 72–3.

30 Kant does acknowledge that in a highly improbable situation an attenuated form of revolt consented to by the sovereign might be justified. But even in this situation Kant insists that citizens never have the right to punish the sovereign for any prior acts because "as the source of law, he can do no wrong." MS, 321n: MoM, 464n. It would seem that sovereigns who violate

Thus Kant's insistence on the ultimate authority of the sovereign and the duty of the subject to obey would appear to support Eichmann's position. A person of Eichmann's limited intellectual comprehension could hardly be accused of bad faith in thinking that his obligation to obey the Führer was sanctioned by the writings of Immanuel Kant himself.

Hannah Arendt takes strong exception, however, to the view that Eichmann could find any justification in Kant for his duty to obey the Führer. She comments: "this was outrageous, on the face of it, and also incomprehensible, since Kant's moral philosophy is so clearly bound up with man's faculty of judgment, which rules out blind obedience."[31] Arendt is right to note that judgment in moral situations must be free and not determined by outside influences. But Arendt simply ignores Kant's own arguments for obedience. Her view is unfortunately contradicted by Kant's discussion in the *Metaphysics of Morals* and "Theory and Practice." We cannot responsibly ignore Kant's repeated and explicit statements and arguments in opposition to the right of resistance or disobedience to the sovereign.[32]

Reared in an age characterized by stability in governments and rulers, Kant witnessed only late in life the first upheavals that adumbrated the volatility of modern times. It is therefore intriguing to speculate whether Kant might have applied to earlier stages in Hitler's career Ladd's argument about the illegitimacy of violence. Observing the violent doctrines and tactics used by Hitler and the Nazi party years before coming to power, could Kant have argued that Hitler's party was illegitimate prior to its election to the Reichstag and Hitler's legitimate designation as Chancellor? Had not Hitler and his party already been guilty of resistance to the legitimate sovereignty of the Weimar Republic?

This line of argument is, perhaps, slightly more plausible than that pursued by Professor Ladd. But it would have provided only a small window of opportu-

---

the laws they themselves have established have in fact by their violation done an injustice. Kant's reasoning here is not convincing.

Kant's abhorrence of revolution was doubtless influenced both by the fact that genuinely despotic and inhumane rulers were rare in Western Europe in his day and by the excesses of the Reign of Terror during the French Revolution. His revulsion at the executions of Charles I and Louis XVI was clearly a major factor in his rejection of the right of revolution. Regicide, Kant argued, "is regarded as a crime that remains forever and can never be expiated (*crimen immortale inexpiabile*), and it seems to be like what the theologians call the sin that cannot be forgiven in this world or the next." Ibid., 321ff.: ibid., 464ff.

31 Arendt, 136.

32 I believe Arendt is right, of course, in thinking that Kant personally would never have supported or even obeyed such orders. Confronted by the abuses of the Third Reich, Kant, I believe, would have changed his mind.

nity for those guided by Kant's philosophy. We can be virtually certain that Kant, as revealed in his writings, would in some fashion have opposed Hitler and the Nazi party up to the time of his selection as Chancellor. Hitler's intentions as revealed in *Mein Kampf* and in the manifestos of the Nazi party should have been denounced and opposed by all Kantians. Whatever Kant himself might have done, however, the historical record shows that those influenced by his philosophy did virtually nothing. Karl Jaspers, perhaps Kant's greatest disciple, was politically inactive prior to Hitler's coming to power and sat out the Hitler years in despair and isolation.[33] And Martin Heidegger, author of a major book on Kant, was so captivated by the spirit of Nazism that he joined the party and spoke favorably of the Führer.

On March 23, 1933, the Reichstag passed the Enabling Act by a majority of 441 to 84. A two-thirds majority would have been assured even if the 81 communist members of the *Reichstag* had been allowed to vote. The sovereignty of Adolf Hitler as Führer had been legitimized by this majority vote of a constitutionally established legislative body.

I have supposed that Kant would have opposed Hitler and the Nazis in their ascent to power. But once Hitler was empowered by the Enabling Act as Führer, would not Eichmann have had the right to claim on the basis of Kant's own arguments the duty to obey along with all other citizens?

Kant would have been appalled by the extraordinary malevolence and criminality of the Third Reich, which had no parallel in Kant's time or at any previous time in western history. Given Hitler's use of all Jews, Gypsies and Germans as means merely, given his subordination of all individuals and all segments of German life to his evil purposes, it is possible – indeed highly probable – that Kant would have rewritten his political philosophy to justify tyrannicide or the right of revolution in a situation so extreme. This revisionism, however attractive, does not absolve the Kant scholar from observing the written record. Unfortunately the record must stand as it was written.[34]

---

33 As Jaspers notes, Kant's view of the philosopher's role in matters of state is the *passive* one of providing advice. Jaspers cites as evidence of Kant's submissiveness his statement in the essay "On Perpetual Peace" that certain kinds of advice should be given to the authorities secretly, for it would appear as belittling were the authorities to appear to be seeking instruction from subordinates, such as philosophers. Jaspers, *Kant: Leben, Werk, Wirkung*, 175–6.

34 But while we cannot rewrite the Kantian text, we must note that the text does not support the view that Kant would have intentionally lent his personal or philosophical support to the Nazi cause. Such a suggestion would also require the rewriting of history.

4 Devilishness as an Actual Mode of Freedom

Reared in the tradition of pietism and educated in the philosophy of the Enlightenment, Kant could not envisage a personality like Hitler just as he could not have imagined a regime of such deliberate and intentional evil as the Third Reich. Kant recognized wrongdoing that results from the impurity and weakness of the human will. Moreover, he granted the possibility of wickedness when the *Gesinnung*, the individual's enduring character or disposition, subordinates the moral law to pathological or sensible motives. But Kant could not even conceive of the possibilities of the demonic – the deliberate and free rejection of reason and its law by reason.[35]

Kant's theory can comprehend the motivations of an Eichmann, a functionary whose efficiency and zeal were motivated almost entirely by careerist concerns; but it cannot illuminate the conduct of a Hitler.

"Only freedom," Kant wrote, "in relation to the internal lawgiving of reason is really an ability; the possibility of deviating from it is an inability. How can the former be defined by the latter?"[36] A human being, Kant writes, transgresses "the inner law *reluctantly*; for there is no human being so depraved as not to feel an opposition to breaking it and an abhorrence of himself in the face of which he has to constrain himself [to break the law]."[37] Could Kant believe that Hitler felt this opposition to breaking the law or this abhorrence of himself? Hitler in fact did not.

Kant fails to take adequate account of the point that when individuals must force themselves to violate the moral law, it is the individuals themselves and no one else who applies the force. This is the case even in situations where such moral transgression conforms to the statutory law of the state, or to edicts from the sovereign. This is not impotence (*Unvermögen*), but the *willful* determination of oneself to do that which one knows to be wrong. Kant uses language that should perhaps have alerted him to the demonic potential in human beings – their power freely to choose evil. Nevertheless he interprets action in opposition to the moral law as impotence.[38]

---

35 For a fuller exposition of Kant's theory of the will and the stages of moral volition from autonomy to devilishness, see Chapters III and X.

36 MS, 227: MOM, 381.

37 MS, 380n: MOM, 512n. The German reads: "*[D]enn es giebt keinen so verruchten Menschen, der bei dieser Übertretung in sich nicht einen Widerstand fühlte und eine Verabscheuung seiner selbst, bei der er sich selbst Zwang anthun muß.*"

38 But there is no evidence Hitler thought his aims, policies and actions were wrong. He passionately enforced his personal views on Germany right up to his suicide.

Eichmann can, of course, be understood in Kantian terms as a person of weak and impure will. He suffered from frequent bouts, not of conscience, but of unconscientiousness. Kant observed that "when it is said that a certain human being *has* no conscience, what is meant is that he pays no heed to its verdict."[39] And Eichmann's opportunity to hear the voice of conscience was diminished by Hitler's program, which discouraged such practices both by propaganda and brute force. Arendt observes, "As Eichmann told it, the most potent factor in the soothing of his own conscience was the simple fact that he could see no one, no one at all, who actually was against the Final Solution."[40]

After Wannsee what little remained of Eichmann's conscience was subordinated to obedience to the Führer.[41] This obedience was now both his duty and his inclination. Obedience to the Führer relieved him, he believed, of all moral responsibility for acts that he clearly recognized were otherwise contrary to the moral law. This very unconscientiousness and weakness of will brought Eichmann eventually to the minimal limits of personality. Ironically, in a dramatic reversal of normal values, the last vestiges of freedom and personality were aroused in him by the Führer's orders. Eichmann, in strict observance of Hitler's orders, defied the orders of his own immediate superiors. In the fall of 1944, he sabotaged to the extent he could Himmler's orders to stop the evacuation of Hungarian Jews to the death camps!

The conventional, pre-Nazi moral and legal framework had in the consciousness of Eichmann been replaced by the perverse "legal" framework decreed by the Führer. As Arendt perceptively says:

> Within this "legal" framework, every order contrary in letter or spirit to a word spoken by Hitler was, by definition, unlawful. Eichmann's position, therefore, showed a most unpleasant resemblance to that of the often-cited soldier who, acting in a normal legal framework, refuses to carry out orders that run counter to his ordinary experience of lawfulness and hence can be recognized by him as criminal.[42]

---

39 MS, 400: MOM, 529.

40 Arendt, 116.

41 In his introduction to the transcripts of Eichmann's pre-trial interrogation, Avner Less claims that Eichmann was aware of Hitler's determination to exterminate the Jews as early as September, 1939. Less, xxii.
It is impossible to be certain that Eichmann, as far removed from Hitler as he was, had any firsthand knowledge of the Final Solution prior to the Wannsee Conference. But Less is almost certainly correct in concluding that Eichmann would have learned of Hitler's intentions from his immediate superiors by 1939.

42 Arendt, 148. The resemblance is unpleasant only because Eichmann experienced the normally unlawful as lawful.

With extraordinary perception, Arendt observes the paradox that "evil in the Third Reich had lost the quality by which most people recognize it – the quality of temptation. Many Germans and many Nazis, probably an overwhelming majority of them, must have been tempted *not* to murder, *not* to rob, *not* to let their neighbors go off to their doom."[43]

Arendt rightly points out that:

> Eichmann was not Iago and not Macbeth, and nothing would have been farther from his mind than to determine with Richard III 'to prove a villain.' Except for an extraordinary diligence in looking out for his personal advancement, he had no motives at all .... He *merely*, to put the matter colloquially, *never realized what he was doing* .... It was sheer thoughtlessness – something by no means identical with stupidity – that predisposed him to become one of the greatest criminals of that period.[44]

In Eichmann, then, we find a personality whose deterioration through moral failure follows the pattern described by Kant's ethical theory: one's personality diminishes along with one's virtue.

It was this complex of qualities – unconscientiousness, weakness, and impurity approaching moral anesthesia – qualities articulated by Eichmann himself in his statement to the court following his conviction, that taught us, in Arendt's famous phrase, "the lesson of the fearsome, word-and-thought-defying *banality of evil*."[45]

Eichmann clearly exemplifies the banality of evil. But what of Hitler? Was he also banal? If Hitler had escaped to Argentina only to be captured by the Israelis and brought to trial in Jerusalem, the Israeli security service would undoubtedly have been looking for a graying, potbellied gentleman in Buenos Aires who charmed his neighbors, was friendly and attentive to little children and who took pleasure in walking his Alsatian dog through the public parks.

But we must not confuse the appearance of banality with banality.[46] Although Hitler displayed many banal traits, and devoid of power might have approached Eichmann in banality, he was from the beginning to the very end of his political career the antithesis of weakness in personality, of subservience, or lack of will.

---

43 Arendt, 150.

44 Arendt, 287–8. As I shall argue, Eichmann, massively guilty as he was, did not rank among the greatest criminals of that period.

45 Arendt, 252.

46 Neither must we overlook, as Arendt most certainly did not, the capacity of persons as genuinely banal as Eichmann to "wreak more havoc than all the evil instincts taken together." Arendt, 288.

In contrast to Eichmann, in Hitler we confront not an absence of self-directed will but, together with Stalin, one of history's ultimate examples of focused, malevolent volition. The power of Hitler's personality imposes itself on ethical theorists as an historical reality to be accounted for in any ethics relevant to human life.[47]

Kant's ethics is inadequate to the understanding of Auschwitz because Kant denies the possibility of the deliberate rejection of the moral law. Not even a wicked person, Kant holds, can will evil for the sake of evil. Such a person's evil, according to Kant, consists merely in the willingness to ignore or subordinate the moral law when it interferes with his or her nonmoral but natural inclinations. The wicked person's evil is expressed in abandoning the conditions of free personal fulfillment in favor of fulfillment as a creature of natural desire. Kant recognizes that an individual may violate his or her moral obligation in pursuit of an object of desire as when, for example, a man steals the property of his parents to support a series of extravagant and short-lived pleasures.

Unlike Plato, Kant recognizes that human beings can knowingly (i.e. intentionally) do evil on the basis of nonmoral motivations. By replacing Plato's theory of a unitary good with a more complex theory of a *heterogeneous* good including moral and natural goods, Kant made plausible the capacity of humans willingly to do evil.[48]

But Kant agreed with Plato in denying the possibility of a person knowingly doing evil for its own sake. By insisting that freedom is a power whose fulfillment depends upon rationality and that irrational misuse is merely an impotence, Kant proposed a theory that rules out the contravening evidence of human experience. Kant not only ignored all literary and imaginative efforts to describe devilish beings who defiantly and powerfully reject the moral law, he even ignored demonic personalities of his own time such as Robespierre, although they are admittedly pale examples in comparison with those that were to emerge with the rise of totalitarianism in our time.

Literary presentations of demonic evil, Kant argued, presuppose a conception of freedom that, lacking a foundation in human experience, is hopelessly transcendent. In human experience, Kant insists, our knowledge of freedom is revealed exclusively by the moral law. The moral law is the *ratio cognoscendi* of freedom. The realization of freedom – that is, the power to act freely – depends upon the incorporation of that law in volition, in free decisions of the will. For

---

47 Hitler's life is a complex set of facts that forces me to believe that devilishness is a possible expression of freedom.

48 I discuss Kant's radical departure from the classical doctrine of ethics at great length in Chapter II.

theoretical reasons, therefore, Kant rejects all speculation about devilish beings: such beings are, on his theory, either transcendent (hence beyond human experience) or, if presented within the bounds of actual human experience, beings whose wickedness results from some degree of impotence.

In *Faust*, Goethe's presentation of Mephistopheles' evil is restricted to the limits imposed by Kant's moral theory. Goethe's Mephistopheles demonstrates the weakness of personality required by Kant's theory.[49] Mephistopheles dutifully serves the moral purposes of God by trying the dispositions of individuals, either to their moral fulfillment or to their damnation. The damnation to which we are led by Mephistopheles involves merely the subordination of the moral law to inclinations, a common human experience amply accounted for in Kant's theory.

The Satan of Milton's *Paradise Lost*, by contrast, exemplifies the transcendent sort of devilishness Kant rejects as a romantic illusion of the heroic grandeur of wickedness. But Milton, in presenting Satan in his solitary defiant rage, consumed by hatred of everything God-like save God-like power, presents a compelling example of the genuinely demonic. Although Milton's portrayal is a work of imagination, it describes accurately the factual evil we confront in Auschwitz – evil that far transcends the conceptual limits of Kant's theory. In Auschwitz and in Hitler we confront not the wickedness that results from impotence but the demonic evil of a powerful though irrational exercise of freedom.

As long as Kant limits the expression of freedom to a rational mode, that is, as long as the irrational is dismissed as a diminution of freedom, it follows that any irrational act or movement must be considered an example of impotence rather than agency. The diabolical becomes merely illusory because on this theory no one can freely and deliberately reject the law. The power – the freedom – to reject anything, Kant insists, derives from the law itself. Kant did not consider the possibility of an irrational assertion of freedom that derives its power from the parasitic use of rationality.

In dismissing as an illusion a person's capacity for freely rejecting the moral law – that is, a person's diabolical potentiality – Kant called attention only to the limitations of his own conception of freedom, not to the limits of human freedom itself.[50]

---

49 See Chapter III, Sections 3–4.

50 In denying that human beings have the power deliberately to reject the moral law, Kant repeated Plato's methodological mistake. Like Plato before him, Kant explicitly considered the data which seemed contrary to his theory and, like Plato, used his theory to dismiss the

In fidelity to the historical record of Auschwitz, we must acknowledge the awful fact of humankind's free power to reject the moral law. We must recognize with Kierkegaard and Nietzsche that human freedom can be diabolically no less than autonomously or heteronomously expressed. We must recognize, in short, that the irrational is a mode of rationality and thus one of the possible expressions of freedom as spontaneity. History turns in part on the deeds of individuals such as Tamburlaine, Napoleon, Stalin and Hitler. Weak personalities cannot marshal the resources and support of the masses to accomplish their destructive goals.

Kant comes closest to addressing the nature of personalities like Hitler in *The Doctrine of Virtue*:

> And it is not only unnecessary but even improper to ask whether great *crimes* might not require more strength of soul than do great *virtues*. For by strength of soul we mean strength of resolution in a human being as a being endowed with freedom, hence his strength in so far as he is in control of himself (in his senses) and so in the state of *health* proper to a human being. But great crimes are paroxysms, the sight of which makes one whose soul is healthy shudder. The question would therefore come to something like this: whether a human being in a fit of madness could have more physical strength than when he is sane. This one can admit without attributing more strength of soul to him, if by soul is meant the vital principle of man in the free use of his powers; for, since the basis of great crimes is merely the force of inclinations that *weaken* reason, which proves no strength of soul, the above question would be tantamount to whether someone could show more strength during an attack of sickness than when he is healthy.[51]

Nowhere does Kant speak in closer accord with Plato. And nowhere does he do greater violence to human experience. The power of the irrational as a mode of free expression is an essential lesson of Auschwitz. Hitler cannot be dismissed as a madman. His cunning, his complex intentions and his malevolence, backed by an iron will, do not accord with Kant's assessment. We must not diminish or underestimate the power of evil and its parasitic use of rationality merely because of our profound aversion to it. We must follow Parmenides, who instructed the young Socrates that we must not deny the form of filth because of our aversion to that which is filthy. Rather we must acknowledge the form in order to understand its nature.[52] We must try, if not to understand, at least to acknowledge the reality of evil in order to avoid it.

---

contravening evidence as illusory. In giving his theory apparent support, Kant exposed its ultimate weakness. See Chapter II, 56ff.

51 MS, 384: MOM, 516.

52 Plato, "Parmenides," 364, 367 (Stephanus 130c-d, 133a).

5 Alternative Explanations of Moral Responsibility

As philosophers, we must also resist pathoepistemic aggression by doctors, psychiatrists and psychologists who would reduce the expression of human personality to the narrow limits of the abnormal or the sick. Hitler must be understood not as a diseased psychopath or crazy man. Hitler's career was an undeterred progression toward one of his life's most dominant objectives – the extermination of the Jews. He consciously chose evil. Fortunately for humankind, Hitler's military power collapsed before he was able to complete his objective, though unfortunately not before he killed most of Europe's Jews. No one as successful in fulfilling his objectives as Hitler can be written off as unintelligent or crazy.[53] Evil genius comes far closer to the mark. And in the case of Hitler there is absolutely no ambiguity about the degree of the individual moral responsibility involved. To the extent that Kant's theory fails to account for Hitler's power to do evil, to that extent his theory is inadequate in practice.[54]

The assessment of the legal and moral responsibility of those involved in the crimes of the Holocaust poses a challenge to ethical theorists and to Kant. What is the moral responsibility of Eichmann, the obedient follower? Arendt notes that Eichmann never realized what he was doing, and asks whether he can he be said to have possessed the *mens rea* or quality of mind requisite for the imputation of legal responsibility.[55] Here she raises again the issue of legal culpability in terms of the assumption current in most western legal systems that "intent to do wrong is necessary for the commission of a crime"; that "where this intent is absent, where... the ability to distinguish between right and wrong is impaired, we feel no crime has been committed."[56] There is also the problem of locating the *actus reus*, the criminal act, which was in fact intended by the criminal. Where do we find *mens rea* and *actus reus* for crimes on the scale of the Holocaust? Should we instead speak of *mentes reae* and *actus rei* in addressing such crimes?

---

53 Sebastian Haffner examines Hitler's entire career from the beginning of his success to his death, not in terms of early success followed by failure, but in terms of an uninterrupted progression toward his lifelong objectives. *Anmerkungen zu Hitler*, available in English as *The Meaning of Hitler*.

54 As surely as Kant was right to borrow as little as possible from anthropology in the development of the foundations of morality, he was also right in insisting that his or any theory of morality must work in practice, that is, that it must apply successfully in anthropology.

55 Arendt, 277.

56 Idem.

These issues were faced squarely by Robert Jackson, the American prosecutor at Nuremberg. He rejected as unsatisfactory a determination to indict and condemn the minor criminals of the Third Reich who committed the immediate deeds of murder, torture and other brutalities while allowing those who gave the orders to go free. But there is no established theory of jurisprudence or ethics by which to determine the degrees of criminality and criminal responsibility as we move away from the functionaries who directly committed specific crimes up through the hierarchy of the Third Reich to the Führer.

The court in Jerusalem placed Eichmann in the middle of that continuum, convicting him for his involvement in a process that extended far beyond him – both far above and far below. In order to hold him responsible, the court had to recognize the special nature of the crime before them – hence the unique character of the criminal "act" in this case. Arendt comments:

> in its judgment the court naturally conceded that such a crime could be committed only by a giant bureaucracy using the resources of government. But insofar as it remains a crime – and that, of course, is the premise for a trial – all the cogs in the machinery, no matter how insignificant, are in court forthwith transformed back into perpetrators, that is to say into human beings.[57]

Although it might be argued that the court in Jerusalem relied on a legal fiction, the court showed great wisdom and respect for the complexity of the facts. It said,

> these crimes were committed *en masse*, not only in regard to the number of victims, but also in regard to the numbers of those who perpetrated the crime, and the extent to which any one of the many criminals was close to or remote from the actual killer of the victim means nothing, as far as the measure of his responsibility is concerned. On the contrary, in general the degree of responsibility increases as we draw further away from the man who uses the fatal instrument with his own hands.[58]

No legal fiction is involved.[59] Rather, the court recognized the context in which all moral and *a fortiori* all criminal activity takes place. I have argued elsewhere that voluntary responsibility cannot be understood apart from the recognition that a sound theory of volition depends upon integrating the concept of volition

---

57 Arendt, 289.
58 Quoted in Arendt, 246–7.
59 In Chapter X I noted the difficulties that follow from Kant's absolute concept of freedom. Every act, whether good or evil, Kant insisted, is done from a state of innocence (RGV, 41: Rel, 36). The court was right to note that the exercise of freedom does not spring from a state of innocence, but from a highly complex context.

with non-volitional factors on which volition depends; that what one does reveals what one is, just as what one is conditions what one does.[60] The *ratio essendi* of one's doing is nothing other than one's being; and one's doing is the *ratio cognoscendi* of one's being. A sound understanding of moral and legal responsibility requires the recognition of the interdependence of being and doing and the interdependence of the moral agent and nature, the state, institutions and fate – all of which combine to establish the context in which moral action takes place.

To comprehend the extraordinary nature and complexity of bureaucratic mass murder, we must revise and supplement established legal and moral theories to provide definitions for such crimes and the degrees of responsibility of their perpetrators. We must develop a matrix of responsibility that accounts not only for the guilt of those directly involved in discrete criminal acts of limited scope but also encompasses, as the degree of responsibility rises, the guilt of those, far removed from specific criminal conduct, who shape the context in which specific acts are carried out. This matrix would describe a continuum of decreasing direct involvement and increasing responsibility. It would take into consideration the institutional networks that enhance the power and scope of individuals in positions of increasing authority.

When the crimes of Auschwitz are examined in terms of such a legal and moral framework, we shall find that there is no paradox involved in the banality of evil of those who commit institutional crimes or in the banality of virtue of those who through institutions do good.[61]

The resolution of this paradox requires the introduction into legal and ethical theory of the concept of the lever. Archimedes said, "give me a fulcrum and I shall move the world." The lever and leverage are concepts that most clearly explain the remarkable capacity of ordinary, even banal individuals to do great evil or good.

We see examples of this every day. A small woman on taking controls of a Boeing 747 extends her power to encompass the enormous forces of that giant machine. The commander of an aircraft carrier who, when out of uniform and off station appears ordinary both in figure and in speech, has power when on the bridge to destroy fleets and cities. Hitler and his associates, accurately described as hoodlums and ne'er-do-wells, once in possession of the levers of power moved the world close to ruin.

---

60 See Silber, "Being and Doing: A Study of Status Responsibility."

61 The banality of virtue, although it has not previously been discussed, is exemplified in the careers of many colorless functionaries who fulfill those tasks that reduce the suffering and increase the enjoyment of quotidian life without exhibiting any qualities of heroic virtue.

Hitler's ability to effect the Final Solution depended not only and not even primarily on the criminal functionaries in Auschwitz. It depended much more on the organizational structure of the SS and its middle managers such as Eichmann. If Eichmann had never joined the SS, he would have been from all we know about him just another everyday failure, banal but not necessarily evil. Eichmann is a historical figure of great evil only because powerful levers were placed in his ordinary hands. Eichmann was both morally and criminally responsible because to a major degree he could have avoided direct participation. He was under no obligation to join the party or the SS; he could have resigned himself to a modest existence as an ordinary private citizen.[62]

Even if we acknowledge that Kant would have recognized the duty to obey the Führer, Eichmann had no right to appeal to Kant in justification of his actions. He could have avoided placing himself in a position where be would be obligated to obey Hitler in the Final Solution. He had only to renounce his personal ambition to get ahead in a system that was evil and that corrupted to varying degrees all those who participated in it. Eichmann could have reduced his culpability in direct proportion to his avoidance of administrative responsibility in the Third Reich.[63]

If Hitler had never become Chancellor of Germany, he would have been innocent of the great crimes for which we hold him morally to account and condemn him. Prior to success in his political career, Hitler was a relatively harmless fanatic who displayed a personality of outrageous virulence. What made Hitler truly exceptional was that a person with his opinions and personality and background should have won the confidence of millions of educated Germans who freely entrusted him with the levers of great power assigned to the head of government in a modern industrialized nation.

The failure of our legal and ethical theories to make use of the concept of leverage – which requires for its understanding the concept of status responsibility – accounts for one of the strangest anomalies in the Nuremberg trials and a remarkable oversight in Jerusalem. The great criminal on whom Hitler de-

---

62 At the time Eichmann joined the SS, he was under the impression that it was only an "escort service" – a bodyguard for top Nazi officials. It is true that many who joined the Nazi party could not have known at the time of their joining about the Final Solution. However, all who joined had to have realized by November 9, 1938 – Kristallnacht – that this was a regime that sanctioned the murder of innocent people. And Eichmann could not have failed to observe the violence of Nazi officials in the decade prior to their gaining power.

63 Robert Lifton claims that most of the Nazi doctors who chose not to become involved in the "euthanasia" program were able to do so – usually by claiming a lack of technical competence. See Lifton, *The Nazi Doctors*, 80–95.

pended more than on any other for his success in the extermination of the Jews received one of the lightest sentences at Nuremberg and held no interest for Simon Wiesenthal or the Israeli judiciary. Albert Speer as Reich Minister for Armaments and Munitions controlled more power and was more responsible than any other single individual for Hitler's survival beyond 1943. Without the organizational genius of Albert Speer, the German industries and economy and the power of the German army to wage war could not have been sustained beyond that time. Assuming his position as Reich Minister in February, 1942, Speer in a matter of a few months substantially increased German war production despite severe day and night bombing by the Allies. He rationalized the system which harnessed foreign slave laborers to German industry and which delivered to German industries the labor, prior to their exhaustion and extermination, of Jews and other inmates of concentration camps.[64]

This arch-criminal was able to evade justice, first, by presenting himself as a man of high moral conscience who lacked the *mens rea* and *actus reus* to be guilty of crimes punishable by death, and, second, by gratuitously accepting in an apparent act of supererogation responsibility for all those crimes which he claimed to know nothing of but about which he acknowledged he should have known. His refinement and apparent "noblesse oblige" deeply influenced the court.

A few years after Eichmann was captured in Buenos Aires, Speer was released from Spandau to live comfortably and get rich on his heavily fictionalized memoirs of the Third Reich. Had Israel wished to bring to trial the criminal who personified evil – neither as banality nor as a virulence bordering on madness – but as the charm and frightful attractiveness of the devil himself, they would have kidnapped Albert Speer from his estate on the Wolfsbrunnenweg in Heidelberg and brought him to Jerusalem.

The record of Albert Speer and his masterly use of the levers of institutionalized power requires the closest attention of philosophers and jurists. By delineating the many facets of his career and the way he moved within the Hitler regime, we may acquire the data necessary to complete a theory of legal and moral responsibility that can function without either legal fictions or moral blinders in the assessment of those responsible for the Holocaust.

In addition to the concept of social leverage, the concepts of status responsibility and collective guilt require attention. Collective guilt is typically regarded as rank error and its use in condemning criminal activities by groups or nations is considered morally perverse. Justice Jackson rejected collective guilt.

64 See Schmidt, 188–98.

In his opening address at Nuremberg, he absolved the German people of blame by considering them captives of the Nazi party and its organization.

Jaspers took a similar line with regard to legal guilt in his "Essay on German Guilt." Published shortly after Germany's defeat, this essay raised the issue of the moral responsibility of the German people for the Hitler regime. Jaspers distinguished criminal guilt, which extended only to the actual perpetrators of Nazi crimes, from other forms of culpability including moral, metaphysical, and political guilt.[65]

These responses, however, are superficial. A sound assessment requires the recognition of concentric circles of involvement in which Hitler, like Dante's Satan, is at the center of greatest influence, and Speer almost his equal. The continuum extends through the ranks of lesser officials to Eichmann and on to still lesser functionaries. It reaches through institutions of finance, business, transportation, and agriculture to those who were minimally involved, such as ordinary private citizens, and finally to imprisoned doctors and other inmates assigned administrative responsibilities in the concentration camps.

There is no reason to doubt the central observation made by Justice Jackson that the German people were, through the violent methods of the Nazi party, captives of Hitler's regime. They could not exist and earn their livelihood in the Third Reich without contributing in some small measure to its continuance. Jackson understood their plight. He recognized that there are times when nothing more can be done than to withdraw as fully as possible from society into "inner exile" on the grounds that resistance is impossible.[66]

But if in such circumstances one chooses life over death, does one not participate freely, even if only to an extremely attenuated degree, in the moral and legal guilt of the Third Reich? It is not guilt by virtue of mere membership

---

65 See Jaspers, *Basic Philosophical Writings,* 397–408.
Regarding moral guilt, Jaspers notes: "In November 1938, when the synagogues were burning and Jews were deported for the first time, the guilt incurred was chiefly moral and political. Both kinds of guilt rested with those who still had power. The generals stood by. In every town the commander could take action against crime, for the soldier is there to protect all, if crime occurs on such a scale that the police cannot prevent it or fail to do so. They did nothing. At that moment they abandoned the once glorious ethical tradition of the German Army." Those Germans – and there were many – who went on about their business as if nothing had happened were morally guilty.
But Jaspers did not deal adequately with the criminal moral and political responsibility of ordinary Germans after the Nazis were in full control, nor did he discuss the responsibility of those in England, France and the United States who, by failing to act, enabled Hitler to obtain the power that eventually was his.
66 See Arendt, 126–127.

in a collective. Guilt is acquired on the basis of one's voluntary acceptance of a status within a society and one's having exercised the power, however limited, that accompanies that status. That is, the concerns that lead thoughtful observers to consider but reject collective guilt can be dealt with more effectively through the concept of status responsibility. For status responsibility entails even at the lowest extreme a minimal degree of freedom and *mens rea* and even an attenuated form of *actus reus*.[67]

An infant or a child incapable of choice is innocent and has no voluntary status. Merely a member without status in the society, the child could not be held morally or legally responsible even to the slightest degree. Any attribution to a child of guilt would have to be based on a grotesque appeal to collective guilt. But the grocer who provides food for a Nazi Gauleiter is, to some minimal degree, an accomplice in the Nazi crimes. The teacher, the judge, the other professionals have a status of even greater involvement as long as they carry on their professional activities – no matter the level of their personal abhorrence of the Nazi program. Their guilt rises with the degree of their support for and their approval of the program. And consider the tragic, fated plight of parents who cannot even consider escape, defiance, or martyrdom without violating their duty to their children. A theory of status responsibility, unlike collective responsibility, can offer an account of the varying degrees of involvement and, hence, degrees of responsibility.

Without regard to what Kant personally might have done – which would involve pure speculation – could one morally justify on the basis of his teaching the individual who concluded that life itself is intolerable in a society as perverse as the Third Reich? That is, from a moral point of view, might one rightly conclude that this was the time to die rather than to acquire the minimal guilt that would follow merely from living in Nazi Germany? Could a person faithful to Kant's point of view justify taking his or her own life rather than participate in the wrongdoing of his or her society? Is this limited resistance to the sovereign justifiable on the grounds that it is self-negating except, perhaps, as an example to others? Or could one justify on Kantian principles the mere failure to complete forms, applications, and the various bureaucratic requirements of Nazi Germany so as to survive in the interstices of involvement or, in the worst case, to be sent to a concentration camp and perhaps to one's death? We must recognize that on a continuum of responsibility, the citizen in this last

67 In the final assessment "guilt" may be nothing more than a moral taint, a responsibility similar to "blood guilt" in ancient Greece.

case would have contributed to his or her own death although to a far lesser degree than if the citizen were directly to take his or her own life.

Kant opposed suicide and held that there was never any duty to sacrifice one's life. I find it difficult to believe, however, that Kant would have considered it morally wrong in these circumstances to expose oneself to the risk of death in service to the moral law.[68]

Would Kant have joined Arendt in denouncing the claim that those who dared to suffer death rather than to tolerate the crimes of Auschwitz had sacrificed their lives in vain?[69]

If Kant were to write a new version of the second *Critique*, might he cite as an example of action in accordance with the moral law, not only Anne Boleyn, but the case of the two peasant boys who, after being drafted into the SS towards the end of the War, were executed when they refused to swear allegiance to Hitler? As one of the boys explained to his parents in his last letter: "We two would rather die than burden our conscience with such terrible things. I know what the SS must carry out."[70] Whether consciously or not, these boys acted in obedience to the categorical imperative.

Any moral theory is gravely deficient that fails to recognize not only the moral rightness of such individuals but also their moral heroism. They knew what to fear – not death, but evil.

In their heroism, those young Germans solved the tragic puzzle of Auschwitz in practice; but it has yet to be solved in theory. Philosophers must remain at Auschwitz until the questions posed by the Holocaust are answered – or at least until they are explored to the limits of human understanding and the inscrutability of evil.

---

68 MS 421–424: MOM, 546–548.

69 Arendt, 232–33.

70 Weisenborn, 149 (my translation).

Kant's Works And Their Abbreviations

The following are the abbreviations used in this volume, both for the original German texts and for the English translations I have chosen.

With the exception of *Lectures on Ethics* and the occasional exception of the *Critique of Pure Reason*, the German texts of Immanuel Kant's that are cited in this volume are those collected in the Akademie Edition:

> *Gesammelte Schriften Hrsg.*: Bd. 1–22 Preussische Akademie der Wissenschaften, Bd. 23 Deutsche Akademie der Wissenschaften zu Berlin, ab Bd. 24 Akademie der Wissenschaften zu Göttingen. Berlin 1900ff.

The following abbreviations are used for individual works. For the German texts, the Akademie volume follows in parentheses. If I have used an English translation I list it following each German reference. Otherwise, translations are my own.

Anth Anthropologie in pragmatischer Hinsicht (AA 07).

AN *Anthropology from a pragmatic point of view*. Translated and edited by Robert Louden. (Cambridge: Cambridge UP, 2006).

Br Briefe (AA 10–13).

Corr *Correspondence*. translated and edited by Arnulf Zweig. (Cambridge: Cambridge University Press, 1999).

EEKU Erste Einleitung in die Kritik der Urteilskraft (AA 05).

CoPJ *Critique of the Power of Judgment*, edited by Paul Guyer; translated by Paul Guyer, Eric Matthews. (Cambridge: Cambridge University Press, 2000).

GMS Grundlegung zur Metaphysik der Sitten (AA 04).

GMM *The Moral Law; Kant's Groundwork of the Metaphysic of Morals*. Translated and analysed by H. J. Paton. (London: Hutchinson, 1948).

HN Handschriftlichcr Nachlass (AA 14–23).

KU Kritik der Urteilskraft (AA 05).

CoAJ *Kant's Critique of Aesthetic Judgement*, translated with seven introductory essays, notes, and analytical index, by James Creed Meredith (Oxford: Clarendon Press, 1911).

CoTJ *Kant's Critique of Teleological Judgement*, translated with an introduction, notes, and analytical index, by James Creed Meredith (Oxford: Clarendon Press, 1928).

KpV Kritik der praktischen Vernunft (AA 05).

CprR *Critique of Practical Reason, and other writings in moral philosophy*, translated and edited with an introduction by Lewis White Beck. (Chicago: U Chicago Press, 1949).

Log Logik (AA 09).

Logic *Lectures on Logic*; translated and edited by J. Michael Young. (The Cambridge Edition of the Works of Immanuel Kant in Translation) (Cambridge: Cambridge University Press, 1992).

MS Die Metaphysik der Sitten (AA 06).

MOM *The Metaphysics of Morals* in *Practical Philosophy* (The Cambridge Edition of the Works of Immanuel Kant in Translation) introduction, translation, and notes by Mary Gregor (Cambridge: Cambridge University Press, 1991).

OP Opus Postumum (AA 21–22).

Päd Über Pädagogik (AA 09).

Ed "On Education" in *Anthropology, History, and Education* (The Cambridge Edition of the Works of Immanuel Kant in Translation) translated by Robert B. Louden and Günter Zöller (Cambridge: Cambridge University Press, 1991).

Prol Prolegomena zu einer jeden künftigen Metaphysik (AA 04).

Prologue "Prolegomena to Any Future Metaphysics: That Will Be Able to Come Forward as Science: With Selections from the *Critique of Pure Reason*" (Cambridge Texts in the History of Philosophy) (Cambridge: Cambridge University Press, 2004).

RGV Die Religion innerhalb der Grenzen der bloßen Vernunft (AA 06).

Rel *Religion Within the Limits of Reason Alone*. Translated, with an introduction and notes, by Theodore M. Greene and Hoyt H. Hudson. (New York: Harper, 1960).

TP Über den Gemeinspruch: Das mag in der Theorie richtig sein, taugt aber nicht für die Praxis (AA 08).

TaP *On the Old Saw: that May be Right in Theory but it won't Work in Practice*. Translated by E. B. Ashton. Introd. by George Miller (Philadelphia: University of Pennsylvania Press, 1974).

Untersuchuung *Untersuchung über die Deutlichkeit der Grundsätze der naturlichen Theologie und der Moral* (AA 02).

Inquiry "An inquiry into the distinctness of the principles of natural theology and morals," In *Critique of Practical Reason*, and other writings in moral philosophy, translated and edited with an introduction by Lewis White Beck (Chicago: University of Chicago Press, 1949).

VPR *Vorlesungen über die philosophische Religionslehre* (AA 28).

LdR *Lectures On Philosophical Theology*; translated by Allen W. Wood and Gertrude M. Clark; with introduction and notes by Allen W. Wood (Ithaca: Cornell University Press, 1978).

WA Beantwortung der Frage: Was ist Aufklärung? (AA 08).

WE "What is Enlightenment?" In *Critique of Practical Reason*, and other writings in moral philosophy, translated and edited with an introduction by Lewis White Beck (Chicago: University of Chicago Press, 1949).

Orientiren Was heißt sich im Denken orientiren? (AA 08)

Orient "What Is Orientation in Thinking?" In *Critique of Practical Reason*, and other writings in moral philosophy, translated and edited with an introduction by Lewis White Beck (Chicago: University of Chicago Press, 1949).

ZeF Zum ewigen Frieden (AA 08)

TEP "Perpetual Peace: A Philosophical Sketch" in *Critique of Practical Reason*, and other writings in moral philosophy, translated and edited with an introduction by Lewis White Beck (Chicago: University of Chicago Press, 1949).

Others:

KrV Kritik der reinen Vernunft; nach der ersten und zweiten Original-Ausgabe neu herausgegeben von Raymund Schmidt. Systematisches Handlexikon zu Kants Kritik der reinen Vernunft, von Heinrich Ratke (Leipzig: F. Meiner, 1930). Also in AA 03.

CpR *Critique of Pure Reason*, translated by Norman Kemp Smith (London: Macmillan and Co., 1929).

VüE Paul Menzer, *Eine Vorlesung Kants Über Ethik* (Berlin: Pan Verlag Rolf Heise, 1924).

LoE *Lectures on Ethics*; translated from the German by Louis Infield; with an introduction by J. Macmurray (New York: Century, 1930).

Other translations of Kant's works

Anthropology from a Pragmatic Point of View by Immanuel Kant, Mary J. Gregor Translated by Mary J. Gregor (The Hague: Nijhoff, 1974).
Critique Of Practical Reason And Other Writings In Moral Philosophy. Tr. and ed. with an introd. by Lewis White Beck. (Chicago, Univ. of Chicago Press, 1949.)
Immanuel Kant's Critique of Practical Reason and Other Works in Theory of Ethics. Trans. by T. K. Abbott, London: Longmans, Green & Co., Ltd, 1873.
Groundwork Of The Metaphysics Of Morals; translated and edited by Mary Gregor; with an introduction by Christine M. Korsgaard. (Cambridge: Cambridge University Press, 1998.)
Lectures on Ethics, tr. Peter Heath and J.B. Schneewind. Cambridge: Cambridge University Press, 1997.
Lectures On Philosophical Theology; translated by Allen W. Wood and Gertrude M. Clark; with introd. and notes by Allen W. Wood (Ithaca: Cornell University Press, 1978).
The Metaphysical Elements of Justice. Translated by John Ladd. Indianapolis · New York: The Bobbs Merrill Company, Inc., 1965.
The Moral Law; Kant's Groundwork Of The Metaphysic Of Morals. Translated and analysed by H. J. Paton (London: Hutchinson, 1948).
On The Old Saw: That May Be Right In Theory But It Won't Work In Practice. Translated by E.B. Ashton. Introd. by George Miller, Philadelphia, University of Pennsylvania Press [1974].
The Philosophy of Law, trans. W. Hastie, (Clifton, New Jersey: Augustus M. Kelley Publishers, 1974).

Bibliography

Adams, Robert M. Introduction to *Religion within the Boundaries of Mere Reason.* (Cambridge: Cambridge University Press, 1998.)

Adickes, Erich. *Kant und das Ding an sich.* Berlin: R. Heise, 1924.

Allison, Henry. *Idealism and Freedom: Essays on Kant's Theoretical and Practical Philosophy.* Cambridge: Cambridge University Press, 1996.

Allison, Henry. *Kant's Theory of Freedom.* Cambridge: Cambridge University Press, 1990.

Anderson-Gold, Sharon. "Kant's Rejection of Devilishness: The Limits of Human Volition." *Idealistic Studies* 14 (1984): 35–47.

Anderson-Gold, Sharon. "Kant's Ethical Commonwealth: The Highest Good as a Social Goal." *International Philosophical Quarterly,* 26 (1986): 23–32.

Ardagh, John. *Germany and the Germans: An Anatomy of Society Today.* New York: Harper & Row, 1987.

Arendt, Hannah. *Eichmann in Jerusalem,* Revised and Enlarged Edition. New York: Viking, 1965.

Aristophanes, *Clouds · Wasps · Peace,* tr. Jeffrey Henderson. Cambridge, Massachusetts · London, England: Harvard University Press, 1998.

Baillie, J. B. *The Phenomenology Of Mind.* New York: Macmillan, 1931.

Barnes, Gerald W. "In Defense of Kant's Doctrine of the Highest Good." *Philosophical Forum* 2, No. 1 (1970): 446–459.

Beck, Lewis W. *A Commentary on Kant's Critique of Pure Reason.* Chicago: University of Chicago Press, 1960.

Beck, Lewis W. *Essays on Hume and Kant.* New Haven: Yale University Press, 1978.

Becker, Carl. *The Heavenly City of the 18th Century Philosophers.* New Haven: Yale University Press, 1932.

Blanshard, Brand. *The Nature of Thought,* Vol. 1. London: George Allen & Unwin Ltd, 1948.

Blanshard, Brand. *Preface to Philosophy.* New York: The Macmillan Co., 1947.

Brewster, Sir David. *Memoirs of the Life, Writings and Discoveries of Sir Isaac Newton Volume 2.* Edinburgh, Thomas Constable and Co., 1855.

Broad, C.D. "Determinism, Indeterminism, and Libertarianism" in *Ethics and the History of Philosophy.* London: Routledge & Kegan Paul, 1952.

Brown, Stuart. "Does Ought Imply Can?" *Ethics,* LX (1950): 275–284.

Burton, J. H. *Life and Correspondence of David Hume, Volume I.* Edinburgh, 1846.

Cassirer, Ernst. *Rousseau, Kant, Goethe.* Trans. by J. Gutmann, P. O. Kristeller, and J. H. Randall, Jr. Princeton: Princeton University Press: June 1970.

Dampier, Sir William. *A History of Science and Its Relations with Philosophy and Religion,* 3rd ed. Cambridge: Cambridge University Press, 1942.

Diderot, Denis. Oeuvres (1875–1877), Vol. 19. Oeuvres complètes de Diderot, [*tome 1, pp. 158–170,*] Éd. J. Assézat Tourneux, Paris, Garnier Frères, 1875.

Doescher, W. O. "Kant's Postulate of Practical Freedom" in *The Heritage of Kant* (ed. by G. W. T. Whitney, Princeton, 1939).

Dostoevsky, Fyodor. *The Brothers Karamazov: A Novel in four Parts and an Epilogue.* Trans. by David McDuff. London: Penguin Books, 2003.

Düsing, Klaus. "Das Problem des höchsten Gutes in Kants praktischer Philosophie." *Kant-Studien,* 62 (1971): 5–42.

Engstrom, Stephen. "The Concept of the Highest Good in Kant's Moral Theory." *Philosophy and Phenomenological Research* 52 (1992): 747–80.

Euripides. "The Bacchae, " trans. William Arrowsmith, in *Euripides V*, eds. Grene and Lattimore. Chicago: University of Chicago Press, 1959.

Ewing, A.C. *Kant's Treatment of Causality*. London: Kegal Paul, Trench, Trubner and Company, 1924.

Fackenheim, Emil. "Kant and Radical Evil" in *The God Within: Kant, Schelling, and Historicity*, trans. by John W. Burbidge. Toronto: University of Toronto Press, 1996.

Friedman, R.Z. "The Importance and Function of Kant's Highest Good." *Journal of the History of Philosophy* 22 no. 3 (1984): 325–342.

Friedman, R.Z. "Virtue and Happiness: Kant and Three Critics." *Canadian Journal of Philosophy* 11 no. 1 (1981): 95–109.

Geismann, Georg and Hariolf Oberer, eds. *Kant und das Recht der Lüge*. Würzburg: Königshausen und Neumann, 1986.

Guevara, Daniel, *Kant's Theory of Moral Motivation*. Boulder, Colorado · Oxford: Westview Press, 2000.

Haffner, Sebastian. *Anmerkungen zu Hitler*. Frankfurt am Main: Fischer Taschenbuch Verlag GmbH, 1978. Available in English as *The Meaning of Hitler*, translated by Ewald Osers. Cambridge: Harvard University Press, 1979.

Hartenstein, G. "Fragmente." *Immanuel Kants Sämmtliche Werke* vol. 8. Leipzig: Leopold Voss, 1868.

Hegel, Georg W. F. *Phanomenologie des Geistes* in *Samtliche Werke*, vol. 2. Translated by J. B. Baillie as *The Phenomenology Of Mind*. New York: Macmillan, 1931.

Heidemann, Ingeborg, "Das Ideal des höchsten Guts," in *Beträge zur Kritik der reinen Vernunft, 1781 * 1981*, Herausgeben von Ingeborg Heidemann und Wolfgang Ritzel. Berlin · New York: Walter de Gruyter, 1981, 233–305.

Horace, *Satires, Epistles and Ars Poetica*, tr. Fairclough. Cambridge, Massachusetts · London, England: Harvard University Press, 1926, 1999.

Hoy, David Couzens. "Hegel's Critique of Kantian Morality." *History of Philosophy Quarterly* 6 No. 2 (1989): 207–232.

Jaspers, Karl. *Kant: Leben, Werk, Wirkung*. Munich: R. Piper & Co., 1975.

Jaspers, Karl. *Karl Jaspers: Basic Philosophical Writings, Selections*, Edited, translated, and introductions by Edith Ehrlich, Leonard H. Ehrlich and George B. Pepper. Athens: Ohio University Press, 1986.

Katz, Steven T., *The Holocaust in Historical Context*. New York: Oxford University Press, 1994.

Kemp Smith, Norman. *A Commentary To Kant's Critique Of Pure Reason*. London: Macmillan and Co., 1923.

Kierkegaard, Søren, *Fear and Trembling and The Sickness Unto Death*, tr. Walter Lowrie. Garden City, New York: Doubleday Anchor Books, 1941, 1954.

Kramling, Gerhard. "Das höchste Gut als mögliche Welt." *Kant-Studien* 77 (1986): 273–288.

Kühn, Manfred. *Kant: A Biography*. Cambridge: Cambridge University Press, 2001.

Lauener, Henri. "The Systematic Significance of the Feeling of Respect in Kant's Ethics." *Acta Philosophica Fennica* 32 (1981): 126–148.

Less, Avner. *Eichmann Interrogated: Transcripts from the Archives of the Israeli Police*, eds., Jochen von Lang, Claus Sibyll. New York: Farrer, Strauss, & Giroux, 1983.

Lifton, Robert J. *The Nazi Doctors: Medical Killing and The Psychology of Genocide*. New York: Basic Books, 1986.

Macmurray, J. "Introduction," in *Lectures on Ethics,* translated from the German by Louis Infield; with an introduction by J. Macmurray. New York: Century, 1930.
Meerbote, Ralf. "*Wille* and *Willkür* in Kant's Theory of Action" in *Interpreting Kant*, ed. Moltke S. Gram. Iowa City: University of Iowa Press, 1982.
Menzer, Paul. "Der Entwicklungsgang der Kantischen Ethik in den Jahren 1760–1785." *Kant-Studien* 2 (1898): 290–322, and 3 (1899): 41–104.
Michalson, Gordon E. "The Inscrutability of Moral Evil in Kant." *Thomist* 51, 1987: 246–269.
Mill, J.S. *Utilitarianism*. New York: The Liberal Arts Press, 1948.
Murphy, Jeffrie. "The Highest Good as Content for Kant's Ethical Formalism." *Kant Studien* 56:1, 1965: 102–110.
Niebuhr, Reinhold. *An Interpretation of Christian Ethics*. New York: Harper & Brothers, 1935.
Ovid, *Metamorphoses Books 1–8*, tr. Miller, rev. Goold. Cambridge, Massachusetts · London, England: Harvard University Press, 1916.
Pap, Arthur. *The A Priori in Physical Theory.* New York: Russell and Russell, 1968.
Paton, Herbert J. *The Categorical Imperative, A Study In Kant's Moral Philosophy.* Chicago: The University of Chicago Press, 1948.
Paton, Herbert J. "An Alleged Right to Lie." *Kant-Studien* 45 (1953–54): 190–203.
Paulsen, F. *Immanuel Kant, His Life and Doctrine*, trans. James Edwin Creighton and Albert Lefèbvre. New York: Frederick Ungar Company, 1972.
Pearlman, Moshe. *The Capture and Trial of Adolf Eichmann.* London: Weidenfeld and Nicolson, 1963.
Piper, Ernst, ed. *Historiker-Streit*, R. Piper GmbH& Co., KG, München, 1987.
Plato. "Gorgias," in *Plato: Complete Works*; edited, with introduction and notes, by John M. Cooper ; associate editor, D.S. Hutchinson. Indianapolis: Hackett, 1997.
Plato, "Parmenides," in *Plato: Complete Works*; edited, with introduction and notes, by John M. Cooper ; associate editor, D.S. Hutchinson. Indianapolis: Hackett, 1997.
Plato. "Protagoras," in *Plato: Complete Works*; edited, with introduction and notes, by John M. Cooper; associate editor, D.S. Hutchinson. Indianapolis: Hackett, 1997.
Plato. "The Republic," in *Plato: Complete Works*; edited, with introduction and notes, by John M. Cooper ; associate editor, D.S. Hutchinson. Indianapolis: Hackett, 1997.
Polanyi, Michael. *Personal Knowledge*. London: Routledge, 1958.
Pope, Alexander, *The Poems of Alexander Pope*, ed. Butts. New Haven: Yale University Press, 1963.
Popper, Karl. The Open Society and Its Enemies. London: Routledge, 1945.
Rosen, Stanley. *Hermeneutics as Politics*. New York and Oxford: Oxford University Press, 1987.
Rosenfeld, Alvin H. and Irving Greenberg. *Confronting the Holocaust: The Impact of Elie Wiesel.* Bloomington: Indiana University Press, 1978.
Schilpp, Paul. *Kant's Pre-Critical Ethics*, 2nd ed. Evanston [Ill.]: Northwestern University Press, 1970.
Schmidt, Matthias. *Albert Speer: The End of a Myth*, translated by Joachim Neugroschel. New York: St. Martin's Press, 1984.
Schmucker, Josef. *Die Ursprünge der Ethik Kants in seinen Vorkritischen Schriften und Reflektionen*. Meisenheim am Glan: A. Hain, 1961.
Schopenhauer, Arthur. *On The Basis of Morality*, trans. E.F.J. Payne. Indianapolis: The Bobbs-Merrill Company, 1965.
Schopenhauer, Arthur. The Basis of Morality, trans. Arthur Brodrick Bullock. London: Swan Sonnenschein, 1903 New York: Macmillan, 1915

Schrader, G. "The Thing in Itself in Kantian Philosophy." *Review of Metaphysics* 2, no. 7 (1949): 30–44.

Schrader, G. "The Transcendental Ideality and Empirical Reality of Kant's Space and Time," *Review of Metaphysics* 4, no. 4 (1951): 507–36.

Seebohm, Thomas. "Kant's Theory of Revolution," *Social Research* 4, Winter (1984): 557–87.

Silber, J. R. "Being and Doing: A Study of Status Responsibility." *The University of Chicago Law Review* 35, No. 1 (1967): 47–91.

Singer, M.G. "The Categorical Imperative." *Philosophical Review* 63 (1954): 577–591.

Singer, Marcus. *Generalization in Ethics: An Essay in the Logic of Ethics, with the Rudiments of a System of Moral Philosophy* (New York: Macmillan, 1961).

Stackelberg, Roderick. *Idealism Debased: From Völkisch Ideology to National Socialism*. Kent, Ohio: Kent State University Press, 1981.

Sullivan, Roger J. *Immanuel Kant's Moral Theory*. Cambridge: Cambridge University Press, 1989.

Thomas, Dylan. "And Death Shall Have No Dominion," in *The Poems of Dylan Thomas*. New York: New Directions Publishing Corporation, 1971.

Vaihinger, H. *Kommentar zu Kants Kritik der Reinen Vernunft*. Stuttgart: W. Spemann, 1881–2.

Velkley, Richard L. *Freedom and the End of Reason: on the Moral Foundation of Kant's Critical Philosophy*. Chicago: University of Chicago Press, 1969.

Viereck, Peter. *Meta-Politics: The Roots of the Nazi Mind*. New York: Alfred A, Knopf, 1941.

Walker, Christopher J. *Armenia, Survival of a Nation*. London: Croom Helm, 1980.

Ward, Keith. *The Development of Kant's View of Ethics*. New York: Humanities Press, 1972.

Weisenborn, Günther. *Der lautlose Aufstand: Bericht über die Widerstandsbewegung des deutschen Volkes*. Hamburg, 1953. Hamburg: Rowohlt, 1954

Weiss, Paul. *Man's Freedom*. New Haven: Yale University Press, 1950.

Weiss, Paul. *Reality*. Princeton: The University Press; London: Humphrey Milford. 1938.

Whitehead, Alfred. *Adventures of Ideas*. New York: Free Press, 1967.

Wiesel, Elie. *Nuit*. Paris: Les Editions de Minuit, 1958; English translation, *Night*. New York: Hill and Wang, 2006.

Wilson, Edward O. *Sociobiology: The New Synthesis*. Cambridge: Belknap Press of Harvard University Press, 1980.

Wood, Allen W. *Kant's Moral Religion*. Ithaca: Cornell University Press, 1970.

Wood, Allen W. *Kant's Rational Theology*. Ithaca: Cornell University Press, 1978.

Yovel, Yirmiahu. "The Highest Good and History in Kant's Thought." *Archiv für Geschichte der Philosophie* 54 (1972): 238–283.

Acknowledgements

Grateful acknowledgement is made for permission to reprint with substantial revisions from the following articles by the author:

"The Context of Kant's Ethical Thought: I," *The Philosophical Quarterly*, Vol. 9 (John Wiley & Sons, 1959).

"The Context of Kant's Ethical Thought: II," *The Philosophical Quarterly*, Vol. 10 (John Wiley & Sons, 1959).

"The Copernican Revolution in Ethics: The Good Reexamined," *Kant-Studien* (De Gruyter, 1959).

"The Ethical Significance of Kant's *Religion*," in *Kant's Religion within the Limits of Reason Alone* (Harper & Brothers, 1960).

"The Moral Good and the Natural Good in Kant's Ethics," *Review of Metaphysics* (Philosophy of Education Society, Inc., 1982).

"The Importance of the Highest Good in Kant's Ethics," *Ethics, An International Journal of Social, Political, and Legal Philosophy* (University of Chicago Press, 1963. Copyright 1962–1963 by The University of Chicago Press).

"Kant's Conception of the Highest Good as Immanent and Transcendent," *The Philosophical Review* (Cornell University Press, 1959).

"Der Schematismus der Praktischen Vernunft" [The Problem of Moral Schematism in Kant's Ethics], *Kant-Studien, Philosophische Zeitschrift der Kant-Gesellschaft* (De Gruyter, 1965).

"Verfahrensformalismus in Kants Ethik," Akten des 4. Internationalen Kant-Kongress; "Procedural Formalism in Kant's Ethics," *The Review of Metaphysics* (1974).

"Kant and the Mythic Roots of Morality," *Dialectica* (Wiley-Blackwell, 1981).

"Kant at Auschwitz," from *Proceedings of the Sixth International Kant Congress*, Vol. 1 (University Press of America, 1991).

Index

Achenwall, Gottfried, 322–323
Adams, Robert M., 83
Adickes, Erich, 40n77, 98n92
Adventures of Ideas, The (Whitehead), 299
aesthetics/aesthetic experience, 28, 44; cognition theory and, 70; empiricism and, 36; judgment and, 225, 229–30; moral feeling and, 272–73; reliance on form as contradiction, 35; the sublime, 273–77
agency, 20, 55, 102–103, 203, 213; form-matter relation and, 41, 44; of individual knower, 38, 41, 42–43; moral law and, 204; natural goods and, 141; of the will, 52, 140, 150, 210. *See also* moral agent
Ahab (character in *Moby-Dick*), 291, 292, 297
Allison, Henry, 109n124
Ammerkungen zu Hitler [*The Meaning of Hitler*] (Haffner), 297, 335n53
analytic method, 28–29, 32
animals, 73, 79, 276, 278
anthropology, philosophical, 14, 67
Anthropology from a Pragmatic Point of View (*Anthropologie*), 22, 215, 229, 245, 307
Antinomies, 295
Antinomy, Third, 81, 87
a posteriori propositions, 34, 35
appearance, 34, 36, 38, 81. *See also* phenomenal order
a priori judgments/principles, 29, 30, 31, 32, 34, 37–38; ethical concepts and, 45; knowledge and, 41; morality and, 26; possibility of, 28, 43
Archimedes, 337
Arendt, Hannah, 317, 319, 320–21, 330, 342; on "banality of evil," 331; on Eichmann's moral responsibility, 335, 336
Aristophanes, 6
Aristotle, 34, 159, 305, 313, 317
Armenian genocide, 316n3
art, 24, 28, 36, 254, 280
assertoric imperative, 130
Augustine, St., 8, 108
Auschwitz, 314, 318, 332, 337, 342; categories of victims at, 316–17; demonic evil of, 333; irrational as mode of free expression and, 334. *See also* Final Solution; Holocaust; Jews, Nazi extermination of; Nazi Germany
autonomy, 53n20, 66, 73, 110–11, 189; dignity of human nature and, 128, 129; as freedom in fulfilled mode, 283, 286; *Gesinnung* (disposition) and, 106; as good, 114; impossibility of conflict in duties and, 247; judgment and, 245; as mode of freedom, 76; of moral agent, 220, 222; moral feeling and, 92; sublime and, 273; universality of reason and, 75, 235, 236, 284; as *Wille*, 113. *See also* freedom, transcendental
Autonomy, Formula of, 233, 236

Bacchae (Euripides), 4
Basis of Morality, The (Schopenhauer), 17
Baumgarten, A. G., 157, 159, 160–61, 162, 163
beautiful, the, 28, 270, 302
Beck, Lewis, 151, 170n53, 306
Becker, Carl, 3, 4, 5, 6, 8, 281–82
behaviorism, 228
Berkeley, Bishop George, 6
Bible, 6, 258
Blanshard, Brand, 36n71, 248n49
Boleyn, Anne, 306, 342

Callicles, 56, 108
categorical imperative, 19, 68, 69, 130, 256–57; as contradiction, 253–54; formula of morality and, 287; Holocaust and, 318, 320, 321, 323, 342; incentives and, 302, 303; judgment and, 231–37, 245–46; moral feeling and, 261, 266; moral law as, 77, 81; obligation of will to object, 62, 155; possibility of, 65, 66, 70, 109–10, 292, 293; procedural formalism and, 258, 288–89; singularity of, 231, 246–47, 248, 253; theory of the good and, 155; three formulae of, 232–33, 234,

241–43; violation of moral law and, 290; voice of God and, 299
causality, 31, 40, 52, 262–63; freedom and, 70–71, 102, 112, 178; heteronomy and, 76; natural laws and, 85; phenomenal order and, 84; principle of finality and, 86; time (temporality)and, 206, 237; two standpoints theory and, 81; will and, 65
Chamberlain, Houston Stewart, 317n6
choice, 53n20, 63n50, 73, 89, 284, 287. See also *Willkür*
Christianity, 7, 288, 299; Christian versus Newtonian/scientific worldview, 3–10, 281–82, 312; mythic roots of, 8; orthodoxy in religious education, 309
civil society, 322, 323, 324, 325
cognition, 21, 70, 227, 228, 271, 272
common sense, 21, 27, 113
community, 21–22, 23, 24, 33, 43
concepts/the conceptual, 38, 205, 207, 208, 274; intuitions and, 213, 233; material and formal, 47; *a priori*, 216
conscience, 56, 106, 255, 305; of Eichmann, 330; guilty, 94, 303; moral perfection and, 161; *Willkür* and, 108
consequences, appeal to, 239
consistency, criterion of, 256–57
contradiction, 21, 34, 91; categorical imperative as, 253–54; judgment procedure in ethics and, 232; in Kant's philosophy, 84, 85; moral schema as, 211; three premises and, 188, 190–91
Copernican Revolution, in ethics, 12n3, 20, 41, 43–44, 155
Copernicus, Nicolaus, 222
crime, 145, 334, 335–36
Critique of Judgment (third *Critique*), 182, 215; on goodness and desire, 160; "Introduction" to, 16, 192n59; on prejudice as heteronomy of reason, 236; on science, 85, 86; symbolic schematism in, 219; on taste, 229–30; on varieties of delight, 302
Critique of Practical Reason (second *Critique*), 20n29, 64, 215, 219, 233–34, 282; on categorical command of morality, 252; centrality of doctrine of the good, 153–55; definition of the good, 46, 47–48; on freedom and moral law, 66; on heterogeneity of the will, 113; highest good in, 152, 171–72, 184; Nazi evil and, 318, 342; on perfection, 161–62; on science, 85, 86; synthesis of Christian and Newtonian worldviews, 286; temporality in, 83; unity of reason and, 16; on will, 67–69
Critique of Pure Reason (first *Critique*), 8, 16, 183, 219, 281; on "absolute" as term, 125–26; on experience, 27, 33; highest good in, 152; on knowledge, 11; on metaphysical knowledge, 25; moral philosophy in, 13; on phenomena and noumena, 81, 87; on primacy of moral philosophy, 20; on schematism, 214, 215; Schopenhauer's view of, 17–18; on science, 85, 86; synthetic method, 30; unitary examination of reason, 15
Crito (Plato), 324

Dante Alighieri, 3, 340
Darwin, Charles, 309
death, 276–77, 341–42
deontology, 152
Descartes, René, 3
desire, faculty of, 48, 54, 159–60, 205n7, 262; conditions of willing and, 164; determination of the will and, 264; evil and, 108, 109; good and bad desires, 55; happiness and, 165; in Hegel's interpretation, 254; higher and lower, 49, 50; highest good and, 209; judgment and, 241; moral feeling and, 268, 269, 270; moral law and, 70; moral schematism and, 223; natural goods and, 129–31, 133–34, 139, 140; particular natural goods and, 134, 136, 138; perfection and, 163; reason and, 122; sublime and, 274; transcendental freedom and, 73, 74; universality and, 167; will and, 68, 69, 156, 283, 300; *Willkür* and, 79, 89
determinism, 71–72
devilishness (absolute evil), 110, 111, 290, 293, 295; freedom in, 298, 332n47;

transcendence or impotence of, 333. *See also* evil
Dewey, John, 239
dialectic, 12, 251
Dialogues Concerning Natural Religion (Hume), 6, 7
Diderot, Denis, 7–8, 281, 286, 287, 288, 300, 307
dignity, 145, 286, 305, 321, 322n22; autonomy and, 221, 222, 273; freedom and, 312; of human nature, 128, 129; moral feeling and, 265; moral pilgrimage and, 309; price and, 125, 126, 127; of virtue, 141
Doctrine of Virtue, The, 334
Dostoyevsky, Fyodor, 311
Dunciad (Pope), 5
duty, 9, 19, 48, 55, 148; awareness of the noumenal and, 40; conflict of duties, 246–47, 248; definition of the good and, 49; deontology and, 152; desire in conflict with, 282–83; doctrine of, 44; evil and neglect of, 99; free beings and, 189; happiness and, 132; in Hegel's interpretation, 255; heterogeneity of the good and, 60; highest good and, 200; homogeneity of the good and, 149; imputed action and, 123; judgment and, 226; material concepts and, 47; moral capacity and, 192; moral education and, 279; natural hindrances to performance of, 139; perfection and, 158; pleasure in fulfillment of, 261, 264, 301; procedural interpretation of, 290; theory of the good and, 155; universality demanded by, 23; value of natural good and, 131, 135; will and, 200. *See also* categorical imperative; obligation

education, moral, 9, 279, 303–7, 310–11
egoism, 22–23, 36
Eichmann, Adolf, 317, 318–22, 325, 339, 340; appeal to Kantian ethics, 317, 320–23, 325, 328; moral responsibility of, 335, 336, 338; motivations of, 329; obedience to Hitler, 320, 322, 327, 330, 338
Einstein, Albert, 6, 309
empiricism, 34, 35–36, 38, 50, 302; rejection of radical empiricism, 35; scientific method and, 4
End in Itself, Formula of the (Formula II), 232, 236, 241–43, 248. *See also* categorical imperative
Engstrom, Stephen, 152
Enlightenment, 3–10, 317, 329
Epicureans, 55, 145n84, 163
epistemology, 2, 37, 41, 233
error, 21, 22, 36
"Essay on German Guilt" (Jaspers), 340
essence, 37
ethics, 1, 25, 116, 183, 220; contribution of Kant's *Religion* to, 114–15; duties of, 246; form and content in, 256; intellectuals and, 2; judgment and, 26, 227–28, 231–46; leverage and, 337, 338–39; moral incentives in, 298–307; science and, 81; theory and practice, 203
Euripides, 4
evil, 9, 61, 64, 76, 103, 153; "banality of evil," 331, 337; evil will, 120; free choice and, 284; *Gesinnung* (disposition) and, 100, 104, 107, 107–11; of the Holocaust and Nazism, 315, 329, 331, 337; judgment and evil object, 271; origin of evil, 97–100, 284n7. *See also* devilishness; wickedness
evil, moral (*das Böse*), 59n40, 116, 139, 140
evil, natural (*das Übel*), 59n40, 61, 116, 140
experience, 14, 21, 40n80, 73, 176; cognitive, 40, 43; embodiment of highest good in, 220; ethical theory and, 204; homogeneous order of, 211; irrationality and, 292; as means of testing propositions, 34; metaphysical knowledge and, 25; moral philosophy grounded in, 182; moral principles and, 25–26; noumenal order and, 87; "object" of, 38, 39–40; phenomenal, 27, 40; as subjective consciousness, 26–27; symbolic schematism and, 223–24; synthetic *a priori* judgments and,

31, 38; transcendental deduction and, 32; two standpoints theory and, 81, 84. *See also* moral experience

faith, age of, 3–4
fanaticism, 23, 87, 88n65, 218, 289
Faust (Goethe), 112–13, 333
Fear and Trembling (Kierkegaard), 288
finality, principle of, 85–86, 175, 215
Final Solution, 315, 318, 319, 320–23, 330, 338. *See also* Auschwitz; Holocaust; Jews, Nazi extermination of; Nazi Germany
forgiveness, 294, 296, 296n30
formalism, 35n66, 260; non-logical character of, 253–57, 288; non-substantive character of, 246–53; procedural character of, 258–60, 288
form-matter relation, 33, 35, 36, 245; in artistic experience, 43; epistemological distinction between, 37, 41; moral experience and, 44
freedom, 43, 52, 64, 69–78; absolute concept of, 290–98; awareness of, 61, 110, 149; clarification of concept of, 283–86; decline of, 115n129, 290; determinism and, 71–72; diminution of, 333; evil (devilishness) and, 298, 332–33; *Gesinnung* (disposition) and, 100; happiness and, 241; heteronomous will and, 65, 68; incomprehensibility of, 96, 223, 305; limits of, 193, 195, 333; metaphysics and, 176, 177, 179, 183; moral feeling and, 265; moral good and, 121; as natural end of humankind, 312–13; as philosophy of morality, 15; principle of finality and, 86; reason/rationality and, 66, 75, 77; responsibility and, 123, 143; as spontaneity, 76, 77; theoretical explanation of, 263; transcendental deduction of, 27n51, 88; unconditionedness and, 54, 62, 119, 128–29; universality in action and, 235; violation of moral law and, 329; virtue and, 144, 190; *Willkür* and, 79, 102. *See also* will, freedom of the
freedom, transcendental, 72–74, 80, 89, 90, 113, 283; demonic evil and, 332; as freedom in negative sense, 66. *See also* autonomy; heteronomy
Freud, Sigmund, 309

genocide, 315, 316, 319
Gesinnung (disposition), 78, 100–114, 115, 286, 329
Glaucon, 56
God, 155, 163, 170, 187, 212; absence of proof of, 304; establishment of postulate of, 185–86, 188; existence of, 3–4, 180–81, 182, 282, 284; explained in religious education, 308; external impositions of, 222; Holocaust and, 314, 315; metaphysics and, 176, 177, 178–79, 183; obligation to commandments of, 65; Satan and, 112–13; voice of, 299
Goethe, Johann Wolfgang, 112, 333
good, heterogeneity of the, 63, 116, 117–18, 142, 149, 155; capacity of willing to do evil and, 332; classical tradition and, 54–61; Hegel, G.W.F.'s criticism and, 255; obligation and, 58, 59, 164, 282; will torn between duty and desire, 282–83
good, highest (*das höchste Gut*), 149, 204–5, 260; as canon of pure reason, 173–83, 198, 202; centrality in Kant's ethics, 151–56; constitutive and regulative employment of, 198–202; happiness as component of, 163–66; immanence of, 184–91, 196–202; judgment and, 227–28; perfection (moral good) as component of, 156–64; symbolic schematism of, 211–24, 225, 237; terminological problems and, 116, 117, 118; transcendence of, 191–202; two standpoints theory and, 82; as union of happiness and virtue, 116, 117, 118, 223; unity of perfection and happiness in, 166–71
good, moral (*das Gute*), 54, 61, 261; as component of highest good, 155–63; as expression of freedom, 138; good will as sole moral good, 63, 164; happiness in

relation to, 60; highest good and, 169, 170; intrinsic goodness of, 119–21, 125–29; natural good distinct from, 59, 120, 124, 149; natural good qualified by, 141–48, 150, 256; temptation to reject, 60, 61; terminological problems and, 116, 117, 118; as virtue, 153. *See also* perfection
good, natural (*das Wohl*), 61, 124, 261, 282; happiness as, 60; intrinsic goodness of, 119, 121–29, 148–49; moral good distinct from, 59, 120, 124, 149; particular natural goods and, 129–34; particular natural goods as extrinsic, relational goods, 134–41; qualified by the moral good, 141–48, 150, 256; sensible nature as ground of, 142, 146, 164; terminological problems and, 116, 117
good, the: absolute and unconditional, 121, 124; complete good (*das vollendete Gut*), 39, 168; definition of, 46–50, 53, 54, 158; desire and, 159–60; as material object of the will, 156; moral versus natural good, 59; as object of moral law, 61–63; as object of volition, 44; Platonic view of, 64; pleasure or delight in good object, 270, 271; supreme good (*das oberste Gut*), 142, 168–70; will in relation to, 48, 49; *Willkür* and, 107. *See also* good, heterogeneity of the
good will, 7n15, 62–63, 120, 123, 148; as good without qualification, 282; happiness and, 285; moral good as, 133, 164; moral value of, 128; particular natural goods and, 137
grace, 295, 296, 297n30, 300, 307
Grand Inquisitor, Dostoyevskian, 311
Greeks, ancient, 1, 6, 54
Greene, Theodore M., 88n65, 96n86, 222n44
Groundwork of the Metaphysic of Morals (*Grundlegung*), 16, 25, 64, 153; Christian worldview and, 282; on dignity, 128; Eichmann and, 318; on freedom, 66; on primacy of metaphysics, 20; procedure of judgment in, 231, 233–34; Schopenhauer's view of, 17–18; will defined in, 65
guilt, 68, 77, 114, 201; absolute freedom and, 294–95, 296, 297n30; collective, 339–41
Gypsies, Nazi extermination of, 316, 318, 328

habits, 34, 73, 74
Haffner, Sebastian, 297, 335n53
happiness, 15n15, 39, 47, 99; as component of highest good, 164–67; desire for, 56, 115, 142; egoism and, 23; freedom and, 241; intrinsic goodness of, 131, 243; moral feeling and, 268; natural desires and, 59; natural good and, 60, 121–22, 124, 127, 133, 150; non-moral goods and, 121; obedience to moral law and, 94, 267; of other human beings, 82, 131, 132, 166, 167; particular natural goods and, 140; perfection and, 50–51, 167–72; principle of personal happiness, 50; virtue identified with, 34, 54, 58, 60; virtue in proportion to, 147–48, 153, 170, 171, 182; worthiness of, 143, 144–45. *See also* good, highest
health, 72n28, 118, 143, 275; crimes and, 334; happiness and, 59, 120; as natural good, 127; of the soul, 56
Hegel, G.W.F., 37, 258, 264n15, 313; on logical formalism, 253–57; on substantive formalism, 249–53
Heidegger, Martin, 328
hermeneutics, 76n33
Herz, Markus, 15, 19, 205n7
heteronomy, 78, 106, 111, 222, 290; of action, 291n19; of choice, 53n20; as evil, 114; as mode of freedom, 66, 67, 68, 69, 76, 283–84; moral agent and, 220; of reason, 236; transcendental freedom and, 73–74; of willing, 244
Heydrich, Reinhard, 315, 319
Himmler, Heinrich, 315, 319
Hindenburg, Paul, 326
Hitler, Adolf, 291, 292, 296–98, 317, 325, 329; coming to power of, 326, 327, 328; demonic evil of, 333; dependence on

functionaries, 338–39; Eichmann and, 319, 321, 322; Final Solution and, 315, 316, 320, 321, 338; lever of power and, 337; personality of, 331–32, 334, 338; Platonic program and, 311n68, 312
Hobbes, Thomas, 324
holiness, 186, 196, 197, 218
Holocaust, 314–15, 317, 335, 339, 342. *See also* Auschwitz; Final Solution; Jews, Nazi extermination of; Nazi Germany
human nature, 65, 105, 128, 131, 133, 222–23
Hume, David, 6, 7, 19, 29, 34
Hutcheson, Francis, 19, 50
hypothetical imperative, 19, 65, 69, 111
hypotyposis, 215–16, 217, 230

Iago (Shakespearean character), 140, 331
identity, principle of, 37
ideology, ethics and, 2
imagination, 28, 35, 75, 206, 240; categorical imperative and, 242; formula of morality and, 287; judgment as, 216, 223–24, 238; moral schemata and, 237–38; sublime and, 274, 275; taste and, 230
immanence, 198, 199, 202, 220
immortality, 176, 177, 179, 183, 187, 282; absence of proof of, 304; commitment to rational universe and, 285; establishment of postulate of, 185, 186, 188; freedom of moral agent and, 284; proof of, 180–81
impulses, 75, 79
incentives, moral, 70, 154, 298–307, 311; evil disposition and, 108; limits of reason and, 312; moral feeling and, 92; *Willkür* and, 79, 80, 103
individuality, 71, 75
integrity (*Wahrhaftigkeit*), 236, 241, 285, 289
intellectuals, 2, 6
intelligence, as natural good, 72n28, 121, 137, 140
intention, 59, 85, 103; *Gesinnung* (disposition)and, 104, 106; as practical principle, 46; will and, 72; *Willkür* and, 102, 103
Interpretation of Christian Ethics, An (Niebuhr), 300
intuition, 28, 41, 42, 83, 178; concepts and, 213; epistemology versus ethics and, 233; noumenal order and, 88; phenomenal order and, 87; *a priori*, 12; symbolic embodiment of highest good and, 219; theoretical formulations and, 203; time (temporality) and, 206, 207–8
irrationality, 76, 292

Jackson, Robert, 336, 339–40
Jaspers, Karl, 328, 340
Jews, Nazi extermination of, 316, 317, 328, 330; as dominant objective of Hitler's life, 335; Eichmann's invocation of Kantian ethics and, 318–23. *See also* Final Solution; Holocaust; Nazi Germany
judgment, 21, 75, 195, 206, 259; *Gesinnung* (disposition) and, 104, 105; hypotyposis and, 216; moral feeling and, 261–71, 272, 280; moral incentives and, 300; *a posteriori*, 37; as practical reason, 263, 271; *a priori*, 25, 34; procedure in all employments, 225–31; procedure in ethics, 231–46; schematic and symbolic roles of, 217; time (temporality) and, 207
justice, 47, 56, 144n84, 306, 339
Juvenal, 147

Kaltenbrunner, Ernst, 315
Kant, Immanuel, works of: *Anthropology from a Pragmatic Point of View* (*Anthropologie*), 22, 215, 229, 245, 307; *The Doctrine of Virtue*, 334; *Lectures on Ethics*, 306; *Logik* (*Logic*), 11, 14n13, 30; *Metaphysics of Morals*, 18n20, 20n29, 162, 249, 293, 327; *Prolegomena to any Future Metaphysics*, 17n20, 29; "On a Supposed Right to Lie," 249; "Theory and Practice" ("Theorie und Praxis"), 98n92, 100n97, 124, 321, 327; *Theory of the Law*, 248; *Über die Pädagogik* (*On Pedagogy*), 304. See also *Critiques*; *Groundwork of the Metaphysic of Morals*; *Religion within the Limits of Reason Alone*

Karamazov, Ivan (Dostoyevsky character), 294n25, 296
Kierkegaard, Søren, 288, 291, 334
Kingdom of Ends, Formula of the (Formula III), 232, 234, 244, 245. *See also* categorical imperative
knowledge, 24, 160; agency of knower, 38, 42; error and, 36, 37, 41; ethical, 19; evil and, 108; existence of, 24–25; finitude (limits) of, 8, 87, 97, 175, 244, 281; of freedom, 111; historical, 11; material and formal, 47; on matters of fact, 35; metaphysical, 182; noumenal order and, 81; phenomenal order and, 87; *a posteriori*, 35; practical, 15; quest for, 1, 2; rational, 11–12; regulative and constitutive, 200; self-knowledge, 36; speaking the truth and, 250; subjective mode of origination, 11; synthetic *a priori*, 43; taste and, 27; theoretical, 9, 13, 206, 207; unity of, 37; virtue and, 64
Kühn, Manfred, 20n29, 181n28, 222n44

Ladd, John, 326, 327, 328
Lectures on Ethics, 306
Leibniz, Gottfried Wilhelm, 35, 82
Lenin, Vladimir, 312
leverage, social, 337, 338–39
"Limits of Sensibility and Reason, The," 19n26
Lisbon earthquake (1755), 7n13
logic, 75, 160, 228, 229; as formal philosophy, 24; irrationality and, 292; requirements imposed by, 21; sensibility and, 254; universality in, 22
Logik (*Logic*), 11, 14n13, 30
Luther, Martin, 289

Mao Zedong, 312
Marx, Karl, 312
mathematics, 4, 5; analytic propositions and, 29; givenness of, 25; rational knowledge and, 12; sublime and, 274; synthetic *a priori* judgments and, 30
matter, form and. *See* form-matter relation
maxims, 47, 80, 127, 146; categorical imperative and, 81, 234, 237; of common human understanding, 229, 242, 245; evil, 98, 100; form and content of, 256; *Gesinnung* (disposition) and, 100–101, 106; judgment and, 229–30; perfection and, 160; of prudence, 122, 159; self-preservation of reason, 236; on speaking the truth, 250; universal law and, 90, 128, 165, 287, 288, 297
Meerbote, Ralph, 79n37
Mein Kampf (Hitler), 328
Melville, Herman, 291
Menthon, François de, 316
Menzer, Paul, 18, 19
Mephistopheles, in *Faust*, 112–13, 333
Metaphysical Elements of Justice (Ladd), 326
metaphysics, 2, 5, 9, 254; knowledge and, 14, 15; as material philosophy, 24, 28; objects of inquiry for, 176–77, 183; as pure philosophy, 20; as science, 25
Metaphysics of Morals, 18n20, 20n29, 162, 249, 293, 327
Mill, John Stuart, 49n12, 239
Milton, John, 112, 296, 333
Moby-Dick (Melville), 291, 292
moral agent, 54, 156, 195, 205, 259–60; appeal to consequences and, 239–40; autonomy of, 222; categorical imperative and, 241, 242, 289; duty and, 60, 203; freedom of, 62, 248, 284; good as object of desire for, 55; heterogeneity of the good and, 59, 60; highest good and, 182, 199, 200, 202, 214, 219; judgment and, 226, 238, 244; moral law and, 61, 208, 209; moral schema and, 212; obligation to embody the good, 47; responsibility of, 288, 337; sensibility and, 210; will and, 52. *See also* agency
moral experience, 1, 25, 33n62, 56, 114; categorical imperative and, 70; classical tradition and, 59; duty and, 61; form-matter relation and, 43, 44; freedom and, 67n11, 96, 178; *Gesinnung* (disposition) and, 101–2; heterogeneity of the good and, 61, 63; human nature and, 132; judgment and, 230, 237;

moral feeling and, 265; obligation and, 26, 130; pleasure and pain in, 271; schemata and, 209; symbolic representation and, 217; time and, 83, 87, 88; two standpoints theory and, 81
moral feeling, 50, 68n15, 92–97, 305, 307; cultivation of, 272–80; freedom and, 312–13; judgment and, 261–71; origin of evil and, 98; *Wille* and, 90, 91, 266
moralists, English, 18, 50
morality, 6, 15, 21, 142, 222; community and, 24; euthanasia (quiet death) of, 95, 107; as final end of human-kind, 43; first principles of, 25–26; between good and evil, 103; judgment and, 225; knowledge of, 181; as practical without qualification, 13; rational foundation for, 8; self-love and, 58; supreme principle of, 46, 265–66, 281, 284, 317; ultimate end of, 20; will in conflict with, 142
moral law, 57, 61, 90–91, 213; action required or proscribed by, 9; aesthetics/aesthetic experience and, 273; autonomy and, 284; awareness of, 149; as categorical imperative, 68, 81, 111, 233, 245; Copernican Revolution in ethics and, 155; definition of the good and, 54–55; as fact of consciousness, 26; freedom and, 61, 69, 176–77, 189, 194, 198–99; good as object of, 61–63; guilty conscience and, 94; happiness and, 170; heterogeneity of the good and, 56; highest good and, 167, 179–80, 192–93, 208; judgment and, 225, 227–28, 261, 262, 277–78, 280; material concepts and, 47; material object of volition and, 204; maxims of, 146; moral good and, 119, 127, 164; moral schematism and, 223; obligation and, 60; perfection and, 157, 160; personality and, 76–77; philosophical system based on, 16; practical reason and, 203; rejection of (opposition to), 65, 66, 111, 166, 185, 291–92, 332, 333–34; reverence or respect for, 128–29, 264; sensibility and, 235; time (temporality) as schema for, 210; universality of, 2, 165, 287; value of particular natural goods and, 135, 137; violation of, 72, 290, 293, 294, 296, 329; *Willkür* and, 80, 89, 101, 107; worthiness of happiness and, 145
"moral sense" theorists, 95
moral task, 224, 225, 246, 253; as creation of moral schemata, 202–10; willing of moral action and, 261
moral volition, 98n92, 167, 210, 227; decline of, 108; faculty of desire and, 209; highest good and, 156, 171, 182–84, 187, 189, 191, 198, 199, 201, 202, 204; incentives and, 303–4; judgment and, 241–42, 245–46; maxims and, 244, 252; moral act identical with, 133; natural good and, 138, 140; perfection and, 159, 161, 162, 163; phenomenal-noumenal interaction and, 82; time (temporality) and, 83, 220; *Willkür* and, 107
moral will, 133, 138, 205n7, 218; holy will distinguished from, 67, 68; moral good as, 63; natural good and, 122; phenomenal-noumenal interaction and, 87
motives, 51, 80, 104
Murphy, Jeffrie, 152, 155n7

Napoleon I, 291, 334
natural law, 6–7, 46, 91, 238
natural sciences, 2, 85
nature, 4, 86, 143, 158; beauties of, 272–73, 280, 303, 308; control of, 6, 275, 276; as expression of God, 7; laws of, 52, 73, 85, 257, 263; moral ordering of, 213; philosophy of, 15; reason and unity of, 175; religious education and, 308; state of nature, 162, 221, 323; sublime and, 275; understanding and, 16; unity of, 215; universal law of, 238, 239
Nazi Germany (Third Reich), 296–98, 314, 339; criminal responsibility and, 336, 340–41; Eichmann and, 318–23; evil of, 329; founding of, 326; Kant's philosophy used in support of, 325; Platonic program and, 311n68, 312; resources committed to Final Solution,

315–16. *See also* Auschwitz; Final Solution; Holocaust; Jews, Nazi extermination of
negation, 37, 40
Newton, Isaac, 3, 5, 8, 85; law of gravity, 30; on laws of nature, 7; *Principia*, 4; Rousseau compared to, 221
Niebuhr, Reinhold, 243n37, 289, 300, 307
Nietzsche, Friedrich, 291, 334
noble savage, ideal of, 221–22
non-contradiction, law of, 77
noumenal order, 38, 80, 290; awareness of duty and, 40; two standpoints theory and, 81–89; *Willkür* and, 102
Nuremberg trials, 336, 338, 339–40

objectivity, 37, 42, 288
obligation, 26, 27, 50, 57, 63, 149; absolute freedom and, 296; awareness of, 61; categorical nature of, 111–12; in Christian tradition, 64–65; constitutive, 200, 214; definition of the good and, 46; disregard of, 64; empiricism and, 36; freedom and, 47n7, 178, 179, 194–95, 198–99 263; heterogeneity of the good and, 58, 59, 282; highest good as, 170, 187–89, 191, 198, 200; humanity's dual nature and, 223; moral law and, 60, 153; moral task and, 224; natural goods and, 131; rational account of, 70, 95; sensible intuition and, 88; transcendental freedom and, 78; *Willkür* and, 79, 81. *See also* categorical imperative; duty
"On a Supposed Right to Lie," 249

pain, 28, 264, 265; of criminal's punishment, 145; good and bad in relation to, 116; judgment and, 262; misdeeds and, 57, 267; moral feeling and, 266, 268, 269; moral incentives and, 301
Pap, Arthur, 29n55
Paradise Lost (Milton), 112, 333
Parmenides, 334
particularity, 43
Paton, Herbert J., 83, 233, 249
Paul, St., 68, 105–6, 108, 291, 309
percepts, 205
perfection, 50–51, 165, 245, 296; as component of highest good, 156–64; as holiness, 186, 196; symbolic schematism and, 218, 219; united with happiness in highest good, 167–72
personality (*Persönlichkeit*), 70, 78, 99, 113, 265; abnegation of, 109; decline of, 290; free will as ground of, 178; fulfillment of, 77; inner freedom of, 223; soul as personality, 299; war and, 276–77; weakness of, 109, 110, 111, 333; *Willkür* as core of, 80
phenomenal order, 38, 80, 208, 288; judgment and, 238; sensibility and, 254; symbolic schematism of highest good and, 219; two standpoints theory and, 81–89; *Willkür* and, 102
Phenomenology of Mind (Hegel), 249
philosophes, 8
philosophy, 2, 4, 46; cosmopolitan conception of, 17, 18, 20, 44; discursive nature of, 24; Kantian conception of, 11–20, 24, 43; natural philosophy in ancient Greece, 6; scholastic, 7, 17, 46; ultimate end of, 13
physics, 25, 30
Plato, 1, 65, 68, 144, 313, 334; on essence and existence, 34; on evil intention, 109n123, 291, 332; freedom identified with rationality, 77; on the Good, 64; on injustice, 293; on moral feeling, 272; punishment of crime and, 144n84; rulership in civil society and, 324; totalitarian education project of, 310–11; on tyrant who does evil, 297
pleasure, 28, 48, 69; faculty of desire and, 49; in fulfillment of duty, 261, 264, 301; moral feeling and, 268, 269–71, 280; pathological and moral, 95, 96; sublime and, 274; *Willkür* and, 79n36, 95
politics, community and, 24
Pope, Alexander, 3, 5
positivism, 97
practical principle, 46–47, 48, 49, 53
practical reason, 2, 157, 233, 256, 257, 299; autonomy and, 66; *Gesinnung*

(disposition) and, 108; highest good and, 154, 185, 190, 192; judgment and, 238, 263, 271; methodology of, 155; moral feeling and, 265–66, 267, 280; primacy of, 20, 173, 291; respect for the law and, 265; sublime and, 277; unity with theoretical reason, 16; will as, 65, 114. See also *Wille* (rational will)
predicates, 35, 38
prejudice, 236
price, dignity and, 125, 126, 127
Principia (Newton), 4
principles, 205
Prolegomena to any Future Metaphysics, 17n20, 29
property, 93, 111n27, 138; stealing of, 254, 257; *usucapio* right and, 248
prudence, 122, 160, 279, 291
pure practical reason. *See* practical reason
pure reason, 2, 15, 84, 224; highest good and, 152, 163; highest good as canon of, 173–83; moral law and, 27, 66; obligation and, 88; practical employment of, 204; theoretical task of, 205

rationalism, 4, 33–34, 35, 37, 163
Raveh, Judge Yitzhak, 320
reason (rationality), 9, 21, 43, 114, 151, 158; community and, 21–22; as faculty of desire, 163; freedom and, 16, 66, 75, 77, 91, 333; Hegel's criticism of, 249–53; highest good and, 190; hypotyposis and, 217; judgment and, 206, 228–29; limits of, 13; metaphysics and, 176–77, 182; morality as ultimate goal of, 24; moral task of, 214; negation of, 75; practical employments of, 174–75, 176; procedural interpretation of, 231; prudence and, 122; rejection of moral law and, 291–92; rejection of reason, 290; schematism and, 215; self-preservation of, 23; sensibility and, 142, 223, 244; in service of human-kind, 16, 24; social contract and, 323; as spontaneity, 76, 77, 173; unity of, 15–16; universality of, 21, 75, 251, 252; value of natural good and, 130, 138; will and, 68; *Willkür* and, 114; worth as judgment of, 144. *See also* practical reason; pure reason
Reason, Age of, 3, 17
reciprocity, 207
relativism, ethical, 310
religion, 5, 14, 28n53, 220; demythologized, 298–99, 309; ethical orthodoxy in religious education, 307–13; ethics and, 2; moral experience and, 33, 88n65; pietism, 3, 222n44, 299, 312
Religion within the Limits of Reason Alone, 69, 89, 282; contribution to ethics, 114–115; on decline of virtue and personality, 290; *Gesinnung* concept in, 100; phenomenal-noumenal interaction and, 83, 88; theoretical background and importance of, 64–69
representation (*Vorstellung*), 39n74, 206–7, 210, 274
Republic (Plato), 59, 324
respect, 127–28, 265, 278
responsibility (accountability), 41, 72n28, 138; absolute, 295–96; delegation of, 258–59; freedom and, 123, 143, 189–90; *Gesinnung* (disposition) and, 100; highest good and, 196; Holocaust and Nazi criminality, 318, 335–37, 339; leverage and status responsibility, 338–39, 341; loss of capacity for, 112; as mark of personality, 70–71; of moral agent, 222; universal law and, 75; *Willkür* as core of, 80, 103
revolution, right of, 318n7, 323, 327n30
Rosen, Stanley, 76n33
Rousseau, Jean-Jacques, 13n9, 18, 19, 162, 221–22, 309n65

Satan, 112–13, 333, 340
schema, 206, 209, 210
schematism, 43, 44, 237; judgment and, 227, 228, 245; symbolic, 211–24
Schilpp, Paul, 18–20, 222n44
Scholastics, 54
Schopenhauer, Arthur, 98n92, 239, 264n15; on Kant's second *Critique*, 17–18, 20n29, 152; on moral law, 26

science, 2, 28, 75, 160; Christian versus scientific worldview, 3–10, 281–82, 309, 310; community and, 24; ethics and, 81; experience and, 34, 36; judgment and, 225, 227, 228; Newtonian, 3; principle of finality and, 85–86; reason and, 174; scientific method, 4, 21, 29, 227; sensibility and, 254; synthetic *a priori* judgments and, 29, 30–31; theory and practice, 203; totality as guiding principle for, 215
Seebohm, Thomas, 314n1, 322n23
self-determination, 71, 72, 73, 109
self-interest, 56, 58, 93n78, 244, 317n6
self-love, principle of, 50, 58, 59, 165, 267
sensibility, 38, 42, 74, 114, 151; categorical imperative and, 156; conditions of willing and, 164, 166; diversity of, 233; happiness and, 154; in Hegel's interpretation, 254, 255, 256; hypotyposis and, 215–16, 217; imputed action and, 122; judgment and, 238, 241, 242; knowledge of phenomena and, 87; of moral agent, 208; moral feeling and, 268, 275; moral law and, 208–11, 235; moral task and, 205, 210; pleasure in, 301; rationality and, 142; reason and, 223, 244, 254–56; sublime and, 274; understanding and, 173, 219; *Willkür* and, 114
Shaftesbury, Anthony Ashley Cooper, Earl of, 19, 50
Singer, Marcus, 233n24, 249n50, 288n16
social contract, 323
socialism, 312
Socrates, 1, 11, 24–25, 258, 267, 334; on happiness, 56–57; on individual in society, 324; paradox of willing nothing and, 163; thesis on the good, 58; on virtue and happiness, 55
Sophism, 13
soul, 176, 177, 178, 293, 334; as correlate of freedom, 178; immortality of, 182, 185, 186, 285; as personality, 299
sovereign, authority of, 324, 326–27
space, 23, 83, 84, 205–6, 220, 237
speech, freedom of, 22
Speer, Albert, 298, 315, 339, 340
Spinoza, Baruch, 2, 313
spontaneity, 41, 102, 174; form-matter relation and, 43; freedom as, 334; knowledge and, 42; reason as, 75–76; transcendental freedom and, 66, 73; understanding as spontaneous activity, 173; *Willkür* and, 80
Stalin, Joseph, 291, 292, 312, 316n3, 332, 334
Stoics, 50, 55, 59, 144, 145n84; on origin of evil, 99; paradox of willing nothing and, 164
subjectivism, 36
sublime, the, 273–77, 278, 280, 303
sufficient reason, 21, 22, 30, 286, 300
suicide, 341–42
superstition, 23, 87, 88n65, 317
synthetic method, 28, 29, 31, 32, 38

Tamburlaine, 334
taste, 27, 75; egoism and, 22, 23; judgment and, 228, 229–30; moral feeling and, 273. *See also* aesthetics/aesthetic experience
teleology, 85, 86n60, 215
Tertullian, 4
theology, 4, 64, 308
"Theory and Practice" ("Theorie und Praxis"), 98n92, 100n97, 124, 321, 327
Theory of the Law, 248
thing-in-itself (*Ding an sich*), 39, 42, 81, 87, 290. *See also* noumenal order
Third Reich. *See* Nazi Germany
Thomas, Dylan, 276
Thomas Aquinas, St., 3
Thomism, 8
Thrasymachus, 107
time (temporality), 23, 83, 84, 205–6, 207; absence as moral schema, 208, 209, 211; moral schemata and, 220, 237; *Willkür* and, 88
totalitarianism, 310–11, 332
totality, 21, 175, 202, 212; categorical imperative and, 234; as guiding principle for science, 215; imagination and, 274; judgment and, 244; of

sensible world, 180; understanding and, 174, 211

transcendence, 2, 74, 217, 284; of highest good, 198, 199, 200, 202; self-transcendence, 42; symbolic schematism and, 220

transcendental deduction, 30, 31, 32, 66n9, 70

transcendental method, 24, 28–29, 38, 43

truth, 23, 24, 88n65, 259; of cognitions, 13, 21; contradiction and, 254; empirical, 174; of experience, 40; logical criteria of, 24; maxim of speaking truth, 250; *a priori* judgments and, 34; science and, 25, 30; universality and, 22; virtue and, 7

Über die Pädagogik (*On Pedagogy*), 304

understanding (*Verstand*), 16, 21, 40, 158; abstraction and, 35; aesthetic experience and, 274; egoism and, 22; good in relation to, 49; imagination and, 28; irrationality and, 292; judgment and, 228; knowledge and, 87; perfection of, 161; schematization of reason and, 215; sensibility and, 173, 219; space and time in relation to, 206, 207, 208; totality and, 174, 211

universality: as determining ground of the will, 53; duty and, 23, 255, 290; judgment and, 235, 244; synthetic *a priori* knowledge and, 43

universal law, 66, 74, 75, 128; judgment and, 105, 231, 232; *Wille* and, 90

Universal Law, Formula of (Formula I), 231, 234–35, 236, 237, 241. *See also* categorical imperative

Universal Law of Nature, Formula of the (Formula Ia), 233, 237, 239–41. *See also* categorical imperative

Untersuchung über die Deutlichkeit der Grundsätze der Theologie und Moral, 18

usefulness (*Nützlichkeit*), 12, 14

usucapio, right of, 248

utilitarianism, 239

Vaihinger, H., 33

value neutrality, 310

Velkley, Richard, 13n9, 15n15

virtue, 1, 8, 9, 20n29, 56, 99; banality of, 337; decline of, 115n129, 290; desire for, 115; diminution of, 109; duties of, 246, 247; freedom and, 144, 190; happiness identified with, 34, 54, 58, 60; happiness in proportion to, 147–48, 153, 170, 171, 182; humanity's moral limitations and, 185, 186; intrinsic goodness of, 131; knowledge and, 64; perfection and, 158, 161; proof of, 289; as supreme good, 141, 167; *Willkür* and, 80. *See also* good, highest

volition, 70, 83, 102, 145, 156, 267; categorical imperative and, 78, 234, 237; criminal responsibility and, 336–37; decline of, 108–9, 115; duty and, 285; *Gesinnung* (disposition) and, 103; good will and, 282; irrationality and, 292; judgment and, 223, 225, 237; malevolent, 332; material content of, 245; of moral agent, 62, 239, 240, 248, 253, 259; moral law and, 111, 165, 181, 182, 210, 261, 265, 332; moral worth and, 284; particular natural goods and, 140; perfection and, 162; phenomenal order and, 82; rationality of, 236, 258; responsibility and, 336–37; singular faculty of, 114, 119n11; social contract and, 323; subjective practical principle and, 46; will as faculty of desire and, 208; *Wille* and, 89, 91; willing as exercise of, 132; *Willkür* and, 91, 92, 100, 104, 105, 107, 113. *See also* moral volition

volition, object of, 53n23, 61–62, 70, 74, 150, 164; categorical imperative and, 156; desires and, 74, 75; evil will and, 109n123; good as, 44, 157, 170; highest good and, 154, 180, 184–87, 190–92, 195, 198, 200–201; intention of the will and, 157; judgment and, 227, 267; known and willed, 261; maxim of the will and, 283; of moral agents, 62; moral law and, 166–67, 204, 213n25, 225; necessity for, 72; perfection and, 159, 161–62; practical principles and,

46; pure practical reason and, 157; self-determination and, 73; unconditioned free willing and, 75; virtue and, 99

Wannsee Conference, 320, 330
war, 23, 68, 276–77
wealth, 48, 121, 122, 143, 144
Weimar Republic, 326, 327
well-being, 134, 140, 251; heterogeneity of the good and, 59; natural good and, 122; of ordinary people, 1; perfection of natural capacities and, 160; physical, 117–18
Weltanschauung (worldview), Christian versus Newtonian/scientific, 3–10, 281–82, 286, 309
Whitehead, Alfred North, 299
wickedness, 8, 107–12, 115n129, 192, 204; loss of worthiness to be happy and, 292–93; as weakness, 290, 329. *See also* evil
Wiesel, Elie, 315
will, 64, 68, 78; absolute worth of, 125; agency of, 52, 210; categorical imperative and, 65, 68, 111; definition of, 53, 65, 68; as faculty of desire, 68, 69, 114, 138; as faculty of freedom, 283; good in relation to, 48, 49, 51–54; holy, 67–68, 235, 261, 284, 300; incentives of, 154; moral good and, 133; obligation to object of volition, 62; predisposition to personality, 90, 91; pure will, 27; struggle for control of, 261; two standpoints theory and, 81–89; unconditionality of, 63, 75; unity of, 89; virtue as goal of, 157. See also *Gesinnung*; moral will
will, determination of the, 53, 235, 256; desire and, 50; moral feeling and, 267; practical principle and, 46
will, freedom of the, 47, 54, 58, 66–67, 71, 121; consciousness of moral law and, 193; highest good and, 201; moral incentives and, 301–2; moral value of good will and, 128; obligation and, 263; realization of freedom and, 332; sublime and, 275; temptation and, 123. See also *Willkür*
Wille (rational will), 67n13, 78, 89–91, 92, 92n77, 115; *Gesinnung* (disposition) and, 106; incentives and, 300, 302; moral feeling and, 90, 91, 266; moral law identified with, 120; origin of evil and, 98; *Willkür* in relation to, 89–92, 93n77, 106, 108–9. *See also* pure practical reason
Willkür (choice, elective will), 78, 79–80, 115, 192, 293; definition of, 67n13; forgiveness and, 294; *Gesinnung* (disposition) and, 100–109, 113–14; incentives and, 300, 302–3; moral feeling and, 93–96, 266; natural goods and, 139; origin of evil and, 97–99; phenomenal-noumenal interaction and, 88–89, 95n80; unconditionedness and, 120; *Wille* in relation to, 89–92, 93n77, 106, 108–9. *See also* choice; will, freedom of the
wisdom, 12, 13, 212
Wolff, Christian, 35, 50, 96, 157; on goodness and perfection, 159; rationalist ethics of, 163
Wood, Allen, 109n124, 111, 180n28; on guilt and forgiveness, 297n30; on Kant's view of rebellion, 322n22; on promoting moral good of others, 221n40
world, idea of, 176, 177

Bei Fragen zur Produktsicherheit wenden Sie sich bitte an:
If you have any questions regarding product safety,
please contact:

Walter de Gruyter GmbH
Genthiner Straße 13
10785 Berlin
productsafety@degruyterbrill.com